Death Investigation

Death Investigation

An Introduction to Forensic
Pathology for the Nonscientist

Ann Bucholtz

Routledge
Taylor & Francis Group

LONDON AND NEW YORK

First published 2015 by Anderson Publishing

Published 2015 by Routledge
2 Park Square, Milton Park, Abingdon, Oxon OX14 4RN

and by Routledge
711 Third Avenue, New York, NY 10017, USA

Routledge is an imprint of the Taylor & Francis Group, an informa business

Acquiring Editor: Sara Scott
Editorial Project Manager: Marisa LaFleur
Project Manager: Punithavathy Govindaradjane
Designer: Russell Purdy

Library of Congress Cataloging-in-Publication Data

Bucholtz, Ann.
    Death investigation / Ann Bucholtz.
        pages cm

1. Dead–Identification. 2. Forensic pathology. I. Title.
    RA1055.B83 2014
    614'.1–dc23

                                                                                    2013038466

British Library Cataloguing in Publication Data
A catalogue record for this book is available from the British Library

ISBN 978-1-4557-7437-1 (pbk)

Transferred to Digital Printing 2016

Dedication

To my son, Lucas Hartsough, a source of constant encouragement and inspiration. To my editor, Sherrie Saint, for her friendship and patience. Thank you to my family and colleagues for their contributions of photos and data.

Contents

Digital Assets

Thank you for selecting Anderson's *Death Investigation*. To complement the learning experience, we have provided a number of online tools to accompany this edition. Two distinct packages of interactive digital assets are available: one for instructors and one for students.

Interactive resources can be accessed for free by registering at: www.routledge.com/cw/bucholtz

FOR THE INSTRUCTOR

- **Test Bank** Compose, customize, and deliver exams using an online assessment package in a free Windows-based authoring tool that makes it easy to build tests using the unique multiple choice and true or false questions created for *Death Investigation*. What's more, this authoring tool allows you to export customized exams directly to Blackboard, WebCT, eCollege, Angel and other leading systems. All test bank files are also conveniently offered in Word format.
- **PowerPoint Lecture Slides** Reinforce key topics with focused PowerPoints, which provide a perfect visual outline with which to augment your lecture. Each individual book chapter has its own dedicated slideshow.
- **Instructor's Guides** Design your course around customized learning objectives, discussion questions, and other instructor tools.

FOR THE STUDENT

- **Self-Assessment Question Bank** Enhance review and study sessions with the help of this online self-quizzing asset. Each question is presented in an interactive format that allows for immediate feedback.
- **Case Studies** Apply what is on the page to the world beyond with the help of topic-specific case studies, each designed to turn theory into practice and followed by interactive scenario-based questions that allow for immediate feedback.

CHAPTER 1

History of Death Investigation

Learning Objectives

- Differentiate the roles of a forensic pathologist versus a hospital pathologist in the performance of autopsies.
- Compare and contrast the coroner system versus a medical examiner system.
- Identify and review the death investigation system in your state. Demonstrate knowledge of the state laws for reportable deaths in your jurisdiction.
- Compare the list of reportable deaths in the Model Post-Mortem Act to the laws in your state. Discuss the additions and deletions and the impact you think they might have for death investigations.
- Discuss the works of Washing Away of Wrongs and what impact it had on the beginnings of death investigation.
- Describe the benefits and drawbacks to professional certification in an area of expertise, such as forensic pathology, forensic nursing, death investigator, or criminalist.

Key Terms

Locard's exchange principle
Center for Disease Control
Alphonse Bertillon
Model Postmortem Act
Coroner
Medical examiner
Forensic pathologist
Hospital pathologist

Chapter Summary

In this chapter we discuss some of the historical origins of forensic medicine, criminalistics, and the coroner system. Also discussed are the multiple supporting organizations that provide credentialing, networking, and continuing education opportunities. The basis of laws regarding death investigation in the United States are examined, which are centered on the 1954 Model Postmortem Act in which suspicious, unusual, or unnatural deaths are investigated to provide information for prosecution, accurate determination of death, and protection of the public against health hazards.

INTRODUCTION

Forensics, derived from the word "forum," refers to the application of various fields of science and medicine in the resolution of legal proceedings. The beginnings of forensic science were crude and rudimentary but formed the basis of areas of research and progress to modern-day use of lasers, sophisticated laboratory equipment to identify particles and drug identification, and computerization to improve response time to locate the answers to questions asked by investigators, some in near real time. This chapter reviews the historical beginnings of forensic medicine and its parallel in criminalistics, contrasts the **coroner** and **medical examiner** investigation systems, as well as provides insight into governing bodies for accreditation, certification, and licensure.

MANDATES, JURISDICTION, AND LAWS

Forensic science has its origins in early China and was documented in an early transcript of text, *Washing Away of Wrongs* by Sung Tz'u written in 1248. He was a criminal affairs officer who wrote the book based on personal experiences. Within the text he described a scenario of a local village murder by a sickle used to harvest grain. The murderer was unknown and the investigator had each farmer bring their tools to the village to be examined. It was noted that flies were attracted to one particular sickle. This was apparently due to adherent tissue and blood on the tool and ended with the farmer admitting to the crime. The story has roots for the basis of forensic entomology with its observation of the relevance of insects and their relationship to the cycle of death. He described handling of male corpses by local men of low social standing and the female corpses were managed by local midwives.

The early Greeks performed anatomical dissections in an attempt to understand the workings of the body and organ relationships. However, it wasn't until the late 18th century when a book written by Giovanni Morgagni that described autopsy dissections with descriptions of disease processes that they gained acceptance in the West. This served as a framework in the late 19th century for Dr. William Osler, the acclaimed physician and educator, supporting the autopsy as a great teaching method for physicians to learn about their patient's disease and to see for oneself the disease process. His work and influence served as the basis for medical training that still is in existence today. The period after World War II showed extensive interest in autopsies, and most were done in the hospital setting to gain knowledge about the effectiveness of new treatments, as well as learn about the disease itself. Hospital autopsies were done for approximately 50% of deaths.

In 1954 the United States passed the **Model PostMortem** Act, which outlined general classes of deaths that need to be further investigated and certified by a government body rather than a **hospital pathologist** or treating physician (Figure 1.1). This act was used as a framework for each state to develop its own particular laws regarding death investigation. The act outlines reporting of all violent deaths; unusual, unnatural, or suspicious deaths; all prison deaths; and any death thought to represent a public health hazard. Over the years, each state has modified their laws to adapt to advances in the medicolegal system, but for the most part they read as they were originally written and reflect these guidelines.

Today, it is estimated that hospital autopsies are done in less than 10% of hospital deaths. The decline is related to multiple influences, including the deleted

---

1954 Model Postmortem Examinations Act

Section 4. [Deaths To Be Investigated.] The Office of Post-Mortem Examinations shall investigate all human deaths of the types listed herewith:
(a) Violent deaths, whether apparently homicidal, suicidal, or accidental, including but not limited to deaths due to thermal, chemical, electrical or radiational injury, and deaths due to criminal abortion, whether apparently self-induced or not;
(b) Sudden deaths not caused by readily recognizable disease;
(c) Deaths under suspicious circumstances;
(d) Deaths of persons whose bodies are to be cremated, dissected, buried at sea, or otherwise disposed of so as to be thereafter unavailable for examination;
(e) Deaths of inmates of public institutions not hospitalized therein for organic disease;
(f) Deaths related to disease resulting from employment or to accident while employed;
(g) Deaths related to disease which might constitute a threat to public health.

Outlined purpose by the Commissioners:
The purpose of the Model Post-Mortem Examinations Act is to provide a means whereby greater competence can be assured in determining causes of death where criminal liability may be involved.

Drafted by the
NATIONAL CONFERENCE OF COMMISSIONERS ON UNIFORM STATE LAWS, 1954
http://babel.hathitrust.org/cgi/pt?id=mdp.39015082088835;view=1up;seq=3

FIGURE 1.1
The 1954 Model Post-Mortem outlined the recommended state mandated reporting of cases to a central investigative agency for adoption of individual state laws.

requirement by the Joint Commission of American Hospitals (their accrediting body) for a minimum autopsy rate and reimbursement to the hospital for this service, as well as improved radiologic methods for patient evaluation [4]. The interesting finding, however, is autopsies discover 22–33% findings that were not previously known even with the current technology [4]. They provide answers to families and further understanding to medical science, but unfortunately continue to decline in the hospital community.

Caseloads for medical examiners and coroner offices continue to increase as the population increases. With shortages of **forensic pathologists** and limited tax-based funds, death investigation offices must limit autopsies performed to those mandated by law. This creates a void for hospitals and families wishing for answers. Hospital pathologists rarely perform them, and in modern hospitals, morgues are no longer included as an essential area of the laboratory department. Those autopsies not falling under jurisdiction of the state's death investigation laws require signed family permission to proceed. State laws even outline the family members who may give this permission, usually following the order of spouse, adult children, parents of the deceased, adult siblings, a legal guardian, and then the individual charged with the disposition of the remains.

In the situation of religious objections and deaths falling under the jurisdiction of the death investigator, an autopsy may proceed without family permission. However, it is best for public relations to work with the family and try to abide by their wishes or perform the autopsy within their religious constraints if at all possible. This may require a rabbi to be present during the procedure, collection of all body fluids to return with the body, or particular religious practices to be performed before or after the procedure. Muslim and Jewish religions request burials prior to sundown of the day of death if at all possible. Some religions forbid embalming. Some families request no autopsy because they wish to have an open casket and viewing of the decedent. With education about the procedure, they can be reassured that the incisions will be done in locations that will not preclude viewing, embalming, and open-casket funerals if the body was not damaged extensively by trauma prior to the autopsy. Objections can be overcome with meaningful conversations between the family and the death investigator or pathologist.

There is no universal body governing the death investigation system at a national level, and each state performs death investigations differently from its neighboring state. Many deaths reported to a death investigation office involve sudden death due to unknown mechanism. They represent natural diseases not previously or well documented prior to death, or the treating physician may be unavailable to sign for a patient with a well-documented history. Generally, there is a time limit in which a death certificate needs to be filed with a local health department after death. For this reason, the medical examiner serves as a resource to fill these gaps. The pathologist can issue meaningful causes of death based on medical records and external examination of the body without the need for an internal examination and full autopsy.

The local health department is the governing body that filters all death certificates to the National Bureau of Vital Statistics. They review and numerically code the causes of death into categories so that trends in causes may be recognized to adjust surveillance, prevention, and treatment practices. The local health department also issues burial or cremation permits to funeral homes after a valid death certificate is filed. They supply copies of death certificates, which are usually public record and can be obtained by anyone. The 1992 Model State Vital Statistics Act and Regulations serves as a template for each state to model their vital records practices and can serve as a reference to answer unusual questions when completing a death certificate [12].

The coroner system has been in existence since organized colonization began in 1492 when the concept was imported with the settlers from England. The first medical examiner office was established in New York City in 1918, and it was the first government division of its kind in the United States [5]. They were also responsible for the first toxicology laboratory in 1918 [5]. The first chief medical examiner in the New York office was Dr. Charles Norris. This was followed by New York University establishing the first department of forensic medicine in 1933.

The **Center for Disease Control** maintains a list of the medical examiner and coroner jurisdictions within the United States, shown in Figure 1.2 [2].

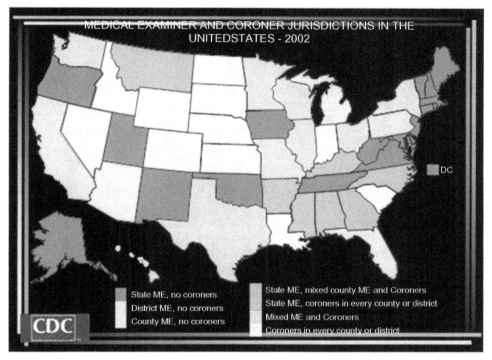

FIGURE 1.2
This map illustrates the various combinations of coroner and medical examiner system jurisdictions within the United States.
Source: Published by the Center for Disease Control.

HISTORY OF CRIMINALISTICS

Parallel to the development of forensic medicine and autopsies, the world of criminalistics was also developing and spurring forward the science of evaluating evidence and tracking criminals. **Alphonse Bertillon** was a French law enforcement officer in the late 19th century who performed research in anthropometry, which is a study of physical characteristics of a person that make him or her unique. His study involved recording measurements of various body regions, such as forearms, trunks, ears, fingers, and faces, to differentiate one person from another (Figure 1.3). This had applications for differentiating criminals from each other, because the usual method had been for station police officers at the entrance to the jail to make visual identifications, which were sometimes inaccurate. The main purpose was to separate repeat-offender prisoners from first offenders. At the time, it was a huge scientific advancement and was thought to be reliable until the early 20th century when it failed to differentiate a case of twins. Although these particular measurements were eventually found to be unreliable, they formed the basis for the science of biometrics that utilizes a similar idea of individualizing characteristics but includes more detailed,

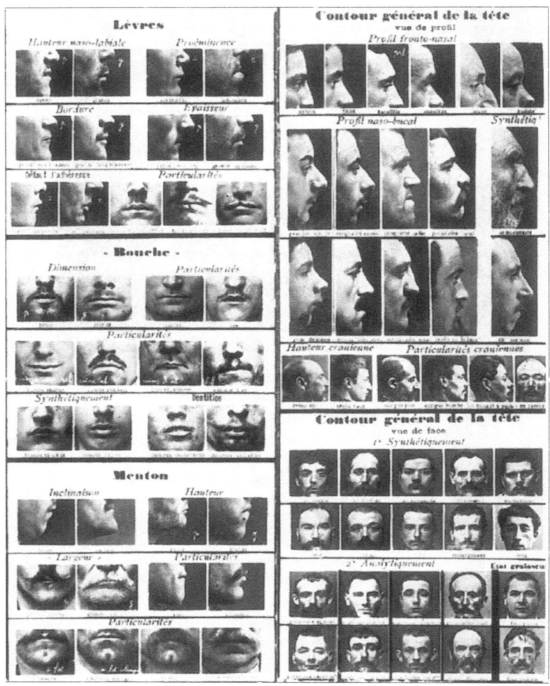

FIGURE 1.3
(A) Various physical characteristics used by Alphonse Bertillon in his research on anthropometry.

FIGURE 1.3, cont'd
(B) An example of the type of measurements he performed to characterize individuals. It shows a striking similarity to our current method of figuring stature from femur bone lengths.
Source: http://www.nlm.nih.gov.

patterned relationships, such as iris scans, fingerprints, and facial-recognition software used in security programs.

Another notable hallmark in criminalistics was the work of Edmond Locard in the early 20th century. He too was a Frenchman but with a background in medicine and law. He became interested in forensics during his studies and eventually formed the first criminalistics laboratory in Lyon, France, in 1910. He is best known for **Locard's exchange principle**, which states that whenever two items come into contact they exchange material between them. This is the principle used to recover evidence and particular trace evidence on the body or other items in a crime scene and link it to the individual who left it. The importance of this principle is that no scene is without trace evidence; it is the job of the investigator to locate it and collect it. Locard was also extremely interested in fingerprints, and through his work in microscopy, he detailed characteristics of them that are used today in fingerprint identification. He is generally considered the first criminalist.

In 1923, August Vollmer, chief of the Los Angeles, CA, Police Department, established the first American crime laboratory. The second crime laboratory was established in 1929 by Calvin Goddard (well known for his work in ballistics) at Northwestern University in Chicago, IL.

Coroners

Coroners are elected officials and in most jurisdictions the only credentials required for being placed on the ballot are a high school diploma and a voter registration card. Medical, science, or law enforcement background is not required. In some jurisdictions, the position has been combined with the sheriff position to decrease administrative overheads. In this case, sworn law enforcement deputies may rotate through the positions of death investigator and not be specifically trained in death-scene evaluations. There can be a public question of conflict of interest when investigations cross into departmental operations. Other jurisdictions utilize a separate department with a chief coroner and deputy coroners. Coroner positions may also be linked to local funeral homes as experienced personnel in dealing with the dead.

The history of the word "coroner" originates in England from the word "crowner," a tax collector for the dead. In old England, coroners were given the task of investigating any local event that might result in revenue for the Crown. Death was a potential source of money, and suicides, fires, shipwrecks, and others all were levied taxes or goods were confiscated by the Crown as fines. After the conquest of the Normans, the countryside continued to kill Normans. To discourage this, a heavy fine was levied against a community in which a Norman was found dead. It became the job of the coroner to determine the origin of the dead person, and they largely assumed the person was a Norman and levied the tax unless someone could prove the decedent was English. This tax levy was known as "murdrum'" and became the origin of the word "murder" [1]. The concept of coroners and sheriffs was brought to the United States with the colonists when it was initially settled. It spread throughout the United States as colonies developed and the need for investigation and management of the dead became a necessity.

The United States varies from state to state in a mixture of medical examiner and coroner jurisdictions and combinations thereof [2]. Because coroners are not physicians, they are unable to perform autopsies. This is contracted to forensic pathologists who supply a cause of death to the coroner. The coroner then has the legal ability to certify the cause and manner of death on the death certificate. Most times, the coroner will agree with the cause of death, but if not, he or she may place any cause on the certificate or rule the manner as he or she wishes. Being a political position can have some bearing on this decision and is a potential downfall of the coroner system. Most times the job is performed justly and accurately in conjunction with the science of the autopsy in mind. In some jurisdictions, mainly ones where the position is combined with the sheriff department, the coroner is also a law enforcement officer with the ability to carry a weapon. Strict coroner office personnel are generally unarmed.

The chief coroner serves as an administrator and leader of the office for death investigations. Most times, he or she hires additional lay persons, many with a medical or law enforcement background, as deputy coroners who are responsible for day-to-day investigations. Because these positions are based on the county divisions of a community, a coroner's office can be a small operation. The deputy coroner may have a varied job description, including crime scene investigation, preparation of death certificates, body transport, and autopsy assistance.

Medical examiners

Medical examiners are forensic pathologists with education as a medical doctor (either an M.D. or D.O.), completion of at least 4 years of anatomic pathology (5 years if also trained as a clinical pathologist), and at least 1–2 years of subspecialty training in forensic medicine. In total, approximately 13–15 years of training after high school is needed to become a forensic pathologist.

Medical school includes the study of basic medical science, including pharmacology, pathology, biochemistry, human physiology, and anatomy, as well as patient care and skills necessary for the practice of medicine. Following medical school, medical students enter a residency program where they specialize in an area of interest. The residency begins with a general year that previously was known and perceived by the public as an internship with continued responsibility and in-depth learning of the specialty over at least 3 years (family medicine, internal medicine) to surgery and pathology (5 years). Because the study of medicine has become so complicated, large branches of medicine have subspecialized into even smaller groups, such as cardiology (internal medicine), head and neck (surgery), and forensic medicine (pathology).

There are a couple of clinical forensic medicine programs in the United States that are areas of subspecialization within emergency medicine but these are not common. Currently in the United States, there are approximately 500–600 board-certified forensic pathologists and 30–40 in training each year [3]. Unfortunately, the number training is less than the greater number of pathologists who are retiring, and there is a projected severe shortage as the number of pathologists continues to age and retire. Even though the number of hospital pathologists performing autopsies has greatly declined, the number of medicolegal autopsies continues to increase as the population increases.

A medical examiner office is typically under the direction of a chief medical examiner who reports to a board of supervisors, state legislature, or the department head of the public health department. Under the chief may be an additional forensic pathologist. Current recommendations are the performance of

250 autopsies per year and no more than 350 per year per forensic pathologist. In large population cities, more than 7,000 deaths are reported to a medical examiner office with at least 4,000–4,500 cases accepted for jurisdiction. Not all cases accepted are necessarily autopsied and may be certified by history or external examination. The autopsy rate is generally at least 60% and more commonly greater than 70–75% depending on staffing and workload. At 4,000 cases, more than 10 pathologists are needed to comply with the accreditation standards. It is clear that even by present-day availability there is a shortage of forensic pathologists and current training will be inadequate to meet future society's needs.

Notable forensic pathologists

Milton Helpern was the second chief medical examiner of the New York City medical examiner office. His support of research and teaching led to many forensic pathologists to later become chief forensic pathologists in other locations, spreading the concept of forensic medicine throughout the United States.

Dr. Thomas Noguchi is a modern-day pathologist who is best known as the "coroner of the stars" and formed the basis of the TV show "Quincy." This notoriety and positive portrayal of death investigations improved the public's perception of the science of forensic medicine. Present-day TV shows similarly dramatize the work of crime scene investigators (CSIs), criminalistics, autopsies, and courtrooms. These shows are not totally realistic but have raised an awareness of the science to most households. The negative side is the "CSI effect," in which juries expect similar results on cases presented to them even though the real forensic science does not support many of the concepts dramatized nor operate under the same time and money constraints as TV laboratories.

Medicolegal death investigators

Medicolegal death investigators serve as observation personnel and key assistants to the forensic pathologist at scenes. It is not possible for the forensic pathologist to visit all scenes and observe the body as it was found. It would be ideal, but just not possible. Death investigators are trained personnel with skills in observation, photography, and social skills to deal with the public during difficult situations. Their backgrounds are diverse and a cross-section of skills is helpful in any office. Some investigators have a funeral home background as funeral directors, others are emergency medical personnel, nurses, retired law enforcement officers, or physician assistants.

The ability to speak to physicians and understand medical terminology is an essential skill. Rudimentary photography skills are also very useful, as well as basics in evidence recovery and management. The ability to explain medical findings to families in lay language and serve as an intermediary between the pathologist and family is essential. Report writing skills, including grammar, are also necessary. Formal education can vary from a high school education to graduate school. Most offices now will not hire an investigator without a college degree. They are also not eligible for board certification via the American Board of Medicolegal Death Investigators (ABMDI) without at least an associate's degree. The ability to become a good death investigator resides more on the personality of the person than a particular degree or level of education. Many of the skills are learned on the job or through various continuing-education and certification courses. They generally work on a shift basis and are available to receive death calls 24 hours a day. In some offices, the death investigator also serves as a body transport team. In others, removals from the scene are contracted to local removal services or funeral homes. Typically, medicolegal death investigators are unarmed and do not serve as law enforcement officers unless they are part of a sheriff–coroner system.

PROFESSIONAL AND CERTIFYING AGENCIES IN THE UNITED STATES
American Board of Pathology

The American Board of Pathology [6] is the body that certifies a pathologist in general anatomic and clinical pathology and its various subspecialties including forensics. Other subspecialties include surgical pathology, cytology, hematopathology, pediatric and neuropathology, among others. There are rules about the prequalifications necessary to apply for certification, including successful completion of a residency in pathology, a valid medical license, a minimum number of 50 autopsies performed, and exposure to subspecialties to ensure general competence in general diagnoses. It includes a substantial application fee and attendance at a testing station in Florida where the exams are given in computerized format.

Anatomic examination includes a written, image recognition, and microscopic examination done over one and a half days. Clinical pathology has a similar three-part exam over an additional one and a half days. To qualify for forensic pathology certification, anatomic pathology certification must be attained. Clinical pathology is not necessary to qualify for forensic pathology certification, but it may be necessary to run a lab and is useful when evaluating toxicology and microbiology results. The forensic pathology exam is a written exam in addition to a combined image exam that includes microscopic exams; it is completed in one day. Most jobs for forensic pathologists require board certification within a certain period of the hire date or may require it prior to being hired. Board certification is desired for court testimony and is used to establish a basis for basic level of competence in the field. The exams are difficult and are usually offered once or twice per year, which can lead to difficulties in one's career if they are not passed successfully.

Some pathologists perform forensic exams and are not board certified but may be prohibited from performing homicides, child deaths, or complicated autopsies because of it. Forensic exams are also sometimes performed by general hospital pathologists with no additional training in rural areas.

Since 2006, the American Board of Pathology has instituted a mandated continuing-education program called MOC (Maintenance of Certification) that requires recertification in each area every 10 years by demonstration of approved ongoing continuing education. Those certified prior to that have grandfathered certificates not needing this requirement.

Forensic pathology has been recognized by the American Board of Pathology as a subspecialty since 1959. The board has a request form available for confirmation on the board certification status of each member who has applied for certification, which can be confirmed by a form and fee for those doing background checks on pathologist applicants.

American Board of Medicolegal Death Investigators

The American Board of Medicolegal Death Investigators (ABMDI) [7] was established in 2005 as an organization to ensure basic skills and knowledge as a death investigator. There are two levels of certification: an entry level that requires on-the-job experience and completion of a written exam and skill checklist, and an advanced level, which requires a minimum of an associate's degree and more extensive work experience, as well as completion of the basic level of certification. The examination and principles of the certification were established by seasoned death investigators who contributed extensively to the NIJ publication of *Death Investigation: A Guide for the Scene Investigator*, as well as a training manual with the same title. The certification process allows members to state their credentials in court with a basis for national standards as a background.

National Association of Medical Examiners

The National Association of Medical Examiners (NAME) [8] is a national professional organization that was established in 1966. It encompasses not only physician medical examiners as members, but also includes an affiliate membership of medicolegal death investigators and administrators who support and supply knowledge to the process of quality death investigations in the United States. Members can participate in an annual continuing-education meeting for maintenance of licensure and board certification for both medical examiners and death investigators. It operates via presentation of numerous scientific papers of current events and studies important to furthering forensic science and death investigations. They also sponsor a voluntary accreditation program in which an office is evaluated regarding policies, procedures, and performance of quality death investigations as outlined by a multilevel checklist and evaluated by a visiting forensic pathologist. Successful completion allows certification for five years.

In addition to the peer-reviewed accreditation process, NAME is actively supporting periodic routine quality assurance reviews of autopsy reports and findings as a means to ensure basic evaluation of quality documents supplied to the public and judicial system.

American Academy of Forensic Sciences

American Academy of Forensic Sciences (AAFS) [9] is a large diverse organization representing the various aspects of forensic science applications and the law. It was established in 1948 and includes all divisions of criminalistics, anthropology, dentists, attorneys, forensic pathologists, physicists, engineers, and others interested in furthering the science and practices. It sponsors a yearly educational meeting with the presentation of 700–800 scholarly papers to peers in the various specialties. Because of the large diverse membership, it allows sharing of research and ideas across specialties and decreases barriers to advancing research. Membership requirements include recommendations from current members, as well as completion of qualifications established by each subsection of the organization.

American College of Forensic Examiners Institute

The American College of Forensic Examiners Institute (ACFEI) [10] is a relatively new organization and is composed of a diverse group of specialists within forensic investigations. They support a credentialing process through an online course and issue a certificate of completion for criminal investigators, forensic nurses, forensic social workers, and forensic accountants. They support a yearly summit meeting for the presentation of papers by various backgrounds within these forensics specialists.

International Association of Coroners and Medical Examiners

The International Association of Coroners and Medical Examiners (IACME) [11] is an international body that encompasses both coroners and forensic pathologists to foster communication and further quality death investigations to aid the public and law enforcement. The group supports the development of state coroners associations, which offer continuing-education classes, as well as an opportunity to standardize practices throughout the state across jurisdictional lines. The international group also offers a yearly continuing-education meeting and an office accreditation process that if satisfactorily completed is valid for five years.

PHYSICIAN LICENSURE

Physicians undergo a general licensure examination process called the United States Medical License Exam (USMLE). It is given in three steps with the first two completed in medical school and the third in the first or second year of residency. Upon successful completion, an unrestricted medical license is issued in the state of the residency rather than the state where medical school was completed. After the initial licensure, other states generally recognize the presence of a license and will issue their license to an applicant in good standing if he or she meets all the qualifications. Each state will have various pass scores required on the USMLE, and letters of good standing from each state the applicant has a current medical license with, which means no malpractice claims, problems with hospital credentials, felonies or arrests, etc. Application for licensure in another state also requires submission of transcripts from college, medical school, and letters of recommendation, and is quite paper-intensive. To aid some of this, the Federation of State Medical Boards has an affiliated agency called Federal Credentialing Verification Service (FCVS) where all these documents may be submitted for verification from their source as a one-time submission. Any further requests from these documents can be supplied from FCVS at a much faster turnaround, and the recipients of the documents can be assured they are true copies of originals. This service also includes an online application process for some state licensure applications and can be used as part of background checks for job applications and credentialing for hospital privileges.

REFERENCES

[1] History. The Coroners' Society of England & Wales. Retrieved from http://www.coronersociety.org.uk/history. [July 2013].

[2] Hickman M, et al. Medical Examiner and Coroners' Offices, 2004. US Dept of Justice, NCJ 216756. Retrieved from http://www.bjs.gov/content/pub/pdf/meco04.pdf. [July 2013].

[3] Hanzlick R, et al. Selecting Forensic Pathology as a Career: A Survey of the Past with an Eye on the Future. Am J Forensic Med Pathol 2008;29(2):114–22. Retrieved from PubMed.gov, http://www.ncbi.nlm.nih.gov/pubmed/18520476. [July 2013].

[4] Rosenbaum G, et al. Autopsy Consent Practice at US Teaching Hospitals: Results of a National Survey. Arch Intern Med 2000;160(3):374–80. Retrieved from http://archinte.jamanetwork.com/article.aspx?articleid=485226. [July 2013].

[5] History of the Office of Chief Medical Examiner. New York City Office of the Chief Medical Examiner; 2013. Retrieved from http://www.nyc.gov/html/ocme/html/about/about.shtml. [July 2013].

[6] Examination Information. The American Board of Pathology; 2013. Retrieved from http://www.abpath.org/. [July 2013].

[7] American Board of Medicolegal Death Investigators. Retrieved from http://abmdi.org/. [August 2013].

[8] National Association of Medical Examiners. Retrieved from https://netforum.avectra.com/eweb/DynamicPage.aspx?WebCode=LoginRequired&Site=NAME. [August 2013].

[9] American Academy of Forensic Sciences. Retrieved from http://aafs.org. [August 2013].

[10] American College of Forensic Examiners Institute. Retrieved from http://www.acfei.com/. [August 2013].

[11] International Association of Coroners and Medical Examiners. Retrieved from http://www.theiacme.com/home2.html. [August 2013].

[12] Taylor P (chairperson). Model State Vital Statiscs act and Regulations; 1992. US Dept of Health and Human Services. Retrieved from www.cdc.gov/nchs/data/misc/mvsact92b.pdf. [October 2013].

CHAPTER 2
Death Scene Investigation

Learning Objectives

- Apply what you know about making death notification to family members from the point of them answering the door to answering common questions they may ask you. Write out your responses and practice them with a colleague or classmate.
- Outline three ways to ensure quality death investigation and standardize your individual practices.
- Propose two methods of peer review that might be useful for death investigator practices.
- Prepare a simple reminder checklist for overall scene investigation to review prior to leaving a scene and arriving at the office.

Key Terms
Quality assurance
Peer review
Chain of custody
Next of kin
Notification

Chapter Summary

This chapter deals with how the death scene investigator approaches the problem of retrieval of the decedent while properly handling the family and the preservation of evidence on and around the body. A scene is a three-dimensional area that needs to be evaluated to assist in the collection of evidence and properly documenting the scene using photographs. This allows a snapshot view for the pathologist and other investigators to later review so the proper conclusions can be reached in cause and manner determination. It is also the first time the investigator will interact with the **next of kin** and many times law enforcement, so it is important that he or she is organized, systematic, and courteous. Family members can be distraught and not at their best, so it is best to have documents ready to leave with them for contact information and instructions on the process so they can later refer to it. This process of investigation is a one-shot deal and can never be duplicated to the level that it is on the initial visit. It is important for the investigator to consider a differential cause of death using observations, document key features, and resist being closed-minded with preconceived notions. An investigation is a fluid process, and as it progresses, small details may be the necessary key to properly determine the cause of death.

INTRODUCTION

The responsibility of death scene investigation varies across the United States. In some locations it may largely fall upon the coroner office, medical examiner office, or a combined coroner–medical examiner system. In some jurisdictions, the coroner office has been joined with a law enforcement department forming a joint sheriff–coroner division. These investigations involve working with multiple different jurisdictions and office policies. It is important for the death investigator to be aware of basic protocols at all death scenes and be able to adapt to other agency requirements.

The body itself is generally under the jurisdiction of the coroner/medical examiner, but the scene generally is under jurisdiction of the corresponding law enforcement agency (which may be a city police department or sheriff office). Some evidentiary materials overlap into both jurisdictions, so it is important to cooperate during the investigation process. Good death investigation means working as a team within a scene so that evidence in and around a body can be preserved so both cause and manner of death may be determined. Law enforcement often conducts witness interviews, collects crime materials, and takes photographs. Death investigators excel at understanding body changes with death, evaluation of wounds, and relationship of the body to surrounding materials relevant to determine cause of death.

Case Study

A 32-year-old male was found dead in bed during a welfare check after he failed to appear at work. Officers responding to the scene noted a secure residence and no obvious trauma. Because of the age and circumstances, the death was reported to the medical examiner's office. The responding death scene investigator obtained the usual intake demographics from the patrol officers (the only ones who responded to the scene). The officers reported no weapons; the residence was in order and no drug paraphernalia was found. Body examination by the death investigator showed a young male, normal body habitus, without injuries or evidence of drug use. The home was of normal temperature, the refrigerator contained food, and there was no obvious cause of death. Pictures were obtained of the decedent from multiple views in the room. Photos of the medicine cabinet and living areas were obtained. Upon opening the closet, the investigator noted four unmarked brown plastic bottles on the shelf with an insulin syringe, which he photographed and confiscated.

An autopsy examination showed no anatomic cause of death with normal heart, slightly heavy lungs, and normal brain. Cause of death was pending further investigation. Six weeks later, after review of organ biopsies (microscopic examination) and a toxicology report negative for the routinely tested substances, the cause of death was still undetermined. The pathologist noted the brown bottles and syringe in the scene photos and consulted the toxicologist. Some substances are not detected during a routine toxicology examination and the materials were sent to a reference laboratory. Huge levels of anabolic steroids were detected in the toxicology. They were not previously detected because steroids are a naturally occurring material in the body and require special testing procedures to determine if they are used illicitly as a body-building effort. The cause of death was certified as "drug intoxication due to anabolic steroid use" and the manner of death as "accident."

Without the observation powers of the death investigator, the proper cause of death may not have been determined, resulting in an "undetermined" cause and manner of death. Subtle findings and routine evaluation of a decedent by a seasoned death investigator is extremely helpful to both the forensic pathologist and law enforcement to routinely document necessary findings and differentiate artifacts from potential relevant findings important in determining the cause of death. The death investigator needs to be accompanied by law enforcement when he or she is looking around the scene, not only for safety but also for jurisdiction to do so. In some states, the only jurisdiction a death investigator may have is that surrounding the body and he or she is not allowed to search within the residence or property. This death investigation jurisdiction usually extends to medications in the name of the decedent and to those items immediately surrounding them. It is important that the investigator collects these medications at the time as well as information for locating next of kin, because he or she cannot return to the scene after leaving it. Law enforcement will not be able to reenter either without a search warrant or family consent. Any items removed can be returned to the family with the body, but not having something needed or discarded by family will make the case much more complicated.

REVIEW OF LITERATURE

Death investigations are performed by individuals with various levels of expertise, experience, and training. Death investigators may have limited experience with dead bodies, crime scenes, anatomy, medical background, or trauma.

The National Academy of Sciences in their report to the National Institute of Justice in 2009 noted this disparity and has recommended it be addressed for a more uniform approach to death investigations across the United States. They cite that various perspectives and backgrounds of individuals are conducting these investigations, from the lay investigator with little or no training in some regions, to criminalists or crime scene investigators specifically trained in scene evidence recovery. The concern by the report is that inexperience and various policies, procedures, and focuses of the investigation may lead to bias with inappropriate convictions or acquittals [2]. This document reviews each area of the evidentiary process and concludes with recommendations for future improvement of the forensic science field. This document has proven important for advancement of grant funding as well as public awareness of issues faced by many departments. It has been the spearhead of accreditation of medical examiner/coroner offices and forensic laboratories, as well as individual certification and **quality assurance** programs.

Quality assurance programs take multiple forms and may involve subscriptions to accrediting bodies. Some examples are sets of case studies reviewed and submitted for grading, unknown lab samples sent to a central laboratory for grading with required results in an acceptable range to "pass," **peer review** of entire files by others within the office with a similar job description, and continuing-education requirements to maintain certification. Some offices also conduct public surveys of service satisfaction that may factor in yearly evaluations and salary adjustments. Other offices seem to be moving toward database tracking of number of cases per investigator, laboratory scientist, or pathologist, with turnaround times for completion to monitor satisfactory performance.

The American Board of Medicolegal Death Investigators is a governing body associated with the National Association of Medical Examiners and has developed a certification process to ensure basic knowledge of entry- and advanced-level death investigators in an attempt to create a basic uniformity in investigative procedures [3]. The certification process involves demonstrating a physical skill set to a forensic pathologist, as well as investigative procedures of various basic death scenarios with a written examination. Advanced certification requires a college degree and an additional written examination. Certification does not imply that errors will not be made; however, it might raise the basic level of investigations to a national baseline. Part of the maintenance of certification is a continuing-education requirement that helps ensure that the relationship to peers for informal assistance and awareness of advancing technology is maintained.

Because of the wide backgrounds and exposure to training, the National Institute of Justice published a guide to aid death investigators in basic knowledge of the process and collection of the necessary data. This guide, *Death Investigation: A Guide for the Scene Investigator*, can aid the investigator who rarely does death investigations or needs assistance [1].

The National Association of Medical Examiners has instituted an accreditation program that is maintained by forensic pathologists peer-reviewing the operation of both medical examiner and coroner offices within the United States [4]. The process involves an entire review of an office involved in death certification to ensure that minimum standards are being met and that the workload is manageable. The checklist used is available to the public and is helpful when reviewing current office policies and procedures to make sure they have been updated to current standards elsewhere. Also available are autopsy performance standards, which can help guide basic case management and provide direction, as well as serve as a quality assurance standard.

Equipment for scene evaluation has become more sophisticated. Although paper, pencil, and tape measures are still used, sophisticated computer programs can now render scene diagrams based on these measurements. Other instruments include a variation on the surveyor's tripod computing distances outdoors and recording them to drop into the computer program. Many can work on three dimensions, which can save hours processing the scene. However, they are complicated devices and require upfront training and routine use to remain proficient. These devices are also extremely expensive and most medical examiner offices cannot afford to purchase them.

PRESERVATION OF EVIDENCE

The first arriving officer is in charge of the scene until a higher-level investigator arrives. The first officer prevents disturbance of the body and isolates any witnesses so they may be interviewed by the death investigator and/or detective. In homicide scenes, yellow tape is usually placed to prevent free movement in and out of the scene. When arriving at these types of scenes, a scribe noting the name, time of entry, and exit will be at the perimeter and is a good place for the investigator to check in to notify officers of his or her arrival.

Other scenes may be more relaxed and lack the tape or scribe with only a single or pair of patrol officers waiting for the investigator's arrival. It is best for him or her to check in with the officers and gain a basic understanding of the situation prior to entry into the area of the dead body. This is extremely important, as sometimes there is evidence that may be stepped on and damaged just past the officers. They can relay information about resuscitative efforts and how the body was found.

With gunshot deaths, it is always a safe practice to secure the hands by placing brown paper bags over them prior to transport. This allows closer examination later for areas of soot or gunshot residue collection if necessary. It is best to secure the bags with tape rather than rubber bands as the bands create the false impression of a ligature on the wrists. Companies also make special paper-type bags that secure with a light string.

To protect against loss, any large quantities of money on the decedent should be counted with a witness, photographed, then placed into an envelope and sealed with initials of both parties on the envelope. Jewelry, even if it appears not especially valuable, may have sentimental value to a family, and needs to be documented via photographs at the scene. Things on the body are best left there and removed at the time of examination. This allows the pathologist to assess any patterned indentations or marks and correlate them with the jewelry that was in place. It also allows the jewelry to be released to the proper next of kin after that is established either at the funeral home or at the office. On occasion a next of kin will request that the jewelry be removed from the decedent prior to the body being transported to the office. If they are insistent on it, it needs to be photographed and written down on a personal effects form and have the family member sign for it along with a law enforcement officer as a witness. Examples of property forms are located in the Appendix.

Upon leaving a residence, the law enforcement officer will secure the house and lock it. Cars may need to be towed to an impound lot. Travel bags or belongings may need to accompany the decedent or be impounded by the police if they are not in a secure position.

Medications with the name of the decedent or ones in their possession need to be collected and removed from the location where the body was found. This gives the investigator valuable information about what diseases they were being treated for, pain medication use, whether they were being taken as prescribed, and the name of the physician treating the decedent to obtain medical history and possibly next of kin. Most medical examiner offices have a form to be filled out regarding medications (Figure 2.1). It is used to document the medication including the Rx number, date prescribed, medication prescribed, how many pills were dispensed and how many were left, prescribing physician, and the

DATE _____   **MEDICATIONS LOG**   ML# _____
                                                                      NAME _____

ITEM# _____PRESCRIPTION# _____MEDICATION _____
PHARMACY _____PHONE# _____DOCTOR _____
DATE FILLED _____NUMBER REMAINING _____NUMBER ISSUED _____
COMMENTS/DOSAGE _____
_____

ITEM# _____PRESCRIPTION# _____MEDICATION _____
PHARMACY _____PHONE# _____DOCTOR _____
DATE FILLED _____NUMBER REMAINING _____NUMBER ISSUED _____
COMMENTS/DOSAGE _____
_____

ITEM# _____PRESCRIPTION# _____MEDICATION _____
PHARMACY _____PHONE# _____DOCTOR _____
DATE FILLED _____NUMBER REMAINING _____NUMBER ISSUED _____
COMMENTS/DOSAGE _____
_____

ITEM# _____PRESCRIPTION# _____MEDICATION _____
PHARMACY _____PHONE# _____DOCTOR _____
DATE FILLED _____NUMBER REMAINING _____NUMBER ISSUED _____
COMMENTS/DOSAGE _____
_____

ITEM# _____PRESCRIPTION# _____MEDICATION _____
PHARMACY _____PHONE# _____DOCTOR _____
DATE FILLED _____NUMBER REMAINING _____NUMBER ISSUED _____
COMMENTS/DOSAGE _____
_____

ITEM# _____PRESCRIPTION# _____MEDICATION _____
PHARMACY _____PHONE# _____DOCTOR _____
DATE FILLED _____NUMBER REMAINING _____NUMBER ISSUED _____
COMMENTS/DOSAGE _____
_____

FIGURE 2.1
Example of a medication log form to inventory medications recovered from a decedent. Seized medications should be promptly inventoried, then discarded by the office protocol.

pharmacy information. Medications are discarded after they are documented and not returned to the family. Medications should not be discarded down the sink and usually require burning through biohazard companies or law enforcement disposal.

Scattered remains can present their own difficulty. This is seen in traffic, airplane, and train accidents where body tissues may be scattered over terrain. It can be especially challenging to collect if more than one decedent is involved. In that case it is best to make a diagram and label the tissues in separate bags. The main section of the residual body can form in one case number and the main section of other(s) can be in other separate body bags. Identification is going to be challenging in these types of cases, so attention to detail for teeth, jewelry, and personal effects will aid the identification and separation of tissues. If possible names are known, search for any local law enforcement prints or records (many have lists of tattoos as well), which will assist with the timely identification and **notification** of the family. If a circumstantial identification is known, it may be necessary to enlist the family to aid the identification process. The family can be informed that remains with the name of their member have been found and the process is beginning for identification to verify it is that person. They may have information for locating dental or medical records or knowledge of identifying scars, marks, or tattoos.

PHOTOGRAPHING THE DEATH SCENE

One of the hardest parts of photographing a death scene is keeping the photos straight, going from one scene to the next, and not having an opportunity to download them from the camera. It helps to become systematic in the photographic process and routinely repeat the same views and add additional views showing other pertinent details.

One suggestion to divide the photos among cases is to photograph a 3 × 5 card or small dry-erase board with the address location (or GPS coordinates), photographer last name, date, and case number, if it has been assigned. Alternatively, a separate SD card can be utilized for each case. Another photo that is useful is of the front of the house showing the location number so that it can be linked to a file. Some of the newer digital cameras allow programming of the filename so that the photographer's initials can form part of the photo file and verify who took the photos.

Photographing a death scene is basically documenting what the investigator sees on a walkthrough of a residence, into a room, and around a body. Rather than randomly taking photos, it is best to be systematic beginning with the front door and moving to the entrance of the room where the body is located with a view from the doorway. An overall view should be obtained from all four corners of the room where the decedent is located. This can be difficult in confined spaces like a bathroom and may need to be modified to using two or three views depending on the circumstances.

Following overall views, medium range and closer views of the body from sides, top, and bottom should be done if possible. Back and front views need to be done. Close-ups of any valuables are important to document their presence in case they are lost at some point or were not present on the body.

Relationships of the body to any objects or surfaces that may have created any injuries noted on the body are useful. The location of knives and knife stands, and presence of blood on them, is important in stabbings. If a gun is located, its position in relationship to the decedent is important, prior to moving it. Handling a gun requires a certain amount of knowledge of firearms, and law enforcement officers can assist with its examination and making it safe as it is secured as evidence. With revolvers, the cylinder should be photographed as it is ejected from the firing position. In semiautomatic handguns, photos of the cartridge and presence of bullets in the chamber and magazine need to be noted. All weapons need to have their serial numbers and both sides photographed after they are made safe. It is useful also to photograph the barrel end of a weapon to document presence or absence of blowback of tissue, blood, or foreign materials into the end of the weapon (again, be sure the weapon has been made safe and emptied of all bullets before doing this).

The surrounding surfaces that may be disturbed by moving the body or by the transport gurney need to be secured and photographed. This will also allow an entry and exit of the body from the scene. The sooner this can be done, the easier it will be to process the remainder of the scene and speed up the process. Preservation of the body as soon as reasonably possible will assist the later examination by the pathologist. By allowing the death investigator and/or pathologist to view the body may add insight into what type of death it is, and aid what photographs or investigation needs to follow. It is important that if the weapon, such as a knife, arrow, etc., is still embedded in the decedent, if possible the investigator needs to leave this weapon in the decedent and just secure it to the body. Any ligatures around the neck need to be left in place to allow the pathologist to view and remove these items. The investigator should disturb the surface of the decedent as little as possible.

After the body is photographed, it can be examined with photographs of any necessary valuables, injuries, or underlying evidence, then the body can be secured for transport. After the body is removed, it is important to photograph the surface where the body was resting. Photographing and securing any new pertinent evidence may be needed at this point using information gleaned from the external examination. The location of medications in relation to the body, bullet strikes, surrounding surfaces, the interior of a vehicle, etc. all need to be photographed as part of the scene investigation process and possible later review.

EVIDENCE COLLECTION TECHNIQUES

Whole books and treatises are written about evidence collection. Here some basic rules of thumb will be discussed that can easily be remembered. It is best to know crime lab technicians' recommendations and use them as a definitive resource because they are the ones doing the actual testing. If an investigator has something unusual, he or she should give them a call and ask them how it would best be collected.

On routine things, if it is a wet specimen, it needs to be collected onto something so it can dry since wet specimens deteriorate and may become unusable. So a wet blood spot needs to be collected with a cotton applicator (basically a large Q-tip) and placed into a specimen container to protect it and later dry. Wet clothing needs to be left on the body and removed during the autopsy. Clothing is usually placed into brown paper bags for transport and into a biohazard transport bag to prevent external contamination seeping through. As soon as possible, clothing needs to be hung to air dry in an area where the items will not be cross-contaminated by people passing by. Most departments have a clothing drying room with separate lockers per case, or special air-drying cabinets. When the clothing is dry, it can be placed into brown paper bags and stored. During the process of drying, each case must be marked with the name and case number to prevent mix-ups.

Dry specimens have more options and depend on the object. Basically, choose the smallest size container based on the size of the specimen, without stuffing it tightly. Guns, knives, and hazardous things like syringes have specialty boxes or plastic containers for secure transport, and to prevent injuries to others who unwittingly handle the contents.

Tape ligatures, gags, plastic wrap, and trash bags

These items present a collection issue because they will stick to the inside of a paper bag or plastic. The cut or torn ends need to be preserved during removal to use as a potential match for a recovered roll of tape. Tape also has potential for fingerprints and vast collection of trace evidence from the scene when it was placed on the decedent (Figure 2.2). Photograph the gag or ligature from the front, sides, and back, if possible, to document its placement. To remove it, use a scalpel (protect the underlying skin with the edge by a ruler or clean scalpel handle slipped under) or a scissor at a point away from the tape edges. Pull the edge of the tape back and document the underlying skin or gag within a mouth and how deeply it was embedded in the skin. The ligature can then be gently removed using forceps and dropped into a pizza or gun box for transport to the lab.

Plastic-wrapped bodies can also be treated similarly but the container for transport may need to be larger, such as a clean banker or file box. Again, fingerprints may be on the layers of plastic as it was applied, so gentle handling is needed. If the top/bottom or inside/outside are difficult to differentiate, discrete small marks can be made with an indelible marker.

Trash bags are also extremely good for fingerprints and need to be handled carefully in areas where there are ties or the edges used to place it over the decedent's

A

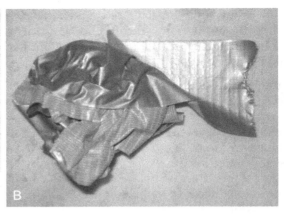

B

C

FIGURE 2.2
(A) The variety of tape that may be characteristic in an investigation to link a suspect to a decedent's death. (B) Tape can be difficult to package because it is sticky, therefore it is best placed inside a box rather than a paper bag if at all possible. (C) The margins of the tape tear can be characteristic and also could be the location of fingerprints. It is important when handling tape evidence to cut it off away from ends or areas where evidence may be best retrieved [5].

body parts. It is best to cut the bag with scissors to open it, leaving the tie intact. It can be laid out for photographs if necessary on a clean sheet then dropped into a brown paper bag for transport. Any questions about how to handle a unique piece of evidence is best managed by calling the crime laboratory where it will be submitted and asking for advice. It makes the processing much easier if they are involved and it is submitted correctly.

Each specimen needs to be labeled properly before removal from the site of collection. In a controlled environment, this can be done with adhesive labels run off on the computer and attached to the outside of the receptacle. These labels typically include the agency case number, name of the decedent, and current date. In the morgue situation it includes the pathologist name in charge of the case, or in law enforcement, the agency name. Below this information, the type of specimen, time collected, and initials of the person collecting it can be written.

For permanent storage, all evidence must be sealed prior to storage to ensure that it has not been tampered with or cross-contaminated. Special evidence tape is used for this purpose.

Occasionally law enforcement will request a sexual assault exam at the scene. It is best to contact the forensic pathologist who will conduct the exam for direction on how to proceed. If it is evident that the decedent has been sexually assaulted, it is a good practice to contact the forensic pathologist on-call and have him or her respond to the scene since swabs collected by the investigator may not withstand scrutiny in court.

CHAIN OF CUSTODY

A **chain of custody** is a form listing any seized evidence in sequence and noted in the same fashion as the identifying marks on the packaging (Figure 2.3). At the bottom of the form is a place for the signature of the person who collected the evidence and turned it over to the next person, who then is in charge of the material. It basically forms a branching tree so the origin of the results can be traced to the person who originally collected it from the site of the crime or from the body. If at any point the chain is broken, the evidence can become inadmissible to court and useless. To prevent any confusion as to which item is which the terminology used on the packaging (e.g., "bullet from head," or item 16 jeans) must match the description on the form.

CHAIN OF CUSTODY

DATE _____   ML # _____

NAME _____   AGENCY/# _____

FROM   TO

_____   _____TIME _____ DATE _____
_____   _____TIME _____ DATE _____
_____   _____TIME _____ DATE _____

FIGURE 2.3
A chain of custody serves as written documentation of each person who has handled a piece of evidence from its site of origin to its final storage destination. It links the piece of evidence to a produced report regarding the evidence, how and where it is stored and its location prior to the evidence being heard in court. It is important that each person linking the evidence to the next person be intact to verify that custody has been maintained and the evidence not tampered or contaminated.

MEDICOLEGAL DEATH INVESTIGATOR SCENE RESPONSE

Types of deaths requiring response

Obviously, it is best if a death investigator can respond to all death scenes, including hospital deaths, and depending on the jurisdiction, the death investigator may be serving the dual service of investigator and body removal. Each jurisdiction is designed slightly different and may utilize law enforcement for information to a varying degree. Also a variable is the body removal service, and whether it is supplied by the office or by a contract service. If it is the office, it may be a crew who does the removal service or it may be done by the death investigator.

In those instances where the death investigator is not the removal person, latitude in judgment or department policy will dictate scene response. Acute deaths where scene response is usually required are those including death in custody, firearm deaths, children, fire deaths, high-profile officials or visitors, aircraft, hangings, and suspicious deaths where law enforcement requests assistance or something seems unusual. Obviously, daytime response is much easier and should approach 100% on these types of deaths, but after-hours or weekend response may become an issue due to financial constraints or shortage of manpower.

Investigation briefcase

Death investigation is getting more sophisticated every day. Many have found durable laptop computers with roving Internet linkage to greatly expedite input into the office database directly from the scene, allowing real-time information to be relayed, as well as freeing the investigator to move to the next scene if need be. With digital photography, photographs can be downloaded and sent to the pathologist to be reviewed over a secure web line.

Even if the office is more basic, a laptop computer can be a real boost to an office. This allows the investigator to enter a case into the template and print it when he or she returns or upload it into the server. A paperless office can consist of a case file folder (much like a chart folder) on a server containing subfolders with the paper documents and one for the photos. It is also possible to have medical records transmitted in PDF format via a general investigator mailbox. Hospitals or doctor offices can do this from their paperless system or via paper directly onto a fax machine. Many copy machines now have the ability to convert paper to PDF-type files. Another useful item is a portable scanner or printer in case a form needs to be printed or if there are documents at the scene that need to be copied but may not be able to be seized by the death investigator (e.g., suicide notes).

Even with these sophisticated abilities, an investigator is going to need a pad of paper to record proper name spelling, date of birth, date and time of death, medications, medical history, who found the decedent, exact address, and next of kin information. An office might find it useful to utilize card form that is easily written on and can be placed into a pocket. There are examples of paper forms for retrieving the necessary intake information in the Appendix.

A digital camera is a must. It is useful to learn the various settings on the camera and practice its use so the investigator is able to adapt to various scenarios. A few difficult situations are those in rain or snow because the flash will reflect off the droplets. Photographing a body inside a motor vehicle is difficult because the investigator can be seen in the reflection of the window. Another is darkness with difficult lighting because the flash is not able to compensate using typical settings. It may be necessary to go manual and use a tripod to allow the aperture to remain open longer. Decomposed bodies in dark backgrounds are also challenging.

Other supplies needed are bags to collect and seal medications or large amounts of money, evidence collection bags of various sizes, lots of gloves, and clean collection instruments like forceps in a sealed clean pouch, paper towels, hand sanitizer, business cards, office brochures, or contact information.

Equipment list

The following is a handy list of items that are good to have when responding to a death scene:

- Camera
- Gloves
- Evidence bags
- Spare SD card and batteries for camera
- Business cards
- Small tablet for note taking
- Sudden Unexplained Infant Death Investigation (SUIDI) forms
- Chain of custody forms
- Paper case form (in case computer is not working)
- Clean forceps for evidence collection
- Pocket knife
- Body identification bracelet or tag
- Black magic markers
- Extra pen
- Hand sanitizer
- Paper towels
- Small biohazard bags and one or two large bags
- Multifunction pocket tool
- Flashlight
- Cut-resistant gloves
- EMT scissors to cut through ligatures, seat belts, etc.

Response vehicle equipment

The response vehicle should serve as a resource for restocking the briefcase and for holding items not commonly used. Typical things that should be stored in the vehicle are:

- Safety vest and flares for roadway scenes
- Body bags: regular, infant; heavy-duty with straps; extra large
- Extra body tags/bracelets
- Personal protective equipment (mask, coveralls, shoe covers, hair covers or ball cap)
- Tape measure
- Extra gloves
- Extra evidence bags and biohazard bags
- Small tarp
- Small shovel
- Pruning shears/bolt cutter
- Rope
- Bottled water
- Bug-collecting equipment (plastic containers with holes in lids, cat food, and large aquarium net or small butterfly net)
- Extra batteries for camera/flashlight
- Backup point-and-shoot camera

The response vehicle needs to reliably start, have a full gas tank before each shift, and be properly maintained, including routine cleaning inside and out. It is a good practice to keep a can of some type of sanitizing spray so that the investigator can spray the bottom of his or her shoes prior to getting into the vehicle at the scene. This will decrease cross-contamination to the vehicle or to other scenes that follow that day. It is also a good practice to wipe down the camera after every scene to make sure there are no biohazards on the camera equipment. Keeping an extra set of clothing including shoes inside the vehicle is helpful in cases where the investigator has become contaminated and has to discard his or her clothing at the scene.

MEDICAL AND SOCIAL HISTORY

The reporting party, such as roommate, spouse, or family member, may have some information about the current or past health of the decedent or his or her habits. It is important to ask about any current complaints, drinking, drug use, smoking, occupation, recent hospitalizations or visits to the doctor, and prescription medication use. Family history, including sudden death or other ill family members, may also be important. Pertinent observations, such as antacid use, over-the-counter medication use, examination of the trash, alcohol bottles, drug residue, etc., are important to include in the report. Even the presence or absence of a secure residence is an important finding, as are the circumstances the decedent was found (e.g., witnessed collapsed, welfare check, routinely returning to residence, etc.). The name of a treating physician is important to routinely request medical records. If it is an older individual, the death may have been expected and that physician may be willing to sign a death certificate if the death appears natural without trauma.

With decomposed bodies, law enforcement officers may know if fingerprints are available for identification verification. It may be efficient to explore with the family or a physician if the decedent had recent X-rays that might be used to confirm identification or if the decedent used a dentist.

NOTIFICATION OF NEXT OF KIN

Death notification to family or close friends of the decedent is not the easiest part of the job for death investigators. Many of the deaths are sudden and family members may be shocked, angry, or have some feelings of guilt or regret. Families are not at their best during these trying times. Violence, sudden collapse, threats, or just intense grief with apparent lack of cooperation may erupt. It is important to always have a situational awareness in case the situation deteriorates.

Notification is best made in person. If personally done, coworkers should be aware of the investigator's location or a coworker or law enforcement officer should accompany him or her to the site of notification. With the transient society we live in, many times this is not personally possible if the next of kin lives a distance away. It may be necessary to activate their local law enforcement agency to notify them and have them call for details. State law usually indicates the order of next of kin notification, which can be in the order of spouse, father, mother, siblings, and children. Obviously not all of them need to be notified, but the closest next of kin needs to be located for further demographic information, final disposition details, medical history, etc.

WRITTEN REPORT FORMATS

The written report should contain a concise summary of the course of events that surrounded the time of death. It needs to be grammatically correct, spell checked, and have a logical flow of information. Saying too much and being overly interpretive is as bad as or worse than leaving out pertinent information. It is best to utilize a framework for each report so information within it can be located quickly to answer pertinent questions (Figure 2.4).

CASE FLOW

Steps in the process of how a body is handled and paperwork flow can be office-dependent. However, all offices have certain aspects in common, and it is helpful to understand this process so it can be explained to a decedent's family members or an outside agency.

Initial Written Report Format
Case #: LAST NAME, First Name
Response date & time: Information source: Circumstances of death: Past medical history: Treating physician Medications: Identification: Notification Body Exam: rigor, livor, body position, areas of trauma
Report Amendments Update identification confirmation if needed Final Disposition: Funeral home, relative authorizing release, date released Follow up history or investigation information

FIGURE 2.4
Summary of key topics needed in every report. Other information can be added within these areas to summarize the course of events.

How does a case come to the attention of an investigator?

State law mandates reporting certain cases by anyone having the knowledge of a death within the statutes. In summary, these include all unnatural, suspicious, or unusual deaths, and those posing a public health hazard. Various smaller categories exist within the law and will clarify the general description. Each office will have a policy on which cases require a scene response and which cases may be managed over the phone. A rule of thumb is all traumatic deaths dead at a scene, those with no attending physician, and those under suspicious circumstances like drug use require a response. Those found outside a residence, inside a vehicle, or if the officer at the scene needs assistance are also common response scenes. Older persons (usually over 70–75 years) or those dying in a hospital are not as high priority to respond and visually view the body. Children dead at a scene should have a response, and, if possible, children dead in a hospital without trauma, medical history, or those with trauma not related to motor vehicle accidents should have a scene response by the investigator or law enforcement to assess the home situation and photography.

Basically, a call comes from outside the office to say there is a death in a particular location. Depending on who makes the call—a dispatcher, a patrol officer, an adjacent county investigator/coroner—will reveal more or less information. Sometimes all that is communicated is an address and request for an investigator to respond. This means the investigator has to be ready for anything from a child, to a homicide, to skeletal remains, to a buried body, to a traffic accident, etc. The response briefcase and vehicle need to be prepared to address questions law enforcement may have and to deal with all these scenarios. The vehicle needs to always be restocked when the previous investigator has returned to the office and used something from the vehicle. Periodic inventory needs to be done to ensure the vehicle and briefcases are stocked.

Other times, the caller may state that the decedent is older with no evidence of foul play or trauma and is under the current care of a physician. Office policy will guide the investigator if a scene response is needed in these types of cases.

Scene response is not something delayed by multiple distractions. When the call comes, the investigator should be organized to respond out the door within five minutes. Many times, officers are being held up at the scene of death while other response calls come to their department. Roads may be closed, trains stopped, or airports closed until the body is removed and the scene is cleared. It is important for the investigator to take the direct route and be timely.

GPS systems are highly advised to not only get the investigator there by the most direct route, but also in remote areas, GPS coordinates can be used for recording on the paperwork as the site of death. Getting to a scene may be complicated by backed-up traffic due to the scene. The local police department dispatch may be able to assist and recommend the best route into the scene, which may mean going to an exit and up the wrong way on a closed road, or to request a police escort. Dispatch can also pass a call to the officer at the scene and let the investigator talk to him or her directly if the investigator is lost or having difficulty. Many times the officer will post a flare or park a unit at a turn-off to guide others in.

What does an investigator do when he or she arrives?

An officer will be at the scene when the investigator arrives and he or she is the first point of contact for information. If the scene is a homicide, there will be a sign-in process to enter the scene and proceed beyond the yellow tape. A detective will escort the investigator in and brief him or her. The investigator should pay attention to areas on the floor and the small flags adjacent to items of evidence so as not to disturb them. Entry into a scene like this requires use of gloves and shoe covers at a minimum. The investigator should follow the lead of the detective who meets him or her, and not pick things up and look at them until the investigator is briefed. Before removing anything, the investigator should ask if it has been photographed and documented. The detective will do a walk-through and explain the case and areas of importance. There is no need to photograph or document anything until this is complete. The investigator should ask about logistics and if there is a clear path to the body. He or she should begin to formulate a plan for approaching the body, as well as what items will be needed to preserve and answer the questions law enforcement officers may have. The investigator should consider the amount of time and when he or she needs to call for body removal service. The investigator wants to be at the scene the shortest amount of time possible (in case there is another scene response) and does not want to wait on the arrival of the body removal service after the body is in the body bag. He or she should begin to fill out the paperwork demographics with the information that is known. In addition, he or she should gather the materials needed to examine the body, including being prepared to protect the hands with brown paper bags, photograph the body, put on the identification band for the body, and have a plan for placement of the body into a body bag. Sealing the bag in the presence of law enforcement documents that the bag has not been breached prior to it being opened by morgue personnel.

How does the investigator start gathering the info?

The scene information will tailor the various specific pieces of information that need to be documented. All scenes get the basic information of demographics, what happened, overall photographs, and examination of the body for rigor, livor, and gross documentation of injuries. Specific documentation of each injury will be documented by the doctor, but some evaluation needs to be made to assess if the injuries are matching the scenario that law enforcement has provided. Discrepancies need to be communicated to them and it should be decided together how best to proceed. It may require the forensic pathologist to respond if law enforcement needs information to proceed. The body needs to be checked for weapons so they may be removed and given to law enforcement prior to transport. The body always needs to be placed on its back to transport so as not to distort the facial features. Wrapping the body in a sheet will minimize the amount of blood welling up in the bag and soaking the clothing, especially for gunshot and stab wounds.

How does the investigator get the body to the office?

Some offices have investigators do their own transport. Other offices have employees in a separate unit do the transport, or in combination with the investigator as an assistant. Other options include local transport services under contract that typically also transport for funeral homes.

What happens to the body when it gets to the office?

The body is logged into the system. Office policy will determine if the body can be prepared for an autopsy or if the bag must remain sealed until the autopsy begins. It is possible to X-ray the body through the bag without opening it, which is helpful in homicides. If the bag can be opened, the property and clothing may be removed and documented on routine cases. Other offices keep the bag closed until the time of the autopsy and all is documented at that time. Height and weight are recorded.

What happens during the autopsy?

The forensic pathologist will take notes about property, weight, and height, and examine the body for injuries. All will be recorded for later transition into a written report. Some cases may be certified only on external examination based on history and observations from the examination. X-rays may be used to examine the body for trauma, enlarged heart, pneumonia, or foreign objects. Toxicology and DNA sampling is obtained on most bodies. Fingerprints are also obtained for retention in the office file as well as a copy forwarded to law enforcement to close records. Using these observations, the doctor will determine if he or she can certify a cause of death upon exam only or decide if an autopsy needs to be done.

An external exam usually takes 15–30 minutes depending on the extent of injuries. A routine autopsy for a natural death or drug intoxication death requires an hour or two to complete. Homicides or complicated cases take generally at least two hours and can extend up to six hours. Child abuse cases can be multistaged over a couple of days and an estimated date for release of the body to the family needs to be coordinated with the pathologist.

What does the investigator do when he or she returns to the office?

The investigator needs to begin a report and enter the demographic data needed into the database, transfer the photographs from the camera to a disk/computer system, and coordinate with the pathologist and morgue staff regarding the case for potential autopsy, need for X-rays, etc. If the office is operating within an online death certificate system, it usually falls to the investigator to begin the data entry for its completion. Generally, this includes the name, date, time, and location of death and time of injury if known. The pathologist will document the cause and manner. It is helpful to chat with the pathologist about his or her findings so they can be relayed to the family. Medications from the decedent need to be counted, recorded, and prepared for discard and should not lie about the office.

What happens after the autopsy?

It is good practice to contact the next of kin after the exam or autopsy to relay the cause of death and findings. If the cause and manner are pending toxicology or further investigation, it is a good time to ask the family further questions needed by the pathologist and about medical history, or gather other information needed to determine the manner of death. The family can be given a time estimate for completion of the cause and manner and the process for them to receive reports, amended death certificates, etc.

How does the body get back to the family?

A family will generally ask how to get the decedent back and this topic is easily addressed during the call made by the investigator after the autopsy/exam. It is a great opportunity to request their funeral home of choice and relay that the decision needs to be made as soon as possible. If families cannot make a decision due to conflicts or are unable to afford a funeral home, it is good to be aware of social services available.

What happens at the funeral home?

It is always a good idea to get the family funeral home choice relayed to the office in writing and verify that the decision was made by the family member who has the authority to do so. Sometimes families do not communicate well and conflicts will become apparent. It is important the office depends on the person with the legal authority and have proof of this to avoid having to assume the cost of transport to another funeral home.

The appropriate funeral home or their transport company will arrive at the office to retrieve the body. It is important that all clothing and personal effects be released with the body. Verification of the personal property, valuables, and identity of the decedent with signatures on all forms is required before the body may leave the building. Visually checking the name on the identification band on the decedent and the case number, by both the morgue personnel/investigator and the funeral home personnel, is imperative to prevent the wrong body being released. It is even more imperative if there is more than one decedent with the same last name.

Valuables and large amounts of money need to be counted and verified plus signed for before release. The office will have a paperwork system to deal with the property and body release (Figure 2.5).

What happens with the paperwork?

Most offices still maintain some form of paper file. Many offices are converting to a paperless office at least to some degree so many reports are present in both formats. A file generally includes standard documents for the investigative report, pathologist report, copy of death certificate, requests for copies of the reports, fingerprints, backup X-ray and photo disks, property, and body release forms. Other information such as chain of custody or medical records may be included. Files are generally filed by case numbers.

How does the family or agencies get copies of the paperwork or file contents?

Each office will have a policy regarding release of documents based on what has been deemed public record by state law. The county or state attorney representing the office usually assists with making decisions about unusual requests like review boards. In most states, the completed death certificate is public record and anyone may retrieve a copy from the health department. Releasing cause and manner information over the phone to press and other entities not related to next of kin may need supervisor approval or need to be referred to the law enforcement agency public information officer/detective in sensitive cases.

State law also may mandate that copies of certain reports, such as homicides, be relayed to particular agencies such as the county or state attorney. Each state varies whether the autopsy report is considered public record and released to all requestors. Knowledge and understanding of this policy needs to be reviewed in

PROPERTY RECEIPT

Date: _____

Name of Deceased: _____ Case # _____

PROPERTY:	Received	Amount		Total	Received
_____	_____	$ 0.01 x _____	=	0.00	_____
_____	_____	$ 0.05 x _____	=	0.00	_____
_____	_____	$ 0.10 x _____	=	0.00	_____
_____	_____	$ 0.25 x _____	=	0.00	_____
_____	_____	$ 0.50 x _____	=	0.00	_____
_____	_____	$ 1.00 x _____	=	0.00	_____
_____	_____	$ 2.00 x _____	=	0.00	_____
_____	_____	$ 5.00 x _____	=	0.00	_____
_____	_____	$ 10.00 x _____	=	0.00	_____
_____	_____	$ 20.00 x _____	=	0.00	_____
_____	_____	$ 50.00 x _____	=	0.00	_____
_____	_____	$ 100.00 x _____	=	0.00	_____
_____	_____		Total =	0.00	_____

Checks: Amount   Received

_____ $_____ _____

_____ $_____ _____

_____ $_____ _____

_____ $_____ _____

_____ _____

Signature, Person releasing property   Witness

_____

Signature, Person receiving property   Date / Time   By

_____

Print Name   Relationship to the decedent (Mortuary, Family, Etc.)

FIGURE 2.5
Basic property documentation form. The articles of clothing and personal effects can be listed and the money itemized. At the bottom are signature areas for those releasing and then receiving the property so that a chain of custody is maintained.

the procedure manual or state law regarding which documents may be released and to whom. Photographs from the autopsy are similar in their status and are not generally released to the press due to their sensitive nature and invasion of privacy. In high-profile cases, the press frequently will seek them under the First Amendment. In Florida, the Earnhardt Family Protection Act, also known as the Earnhardt Law, was passed in response to the press wishing access to the autopsy photos of Dale Earnhardt, Sr., who died during the Daytona 500 auto race. The Florida law states that autopsy photos, videos, and audio recordings are confidential and should not be released without a judge's approval. Failure to comply with the law is a felony punishable by a $5,000 fine. A surviving spouse, parent, or child may view the photos and the medical examiner or other state agencies may utilize them in the course of their duties without the judge's permission, but the identity of the decedent must remain confidential. Other states have adopted similar restrictions. Families may request to see the autopsy photos. This can be traumatic for them to review, and whenever possible, the investigator needs to explore what answer they are seeking to see if the question can be answered in some other fashion.

Attorneys commonly request copies of autopsy and toxicology reports and possibly photos. Office policy needs to outline the procedure for this. A good practice is for the request to be submitted in writing on company letterhead with the request outlining which documents they wish to obtain. There may be fees associated with this request and those will need to be communicated to them. Occasionally they will submit a subpoena or a *duces tecum*, which outlines a request for the entire record, including investigative reports, toxicology, worksheets, chain of custody, and internal documents that form the file. Many offices exclude reports from outside agencies (e.g., medical records, police reports) as they were not generated by the coroner/medical examiner office and should be retrieved from the originating source. It is best if the chief coroner or medical examiner outlines which documents are to be included in each type of request (*duces tecum*, subpoena, letter request) and approve any outlying ones. This list can be preapproved by the office attorney to make sure it is in compliance with state laws.

The length of time to completion of an autopsy report will vary based on a number of factors. It can be dependent on information from the crime laboratory, further investigation, confirmation of the identity of the decedent, toxicology results, medical records, and review of microscopic tissue biopsies that need review by the forensic pathologist. It is generally at least one month for a report and can extend to six months or even a year depending on the workload and the difficulties of the case. It is best not to promise an exact date, but to have the families or other interested parties call back at intervals.

Case Study

A call comes to the office requesting an investigator to respond to a possible suicide at 399 Harbor Street in your local jurisdiction. Upon arriving at the scene, the investigator is met outside the residence by a patrol officer and a detective. They relate that a 25-year-old male was found by a friend on the patio of the decedent's residence. He was found sitting in a chair with a gun on his lap beside his right hand. EMS was called, documented a gunshot wound to the head, and moved him to the ground, but he was unable to be resuscitated. The officers state he had recently been found to be having an affair with his wife's best friend, had been accused of embezzling money from the office where he worked, and was being investigated by undercover police for drug trafficking.

The death investigator asks the usual demographics, including name, age, date of birth, next of kin, time of pronouncement, when he was last seen alive, how he was identified, as well as the detective's name and contact information. The family has not arrived outside the residence and the investigator inquires about the whereabouts of the wife. Further questioning can be about the ownership of the gun, where it was stored, where the ammunition was stored, how long he had the gun, how familiar he was with gun usage, was he right- or left-handed, and what prompted the friend to come visit.

At this point, it is time for the investigator to consider calling for transport so they will arrive about the time she is ready to place the body in the bag. The investigator has a fully stocked briefcase including a working camera, gloves, brown paper bags, and body bag with a seal to carry to the patio for the examination. This is the best time for her to put two pairs of gloves on before entering. It is also helpful for her to snap the baseline photo of the location on a white board as well as the house number before proceeding inside the house. She should place booties on her feet to prevent tracking blood back through the house, and it is also a good time to ensure her hair is confined and all necessary clothing protection is in place.

The detective then escorts the investigator to the patio for the survey. The decedent is visible lying on the ground next to a metal chair and a large pool of blood is at the base of the chair and under the decedent's head. The pool of blood at the base of the chair contains a peripheral fine spray of blood spatter. The gun is lying on an adjacent picnic table and has been made safe by the patrol officer upon his arrival. According to the detective, the 9-mm handgun had an empty chamber and empty magazine. Blowback is visible within the barrel of the weapon. The gun had been stored in a case in an upstairs bedroom and the case was found open on the bed. A new box of ammunition was on the dresser and showed a single missing bullet in the package. A receipt for the ammunition was lying beside the box and dated the previous day.

The investigator proceeds to photograph the scene from four points around the decedent, followed by midrange views of the top and sides of the body. Photos of the gun on the table, including serial number and blood transfer on the barrel, need to be documented. Midrange views need to be obtained of the blood spray at the base of the chair. Photos of the decedent's hands showing any soot deposition, as well as mid- and close-range views of the gunshot wound need to be documented. Valuables including necklaces and rings need to be visible in the photos. It is always helpful and courteous for the investigator to assist law enforcement with any photos they may need during this process.

Before touching the body, it is good for the investigator to pull out brown paper bags and tape so she can secure these in place before handling the body. As they are slipped on, it is a good time to examine the hands for injuries. Handling the arms also gives information about the rigor, body warmth, and livor. Before getting gloves bloody, it is good to assess livor on the torso, and assess the chest and remainder of the body for any other injuries. Pockets can be patted for identification, wallets, potential weapons, and drugs. It is good practice to pat the pockets before putting hands into them. This will avoid the investigator being stuck by needles or any other sharp objects that might be in the pockets. The last step is to make a close examination of the head including the eyes for petechiae, the mouth for injuries, and the neck. The goal is to differentiate entrance and exit wounds, if possible, and note any other injuries. If entrance and exit wounds are unable to be determined by the investigator, it is better to be noncommittal. The presence of soot or a muzzle abrasion in this type of case will let the detective know it was a contact or near-contact wound. If an exit wound is identified, the detective will want to try to locate the expended bullet, if possible. So it will be necessary to palpate the scalp to locate it. The wounds should never be probed. If the face is distorted by trauma, it is helpful for the investigator to ask law enforcement to check for availability of fingerprints on file for confirmation of identity.

Officers may be willing to assist rolling the body to view the back so both parties can obtain photos. Or it can be done when removal arrives to help move the body into the bag. Either way, photographing the body when it is rolled onto

Continued

the side is a good way to not only document the back for injuries, but also note any jewelry pendants that are on the back of a necklace, and the ground under the decedent. If the blood is flowing freely, a towel can be used to wrap around the head and contain the mess. An open body bag can be tucked under the body while on its side and when it's rolled back it will be within the inside of the bag ready for transfer to a gurney and removal. The identification band can be attached and any related property can be contained in the bag. At this point, bloody gloves can be peeled off and placed in the bag, or a small biohazard bag in the briefcase.

It is time to photograph the gun case and ammunition box, as well as search for a note or medications related to the decedent. As the house is surveyed, items used to date the last known alive point are noted including cellphone texts, etc. The investigator gathers this information and inquires about the notification of the wife. The detective has already spoken to her and told her of the husband's death via phone. She is en route to the residence.

Removal service has arrived and is ready to remove the body to the office. The investigator assists with logistics of escorting them to the decedent and ensures the bag is sealed. The detective has boxed the firearm and the ammunition and ejected casing. A bullet was not located. After the body has exited the scene, the ground around the body can be photographed.

The body arrives at the morgue and is logged in by the personnel. A head X-ray is obtained through the body bag and a projectile is noted. The forensic pathologist is briefed and it is decided the autopsy will be done in two hours. The detective is called and notified that the bullet is present in the head and the pathologist is doing an autopsy in two hours. The detective has confirmed a previous arrest record and fingerprints are on file if needed. The wife is located at the residence phone and the investigator makes contact to confirm notification and obtain psychological history.

The pathologist confirms the contact gunshot wound of the head and findings consistent with suicide. Toxicology specimens are obtained and sent to the laboratory. Fingerprints are also obtained during the autopsy and ready to be sent to law enforcement for confirmation of identity. The investigator scans and arranges to email them or deliver them to law enforcement for positive identification.

The investigator calls the wife and notifies her of the cause of death and answer her questions. Other family members inquire about clean up and the investigator refers them to cleaning services in the community that deal with such matters. They inquire how to obtain a death certificate and the investigator relays that it will be given to them at the funeral home. The family supplies the name of the funeral home and the investigator requests that the funeral home send that authorization to the office and the decedent can be released with property and valuables.

The investigator completes the written report, downloads the photos, and records any medications to finalize the investigation. Follow-up information is usually placed onto addendum reports.

RESOURCES

Many state crime laboratories and the FBI publish an evidence handling manual. Here are a few helpful versions:

Missouri. http://www.mshp.dps.missouri.gov/MSHPWeb/Publications/Handbooks-Manuals/documents/SHP-145.pdf.

Texas: Physical Evidence Handbook. http://www.txdps.state.tx.us/CrimeLaboratory/documents/PEHmanual.pdf.

FBI: Handbook of Forensic Services. http://www.fbi.gov/about-us/lab/handbook-of-forensic-services-pdf/view.

Schoebel PJ, Weiss S. Photography of medicolegal and forensic autopsies. Evidence Technology Magazine 2009;10–13:28.

Body diagrams. http://www.afmes.mil/index.cfm?pageid=resources.autopsy_diagrams.

REFERENCES

[1] National Medicolegal Review Panel. Death Investigation: A Guide for the Scene Investigator. Technical update. National Institute of Justice; 2011. Retrieved from https://ncjrs.gov/pdffiles1/nij/234457.pdf. [16 August 2013].

[2] National Research Council of the National Academies. Strengthening Forensic Science in the United States. National Academies Press; 2009. Retrieved from http://www.nap.edu/catalog.php?record_id=12589. [22 August 2013].

[3] American Board of Medicolegal Death Investigators. Retrieved from http://abmdi.org/. [23 August 2013].

[4] NAME Accreditation Checklist 2009-2014. National Association of Medical Examiners Inspection and Accreditation Documents. Checklist and Autopsy Standards. Retrieved from https://netforum.avectra.com/eweb/DynamicPage.aspx?Site=NAME&WebCode=PubIA. [23 August 2013].

[5] Pressure Sensitive Tape. Missouri State Highway Patrol. Retrieved from http://www.mshp.dps.missouri.gov/MSHPWeb/PatrolDivisions/CLD/TraceEvidence/tape.html. [16 August 2013].

CHAPTER 3
Death Certification

Learning Objectives

- Distinguish cause of death from a manner of death and give examples of each.
- Identify a cause of death that might need further investigation and outline the reasoning why it would need to be investigated, as well as the questions that would need to be asked to determine if jurisdiction would be needed.
- Discuss the purpose of a death certificate and its role in vital statistics and final affairs of the decedent.
- Research the state laws for the definition of a fetus, age of viability, and live birth in your state. Discuss what impact this determination has for the proper certification format (i.e., birth certificate with death certificate versus fetal death certificate).
- Illustrate an example of a therapeutic misadventure and questions that need to be answered to differentiate an accidental manner versus a known complication for a natural disease.

Key Terms
Manner of death
Cause of death
Fetus
Live birth
Therapeutic misadventure

Chapter Summary

Death certification is an important document for families to resolve estates, as well as a means to monitor public health trends and prevention of death. It is important to distinguish causes of death from mechanisms of death, as well as have an understanding of key investigative issues used to distinguish the manner of death. Death investigators usually serve as a final safeguard of questionable causes of death to prevent unreported cases to the death investigation system and serve as a reference for vital records departments and families. It is important to have a working knowledge of causes of death that may have an underlying accidental, suicidal, or homicidal manner.

INTRODUCTION

Death certification is a process of establishing an official cause of death for official purposes. Certificates are completed by a treating physician, by coroners, or by medical examiners (Figure 3.1). State law determines who will be eligible for

U.S. STANDARD CERTIFICATE OF DEATH

LOCAL FILE NO.   STATE FILE NO.

NAME OF DECEDENT — For use by physician or institution

To Be Completed/ Verified By: FUNERAL DIRECTOR

1. DECEDENT'S LEGAL NAME (Include AKA's if any) (First, Middle, Last)			2. SEX	3. SOCIAL SECURITY NUMBER

4a. AGE-Last Birthday (Years)	4b. UNDER 1 YEAR		4c. UNDER 1 DAY		5. DATE OF BIRTH (Mo/Day/Yr)	6. BIRTHPLACE (City and State or Foreign Country)
	Months	Days	Hours	Minutes		

7a. RESIDENCE-STATE	7b. COUNTY	7c. CITY OR TOWN

7d. STREET AND NUMBER	7e. APT. NO.	7f. ZIP CODE	7g. INSIDE CITY LIMITS? ☐ Yes ☐ No

8. EVER IN US ARMED FORCES? ☐ Yes ☐ No	9. MARITAL STATUS AT TIME OF DEATH ☐ Married ☐ Married, but separated ☐ Widowed ☐ Divorced ☐ Never Married ☐ Unknown	10. SURVIVING SPOUSE'S NAME (If wife, give name prior to first marriage)

11. FATHER'S NAME (First, Middle, Last)	12. MOTHER'S NAME PRIOR TO FIRST MARRIAGE (First, Middle, Last)

13a. INFORMANT'S NAME	13b. RELATIONSHIP TO DECEDENT	13c. MAILING ADDRESS (Street and Number, City, State, Zip Code)

14. PLACE OF DEATH (Check only one; see instructions)

IF DEATH OCCURRED IN A HOSPITAL: ☐ Inpatient ☐ Emergency Room/Outpatient ☐ Dead on Arrival

IF DEATH OCCURRED SOMEWHERE OTHER THAN A HOSPITAL: ☐ Hospice facility ☐ Nursing home/Long term care facility ☐ Decedent's home ☐ Other (Specify):

15. FACILITY NAME (If not institution, give street & number)	16. CITY OR TOWN , STATE, AND ZIP CODE	17. COUNTY OF DEATH

18. METHOD OF DISPOSITION: ☐ Burial ☐ Cremation ☐ Donation ☐ Entombment ☐ Removal from State ☐ Other (Specify):	19. PLACE OF DISPOSITION (Name of cemetery, crematory, other place)

20. LOCATION-CITY, TOWN, AND STATE	21. NAME AND COMPLETE ADDRESS OF FUNERAL FACILITY

22. SIGNATURE OF FUNERAL SERVICE LICENSEE OR OTHER AGENT	23. LICENSE NUMBER (Of Licensee)

To Be Completed By: MEDICAL CERTIFIER

ITEMS 24-28 MUST BE COMPLETED BY PERSON WHO PRONOUNCES OR CERTIFIES DEATH	24. DATE PRONOUNCED DEAD (Mo/Day/Yr)	25. TIME PRONOUNCED DEAD

26. SIGNATURE OF PERSON PRONOUNCING DEATH (Only when applicable)	27. LICENSE NUMBER	28. DATE SIGNED (Mo/Day/Yr)

29. ACTUAL OR PRESUMED DATE OF DEATH (Mo/Day/Yr) (Spell Month)	30. ACTUAL OR PRESUMED TIME OF DEATH	31. WAS MEDICAL EXAMINER OR CORONER CONTACTED? ☐ Yes ☐ No

CAUSE OF DEATH (See instructions and examples)

32. PART I. Enter the chain of events—diseases, injuries, or complications—that directly caused the death. DO NOT enter terminal events such as cardiac arrest, respiratory arrest, or ventricular fibrillation without showing the etiology. DO NOT ABBREVIATE. Enter only one cause on a line. Add additional lines if necessary.

Approximate interval: Onset to death

IMMEDIATE CAUSE (Final disease or condition ------> resulting in death)
a. _____
Due to (or as a consequence of):

Sequentially list conditions, if any, leading to the cause listed on line a. Enter the UNDERLYING CAUSE (disease or injury that initiated the events resulting in death) LAST
b. _____
Due to (or as a consequence of):

c. _____
Due to (or as a consequence of):

d. _____

PART II. Enter other significant conditions contributing to death but not resulting in the underlying cause given in PART I

33. WAS AN AUTOPSY PERFORMED? ☐ Yes ☐ No
34. WERE AUTOPSY FINDINGS AVAILABLE TO COMPLETE THE CAUSE OF DEATH? ☐ Yes ☐ No

35. DID TOBACCO USE CONTRIBUTE TO DEATH? ☐ Yes ☐ Probably ☐ No ☐ Unknown	36. IF FEMALE: ☐ Not pregnant within past year ☐ Pregnant at time of death ☐ Not pregnant, but pregnant within 42 days of death ☐ Not pregnant, but pregnant 43 days to 1 year before death ☐ Unknown if pregnant within the past year	37. MANNER OF DEATH ☐ Natural ☐ Homicide ☐ Accident ☐ Pending Investigation ☐ Suicide ☐ Could not be determined

38. DATE OF INJURY (Mo/Day/Yr) (Spell Month)	39. TIME OF INJURY	40. PLACE OF INJURY (e.g., Decedent's home; construction site; restaurant; wooded area)	41. INJURY AT WORK? ☐ Yes ☐ No

42. LOCATION OF INJURY: State: City or Town:

Street & Number: Apartment No.:   Zip Code:

43. DESCRIBE HOW INJURY OCCURRED:	44. IF TRANSPORTATION INJURY, SPECIFY: ☐ Driver/Operator ☐ Passenger ☐ Pedestrian ☐ Other (Specify)

45. CERTIFIER (Check only one):
☐ Certifying physician-To the best of my knowledge, death occurred due to the cause(s) and manner stated.
☐ Pronouncing & Certifying physician-To the best of my knowledge, death occurred at the time, date, and place, and due to the cause(s) and manner stated.
☐ Medical Examiner/Coroner-On the basis of examination, and/or investigation, in my opinion, death occurred at the time, date, and place, and due to the cause(s) and manner stated.

Signature of certifier _____

46. NAME, ADDRESS, AND ZIP CODE OF PERSON COMPLETING CAUSE OF DEATH (Item 32)

47. TITLE OF CERTIFIER	48. LICENSE NUMBER	49. DATE CERTIFIED (Mo/Day/Yr)	50. FOR REGISTRAR ONLY- DATE FILED (Mo/Day/Yr)

To Be Completed By: FUNERAL DIRECTOR

51. DECEDENT'S EDUCATION-Check the box that best describes the highest degree or level of school completed at the time of death.	52. DECEDENT OF HISPANIC ORIGIN? Check the box that best describes whether the decedent is Spanish/Hispanic/Latino. Check the "No" box if decedent is not Spanish/Hispanic/Latino.	53. DECEDENT'S RACE (Check one or more races to indicate what the decedent considered himself or herself to be)
☐ 8th grade or less	☐ No, not Spanish/Hispanic/Latino	☐ White
☐ 9th - 12th grade; no diploma		☐ Black or African American
☐ High school graduate or GED completed	☐ Yes, Mexican, Mexican American, Chicano	☐ American Indian or Alaska Native (Name of the enrolled or principal tribe)_____
☐ Some college credit, but no degree	☐ Yes, Puerto Rican	☐ Asian Indian ☐ Chinese ☐ Filipino
☐ Associate degree (e.g., AA, AS)	☐ Yes, Cuban	☐ Japanese ☐ Korean ☐ Vietnamese
☐ Bachelor's degree (e.g., BA, AB, BS)	☐ Yes, other Spanish/Hispanic/Latino (Specify) _____	☐ Other Asian (Specify)_____ ☐ Native Hawaiian ☐ Guamanian or Chamorro
☐ Master's degree (e.g., MA, MS, MEng, MEd, MSW, MBA)		☐ Samoan ☐ Other Pacific Islander (Specify)_____
☐ Doctorate (e.g., PhD, EdD) or Professional degree (e.g., MD, DDS, DVM, LLB, JD)		☐ Other (Specify)_____

54. DECEDENT'S USUAL OCCUPATION (Indicate type of work done during most of working life. DO NOT USE RETIRED)

55. KIND OF BUSINESS/INDUSTRY

REV. 11/2003

FIGURE 3.1

The U.S. Standard Certificate of Death. It serves as the template for each state to adopt their death certificate in compliance with their state laws. The majority of states and the jurisdictions within them have progressed to online death certification, which appears similar to this format [4].

MEDICAL CERTIFIER INSTRUCTIONS for selected items on U.S. Standard Certificate of Death
(See Physicians' Handbook or Medical Examiner/Coroner Handbook on Death Registration for instructions on all items)

ITEMS ON WHEN DEATH OCCURRED
Items 24-25 and 29-31 should always be completed. If the facility uses a separate pronouncer or other person to indicate that death has taken place with another person more familiar with the case completing the remainder of the medical portion of the death certificate, the pronouncer completes Items 24-28. If a certifier completes Items 24-25 as well as items 29-49, Items 26-28 may be left blank.

ITEMS 24-25, 29-30 – DATE AND TIME OF DEATH
Spell out the name of the month. If the exact date of death is unknown, enter the **approximate** date. If the date cannot be approximated, enter the date the body is found and identify as **date found**. Date pronounced and actual date may be the same. Enter the exact hour and minutes according to a 24-hour clock; estimates may be provided with "Approx." placed before the time.

ITEM 32 – CAUSE OF DEATH (See attached examples)
Take care to make the entry legible. Use a computer printer with high resolution, typewriter with good black ribbon and clean keys, or print legibly using permanent **black** ink in completing the CAUSE OF DEATH Section. **Do not abbreviate** conditions entered in section.

Part I (Chain of events leading directly to death)
•Only **one** cause should be entered on each line. Line (a) **MUST ALWAYS** have an entry. **DO NOT** leave blank. Additional lines may be added if necessary.
•If the condition on Line (a) resulted from an underlying condition, put the underlying condition on Line (b), and so on, until the full sequence is reported. **ALWAYS** enter the **underlying cause of death** on the lowest used line in Part I.
•For each cause indicate the best estimate of the interval between the presumed onset and the date of death. The terms "unknown" or "approximately" may be used. General terms, such as minutes, hours, or days, are acceptable, if necessary. **DO NOT** leave blank.
•The terminal event (for example, cardiac arrest or respiratory arrest) should not be used. If a mechanism of death seems most appropriate to you for line (a), then you must always list its cause(s) on the line(s) below it (for example, cardiac arrest **due to** coronary artery atherosclerosis or cardiac arrest **due to** blunt impact to chest).
• If an organ system failure such as congestive heart failure, hepatic failure, renal failure, or respiratory failure is listed as a cause of death, always report its etiology on the line(s) beneath it (for example, renal failure **due to** Type I diabetes mellitus).
•When indicating neoplasms as a cause of death, include the following: 1) primary site or that the primary site is unknown, 2) benign or malignant, 3) cell type or that the cell type is unknown, 4) grade of neoplasm, and 5) part or lobe of organ affected. (For example, a primary well-differentiated squamous cell carcinoma, lung, left upper lobe.)
•Always report the fatal injury (for example, stab wound of chest), the trauma (for example, transection of subclavian vein), and impairment of function (for example, air embolism).

PART II (Other significant conditions)
•Enter all diseases or conditions contributing to death that were not reported in the chain of events in Part I and that did not result in the underlying cause of death. See attached examples.
•If two or more possible sequences resulted in death, or if two conditions seem to have added together, report in Part I the one that, in your opinion, most directly caused death. Report in Part II the other conditions or diseases.

CHANGES TO CAUSE OF DEATH
Should additional medical information or autopsy findings become available that would change the cause of death originally reported, the original death certificate should be amended by the certifying physician by **immediately** reporting the revised cause of death to the State Vital Records Office.

ITEMS 33-34 - AUTOPSY
•33 - Enter "Yes" if either a partial or full autopsy was performed. Otherwise enter "No."
•34 - Enter "Yes" if autopsy findings were available to complete the cause of death; otherwise enter "No". Leave item blank if no autopsy was performed.

ITEM 35 - DID TOBACCO USE CONTRIBUTE TO DEATH?
Check "yes" if, in your opinion, the use of tobacco contributed to death. Tobacco use may contribute to deaths due to a wide variety of diseases; for example, tobacco use contributes to many deaths due to emphysema or lung cancer and some heart disease and cancers of the head and neck. Check "no" if, in your clinical judgment, tobacco use did not contribute to this particular death.

ITEM 36 - IF FEMALE, WAS DECEDENT PREGNANT AT TIME OF DEATH OR WITHIN PAST YEAR?
This information is important in determining pregnancy-related mortality.

ITEM 37 - MANNER OF DEATH
•Always check Manner of Death, which is important: 1) in determining accurate causes of death; 2) in processing insurance claims; and 3) in statistical studies of injuries and death.
•Indicate "Pending investigation" if the manner of death cannot be determined whether due to an accident, suicide, or homicide within the statutory time limit for filing the death certificate. This should be changed later to one of the other terms.
•Indicate "Could not be Determined" **ONLY** when it is impossible to determine the manner of death.

ITEMS 38-44 - ACCIDENT OR INJURY – to be filled out in all cases of deaths due to injury or poisoning.
•38 - Enter the exact month, day, and year of injury. Spell out the name of the month. **DO NOT** use a number for the month. (Remember, the date of injury may differ from the date of death.) Estimates may be provided with "Approx." placed before the date.
•39 - Enter the exact hour and minutes of injury or use your best estimate. Use a 24-hour clock.
•40 - Enter the general place (such as restaurant, vacant lot, or home) where the injury occurred. **DO NOT** enter firm or organization names. (For example, enter "factory", **not** "Standard Manufacturing, Inc.")
•41 - Complete if anything other than natural disease is mentioned in Part I or Part II of the medical certification, including homicides, suicides, and accidents. This includes all motor vehicle deaths. The item **must** be completed for decedents ages 14 years or over and may be completed for those less than 14 years of age if warranted. Enter "Yes" if the injury occurred at work. Otherwise enter "No". An injury may occur at work regardless of whether the injury occurred in the course of the decedent's "usual" occupation. Examples of injury at work and injury not at work follow:

Injury at work	Injury not at work
Injury while working or in vocational training on job premises	Injury while engaged in personal recreational activity on job premises
Injury while on break or at lunch or in parking lot on job premises	Injury while a visitor (not on official work business) to job premises
Injury while working for pay or compensation, including at home	Homemaker working at homemaking activities
Injury while working as a volunteer law enforcement official etc.	Student in school
Injury while traveling on business, including to/from business contacts	Working for self for no profit (mowing yard, repairing own roof, hobby)
	Commuting to or from work

•42 - Enter the complete address where the injury occurred including zip code.
•43 - Enter a brief but specific and clear description of how the injury occurred. Explain the circumstances or cause of the injury. Specify **type of gun** or **type of vehicle** (e.g., car, bulldozer, train, etc.) when relevant to circumstances. Indicate if more than one vehicle involved; specify type of vehicle decedent was in.
•44 -Specify role of decedent (e.g. driver, passenger). Driver/operator and passenger should be designated for modes other than motor vehicles such as bicycles. Other applies to watercraft, aircraft, animal, or people attached to outside of vehicles (e.g. surfers).

Rationale: Motor vehicle accidents are a major cause of unintentional deaths; details will help determine effectiveness of current safety features and laws.
REFERENCES
For more information on how to complete the medical certification section of the death certificate, refer to tutorial at http://www.TheNAME.org and resources including instructions and handbooks available by request from NCHS, Room 7318, 3311 Toledo Road, Hyattsville, Maryland 20782-2003 or at www.cdc.gov/nchs/about/major/dvs/handbk.htm

REV. 11/2003

FIGURE 3.1, cont'd

Cause-of-death – Background, Examples, and Common Problems

Accurate cause of death information is important
• to the public health community in evaluating and improving the health of all citizens, and
• often to the family, now and in the future, and to the person settling the decedent's estate.

The cause-of-death section consists of two parts. Part I is for reporting a chain of events leading directly to death, with the **immediate cause** of death (the final disease, injury, or complication directly causing death) on line a and the **underlying cause** of death (the disease or injury that initiated the chain of events that led directly and inevitably to death) on the lowest used line. Part II is for reporting all other significant diseases, conditions, or injuries that contributed to death but which did not result in the underlying cause of death given in Part I. **The cause-of-death information should be YOUR best medical OPINION.** A condition can be listed as "probable" even if it has not been definitively diagnosed.

Examples of properly completed medical certifications

CAUSE OF DEATH (See instructions and examples)

		Approximate interval: Onset to death
32. **PART I.** Enter the chain of events--diseases, injuries, or complications--that directly caused the death. DO NOT enter terminal events such as cardiac arrest, respiratory arrest, or ventricular fibrillation without showing the etiology. DO NOT ABBREVIATE. Enter only one cause on a line. Add additional lines if necessary		
IMMEDIATE CAUSE (Final disease or condition ------> resulting in death)	a. Rupture of myocardium Due to (or as a consequence of):	Minutes
Sequentially list conditions, if any, leading to the cause listed on line a. Enter the **UNDERLYING CAUSE** (disease or injury that initiated the events resulting in death) **LAST**	b. Acute myocardial infarction Due to (or as a consequence of):	6 days
	c. Coronary artery thrombosis Due to (or as a consequence of):	5 years
	d. Atherosclerotic coronary artery disease	7 years

PART II. Enter other significant conditions contributing to death but not resulting in the underlying cause given in PART I	33. WAS AN AUTOPSY PERFORMED? ■ Yes No
Diabetes, Chronic obstructive pulmonary disease, smoking	34. WERE AUTOPSY FINDINGS AVAILABLE TO COMPLETE THE CAUSE OF DEATH? ■ Yes No

35. DID TOBACCO USE CONTRIBUTE TO DEATH?	36. IF FEMALE	37. MANNER OF DEATH
■ Yes Probably No Unknown	■ Not pregnant within past year Pregnant at time of death Not pregnant, but pregnant within 42 days of death Not pregnant, but pregnant 43 days to 1 year before death Unknown if pregnant within the past year	■ Natural Homicide Accident Pending Investigation Suicide Could not be determined

CAUSE OF DEATH (See instructions and examples)

		Approximate interval: Onset to death
32. **PART I.** Enter the chain of events--diseases, injuries, or complications--that directly caused the death. DO NOT enter terminal events such as cardiac arrest, respiratory arrest, or ventricular fibrillation without showing the etiology. DO NOT ABBREVIATE. Enter only one cause on a line. Add additional lines if necessary		
IMMEDIATE CAUSE (Final disease or condition ------> resulting in death)	a. Aspiration pneumonia Due to (or as a consequence of):	2 Days
Sequentially list conditions, if any, leading to the cause listed on line a. Enter the **UNDERLYING CAUSE** (disease or injury that initiated the events resulting in death) **LAST**	b. Complications of coma Due to (or as a consequence of):	7 weeks
	c. Blunt force injuries Due to (or as a consequence of):	7 weeks
	d. Motor vehicle accident	7 weeks

PART II. Enter other significant conditions contributing to death but not resulting in the underlying cause given in PART I	33. WAS AN AUTOPSY PERFORMED? ■ Yes No
	34. WERE AUTOPSY FINDINGS AVAILABLE TO COMPLETE THE CAUSE OF DEATH? ■ Yes No

35. DID TOBACCO USE CONTRIBUTE TO DEATH?	36. IF FEMALE	37. MANNER OF DEATH
Yes Probably ■ No Unknown	Not pregnant within past year Pregnant at time of death Not pregnant, but pregnant within 42 days of death Not pregnant, but pregnant 43 days to 1 year before death Unknown if pregnant within the past year	Natural Homicide ■ Accident Pending Investigation Suicide Could not be determined

38. DATE OF INJURY (Mo/Day/Yr) (Spell Month) August 15, 2003	39. TIME OF INJURY Approx. 2320	40. PLACE OF INJURY (e.g., Decedent's home; construction site; restaurant; wooded area) road side near state highway	41. INJURY AT WORK? Yes ■ No

42. LOCATION OF INJURY: State: Missouri	City or Town: near Alexandria	
Street & Number: mile marker 17 on state route 46a	Apartment No.	Zip Code:

43. DESCRIBE HOW INJURY OCCURRED: Decedent driver of van, ran off road into tree	44. IF TRANSPORTATION INJURY, SPECIFY: ■ Driver/Operator Passenger Pedestrian Other (Specify)

Common problems in death certification

The **elderly decedent** should have a clear and distinct etiological sequence for cause of death, if possible. Terms such as senescence, infirmity, old age, and advanced age have little value for public health or medical research. Age is recorded elsewhere on the certificate. When a number of conditions resulted in death, the physician should choose the single sequence that, in his or her opinion, best describes the process leading to death, and place any other pertinent conditions in Part II. If after careful consideration the physician cannot determine a sequence that ends in death, then the medical examiner or coroner should be consulted about conducting an investigation or providing assistance in completing the cause of death.

The **infant decedent** should have a clear and distinct etiological sequence for cause of death, if possible. "Prematurity" should not be entered without explaining the etiology of prematurity. Maternal conditions may have initiated or affected the sequence that resulted in infant death, and such maternal causes should be reported in addition to the infant causes on the infant's death certificate (e.g., Hyaline membrane disease due to prematurity, 28 weeks **due to** placental abruption **due to** blunt trauma to mother's abdomen).

When **SIDS** is suspected, a complete investigation should be conducted, typically by a medical examiner or coroner. If the infant is under 1 year of age, no cause of death is determined after scene investigation, clinical history is reviewed, and a complete autopsy is performed, then the death can be reported as Sudden Infant Death Syndrome.

When processes such as the following are reported, additional information about the etiology should be reported:

Abscess	Carcinomatosis	Disseminated intra vascular coagulopathy	Hyponatremia	Pulmonary arrest
Abdominal hemorrhage	Cardiac arrest		Hypotension	Pulmonary edema
Adhesions	Cardiac dysrhythmia	Dysrhythmia	Immunosuppression	Pulmonary embolism
Adult respiratory distress syndrome	Cardiomyopathy	End-stage liver disease	Increased intra cranial pressure	Pulmonary insufficiency
Acute myocardial infarction	Cardiopulmonary arrest	End-stage renal disease	Intra cranial hemorrhage	Renal failure
Altered mental status	Cellulitis	Epidural hematoma	Malnutrition	Respiratory arrest
Anemia	Cerebral edema	Exsanguination	Metabolic encephalopathy	Seizures
Anoxia	Cerebrovascular accident	Failure to thrive	Multi-organ failure	Sepsis
Anoxic encephalopathy	Cerebellar tonsillar herniation	Fracture	Multi-system organ failure	Septic shock
Arrhythmia	Chronic bedridden state	Gangrene	Myocardial infarction	Shock
Ascites	Cirrhosis	Gastrointestinal hemorrhage	Necrotizing soft-tissue infection	Starvation
Aspiration	Coagulopathy	Heart failure	Old age	Subdural hematoma
Atrial fibrillation	Compression fracture	Hemothorax	Open (or closed) head injury	Subarachnoid hemorrhage
Bacteremia	Congestive heart failure	Hepatic failure	Paralysis	Sudden death
Bedridden	Convulsions	Hepatitis	Pancytopenia	Thrombocytopenia
Biliary obstruction	Decubiti	Hepatorenal syndrome	Perforated gallbladder	Uncal herniation
Bowel obstruction	Dehydration	Hyperglycemia	Peritonitis	Urinary tract infection
Brain injury	Dementia (when not otherwise specified)	Hyperkalemia	Pleural effusions	Ventricular fibrillation
Brain stem herniation		Hypovolemic shock	Pneumonia	Ventricular tachycardia
Carcinogenesis	Diarrhea			Volume depletion

If the certifier is unable to determine the etiology of a process such as those shown above, the process must be qualified as being of an unknown, undetermined, probable, presumed, or unspecified etiology so it is clear that a distinct etiology was not inadvertently or carelessly omitted.

The following conditions and types of death might seem to be specific or natural but when the medical history is examined further may be found to be complications of an injury or poisoning (possibly occurring long ago). Such cases should be reported to the medical examiner/coroner:

Asphyxia	Epidural hematoma	Hip fracture	Pulmonary emboli	Subdural hematoma
Bolus	Exsanguination	Hyperthermia	Seizure disorder	Surgery
Choking	Fall	Hypothermia	Sepsis	Thermal burns/chemical burns
Drug or alcohol overdose/drug or alcohol abuse	Fracture	Open reduction of fracture	Subarachnoid hemorrhage	

REV. 11/2003

FIGURE 3.1, cont'd

FUNERAL DIRECTOR INSTRUCTIONS for selected items on U.S.

Standard Certificate of Death (For additional information concerning all items on certificate see Funeral Directors' Handbook on Death Registration)

ITEM 1. DECEDENT'S LEGAL NAME
Include any other names used by decedent, if substantially different from the legal name, after the abbreviation AKA (also known as) e.g. Samuel Langhorne Clemens AKA Mark Twain, **but not** Jonathon Doe AKA John Doe

ITEM 5. DATE OF BIRTH
Enter the full name of the month (January, February, March etc.) Do not use a number or abbreviation to designate the month.

ITEM 7A-G. RESIDENCE OF DECEDENT (information divided into seven categories)
Residence of decedent is the place where the decedent actually resided. The place of residence is not necessarily the same as "home state" or "legal residence". Never enter a temporary residence such as one used during a visit, business trip, or vacation. Place of residence during a tour of military duty or during attendance at college is considered permanent and should be entered as the place of residence. If the decedent had been living in a facility where an individual usually resides for a long period of time, such as a group home, mental institution, nursing home, penitentiary, or hospital for the chronically ill, report the location of that facility in item 7. If the decedent was an infant who never resided at home, the place of residence is that of the parent(s) or legal guardian. **Never** use an acute care hospital's location as the place of residence for any infant. If Canadian residence, please specify Province instead of State.

ITEM 10. SURVIVING SPOUSE'S NAME
If the decedent was married at the time of death, enter the full name of the surviving spouse. If the surviving spouse is the wife, enter her name prior to first marriage. This item is used in establishing proper insurance settlements and other survivor benefits.

ITEM 12. MOTHER'S NAME PRIOR TO FIRST MARRIAGE
Enter the name used prior to first marriage, commonly known as the maiden name. This name is useful because it remains constant throughout life.

ITEM 14. PLACE OF DEATH
The place where death is pronounced should be considered the place where death occurred. If the place of death is unknown but the body is found in your State, the certificate of death should be completed and filed in accordance with the laws of your State. Enter the place where the body is found as the place of death.

ITEM 51. DECEDENT'S EDUCATION *(Check appropriate box on death certificate)*
Check the box that corresponds to the highest level of education that the decedent completed. **Information in this section will not appear on the certified copy of the death certificate. This information is used to study the relationship between mortality and education (which roughly corresponds with socioeconomic status). This information is valuable in medical studies of causes of death and in programs to prevent illness and death.**

ITEM 52. WAS DECEDENT OF HISPANIC ORIGIN? *(Check "No" or appropriate "Yes" box)*
Check "No" or check the "Yes" box that best corresponds with the decedent's ethnic Spanish identity as given by the informant. Note that "Hispanic" is not a race and item 53 must also be completed. Do not leave this item blank. With respect to this item, "Hispanic" refers to people whose origins are from Spain, Mexico, or the Spanish-speaking Caribbean Islands or countries of Central or South America. Origin includes ancestry, nationality, and lineage. There is no set rule about how many generations are to be taken into account in determining Hispanic origin; it may be based on the country of origin of a parent, grandparent, or some far-removed ancestor. Although the prompts include the major Hispanic groups, other groups may be specified under "other". "Other" may also be used for decedents of multiple Hispanic origin (e.g. Mexican-Puerto Rican). **Information in this section will not appear on the certified copy of the death certificate. This information is needed to identify health problems in a large minority population in the United States. Identifying health problems will make it possible to target public health resources to this important segment of our population.**

ITEM 53. RACE *(Check appropriate box or boxes on death certificate)*
Enter the race of the decedent as stated by the informant. Hispanic is not a race; information on Hispanic ethnicity is collected separately in item 52. American Indian and Alaska Native refer only to those native to North and South America (including Central America) and does not include Asian Indian. Please specify the name of enrolled or principal tribe (e.g., Navajo, Cheyenne, etc.) for the American Indian or Alaska Native. For Asians check Asian Indian, Chinese, Filipino, Japanese, Korean, Vietnamese, or specify other Asian group; for Pacific Islanders check Guamanian or Chamorro, Samoan, or specify other Pacific Island group. If the decedent was of mixed race, enter each race (e.g., Samoan-Chinese-Filipino or White, American Indian). **Information in this section will not appear on the certified copy of the death certificate. Race is essential for identifying specific mortality patterns and leading causes of death among different racial groups. It is also used to determine if specific health programs are needed in particular areas and to make population estimates.**

ITEMS 54 AND 55. OCCUPATION AND INDUSTRY
Questions concerning occupation and industry must be completed for all decedents 14 years of age or older. This information is useful in studying deaths related to jobs and in identifying any new risks. For example, the link between lung disease and lung cancer and asbestos exposure in jobs such as shipbuilding or construction was made possible by this sort of information on death certificates. **Information in this section will not appear on the certified copy of the death certificate.**

ITEM 54. DECEDENT'S USUAL OCCUPATION
Enter the usual occupation of the decedent. This is not necessarily the last occupation of the decedent. Never enter "retired". Give kind of work decedent did during most of his or her working life, such as claim adjuster, farmhand, coal miner, janitor, store manager, college professor, or civil engineer. If the decedent was a homemaker at the time of death but had worked outside the household during his or her working life, enter that occupation. If the decedent was a homemaker during most of his or her working life, and never worked outside the household, enter "homemaker". Enter "student" if the decedent was a student at the time of death and was never regularly employed or employed full time during his or her working life. **Information in this section will not appear on the certified copy of the death certificate.**

ITEM 55. KIND OF BUSINESS/INDUSTRY
Kind of business to which occupation in item 54 is related, such as insurance, farming, coal mining, hardware store, retail clothing, university, or government. DO NOT enter firm or organization names. If decedent was a homemaker as indicated in item 54, then enter either "own home" or "someone else's home" as appropriate. If decedent was a student as indicated in item 54, then enter type of school, such as high school or college, in item 55. **Information in this section will not appear on the certified copy of the death certificate.**

NOTE: This recommended standard death certificate is the result of an extensive evaluation process. Information on the process and resulting recommendations as well as plans for future activities is available on the Internet at: http://www.cdc.gov/nchs/vital_certs_rev.htm.

REV. 11/2003

FIGURE 3.1, cont'd

its completion depending on the circumstances the decedent is found in. This chapter discusses the various portions of the death certificate, definitions of terms used in death certification, and tips for surveillance of problem death certificates.

DEFINITION AND PURPOSE

A death certificate serves two main purposes: as a public document registering an official cause of death that allows estates to be closed and financial matters to be resolved, and as a vital record document in which national statistics are derived and monitored for public health trends for prevention of disease or health hazards. The document consists of demographic information such as official name, date of birth, address, social security number, parents' names, and location of death (Figure 3.2). The next main area consists of the cause and manner of death, as well as particulars of an accidental or unnatural cause of death. Community treating physicians may sign death certificates on their patients if they die of natural causes such as heart or lung disease, strokes, etc. All unnatural causes of death such as falls, suicides, drug intoxications or homicides must be certified by either a forensic pathologist/medical examiner or a coroner depending on the state law requirement. To prevent unnatural deaths from being missed or not examined by authorities, in many jurisdictions death certificates are monitored by the coroner or medical examiner office for causes that may be unnatural.

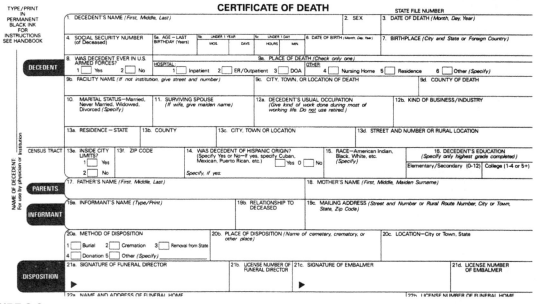

FIGURE 3.2

The top portion of the death certificate showing the required information that needs to be completed. The majority of this portion of the death certificate is completed by the funeral home when the family arrives to make arrangements. The investigator is largely responsible for originating the name, date, time and location of death, and location of where the death occurred. The forensic pathologist completes the cause and manner and how the injury occurred.

CAUSE OF DEATH

Cause of death is a medical description or diagnosis describing why someone is dead. Common causes of death are often abbreviated forms of medical terms (Figure 3.3). It is helpful to have a basic understanding of common medical diagnoses, anatomy and physiology to evaluate death certificates and converse

Common Medical Abbreviations	
AFIB	Atrial Fibrillation
ALS	Amyotrophic Lateral Sclerosis
AMI	Acute Myocardial Infarct
ASCVD	Atherosclerotic Cardiovascular Disease
Asp	Asphyxia
AVM	Arteriovenous Malformation
BFT	Blunt Force Trauma
c	with
CA	Cancer
CAD	Coronary Artery Disease
CABG	Coronary Artery Bypass Graft
CHD	Congenital Heart Disease
CHF	Congestive Heart Failure
CNS	Central Nervous System
CP	Cerebral Palsy/Chest Pain
CRF	Chronic Renal Failure
CT	Computerized Tomography (type of xray)
CV	Cardiovascular
CVA	Cerebrovascular Accident
DM	Diabetes Mellitus
DVT	Deep Vein Thrombosis
Dz	Disease
ESRD	End Stage Renal Disease
ETOH	Ethanol (alcohol)
GSW	Gunshot Wound
HTN	Hypertension (Hypertensive)
ICD	Implantable Cardioverter Defibrillator
ICH	Intracranial or Intracerebral
IHD	Ischemic Heart Disease
MI	Myocardial Infarction
MRI	Magnetic Resonance Imaging
MRSA	Methicillin Resistant Staphylococcus Aureus
Mult	Multiple
MVA	Motor Vehicle Accident
MVP	Mitral Valve Prolapse
(P)	Pending
RA	Rheumatoid Arthritis
s	without
SAH	Subarachnoid Hemorrhage
SDH	Subdural Hemorrhage
SIDS	Sudden Infant Death Syndrome
SUIDI	Sudden Unexplained Infant Death Investigation
URI	Upper Respiratory Infections
UTI	Urinary Tract Infection

FIGURE 3.3
A list of common abbreviations that will be encountered by the death investigator.

with physicians, nurses and emergency medical personnel. Common examples include:

- Myocardial infarction (heart attack)
- Acute intracerebral hemorrhage (stroke)
- Atherosclerotic cardiovascular disease (generalized hardening of the arteries)
- Chronic obstructive pulmonary disease (emphysema and chronic bronchitis)

The cause area has three lines—a, b, c—with each line followed by the term "due to." Vital records do not require that all three lines are completed, but a pathological cause must be listed somewhere within these lines, not just a physiologic one (Figure 3.4). Physiologic causes are, for example, cardiac arrest, hemorrhage, cardiac arrhythmia, respiratory arrest, and renal failure. All these mechanisms of death have an underlying pathologic cause that needs to be listed to be accurate and acceptable.

Here is an example where inaccurate information is supplied and will result in the doctor being called:

a. Cardiac arrest

If this had been certified as the following it would have been approved:

a. Cardiac arrest *due to*
b. Myocardial infarction

Note if placed in the reverse order it would not read properly and would be inaccurate. Since everyone dies of cardiac arrest (i.e., heart stopping), it could also have simply been completed as

a. Myocardial infarction

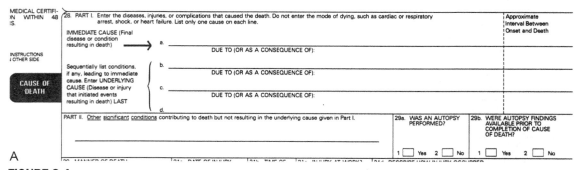

FIGURE 3.4
(A) Demonstrates the three lines available to certify the cause of death. Not all three lines are necessary but at least one line must include a pathological cause of death.

TYPE / PRINT
IN
PERMANENT
BLACK INK
FOR
INSTRUCTIONS
SEE HANDBOOK

TENNESSEE DEPARTMENT OF HEALTH
CERTIFICATE OF DEATH

STATE FILE NUMBER

1. DECENDENT'S NAME (First, Middle, Last)	2. SEX	3. DATE OF DEATH (Month, Day, Year)

DECEDENT

4. SOCIAL SECURITY NUMBER (of Deceased)	5a. AGE – LAST BIRTHDAY (Years)	5b. UNDER 1 YEAR / MOS / DAYS	5c. UNDER 1 DAY / HOURS / MIN	6. DATE OF BIRTH (Month, Day, Year)	7. BIRTHPLACE (City and State or Foreign Country)

8. WAS DECEDENT EVER IN U.S. ARMED FORCES? 1 □ Yes 2 □ No	9a. PLACE OF DEATH (Check only one) HOSPITAL 1 □ Inpatient 2 □ ER/Outpatient 3 □ DOA OTHER 4 □ Nursing Home 5 □ Residence 6 □ Other (Specify)

9b. FACILITY NAME (If not institution, give street and number)	9c. CITY, TOWN, OR LOCATION OF DEATH	9d. COUNTY OF DEATH

10. MARITAL STATUS—Married, Never Married, Widowed, Divorced (Specify)	11. SURVIVING SPOUSE (If wife, give maiden name)	12a. DECEDENT'S USUAL OCCUPATION (Give kind of work done during most of working life. Do not use retired.)	12b. KIND OF BUSINESS/INDUSTRY

13a. RESIDENCE – STATE	13b. COUNTY	13c. CITY, TOWN OR LOCATION	13d. STREET AND NUMBER OR RURAL LOCATION

CENSUS TRACT

13e. INSIDE CITY LIMITS? 1 □ Yes 2 □ No	13f. ZIP CODE	14. WAS DECEDENT OF HISPANIC ORIGIN? (Specify Yes or No—If yes, specify Cuban, Mexican, Puerto Rican, etc.) Yes 0 □ No □ Specify, if yes:	15. RACE—American Indian, Black, White, etc. (Specify)	16. DECEDENT'S EDUCATION (Specify only highest grade completed) Elementary/Secondary (0-12) / College (1-4 or 5+)

PARENTS

17. FATHER'S NAME (First, Middle, Last)	18. MOTHER'S NAME (First, Middle, Maiden Surname)

INFORMANT

19a. INFORMANT'S NAME (Type/Print)	19b. RELATIONSHIP TO DECEASED	19c. MAILING ADDRESS (Street and Number or Rural Route Number, City or Town, State, Zip Code)

DISPOSITION

20a. METHOD OF DISPOSITION 1 □ Burial 2 □ Cremation 3 □ Removal from State 4 □ Donation 5 □ Other (Specify)	20b. PLACE OF DISPOSITION (Name of cemetery, crematory, or other place)	20c. LOCATION—City or Town, State

21a. SIGNATURE OF FUNERAL DIRECTOR	21b. LICENSE NUMBER OF FUNERAL DIRECTOR	21c. SIGNATURE OF EMBALMER	21d. LICENSE NUMBER OF EMBALMER

22a. NAME AND ADDRESS OF FUNERAL HOME	22b. LICENSE NUMBER OF FUNERAL HOME

REGISTRAR

23. REGISTRAR'S SIGNATURE	24. DATE FILED (Month, Day, Year)

CERTIFIER

25a. PHYSICIAN — To the best of my knowledge, death occurred at the time, date, and place, and due to the cause(s) and manner as stated.

1 □ SIGNATURE AND TITLE OF PHYSICIAN	25b. LICENSE NUMBER	25c. DATE SIGNED (Month, Day, Year)

26a. MEDICAL EXAMINER — On the basis of examination and/or investigation, in my opinion, death occurred at the time, and place, and due to the cause(s) and manner as stated.

2 □ SIGNATURE AND TITLE OF MEDICAL EXAMINER	26b. LICENSE NUMBER	26c. DATE SIGNED (Month, Day, Year)

PHYSICIAN OR MEDICAL EXAMINER EXECUTING CERTIFICATE MUST COMPLETE AND SIGN MEDICAL CERTIFICATION WITHIN 48 HOURS.

27. NAME AND ADDRESS OF CERTIFIER (PHYSICIAN OR MEDICAL EXAMINER) (Type/Print)

SEE INSTRUCTIONS ON OTHER SIDE

CAUSE OF DEATH

28. PART I. Enter the diseases, injuries, or complications that caused the death. Do not enter the mode of dying, such as cardiac or respiratory arrest, shock, or heart failure. List only one cause on each line.

Approximate Interval Between Onset and Death

IMMEDIATE CAUSE (Final disease or condition resulting in death)
a. _____
DUE TO (OR AS A CONSEQUENCE OF):

Sequentially list conditions, if any, leading to immediate cause. Enter UNDERLYING CAUSE (Disease or injury that initiated events resulting in death) LAST
b. _____
DUE TO (OR AS A CONSEQUENCE OF):
c. _____
DUE TO (OR AS A CONSEQUENCE OF):
d. _____

PART II. Other significant conditions contributing to death but not resulting in the underlying cause given in Part I.	29a. WAS AN AUTOPSY PERFORMED? 1 □ Yes 2 □ No	29b. WERE AUTOPSY FINDINGS AVAILABLE PRIOR TO COMPLETION OF CAUSE OF DEATH? 1 □ Yes 2 □ No

30. MANNER OF DEATH 1 □ Natural 2 □ Accident 3 □ Suicide 4 □ Homicide 5 □ Pending Investigation 6 □ Could not be Determined	31a. DATE OF INJURY (Month, Day, Year)	31b. TIME OF INJURY M	31c. INJURY AT WORK? 1 □ Yes 2 □ No	31d. DESCRIBE HOW INJURY OCCURRED
	31e. PLACE OF INJURY—At home, farm, street, factory, office building, etc. (Specify)			31f. LOCATION (Street and Number or Rural Route Number, City or Town, State)

NAME OF DECEDENT: For use by physician or institution

BIRTH NO _____

PH-1659
REV. 2-93

RDA 1399

B

FIGURE 3.4, cont'd
(B) Shows the five options for manner of death that are available in most states. "Natural" is the only box that may be certified by private treating physicians. The remaining boxes are to be used only by coroner/medical examiner offices.

It could then be approved by vital records immediately. Many states have mandates for how long a death certificate may be outstanding and unsigned by a private physician. Burials cannot occur without a valid death certificate signed by a physician to allow the proper burial or cremation permits to be issued by vital records departments. It is helpful to review your state law requirements for death certificates and death reporting to the coroner/medical examiner office, and have the laws pertaining to your state readily available for reference.

MANNER OF DEATH

Manner of death is in one of five classifications: natural, accident, suicide, homicide, or undetermined. Some states have an additional category called **therapeutic misadventure** when the death is related to a medical intervention. Private physicians are only allowed by state law to certify natural deaths. The other manners of death are reserved for the coroner or forensic pathologist. It is not always easy to make a distinction to a medical certainty between two or more manners, and in that instance, undetermined is used. In most jurisdictions this classification is used less than 5% of the time.

The distinction between accident, suicide, and homicide is based largely on the concept of intent of an action that caused the death.

INFORMATION NEEDED FOR COMPLETION

It is important to obtain specific information for the death certificate at the time of the investigation, such as the decedent's legal name and proper spelling and date of birth; date and time of death pronouncement; location of death; date, time, and location of incident; home address; next of kin; and social security number if known. Medical history, medications, and physicians are also useful information to be obtained or seized. See Figure 3.5.

INVESTIGATION OF PROBLEMATIC DEATH CERTIFICATES

As part of the certification process, many states are progressing to electronic (online) death certification. This is a wonderful advancement, as it allows data to be transmitted easily between agencies and speeds up the process. It also allows death investigators to review death certificates for problematic causes of death and allow investigations to move forward more promptly. The following causes are common ones that should be further investigated by reviewing medical records and/or discussing the cause with the signing physician.

Pneumonia

Pneumonia can cause death alone or as a complication of multiple other illnesses, including trauma, and is a symptom of health department reportable diseases. When this is the listed cause, it is best to speak with the signing

DATE RPTD. _____

RPTD. BY _____

TRANSPORT _____

TIME RPTD. _____/_____

TIME COMPLT. _____/_____

FIELD AGENTS _____/_____

DOCTOR _____

INVESTIGATOR _____

CASE NUMBER

COUNTY _____ PROCEDURE _____ DATE _____ FORENSIC ANTHRO _____ DENTIST _____

NAME FN _____ MI _____ LN _____

ALIAS _____ M S W D OCC _____

ADDRESS _____ CITY _____ STATE _____ ZIP _____

DOB _____ AGE _____ RACE _____ SEX _____ S.S.N. _____

HT (cm) _____(inches) _____ WT (kg) _____(lbs) _____ HC _____ EC _____

NOK FN _____ LN _____ REL _____ PHONE _____

ADDRESS _____ CITY _____ STATE _____ NOTIFIED Y N

ID (MEANS & NAME) _____

LOCATION FOUND _____

REASON ME CASE _____

MED. HX _____

MEDS. _____

AGENCY _____ CASE # _____ OFFICER _____

INJURY LOCATION _____ WORK Y N

DATE _____ TIME _____ DRIVER _____ PASSENGER _____ PEDESTRIAN _____

WHERE DID DEATH OCCUR? HOSP. _____ ER _____ OR _____ INPT _____ AT SCENE _____ UNKNOWN _____

LSA DATE _____ TIME _____ LOC. _____ BY _____

FD. DATE _____ TIME _____ LOC. _____ BY _____

PRN. DATE _____ TIME _____ LOC. _____ BY _____

FUNERAL HOME _____ BY _____ RELATION _____

PHOTOS: OME ID Y N EXAMINATION OME Y N AGENCY Y N

FINGERPRINTS: _____ PALMS _____ FOOT _____ RADIOGRAPHS _____

_____

_____

_____

_____

_____

_____

_____

_____

_____

_____

_____

_____

_____

_____

_____

_____

_____

_____

_____

RELEASED BY _____ RECEIVED BY _____

FIGURE 3.5

An example of an office intake sheet that after completed will contain the information necessary to complete the demographic and injury sections of a death certificate. The cause and manner of death are determined following examination by the forensic pathologist. Examples of intake sheets can be found in the Appendix.

Case Study

A young male is found with a gunshot wound to his head in a room and a gun nearby on the floor. The cause of death is gunshot wound to the head. However, the manner of death depends on the scenario. One scenario might be that the gun was picked up by a five-year-old child and the gun went off, striking the decedent. In that instance, a five-year-old child would have little knowledge of firearms and the manner would be accidental. Another scenario could be the decedent was shot during a home invasion and the manner of death would be homicide. A third scenario is the gun was placed by the decedent against his head and the manner would be suicide.

The intent is the important distinction to determine the manner. In suicide, the intent is directed against one's self with a willingness to die due to the action. Homicide is the intent and willful action to take another person's life. Accident is where there was no intent to hurt someone but the action resulted in death. The determination of manner by the coroner/medical examiner is distinct from a judicial sense of determining this. Legal definitions may vary and allow the judicial system to impart manslaughter and various degrees of homicide (e.g., first degree, second degree, third degree) based on circumstances of the investigation.

If a gun is used to cause injury to another person, many factors will be needed to determine intent. In the first scenario, the age of the child, the child's knowledge of guns including any formal training, the mental capacity of the child to determine right from wrong, and the child's statements as to how the injury occurred will all need to be understood to make the best judgment for the manner. Normal development reasoning of right and wrong should be accomplished by six to eight years old. Even so, the legal system may bring homicide charges regardless of the determination on the death certificate since they use different criteria than the criteria used by medicine. They also have divided the homicide category into involuntary manslaughter, voluntary manslaughter, first-degree murder, second-degree murder, and third-degree murder. The court system will take multiple factors into account, including previous juvenile offenses, the type of injury, and the heinous nature of the crime, to decide whether the child is tried as an adult or a juvenile. Children have been sentenced to life in prison, and some as young as 13 years old tried as an adult. If the scenario is complex and multifactorial, an undetermined manner should be considered for the death certificate and the courts can decide what charges, if any, are required.

physician and rule out trauma, such as a head injury, motor vehicle accident, fall, or an unexpected illness in a previously healthy person.

Brain hemorrhage

Brain hemorrhages can be of various types and are commonly listed as intracerebral hemorrhage, subdural hemorrhage, subarachnoid hemorrhage, cerebral hemorrhage, or stroke. Some of these can occur due to underlying disease such as hypertension (high blood pressure), or to falls or minimal trauma, especially if the person is on blood thinners (anticoagulants). The distinction is important to make to properly certify the cause and manner of death. It may mean that survivors receive certain benefits if the death is certified as an accident.

The easiest way to begin to sort out the manner is to retrieve the emergency responder report for symptoms the decedent was experiencing, emergency department notes, and CT or MRI scan reports of the brain. It must be noted, however, that a body of literature exists as to the large number of missed diagnoses via these test results. When in doubt, the decedent may need to be physically examined externally for signs of injury, as well as performing an examination of the brain for the site of origin of the hemorrhage. In general, basal ganglia, intracerebellar, or brainstem hemorrhages can be seen commonly in hypertension. Subdural hemorrhages should be considered accidental in origin until further information is obtained. Subarachnoid hemorrhages may be due to natural or accidental origin and may depend on scene investigation or medical history. Distribution of scalp injuries with brain injuries may also aid in distinguishing accidental, homicide, or natural manners of death.

Fractures (hip, rib, spine, osteoporotic, pathological)

Fractures are most commonly due to falls and most need to be reported to the death investigator for evaluation and jurisdiction determination. Factors used to determine if the death is due to accident or natural disease with underlying health problems can be difficult. These factors include the time duration between the incident and death, the mechanism causing death (e.g., pneumonia, pulmonary embolus, myocardial infarction, aspiration of food, decubitus ulcers, sepsis), and if the decedent had a previously active lifestyle that never returned to a normal state following the incident. Some offices make an arbitrary timespan (e.g., six to eight weeks following injury) for these complications to occur due to the accident versus the preexisting underlying disease processes. Basically, each case must be investigated and evaluated on an individual basis.

Other factors that may explain why the fracture occurred with minimal trauma (sitting down, being turned in bed) are osteoporosis (a loss of calcium in bone due to aging) or underlying metastatic bone cancer. Either of these may cause bones to be weak and brittle. Depending on the investigation, the manner may be ruled as a natural manner of death.

Falls

Falls and accidental deaths should be suspected or investigated in alcoholics, the elderly, or those with bruises over bony prominences like the knees, elbows, ribs, and chest, or deformity of the arms or legs, especially shortening and external rotation of a leg. It may require X-rays and/or an autopsy examination to distinguish the cause of death.

Remote motor vehicle accidents, gunshot wounds, or head injuries

Some patients experience a head or spinal injury and survive many months with deficits, eventually dying of a natural disease such as pneumonia, sepsis, or other infection. It is important to recognize these cases so that the death certificate is certified properly and any remaining evidence (old bullets) may be recovered. The bullet may serve as crucial evidence to relate a gun to the injury.

There is no statute of limitations in any U.S. state, so if the perpetrator can be linked to the death, he or she may be charged with homicide. In some states, the original charge of assault may be upgraded to murder if the death is linked to the original injury.

The injury may be very remote and the circumstances of the injury (location, jurisdiction, dates, how it occurred) may not be easily found in medical records, as most hospitals only keep their records for seven years before destroying them. The family can serve as a valuable resource in locating this information, so that follow-up with any necessary law enforcement agencies can be done. It is helpful to obtain recent hospital discharge summaries, X-ray reports, and more recent progress notes from care facilities to evaluate the extent of the injuries and relationship to the original injury. Basically, if the final disease process is related to the original injury, the cause of death is viewed as a complication of the injury regardless of interval. This is where the difficulty lies—finding the connection to the injury as well as defining the disease process resulting in death. The thought process involves whether the decedent's life was shortened by the injury or the life was significantly altered from the way it existed before the accident.

Seizures

Seizures are due to an irregularity of the brain's electrical current causing abnormal movements and breathing. They may result in sudden death. Seizures can also be a pathologic disease process with an unknown etiology. They can be a symptom of another disease, a final terminal death event, alcohol or drug withdrawal, or previous injury to the brain. Because the diagnosis is nonspecific, most of these death certificates need to be investigated further or examined at the office for a possible autopsy.

Children

Pediatric death certificates need to be scrutinized closely for causes that may need to be evaluated through an autopsy or at least external examination by the forensic pathologist. There may be infectious causes that have not been defined by hospitalization, putting fellow family members or the community at risk for a preventable outbreak, a previous injury with a prolonged survival period, ingestion of substances, or injuries or neglect by caregivers or as wards of the state. Conversations with the reporting party may help elicit the information necessary to determine if jurisdiction needs to be enforced.

Miscarriages

Fetal deaths can be very confusing. It is best to review your current state law definition of a fetal death, age of viability, and birth definition. In general, fetal deaths are usually defined as those under 20 weeks' gestation and 350 grams in weight (this may vary slightly depending on your state).

Live births are those with the infant taking a breath and/or having a heartbeat. Some states add pulsations of the umbilical cord to indicate live birth. If the infant has any of these, it requires both a birth certificate and death certificate. The birth certificate will be completed by the delivering physician, and the death certificate can be completed by the forensic pathologist or coroner.

Fetal death certificates also exist for those cases where there was no sign of life before or after 20 weeks of gestation. The complicated distinction comes if the infant is of the age of viability (>20 weeks gestation and/or 350 grams) and there is an incidence of trauma (homicide or accident), drug use of the mother, or other complication resulting in early delivery. Then, the actual age of the **fetus** can be important, and is assessed not only on the weight or computed gestational age, but also by examination parameters by the forensic pathologist, such as foot length, hand length, body weight and length, examination of the placenta, toxicology testing of the fetus, etc. It may be necessary to access the maternal prenatal and delivery records, including toxicology and culture results, to aid the investigation of the death of the fetus. If the mother is living, access to her records can be challenged as a privacy issue. Because the lives of the fetus and mother are so intertwined, it is usually granted but must be recognized if problems arise or state laws prohibit access.

Therapeutic abortion death certificates may also be reviewed routinely by the death investigator. The death investigator needs to be knowledgeable about the state laws governing the gestational age and weight with which they may legally occur.

Children of mixed heritage and race are generally classified by the race of the mother. This was decided by the Standards for Classification of Federal Data on Race and Ethnicity in 1989. It is a statistical fact only; it is not meant to be dogmatic and is only used as a general guideline.

On a similar topic of difficult questions on a death certificate is the gender. On infants it is determined by the internal genitalia. On those seeking transgender, it is usually decided based on the birth certificate classification unless a legal proceeding has been done by the courts to convert the gender designation. In any of these questions, the local health department can update and advise specific issues.

CREMATION AUTHORIZATIONS

Many states require death certificates to be reviewed by the coroner or medical examiner office to evaluate the causes of death for potential causes that were not previously reported for jurisdiction. The review is done to identify causes where the certificate implies an unnatural cause of death or public health hazard falling under the death investigation laws. Prior to authorizing these deaths for cremation or transportation out of the country, any discrepancies need to be clarified by obtaining medical records or conversing with the certifying physician for particulars on the cause of death.

REFERENCES

[1] Hanzlick R, editor. Cause of Death Statements and Certification of Natural and Unnatural Death. College of American Pathologists; 1997. Retrieved from https://netforum.avectra.com/temp/ClientImages/NAME/8c58e7e9-b2fa-44a9-8d1b-3085cd14bf25.pdf. [August 2013].

[2] Hanzlick R. Cause of Death Tutorial. Fulton County Medical Examiner; 1996. Retrieved from http://www.fultoncountyga.gov/cause-of-death-tutorial. [August 2013].

[3] National Vital Statistics System. Center for Disease Control and Prevention. Retrieved from http://www.cdc.gov/nchs/nvss.htm. [August 2013].

[4] National Death Certificate. US standard certificate of death; 2003. Center for Disease Control and Prevention. Retrieved from http://www.cdc.gov/nchs/data/dvs/death11-03final-acc.pdf. [August 2013].

CHAPTER 4
Time of Death

Learning Objectives

- Discuss the factors used to estimate the time of death.
- Illustrate by examples what observations need to be recorded by the investigator to assist with determining the time of death.
- Explain the general methods used to collect insects for entomology consultation.
- Discuss the environmental conditions that can alter the timeline for estimating the time of death.
- Discuss the types of observations of plants at an outdoor scene that may aid estimations for the time of death.

Key Terms
Livor
Rigor
Adipocere
Instar
Mummification
Saponification

Chapter Summary

In this chapter the various physiologic changes that occur within the body during and after death are discussed. These changes proceed through a progression of changes that can be used to estimate the time of death. These parameters are only an estimate and are highly dependent on temperature, body habitus, and other environmental factors. The assessment factors each follow a continuum that needs to be recorded by the investigator prior to the body being removed from the death site. When taken as a whole, these values and investigative information are used to make the best time determination in an unwitnessed death. Various investigative observations may be helpful to add more information concerning the postmortem interval as well as the decedent's lifestyle. Collection of insects, plants, and photographs may be necessary in some cases to aid this determination.

INTRODUCTION

With death, multiple body mechanisms fail and cause various body changes that are used to estimate time of death and the position of the body. This chapter discusses the physiology of these body changes and how these changes can be utilized in a death investigation.

PHYSIOLOGY OF DEATH

In its normal state, the body's heart is beating, circulating blood throughout the tissues, and the lungs exchange carbon dioxide waste for fresh oxygen. Oxygen is then used to maintain the cellular energy state of the body through the use of energy packets called ATP (adenosine triphosphate). When a packet is depleted it is converted to a low-energy state called ADP (adenosine diphosphate) and is in need of oxygen to reform into renewed ATP. ATP is necessary to run multiple microscopic cellular components that maintain the status quo of internal cell versus external cell concentrations of various minerals, enzymes, amino acids, fats, glucose, etc. Without ATP, all the functions of the body's cells fail, causing them to die, which is called **necrosis** in the living body and **autolysis** when cell death occurs after death.

Death is usually defined by individual state law, but in general, includes the cessation of both respiration and cardiac activity. Since the advent of advances in medicine with extended life support, most states have included guidelines as to what constitutes brain death. It was necessary to do so since medicine is now able to maintain someone on artificial respiration for a prolonged period, allowing respiration and cardiac activity to proceed without meaningful brain function. Respiration and cardiac functions are largely centered in the primitive area of the brainstem, whereas critical thinking and awareness are centered in the cortex. It is possible to lose the majority of the cortex and maintain the primitive cardiac and respiratory functions. It is also possible to appear to have no cortical function and be locked in, but unable to communicate in a verbal fashion. The stringent criteria used to pronounce brain death were developed to recognize these differences and make an accurate determination prior to removing life support.

Rigor

Rigor mortis, commonly known as **rigor**, is the postmortem muscle stiffening of the body. It is created because the lack of oxygen to the cells results in lower levels of ATP in the body. ATP is needed for muscle cells to maintain their delicate balance of various chemicals, including calcium used for muscle contraction. The lack of ATP causes the body cells to leak calcium around muscle fibril bundles. This allows the muscle fibrils to bind by cross-linking, resulting in the muscle contracting (i.e., setting) in its present position. ATP is needed to restore the calcium equilibrium, but without oxygen, the muscle bundles bind but are unable to reset [1]. The body remains in the muscular contraction state it was in at the time of death. With death, the body will assume a position of relaxation toward gravity or the object it is resting on.

The muscle bundles will maintain the contraction for a period of time until the muscle fibrils begin to deteriorate, releasing the cross-linking. Contraction is first detected in the smaller muscles of the face or hands and then extends to larger muscles of the arms and legs where it remains the longest. It eventually passes and the muscles will become relaxed, first noted in the small muscles then proceeding to the larger ones. The amount of muscle mass a person has will increase the duration or strength of the rigor (e.g., a body builder has more prolonged rigor than a tiny elderly woman or baby). Also, exercise just prior to the time of death will cause the rigor to begin more rapidly because of the already depleted ATP within the body.

Descriptive terms used are **full rigor**, **easily broken rigor**, and **absent rigor**. Full rigor is seen at the height of muscle rigidity, and at average household temperatures it occurs about six to eight hours after death. In the early post-mortem state and after the peak period it is described as easily broken. Eventually as the body progresses toward a state of early decomposition, it will become absent. It is also absent in the immediate period following death. Full rigor lasts three to four hours in a normal adult, but this depends on a number of factors, including the ambient (surrounding) temperature if in an outdoor environment, a building, a car, a residence, or the shade of a tree. Another factor is the amount of body fat or clothing insulating the body. Environmental heat has the same effect and cooling decreases the rate of decomposition onset. A body that is moved then placed inside a body cooler wrapped in blankets and wearing heavy clothing will continue to decay because of the insulating properties of the clothing and blankets from the cooler air.

Moving a body also affects the determination of the time interval. In the movement process, small bundles are broken and may reset their cross-links or they may break prematurely, which disturbs the postmortem time estimate. The best time to assess rigor is prior to the body being moved. It is important to assess and note the extent of rigor, body warmth, livor, and environmental temperature prior to the body being placed into a body bag.

Livor

Livor mortis, commonly known as **livor**, is the postmortem settling of blood. When the heart stops beating the blood no longer circulates, causing it to pool within the capillaries and small vessels closest to gravity. Because of the cellular disruption, clotting then begins. In the early postmortem interval, the blood will remain liquid, and if the body is moved, the blood will partially realign in the new position of gravity. This pattern is useful to determine if a body was moved prior to its being seen by the death investigator.

If a body is viewed by the investigator with anterior lividity but lying on its back, then the body had initially collapsed in the face-down position. There are many explanations why the body may have been moved. It may be done by the person who discovered the body to assess the decedent's condition; emergency medical or law enforcement personnel; or perpetrators of a potential crime. For transport, the majority of bodies are placed on their back inside the body bag so they may assume a posterior lividity pattern in addition to the initial one. It is helpful to make note of livor routinely at the autopsy and review photographs of how the body was positioned at the death scene.

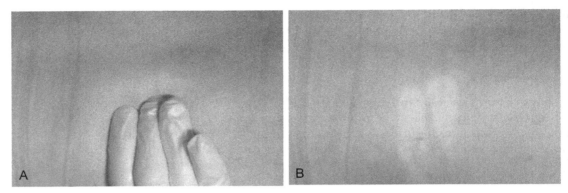

FIGURE 4.1
(A) Generalized lividity over the back of someone found lying on his back. (B) When the skin is pressed in the early postmortem period, the lividity will dissipate and appear pale in the pressure area.

Lividity is not usually uniformly present on the side of gravity. In areas where the body has been resting against an object, lividity is prevented due to the pressure on the surface. It will be seen as a pale area surrounded by pink (Figure 4.1). An example would be an infant found face down in a crib. He or she will demonstrate lividity anteriorly and can have pale areas on a cheek or over the face and mouth areas. When discovered, a caregiver usually moves the baby and resuscitative efforts are begun. Lividity may then begin to change posteriorly and the blanched pale areas will begin to fade. It is very important to photograph the infant's face upon arrival since sometimes the lividity can change rapidly and the pale areas may not be visible later.

The liquid condition of the blood remains for the first three to four hours following death and becomes relatively fixed in position after six to eight hours. Following that, it will no longer move from the initial position. Terms to describe lividity are **blanchable** and **fixed lividity**. Blanchable refers to the early postmortem period where pressure applied by the investigator's hand will dispel the blood in an area of dependent livor and appear uniformly pale, then slowly return to pink. Eventually, the lividity becomes fixed into place and unable to be displaced by applied pressure.

Factors affecting the onset of lividity include the condition of circulation at the period near death. Some people die slowly with the heart gradually assuming a slow heartbeat and the body will begin to pool blood in the peripheral extremities and back prior to death.

Livor may have different colors. Usually it is light pink, and with time assumes a dusky pink. When a body is placed in a cold refrigerator or in an outside cold environment, it becomes bright pink. Bright pink is also seen with carbon monoxide and cyanide poisoning. Poisons such as potassium chlorate, phosphorus, and nitrites give a brown-colored lividity. Hydrogen sulfide gives a bluish-green coloration.

Case Study

A body is found in a field lying on her back with the legs and arms flexed at the elbows and knees. The decedent was noted to have left-side livor. The rigor was present throughout the body and the livor was fixed on the left torso. A gunshot wound was noted of the left scalp.

These findings indicate the body has been moved. Rigor assumes the position of gravity and upward flexion of the extremities is not consistent with the death occurring at that site. Fixed lividity on one side of the body is also inconsistent with the body being on her back at the time of death, confirming the body was moved. The body was in the position for a period of at least six to eight hours or longer prior to being placed into the field where it was found.

Temperature

Environmental temperature has a large effect on the progression of postmortem change. Heat causes rigor and livor to pass through their respective stages more rapidly, and cold slows the progression. Direct sunlight with an environmental temperature over 100 °F will result in the onset of decomposition within a matter of a couple of hours. Cold, such as snow, will slow the onset of decomposition initially until thawing begins. Cold can result in freezer burn–type areas where the body has rested on the ground.

Decomposition

Without preservation a body will deteriorate and progress into an advanced postmortem state. If the body is exposed to the sunlight and air, it progresses more rapidly than if it were buried or within water [4]. This is partially related to the added benefit of insects and carnivores. Insects infest a body in an orderly fashion and particular subspecies are related to the locality within the United States. Generally, flies are the first infesters and they may lay their eggs on fresh bodies. Flies are especially attracted to areas of injury.

The first stage of decomposition is venous marbling (Figure 4.2). This occurs when the blood decomposes within the vascular system and produces brown vessel arborization on the skin. This is followed by red-green discoloration of the skin with fluid-filled skin blebs of decomposition fluid. Rupture of capillaries within the mouth and nose cause oozing of thick dark-red decomposition fluid. The body then progresses to black-green discoloration with subcutaneous gas formation containing hydrogen sulfide gas. This is most pronounced in the face, torso, and genitalia with distortion of facial features.

Skin slippage is evident with glove formation of the hands and feet where actual sheets of skin peel from the body (Figure 4.3). The hand glove can be used to obtain fingerprints to aid identification. The easiest way to do this is to place the entire glove or, if fragmented, the fingertips over the investigator's gloved hand and roll the fingertips onto the ink and put them onto the fingerprint cards. It

FIGURE 4.2
One of the early stages of decomposition called venous marbling, which is caused by decomposing blood within the vascular tree.

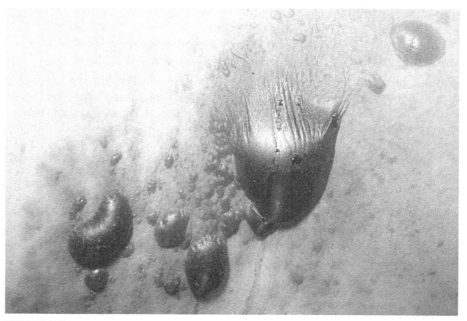

FIGURE 4.3
The beginning of skin slippage and filling of skin blebs by noxious-smelling decomposition fluid.

may take multiple attempts to get a good print. The decomposed hands may be greasy with decomposition fluid and the tips can be blotted with alcohol swabs. Wiping or scraping can destroy the print ridges or tear the skin, so the cleaning needs to be done gently.

The subcutaneous blistering and fluid accumulation along with the skin slippage occurs because the bacteria are breaking down the body fat and proteins into by-products that produce foul-smelling gases, including hydrogen sulfide and methane, which bloat the body. This accumulates inside the body as well as within the skin. The skin begins separating and the fluids accumulate under the skin and drain onto the ground. The blistering makes some mistakenly think the skin has been burned, but this is not true. The decomposition fluid is watery, red-brown, and the early novice investigator may think it is frank blood. Decomposition fluids tend to be more watery or have a mucous slimy quality. Blood when decomposed appears more as a tarry black material. Distension of the genitalia, widening of the anus, and even expulsion of the bowel occurs as a result of the decomposition, and is not necessarily a sign of trauma. Sexual assault swabs can be obtained in these cases, but the bacteria may render the results unable to be interpreted.

Mummification is another decomposition process that occurs in hot, arid environments where the body is partially protected from the sun and the air is blowing across the body and drying it. In this process the skin shrinks and becomes leather-like with a dry, musty smell. Because of the shrinkage, the facial beard may appear to grow and nails lengthen when in reality it is an artifact due to drying. Internal examination will show dried, shrunken organs and no residual body fluids. Identification becomes a challenge because the hands are dried and prints are unavailable. The hands can be processed using various techniques like sodium hydroxide rehydration or soaking the hands in a soap solution to soften them and reinflate the fingertips to allow for fingerprints. When the tips are able to be manipulated, a needle and syringe containing formalin, water, or tissue builder can be inserted under the skin to gently inflate and expand the wrinkles from the surface. The fingertips may need to be gently massaged to distribute the fluid under the surface. It is important not to over-inflate the surface since it distorts the fingerprint ridges.

Saponification is a process of decomposition in cold, wet environments, such as cold lakes, rivers, or basements, and is called **adipocere** (Figure 4.4). It is a form of soap formation by chemically changing the composition of the body fat. The surface of the skin appears chalky white and, when extensive, the skin and soft tissue crumble like plaster. Bodies found in lakes after many years can still retain extensive skin surface with this appearance.

Mold formation occurs in closed environments such as caskets or closets where the body is protected from insects. The mold forms a micro environment within the closed space and the body can be relatively well preserved for years after death.

The postmortem interval to reach either wet decomposition or mummification varies and it can be difficult to assign a definite time. A common estimate is one

FIGURE 4.4
Adipocere formation of the skin and subcutaneous tissue is a form of decomposition found in cold, wet environments.

week in the open air equals two weeks in water, equals eight weeks underground. Skeletal remains are usually devoid of tissue by six months with scavenger activity. The bones will retain odor for at least a year depending on the environment. Recovery of scattered skeletal remains due to animal scavenging can be challenging but may follow terrain features or animal travel routes [3].

There are multiple tales associated with death. One is that the fingernails grow after death, but this is merely an illusion due to shrinkage of the skin on the fingertips due to dehydration. The beard and hair have also been said to grow after death, but the same skin shrinkage accounts for this apparent change. Some are afraid to open the eyes or ask if viewing the eyes will reflect what they last saw and this cannot be done. The eyes work with a complex system integrated with brain activity to register what is seen and our vision of objects are not visible within the eye.

POSTMORTEM CARNIVORE ACTIVITY

Wild and domestic animals including mammals and birds will feed upon a human cadaver. Exposed areas, such as face and hands as well as bloody areas, are prime focus areas. Large carnivores will also select the large muscle mass

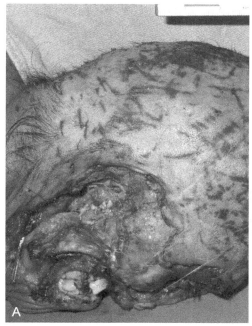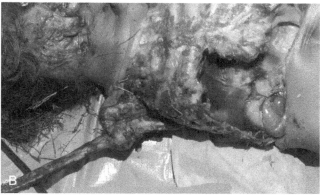

FIGURE 4.5
(A) A typical area of carnivore activity centered around the mouth of a decedent. (B) Loss of flesh from the upper extremity and chest on a decedent from exposure to wild animal activity. Flesh and muscle areas exposed outside of clothing are common sites.

areas of the thighs, legs, and abdomen. This can make identification challenging and may necessitate dental comparison for identity. See Figure 4.5 for examples.

POSTMORTEM INSECT LIFE CYCLE

The first insects to attack a body are flies, usually blowflies. Blowflies are present in the environment to approximately 52 °F [2]. The flies are very orderly in their development from eggs to first through third **instar** stages, to pupa, then hatching as a mature fly. The cycle varies in length depending on the warmth of the environment, but generally in warm weather it takes 8 to 10 days to reach pupa stage (Figure 4.6). As the flies are feeding on the body, various beetles and other insects also feed on the remains (Figure 4.7). Collection and preservation of insects at the point when the body is discovered can allow a forensic entomologist to give an estimate of the postmortem interval. This collection is not always necessary but may be needed in suspected homicides. Because the insects feed on the body, they can be ground and liquefied for a qualitative drug screen if no other fluids or tissue is available.

EMBALMING

Embalming is the practice of removing the blood from the vascular system and replacing it with formalin. In doing so, the evaluation of lividity and rigor are

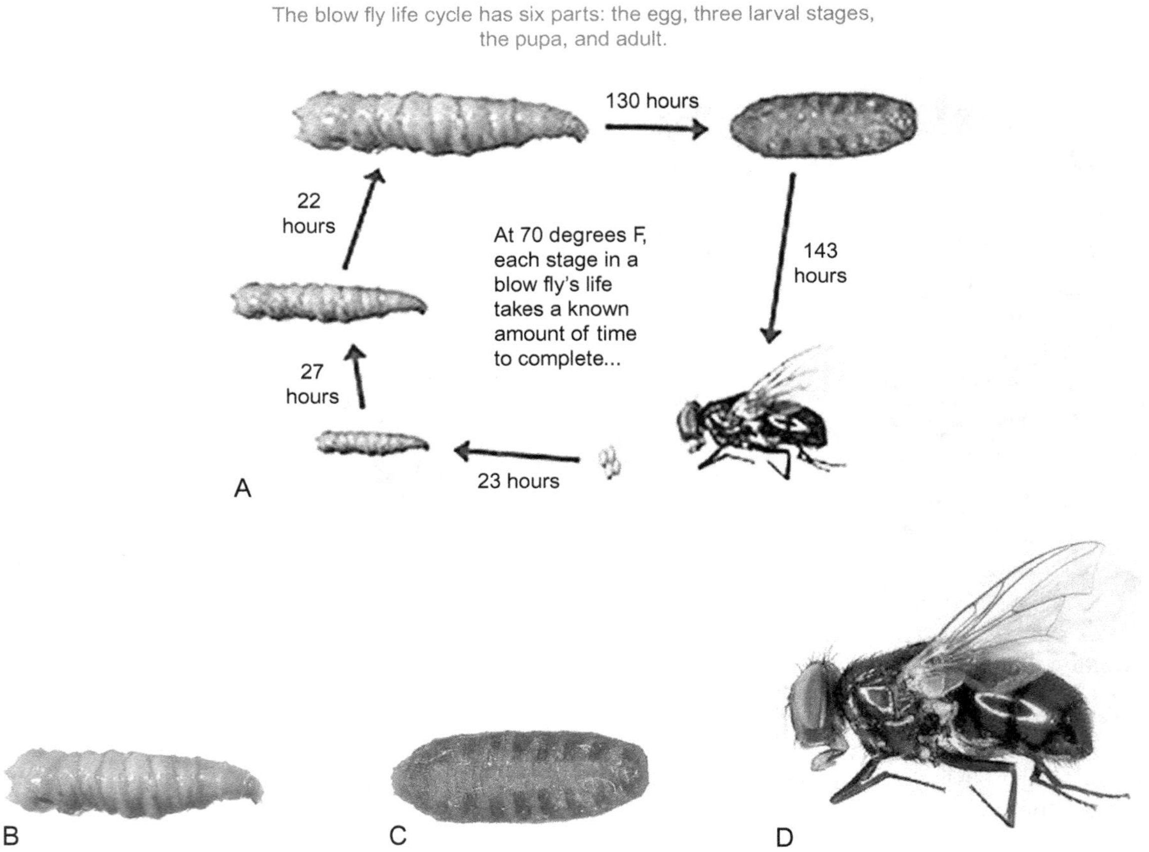

The blow fly life cycle has six parts: the egg, three larval stages, the pupa, and adult.

130 hours

22 hours

At 70 degrees F, each stage in a blow fly's life takes a known amount of time to complete...

143 hours

27 hours

A

23 hours

B

C

D

FIGURE 4.6
(A) The typical life cycle of a blowfly as it matures from a maggot to a full-grown fly. (B, C) It passes through three enlarging cycles of maggots called instars and pupae. (D) The adult blow fly is capable of laying eggs on decomposing tissue to repeat the cycle.
Source: Cleveland Museum of Natural History, http://www.nlm.nih.gov/visibleproofs/galleries/technologies/blowfly.html.

no longer able to be assessed. The embalming procedure involves incisions at the base of the neck to localize the carotid artery and jugular vein. Incisions are also made in the right and left groins to utilize the femoral arteries and veins. Formalin is pumped into the arterial system, which diffuses into the soft tissue, preserving it (Figure 4.8). As it is pumped, the vascular blood is drained via the venous system. The trunk is preserved by inserting a trocar, puncturing the organs, removing body fluids, and replacing them with formalin. Embalming basically removes or contaminates all the body fluids that would be used for toxicology, and the punctures of the organs inhibit making some pathologic diagnoses. For this reason, forensic examinations are best done prior to embalming.

FIGURE 4.7
Other insects will also attack the body. This photo illustrates the irregular waxy abrasions seen secondary to roaches, which were commonly present at the scene.

A body having undergone an autopsy can still be viewed by the family and have an open-casket funeral. The incisions are made in areas covered by clothing or the casket materials. Embalming is done using the same vessels but localized internally. Cavity work is not necessary because of their removal during the autopsy.

Bruises may become more apparent after death especially in dependent areas due to increased lividity, as well as in nondependent areas where the paleness may make them more visible. Sometimes there will be no bruise visible, but after being in the morgue cooler overnight, the bruising will develop either by blanching the surrounding skin or increasing the blood in the area via the blood settling during livor. In some cases it can be useful to review the surface of the body for evaluation of development of a patterned contusion. It is also important to note that some bruises can "disappear" due to lividity, so it is good to photograph visible injuries at the scene for later evaluation. This is especially important in cases of child abuse, in-custody deaths, and homicidal blunt-force trauma.

INVESTIGATIVE TECHNIQUES TO NARROW TIME OF DEATH

Unless it is a witnessed collapse, establishment of a time of death is only an estimate plus or minus hours. If the decedent suddenly collapsed and resuscitative efforts were initiated, the point at which no respiratory or cardiac activity is present can be verified and the person pronounced dead. To make the latter determination, EKG pads are attached and in some jurisdictions require either a physician or EMS guidelines to make that determination. In cases of obvious cause of death (e.g., severe head injuries or body deformities) an office practice

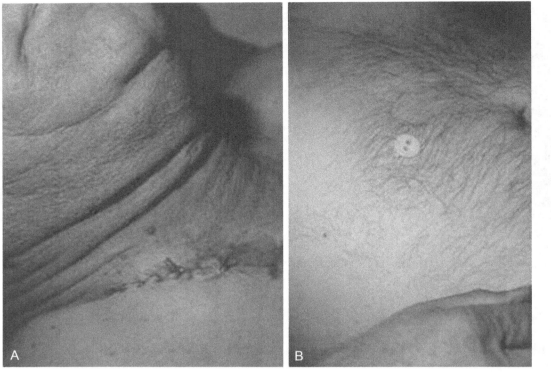

FIGURE 4.8
(A) The typical embalming incision closed by suture and wax at the base of the neck. Other areas that may be used are the groins to perfuse the legs with formalin under pressure. (B) An embalming trochar site for evacuation of the internal food and waste material to slow down the rate of decomposition. Embalming formalin solution is then pumped through the trochar into the torso to promote preservation of the remains.

may be in place to assign a time of death at the arrival of the first law enforcement officer, the coroner, or medical investigator. It is usually formally recorded in the report as the "time of death is (*date*) at ___ hours" and recorded in military time. Also note it is very confusing to use a time such as 1/14/2014 at 00:00 hours. This type of data recording is confusing to decide if the time is unknown, or being established at midnight on the 13th or 14th. To avoid the confusion it is better to record the time as 1/13/2014 at 1159 hours or as 1/14/2014 at 0001 hours. Time of death is important because it can determine by a few minutes whether certain benefits may be bestowed on the family and estate of the decedent.

Clues inside a residence that may be helpful to estimate time of death are food freshness dates in the refrigerator, calendar markings, mail delivery dates, earliest newspaper outside a door, blood glucose monitors for last recorded date, diaries, phone messages, and medical diaries.

In some cases the body may be found with little information and warrant extreme investigation as to how long the person may have been dead. In those cases, pocketed receipts or phone logs may be valuable. Other methods may include collection of insects or noting foliage that has grown or is absent under the body. Details on the receipts may also be useful to understand the lifestyle of the person, previous locations, or what he or she was purchasing. If the interval is relatively short, many stores have video surveillance cameras with recordings that can be reviewed to determine acquaintances near the time of death.

Collection of insects is best coordinated with a forensic entomologist. A basic understanding is needed to collect two types of samples: one living and one preserved. It is best to collect various stages of all the species seen on the body and divide them between the two types of containers. The living ones need to be collected with a food supply and slightly moist with an air supply so they can survive transit. This is most easily done in a plastic container with small holes in the lid and a small chunk of cat food placed in the bottom with a couple drops of water so as not to drown the specimens. If live flies are present, it is also useful to have a small net to capture some of them in addition to sampling the various stages of maggots and beetles. The preserved samples need to have a similar spectrum of insects collected into a separate closed container filled with isopropyl (rubbing) alcohol. Both are submitted to a forensic entomologist for study. The entomologist will examine the preserved specimens to make an assessment of the types of insects, as well as determine what point is their life cycle. If need be, the living specimens can be used to raise a similar stage in the life cycle under similar weather conditions to get a time estimate.

Plants under a decedent may also give a clue. If the grass is dead, the body has been lying on the grass for some time; if yellow, less time. Some plants only grow certain times of the year and their presence under the body can give an idea of when that occurred in that particular climate. It is helpful to use local botanists and entomologists to assist since they are most knowledgeable of the local climate and plant/insect conditions. If none is available and it seems time of death is going to be an extremely important issue, the surrounding environment within 10, 20, and 30 feet can be documented photographically as well as the 360° view of the area under the body once it is removed. Close-up photographs of plants and vegetation can then be submitted when a botanist is located.

Loose plants or seed pods not appearing indigenous to the area can also be important evidence to collect. They may have been transferred to the scene by the decedent or a potential perpetrator. DNA of plants can be as unique as human DNA and seed pods have been traced to a single tree location.

REFERENCES

[1] King M. Tetany and Rigor Mortis; 2013. Retrieved from The Medical Biochemistry Page, http://themedicalbiochemistrypage.org/muscle.php. [August 2013].

[2] Bass W. Outdoor Decomposition Rates in Tennessee. Boca Raton, FL: CRC Press; 1997.

[3] Gleason M. Search for Human Remains. Search and Rescue Tracking Institute; 2008. Retrieved from http://www.sarti.us/sarti/files/SearchForHumanRemains.pdf. [August 2013].

[4] Vass A. Beyond the Grave—Understanding Human Decomposition. Microbiol Today 2001;28:190. Retrieved from http://www.academia.dk/BiologiskAntropologi/Tafonomi/PDF/ArpadVass_2001.pdf. [August 2013].

CHAPTER 5
Autopsy Procedure

Learning Objectives

- Outline the different personal protective equipment items used in death investigation and associate them with the purpose they serve to protect the investigator and the evidence being collected.
- Compare and contrast the Virchow and Rokitansky evisceration techniques and discuss the advantages of each.
- Recognize the various sites to obtain blood for toxicology and discuss the advantages and disadvantages of each.
- Demonstrate with a camera photographing an object from a distance, midrange and close-up views. Note the importance of adding a point of reference to identify the close-up view location.
- Demonstrate with a camera photographing with and without a ruler and at various angles in the relationship of the camera to the object (shallow angle, 90° angle, greater than 90° angle). Note the distortion of the object by the various angles and why it is important to maintain 90°.

Key Terms
PPE
N-95 mask
Bite-mark ruler
Virchow technique
Rokitansky technique
Trace evidence
Vitreous
Femoral blood
Subclavian blood

Chapter Summary

The best autopsies are those where a routine pattern of data collection is obtained and recorded. By performing each autopsy systematically, it allows subtle pathologic changes to be noted easily. Each case may require special modifications to answer a particular question, but the majority of data is obtained in this systematic fashion. This chapter discusses methods of recording the data and routine and special procedures used for dissection and specimen collection. These beginning techniques will serve as a basis to adapt them to a particular case to answer desired questions for determining the cause of death.

INTRODUCTION

The purpose of an autopsy is to systematically dissect and view the organs and their relationships to determine a cause of death. This chapter will discuss the various evidence collection procedures, how an autopsy is performed, and special techniques that may be required to answer specific questions resulting from the injuries or disease process.

PERSONAL PROTECTIVE EQUIPMENT (PPE)

The purpose of protective equipment during an autopsy is to decrease the potential health hazards to those in the room and prevent transmission of those biohazards outside the room to clean office areas. Under the Center for Disease Control Guidelines, all patients and decedents are to be handled by universal precautions. This means that all decedents' body fluids are considered infectious for potential transmission of HIV, hepatitis, and other infectious organisms. To prevent this transmission, those exposed to potential hazards need to wear protective personal equipment.

At a scene investigation, where there is potential for contamination of personal clothing or to prevent contamination of the scene for DNA and evidence collection, the following items should be worn:

- Shoe covers
- **Mask** (N-95 particulate type mask)
- Clean lab coat or disposable jumpsuit
- Disposable gloves

In the morgue where splash and aerosol contamination occur, the following items need to be worn (Figure 5.1):

- Eye protection (goggles, face shields, safety glasses with side shields)
- Surgical gown or jumpsuit over scrubs
- Shoe covers
- Mask (N-95 particulate type mask)
- Disposable gloves, normally two pairs over one another

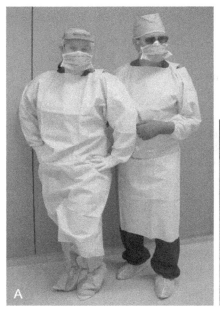
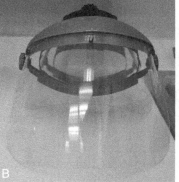

FIGURE 5.1
(A) The personal protective equipment advised during an autopsy. (B) A face shield may be used instead of goggles to prevent eye and face splashes.

Visitors not in direct contact with the body may wear street clothes but put a washable or disposable cover over them during observation. Other items required are eye protection, mask, shoe covers, and gloves if handling any bio-hazardous materials.

Disposable items should be discarded in proper biohazard receptacles prior to exiting the contaminated area, whether it is a scene or the autopsy suite. Sharps, such as syringes or blades, collected at a scene need to be transported in proper evidence containers to prevent injury to others. Medications need to be collected into vinyl evidence pouches and sealed to prevent spilling and contamination of work surfaces. These evidence pouches are marked with the decedent's name, date and time of collection, location, and initialed by the collecting agent.

Trash disposal from a morgue area is placed into biohazard (red or orange) bags inside transmittal receptacles (barrels) and disposed of through biohazard companies. Each state has guidelines as to the number of days the materials can be held inside a facility and how items are to be handled. Most biohazard companies can provide guidance on the particular state guidelines. Needles and scalpels must be placed into special sharps containers and discarded separately from routine trash. Needles are never recapped and discarded. No biohazard trash, including gloves, should go into a routine trash dumpster. Noncontaminated trash, such as packing boxes, can be recycled or placed into routine dumpsters if they do not have biological fluid contamination.

Linen services also must comply with a certain level of biological safety codes for scrubs and towels used in a morgue. These items may have extensive fluid contamination and need to be transported inside impervious bags. State laws may govern needed laundering standards and add cost to potential contracts.

Work surfaces are usually divided into clean and dirty areas. Paperwork that may be in the morgue area needs to remain in the clean areas if at all possible. Many morgues have become paperless to decrease the cross-contamination to other areas within the office. Useful paperless forms include those for toxicology, chain of custody, investigation reports, and weight sheets, which can be viewed and completed on a computer inside the morgue area. Food, drink, and smoking are not allowed in biohazard areas.

BODY ADMISSION TO THE MORGUE

The body is considered evidence and needs to follow similar procedures of evidence transfer. This includes documentation of body removal from the scene, including transportation person, date, and time. When the body arrives at the morgue, it needs to be signed in with identification of name, location removed from, date, time, and person delivering the decedent. To protect property and valuables inside the body bag, it is good practice to seal all body bags until they are opened at the time of the autopsy by morgue staff (Figure 5.2). It is difficult at scenes to always note in a report all jewelry or money that may be on the decedent. This procedure protects all parties, including the decedent from unnecessary loss

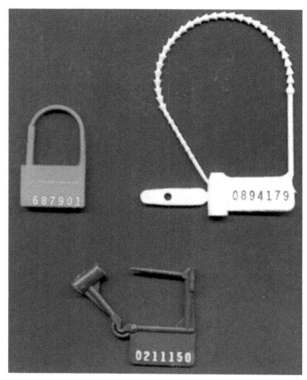

of valuables, which can also become a liability for the office, law enforcement, or the transport company. All large quantities of cash should be counted by two parties and documented in writing prior to it being secured in a safe or transferred with the decedent.

A useful method to secure valuables and money is with a plastic-sealing machine (Figure 5.3). The valuables and money can be secured within the bag and sealed so it is visualized and secured, preventing biohazard materials from spilling in the safe, onto desks, or during transfer to funeral homes and families. The investment in a high-quality machine is well worth the offset of liability with fines from OSHA or loss of valuables in transit. The Appendix contains some examples of paper versions of property sheets.

Body admission includes logging the decedent into the office database, which begins with the official designation of a coroner or medical examiner case number. Some office policies assign this in the field, but others require

FIGURE 5.2
Examples of numbered plastic seals that can be used to secure the zipper on a body pouch to prevent tampering and secure the body as evidence.

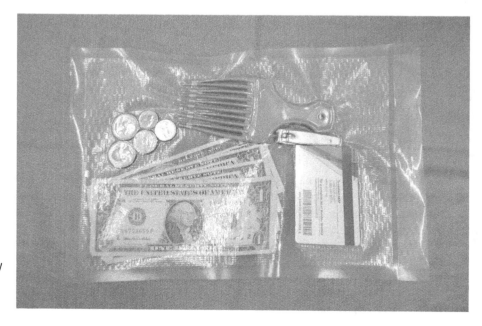

FIGURE 5.3
Plastic vacuum-sealed property that allows easy viewing and verifying of the contents for release to an agency or family.

physical presence of the body for admission numbers. Accurate demographic data entry is extremely important because this sets the stage for multiple articles of paper, toxicology, X-rays, photographs, labels, and transfer of information outside the office including the death certificate. Verification of spelling of the official name as it should appear on the death certificate, date of birth, date and time of death, and location of death are minimum facts that need to be entered. If the decedent's name is unknown or he or she is unrecognizable (trauma, decomposition), office policy will dictate how this type of case should be entered into the database. An example is "Unidentified #_____" or "Doe #_____." This especially applies to traffic accident victims, burned decedents, skeletal remains, and decomposed or other severely traumatized individuals. The pathologist will advise what type of identification method will be necessary, such as prints, dental records, or anthropology consultation (Figure 5.4).

Admission also includes a body weight. This may need to be verified or updated after undressing the decedent and removing extraneous materials such as water, extra clothing, or heavy scene items. Height also needs to be recorded and is obtained from the heel of the foot (from a leg that is not fractured) to the top of the head.

Funeral homes will frequently call and ask if the decedent is "viewable." They are referring to the viewing of a body at a funeral or by family. In traditional viewings, this is usually done from the decedent's right side with viewing of the right face and with the left hand placed over the right hand on the covering blanket. The ability to view a body is a difficult question to answer. Funeral homes have many skills to reconstruct a person's face with makeup and even wax when there is extensive trauma. If the person is decomposed or partially skeletonized on the face it may not be possible to view the body in the traditional sense but families may still want to see their relative. It is best for the investigator to be helpful if possible, but also somewhat hesitant to make that decision.

X-ray procedures

X-rays are done with the decedent still in the body bag and the clothing intact. Bullets can get entangled in clothing and it is important to know how many projectiles arrived with the decedent. X-rays can also help the investigator locate hazards such as needles and knives, personal effects, and even shadows of wallets.

The number and which X-ray views are done depend on the type of case. Homicides and unidentified and decomposed bodies get a typical trauma panel, which includes anterior and lateral head views, anterior views of the chest, and abdomen and pelvis views past the hips. If there are wounds or known prostheses of extremities, those are added. This panel allows an overview of the entire body devoid of extremities showing teeth restorations, spine alignment, and skull and rib contours. A trauma panel can also be useful in traffic accidents. In some offices where traffic accident victims receive an external exam only, X-rays can be useful to demonstrate critical fractures. It is difficult to do lateral views of the torso because of its position on a morgue tray, which makes it harder for

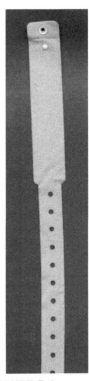

FIGURE 5.4
A simple identification band that can be placed on the ankle of the decedent either at the time of the autopsy or at the scene. It should include a case number and name of the decedent, and is useful to verify the identity of the body at the time it is released to the funeral home.

X-ray penetration. If the search for a bullet is becoming difficult, or multiple gunshot wounds are evident, X-rays can be helpful because they give a third dimension to locate the projectile.

Infant protocols are similar to adult trauma panels except the whole body is routinely X-rayed including extremities. Because more subtle findings are being sought, the infant needs proper alignment to view the extremities. The arms need to be positioned down by the side of the infant, preferably palm upward to view the arms with little rotation of the forearm bones. Medical-care appliances can obscure findings, and in questionable cases, the X-rays may need to be repeated after the appliances are removed by the pathologist. In some cases, sections of healed or recent fractures may need to be excised and X-rayed to better document evidence of healing for dating purposes.

If a gunshot wound is thought to be a result of suicide, a localized view of the area can be done, usually a head or chest X-ray as needed. If the decedent is decomposed, however, it is best to do a complete trauma panel to assure that other gunshot wounds are not missed due to the compromised assessment abilities.

Dental examination X-rays usually require a different X-ray system than the usual body X-ray system. Most modern dentists now use a digital system with digital sensor probes attached to a laptop for visualization and recording the images. The beauty of digital images is the ease with which they can be emailed from the decedent's dentist to the forensic odontologist for comparison to postmortem images. This greatly speeds up the identification process rather than transmission of film images through couriers or mailing.

Current X-ray technology is changing. Film X-ray use is basically obsolete and transition has been made to digital X-rays. Whole-body digital X-ray scanners and CT and MRI scanning now exist for forensic use. These technologies allow images of three-dimensional reconstructions of bullet and knife trajectories, as well as research into application of radiology for a "virtual autopsy." This concept involves high-quality X-rays to document internal injuries, and in some cases, can be used in lieu of a traditional autopsy (e.g., for religious objections or mass disasters). As more offices obtain these technologies, their use will no doubt expand into more applications. Because the decedents are not moving and radiation exposure to the patient is not a consideration, the technology can be less sophisticated, and, in turn, have lower costs than traditional patient instruments. Many times the technology can be obtained secondhand as hospitals upgrade and discard older equipment, and at a much lower cost than cutting-edge equipment.

Photography at the autopsy

The main purpose of photographs is to serve as a permanent record of injuries and injury patterns and for identification purposes. A second purpose is for documentation of clothing and personal effects should a question arise about their loss.

Scene photography is useful to document the position of the body in relationship to its surroundings. When arriving at a scene it is useful for the investigator to begin a series of photographs using an index card with the location, date, and his or her last name. To verify the location, photos of identifying landmarks, such as a street sign or house number, are useful to separate multiple cases on the camera.

Similar documentation separating cases on the camera for autopsies are useful. It can begin with the identifying tag/bracelet on the body and include a photo of the number assigned to that body. The photographic documentation continues upon opening the body bag. Overall, general photographs of the entire body from the sides and top are done prior to removing the clothing. This documents how the body is received at the time of the examination. Close-ups of gunshot wounds are done prior to the clothing being removed. Any necessary evidence from the surface of the body is also retrieved and documented.

The body is then undressed and washed. Overalls, plus more detailed photographs are then obtained (Figure 5.5). At this point it is useful to begin with a close-up view of the face from the mid-neck to the top of the head on a clean background. This can be very useful to verify that the case number corresponds to the face associated with that case number in case there is any mix up of bodies. A photograph with that case number included is also good documentation. Each field of view should include a slight overlap with the previous view taken so there are no missing elements documented. Photographs are taken at right angles (i.e., 90° angle) from the surface of the body to prevent distortion [2]. The following views are standard photographs:

- Overall views from the top and both sides, and possibly the back prior to undressing/washing.

After undressing and washing:

- Identification photograph with and without number, from top of head to mid-neck.
- Overhead of torso from mid-neck to upper thighs.
- Overhead of upper thighs to feet.
- Side view of head to mid-neck, both right and left.
- Side view of mid-neck to thighs, both right and left.
- Side view of thighs to feet, both right and left.
- Back of head to mid-neck.
- Back of torso from mid-neck to base of buttocks.
- Back of legs from buttocks to feet.
- Back and top of feet and hands.
- Midrange photos: These views are used to localize injuries that will require close-up views. They help to localize where on the body the following close-up view will be photographed.
- Close-ups: Any bullet wounds, clean and dirty, with and without scale.
- Any patterned injuries or those related to death, with and without scale.

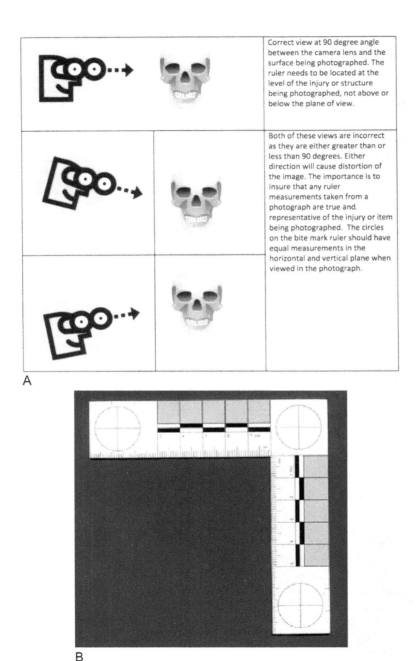

| | | Correct view at 90 degree angle between the camera lens and the surface being photographed. The ruler needs to be located at the level of the injury or structure being photographed, not above or below the plane of view. |
| | | Both of these views are incorrect as they are either greater than or less than 90 degrees. Either direction will cause distortion of the image. The importance is to insure that any ruler measurements taken from a photograph are true and representative of the injury or item being photographed. The circles on the bite mark ruler should have equal measurements in the horizontal and vertical plane when viewed in the photograph. |

A

B

FIGURE 5.5
(A) Demonstrates what happens to the photographed view of an injury or object if the camera is not at a right angle to the object. The purpose of the ruler in the photograph is to substantiate and reproduce the size of an injury or object. (B) A standard photography ruler used during an autopsy and at scenes to document items in two dimensions.

- Collected evidence prior to being placed into a container and sealed (it is helpful to include the identifying label that will be affixed to the container).
- Front and backs of the hands in homicides.

A standard scale used in forensic photo documentation is an ABFO (American Board of Forensic Odontologist) **bite-mark ruler**. It was developed to use on bite-mark wound documentation but has since become the standard photographic reference used in all wounds. It has become so because of three features: it is shaped in a right angle so it gives simultaneous two-dimensional documentation of an injury pattern; it has a gray and white scale to document standard gray and white coloration; and it has circles on the surface to document that the photo was taken at a true right angle from the wound, which prevents misinterpretation of measurements and characteristics.

EVIDENCE COLLECTION DURING AN AUTOPSY

The type of evidence collected during an autopsy is individualized to the type of case and evidentiary requirements determined by the forensic pathologist and investigating law enforcement agency. Common types of evidence collection techniques will be discussed here. Much of the evidence is collected from the hands, and prior to cleaning or collecting it is proper procedure to photograph the front and backs of the hands and nails. The hands of the decedent should never be handled without gloves to prevent transfer of DNA. If **trace evidence**, gunshot residue, or DNA is going to be collected, it is best practice to handle the hands only with a fresh pair of gloves for each hand and minimize contact with the hands until these collections are complete. Sometimes officers wish to perform fingerprints at the scene. It will need to be weighed whether the fingerprint can be done with minimal impact on further collections (digitally on clean screen, inkless fingerprint ink, etc.). The order of collection of materials from the hands after the bags are removed is gunshot residue, DNA swabs, trace evidence, and then fingernail clippings. It is good to bivalve the brown bags so one hand has a clean surface to rest on while working on the other hand between specimen types. To keep the bags sorted, the outside of the brown bag can be marked right and left when the body bag is opened, so when each are passed off to be packaged, there is no confusion.

Gunshot residue collection

Gunshot residue is usually collected using a special kit. There are two major types of kits available depending on the crime lab being used. Both kits require the same precautions and are applied to the backs of the right and left hands separately at the thumb, web of the thumb, and first finger.

Fingernail clippings

Fingernail clippings are usually collected in homicides where there was a physical connection between the victim and assailant. It is hopeful that the debris under the nails would yield DNA linking the two near the time of death. Prior to clipping the nails, it is important to note their condition for evidence of tearing or loss of acrylic nails. The clippings are easily collected into cone-shaped filter papers separately and placed into individual envelopes. Clean clippers and gloves are changed between hands to prevent cross-contamination. It is important to clip only the nail and prevent contamination with the decedent's blood because that can overwhelm the miniscule quantity of assailant DNA that might be present.

Trace evidence

Trace evidence is minute fragments of debris, fibers, hair, vegetation, paint chips, and the like adherent to the body. Paint chips, plastic, and glass fragments are useful in pedestrian motor vehicle accidents, especially a hit and run where the suspect vehicle is unknown. These small fragments may be the necessary evidence to identify a suspect car and link it to the decedent. The other types of materials, such as hairs, fibers, or vegetation, can be useful in a discarded body homicide where very little is known about a suspect or crime scene. These small details may be all that links a suspect to the decedent, especially if the materials are particularly characteristic or embedded within wounds or blood. These fragments are easily collected into a cone-shaped filter paper and sealed inside an envelope.

To sort out foreign hairs from the decedent's hairs, it is useful for the laboratory to receive known head, eyebrow, and/or pubic hairs as exemplars for comparison. These are best retrieved as pulls rather than cuts so as to include the hair roots. They are collected from three to five different regions of the scalp or pubic area to get a general sampling and are placed into a cone-shaped filter paper and sealed inside an envelope.

DNA swabs

With the advances in DNA technology, minute amounts of DNA can be recovered from contact between the victim and assailant. It is best to target areas not overwhelmed from the victim's blood to try to recover this type of DNA. Areas to consider retrieving it are the neck, breasts, thighs, fingertips, and outer labia/penis.

To collect these, packages of sterile cotton swabs and a small cup of sterile saline are used. It is preferable to dry them after collection in a swab dryer available from forensic supply companies.

These collections are done after the hand collections and before the body is washed or handled. The sterile cotton swabs are dipped in the saline and rolled over the upper edge of the cup to remove the excess water. The swab is rolled over the desired surface and placed into the dryer, marked at the edge for the site of collection. A second swab is rolled over the previously dampened area and combined with the previous collection. This is called the wet–dry technique. The first swab loosens any epithelial cells adherent to the skin, which are then picked up by the second dry swab. This procedure is repeated for the desired collection areas. When the swabs are dry, they are packaged in envelopes or small collection boxes, labeled, and released to law enforcement through the chain of custody.

Sexual assault

Sexual assault kits are usually standardized by each state crime laboratory and are available from them or law enforcement (Figure 5.6). It is advisable to have at least two available in the office at all times but may require more depending on the number of cases the office performs weekly. Within the kit are swabs for collection from multiple sites. The order of collection begins with oral swabs with attention to crevices along the gumline and teeth. One swab is rolled onto the accompanying glass slide and marked with the case number and "oral." This is followed by pubic hair combings onto a half-folded paper and includes the comb with the paper into the envelope. This is followed by vaginal swabs that are placed into a swab drying rack to dry prior to packaging. It is necessary to get good views of each orifice to prevent contamination. Generally, a minimum of four swabs is needed for each orifice, as the amount of sperm may be in small numbers. Each location where swabs are to be obtained should be preceded by a change of exam gloves to prevent any cross-contamination. Photographs of traumatized areas can be obtained at the same time as the exam and is easiest if there is a photographer present to assist. After the vaginal exam, swabs can be obtained from the inner or anterior thighs if secretions are visualized. These can be added to the kit in plain, white envelopes and marked by case labels. Anal swabs are obtained next by separating the buttock cheeks to directly view the anal opening for insertion. This is important to prevent contamination from any posterior drainage from the vagina onto the surrounding buttocks. Just as for the oral and vaginal specimens, a single swab is used to prepare a glass slide by rolling it over the surface and labeling it with the case number or site. It is important to keep all the swabs separate and thoroughly dry them before packaging. All items labeled then are placed back into the box and sealed.

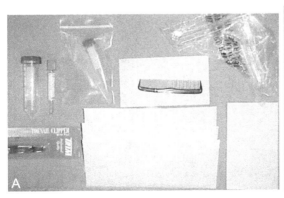
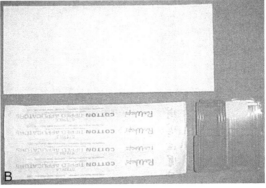

FIGURE 5.6
(A, B) Items in a sexual assault kit. These kits are available from law enforcement and are standardized for the crime laboratory.

Toxicology specimen collection

The types of toxicology specimens tested will be determined by the forensic pathologist and the forensic toxicologist. The quality of the specimens is determined by the condition of the body as well as the skill of the person retrieving them.

The specimens commonly retrieved for an external examination only include **vitreous**, peripheral blood, and urine if available. A clean syringe should be used between each specimen type and the specimen placed directly into the tube/jar and immediately labeled with the patient's name, specimen type, date, time, and initials of the person drawing it (Figure 5.7).

Specimens drawn during an autopsy include vitreous, **femoral blood**, urine (if available), liver tissue (right lobe, about 30 g), and gastric sampling. Brain tissue and head hair are emerging as desired specimens in some cases and, depending on the laboratory, they may be standard collections.

Vitreous is useful as a means of quantifying alcohol and verifying a blood-alcohol level, especially if the decedent received medical intravenous fluids, which dilute blood specimens. They also lag behind blood-alcohol metabolism and

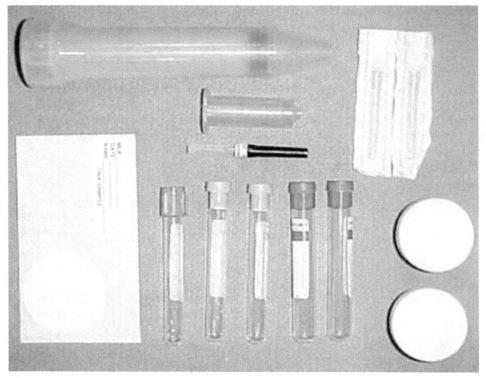

FIGURE 5.7
An example of a toxicology sampling kit for the various specimens on each decedent. It is helpful to have these kits set up for each autopsy to prevent missing a specimen.

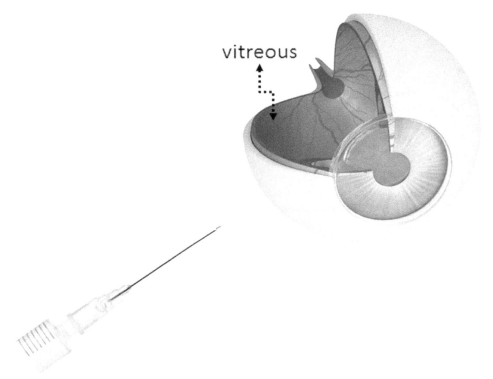

FIGURE 5.8
A diagram depicting the location to obtain vitreous from the eye. The eye is a hollow ball filled with the clear viscous fluid. As the fluid is removed with the syringe and needle, the eye will collapse.

may give a look back in time at a higher level prior to death. For this purpose, vitreous should be placed into a preservative (gray top) tube. Vitreous is also useful to determine predeath electrolytes as postmortem blood is not useful for this purpose. Vitreous glucose is especially useful to evaluate deaths where there has been a history of diabetes mellitus. A small drop can be used in a personal glucometer to evaluate the level. Postmortem, the vitreous glucose value drops quickly to zero, and evaluation upon admission to the morgue can prove useful after the eyes are evaluated for hemorrhages and petechiae. For electrolyte testing, vitreous needs to be placed into a nonpreservative tube (usually a red top, without gel). Vitreous is obtained by placing a 16g needle attached to a syringe or vacutainer into the eye sclera and withdrawing the clear viscous fluid. Total volume from both eyes is usually less than 5 ml and can easily be divided between the two specimens, red-top tube followed by gray-top tube.

Femoral blood

Peripheral blood is the desired specimen, as it is thought to reflect most accurately what the brain and body was experiencing at the time of death. More central blood (i.e. heart blood and even **subclavian blood**) is closer linked to the absorption areas from the arms, neck, or small intestines. In these areas the blood has not passed through the liver or kidneys where drugs are metabolized to a more inactive chemical structure or metabolized to their active structure and quantified values may be less accurate. It is preferred to obtain blood from the most distal area if possible. If it is necessary to encourage blood into the iliac vessels, it is best if milked from the legs proximally rather than from the inferior vena cava. See Figure 5.9.

It is difficult to obtain blood from the femoral system of infants. Cardiac blood is typically used to obtain toxicology, metabolic screens, and cultures. Motor vehicle victims also can have scant femoral blood, but usually one tube can be obtained. The remainder of the specimen can be cardiac blood as needed. Cavity blood should be used only as a last resort because it can be contaminated from the stomach contents and yield inaccurate quantification results. This is especially a hazard in blind sticks for cardiac and subclavian samples in external exams. If it is necessary, the right pleural cavity is preferred since it is furthest from the stomach.

Evisceration techniques

The body is opened using a Y-shaped incision with the upward branches beginning at the top of each shoulder and the stem of the Y extends through the mid-abdomen to the symphysis bone. The branches of the Y are done to protect the viewing area of the neck and chest for the funeral and visitation. If an open shirt or low-cut blouse/dress is used in the casket, the autopsy incisions will not be visible. A midline incision can be devastating for this reason. This technique also spares the neck, which is also visible. For the removal of the chest plate and neck organs the skin is reflected upward to the lower jaw. European countries have a different style and may use a midline chest with extension of the Y branches onto each side of the neck, but in the United States this is not done.

An evisceration technique refers to methods of organ removal from the torso. There are two basic techniques of organ removal from the body: Virchow and Rokitansky styles (Figure 5.10). Each has useful applications, and the method used depends on the style preferred by the pathologist or particular questions that may need to be answered during the examination.

The **Rokitansky technique** is a block style that allows the organs to be evaluated in relationship to their interconnections such as vasculature or ducts. Disadvantages to removing the organ cavity as a whole are the bulkiness of working with the mass of tissue, as well as being heavy and messy. The Appendix contains a photographic overview of the autopsy procedure.

The **Virchow technique** utilizes an organ-by-organ approach that uses the natural retraction of the body itself and allows the connections to be viewed for the majority of cases. It is usually faster, and makes handling the organs alone much easier than block removal. The blood drains naturally into the cavity and prevents a large degree of mess to clean up.

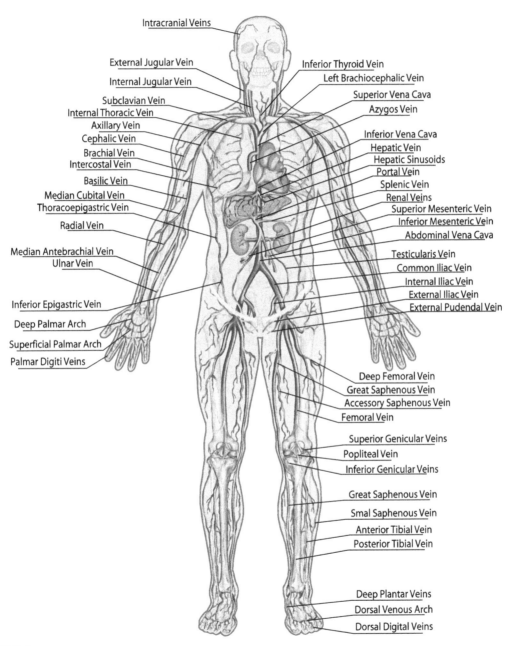

Intracranial Veins

External Jugular Vein
Internal Jugular Vein
Subclavian Vein
Internal Thoracic Vein
Axillary Vein
Cephalic Vein
Brachial Vein
Intercostal Vein
Basilic Vein
Median Cubital Vein
Thoracoepigastric Vein
Radial Vein
Median Antebrachial Vein
Ulnar Vein
Inferior Epigastric Vein
Deep Palmar Arch
Superficial Palmar Arch
Palmar Digiti Veins

Inferior Thyroid Vein
Left Brachiocephalic Vein
Superior Vena Cava
Azygos Vein
Inferior Vena Cava
Hepatic Vein
Hepatic Sinusoids
Portal Vein
Splenic Vein
Renal Veins
Superior Mesenteric Vein
Inferior Mesenteric Vein
Abdominal Vena Cava
Testicularis Vein
Common Iliac Vein
Internal Iliac Vein
External Iliac Vein
External Pudendal Vein
Deep Femoral Vein
Great Saphenous Vein
Accessory Saphenous Vein
Femoral Vein
Superior Genicular Veins
Popliteal Vein
Inferior Genicular Veins
Great Saphenous Vein
Smal Saphenous Vein
Anterior Tibial Vein
Posterior Tibial Vein
Deep Plantar Veins
Dorsal Venous Arch
Dorsal Digital Veins

FIGURE 5.9
An anatomical chart of the venous system. Note the locations of the right and left subclavian vessels, the femoral veins, and the distal internal iliac veins. These are locations where blood is commonly withdrawn for toxicology sampling.

A   B

FIGURE 5.10
(A) Photo commemorating the work of the German pathologist, Dr. Rudolf Virchow. (B) Photo commemorating the work of the Austrian medicolegal anatomist, Dr. Karl Rokitansky. Both contributed to anatomical pathology through their evisceration techniques.

If necessary, a modified Rokitansky technique can be done if a specific area needs to be visualized such as the vasculature of the heart and lungs. The chest can be removed as a block and the remainder of the individual organs via the Virchow method.

Prior to any organ removal or even toxicology specimens, it may be necessary to measure fluids that have accumulated within the pleural or abdominal cavities. This is done by using a ladle to dip each area separately into a measuring device for quantification (Figure 5.11). If large amounts of blood are estimated, it is best to keep the right pleural cavity and not discard it until toxicology is obtained. Cavity blood can be used to perform qualitative assessments and then quantification performed on a single femoral specimen if that is all that is available.

The order of organ removal is based on the traditional teaching of heart removal with draining of blood into the pericardium and chest cavity, releasing the "vascular seal." After the heart is removed, the cranium can then be removed. This order prevents blood from being suctioned into the cranial cavity while the skull is being removed and creating artifact hemorrhage on the brain with misinterpretation of the finding. After the brain is removed, the neck may be examined. This order allows blood to not only drain into the chest cavity, but also from the skull, which in essence creates a bloodless field in the neck vasculature. The finding of hemorrhage of the neck muscles in asphyxial strangulations can be very subtle, and knowledge that it is a bloodless field adds credence that the finding is a real one and not an artifact. It is also important to

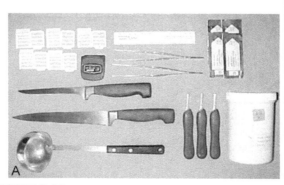
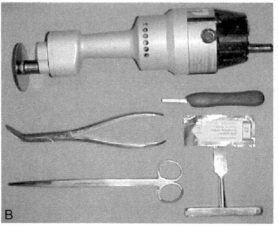

A   B

FIGURE 5.11
(A) The instrument setup for the removal of organs from the trunk. Each pathologist will have special instruments they like available such as hemostats or special scissors. (B) The instrument setup for removal of the brain. The saw is not immersible in water and must only be scrubbed on the blade portion.

retain the skin over the surface of the neck until this final step because the pooling of blood from removal of the chest plate and underlying subclavian/azygous vessels can stain the neck muscles, creating the same distortion. In some cases of asphyxia, the hyoid and thyroid cartilage bones may be intact and the only finding will be hemorrhage. If a technician is assisting the pathologist, it is important to notify them of any hemorrhagic findings prior to the removal of the cranium or the neck organs for the pathologist to view in situ. Intravenous catheter insertion into the jugular veins can result in therapeutic hemorrhage into the neck musculature but needs to be evaluated in situ by the pathologist to make that determination.

Virchow organ removal follows a systemic order. The heart is removed by incising the vessels near the pericardium on the underside of the heart followed by the pulmonary artery and aorta. Each lung is removed by incising through the medial hilum, which frees it from the trachea and vasculature. The right lung will have three lobes and the left will have two lobes. The small and large bowel is removed next and usually can be discarded into the organ return bag if there are no gross abnormalities. The liver is removed by snipping along the diaphragmatic border and cutting its connection from the central vascular/bile duct region. The spleen is usually free floating in the left-upper quadrant and easily cut from its vascular pedicle. The adrenal glands rest on the super and medial portions of each kidney and can be excised for the pathologist, or if the pathologist is prosecting, incised in situ for evaluation. A thin incision can be made on the outer edge of each kidney, which will begin to free the surface membranous capsule. Forceps can be used to strip away the fat and connection tissue and its vascular pedicle will be visualized medially and cut. The bladder and internal female genitalia are identified in the pelvis. The bladder is freed from the symphysis of the pelvis with blunt dissection or scissors. It is important to note the course of the femoral arteries along the rim of the pelvis bilaterally and avoid them during the removal. By using the knife/scissors and staying medial to them with blunt dissection, the sides of the organs (including the ovaries, which will lie near the vessels) will be released. Posteriorly, the organs lie on top of the rectum, which is usually not needed, and if excised causes abundant drainage from the cavity into the bag and casket. Blunt or scissor dissection is useful to free the organs from the rectum. By remaining inside the pelvis and not putting excessive traction on the bladder or uterus, an incision can be made front to back without placing a gaping opening onto the perineum.

The only remaining organs are the esophagus/stomach with pancreas, aorta, and trachea. An incision is made transversely above the vessel bifurcation into the right and left iliac vessels. Each diaphragm is then excised along their contours to the midline. A transverse incision is made through the trachea, esophagus, and great vessels as they exit from the arch of the aorta. It is important to not put too much traction on the arch as the subclavian arteries will snap under the clavicles, making it difficult to embalm the arms and head. The trachea can be used for traction because the remaining tissue is excised away from the spine to the transverse vascular incision near the pelvis.

The Rokitansky technique is basically the Virchow technique from the point of the transverse incision across the vessels of the pelvis, followed by the incision near the clavicles, both diaphragms. The entire organ block can be excised off the spine and given to the pathologist. They may wish the bowel removed prior to the block being excised.

The head is examined by making a continuous incision from behind each ear over the vertex of the head remaining behind a line drawn over the top from ear canal to canal. It is important to not get the incision too far forward since it will be seen in the casket if the person has very little hair, and if the incision is too far posterior it can make reflecting the anterior portion for visualization of the skull extremely difficult or actually split down the top of the head. This is especially difficult if the head is edematous, so care must be taken to not force the skin too quickly. Using blunt dissection and small incisions, the scalp is loosened anteriorly to fold the top and anterior portion over the forehead. The posterior flap is easier to use the scalpel to reflect downward. Photographs may be needed at this point depending on the case. Temporalis muscles are present on the right and left sides of the head that need to be incised downward to make a path for the saw. The saw cut is made about 3 cm above the brow ridge anteriorly and slightly below the occipital protuberance posteriorly. To avoid a totally circular skull cap resulting, these two horizontal lines are offset onto a notch area on both sides of the head so that the skull rests on a shelf. From the beginning, it is helpful to draw a line using the scalpel to follow with the saw. The oscillating saw is relatively safe to the naïve handler as the cutting edge vibrates to create the cut, rather than incising. To give life to the saw it is important to lift and press rather than push the cutting margin in a linear path.

After the circular cuts are made, a skull key can be inserted and turned to begin the separation of the edges and pry it open. If blood is visualized, the pathologist should be notified prior to proceeding. It will be necessary to use scissors to cut the anterior dura margin then insert a hand to support the brain while the skull cap is removed by the other hand. This will prevent tearing of the brain from the brainstem. Photographs may be necessary of any blood or other abnormalities, and while this is being prepared, the brain needs to be supported so it doesn't separate at the brainstem. The brain is then anteriorly lifted gently from the base of the skull and the nerve connections are snipped close to the skull. As the posterior brain is approached the dura forms a shelf under which lies the cerebellum and brainstem. It is important to incise the shelf along each edge where it connects the skull, which will free the posterior fossa and allow visualization of the brainstem. It is important to note any separation of the brainstem from the cortex and inform the pathologist. Reaching with scissors as far into the foramen as possible, the spinal cord is cut from the remaining portion and the brain should lift out to be weighed. The brain is normally very soft and should be kept separate from other organs for the pathologist to evaluate. The dura lining the skull and cap needs to be removed for evaluation of any underlying skull fractures. The pathologist will wish to view both the skull cap as well as the removed dura. If hemorrhage is present on the dura, the pathologist may wish to remove it and take microscopic sections. The head is left open until the neck dissection is complete and the pathologist has given permission for it to be closed. Closure is accomplished by placing the skull cap in place, returning the skin to the normal anatomic position, and tacking with the normal thread. It may be helpful to put some paper towels inside the cranium to absorb blood draining from the face. Some offices cover the head with a bag to prevent extensive leakage.

The neck organs remain and are discussed later under special techniques for tongue removal. The cavities are then dried from accumulated blood and evaluated for fractures that are documented. How to document fractures is also discussed in the "Special Techniques" section.

RECORDING AUTOPSY DATA

Many offices are going to a paperless system and records are kept in an online file for each case. Some of the databases are quite sophisticated, but even a dedicated folder on the office server for each case will suffice. Each folder can contain a subfolder for photos, investigative reports, a chain of custody, an autopsy weight sheet, an autopsy report, and medical records.

External examinations may have their own form that may include only a handwritten diagram or fill-in form depending on the office protocol. An example of one is found in the Appendix.

Records generated during an autopsy include a weight sheet, diagrams, and a chain of custody for any evidence leaving the building, and a toxicology request form. A weight sheet includes an area for each of the major organ systems to record the weight, and areas for the pathologist to record specific findings for dictation. See the Appendix for an example of a weight sheet.

Each organ is weighed individually in grams and the weight recorded on the autopsy record sheet. The pathologist may also have the assistant record various findings throughout the dissection. When weighing the heart, it is important to expunge blood from the chambers so an accurate weight can be recorded, or the weight can be repeated after the heart chambers are opened and drained by the pathologist. Recording volumes from body cavities, bladder, and stomach will require using a ladle to transfer the fluids into a measuring device, usually a 1 L container. It is also possible to measure urine and cavity fluid volumes by weight as 1 ml approximates 1 g in weight. This is useful for estimating clotted blood or volume of fluids within hollow organs by weighing the organ with the liquid intact, emptying the liquid, then reweighing the organ. The difference in weights will give the volume of liquid.

The following is a summary of materials generated during an autopsy or examination.

Cut box or tissue container

This is a small biopsy container filled approximately halfway with formalin and used by the pathologist to retain biopsies for potential microscopic examination.

Some pathologists utilize this container plus "cut in" the biopsies directly to histology containers as they are performing the dissections.

Cassettes for histology

Cassettes are small plastic cages that hold the biopsy specimens for histology. They are labeled with the office case number and begin with 1 or A, a sequential sequence to differentiate one from the next. These cassettes are transferred to a histology department in formalin. They are then placed through a processing machine to infuse the biopsies with preservative. This process usually requires an overnight cycle. The cassettes are removed from the cage and embedded by the histologist into paraffin, which can be cut into very thin slices and placed onto microscopic slides. The slides undergo a series of staining procedures to outline the cells for the pathologist to review under the microscope. If the specimens are sent outside the building, they will require a chain of custody outlining the number of cassettes sent for each case. Formalin is considered a carcinogen and the transfer container should be one that will not leak, placed inside a plastic bag inside a cooler for the courier.

Retention of brain for later dissection

In some cases, the pathologist will wish to retain the entire brain for formalin fixation, later dissection, and review. It may require transfer to a neuropathologist for dissection. The brain is removed, weighed, and placed into a 15–20% formalin solution (a higher concentration than normal because of its higher water content). It will require a container large enough to cover the surface with formalin, usually at least a gallon-size container one-quarter to half full with formalin. The brain is lowered into the formalin and secured to the top by a string around the brainstem or floated inside a hairnet to prevent flattening by resting on the bottom of the container. It usually requires 7 to 10 days for the brain to be "fixed" and ready for dissection. If the brain is bisected, fixation will occur much quicker. The pathologist will require cassettes for obtaining biopsies from the fixed brain for microscopic review. Cases where the brain may be retained for fixation are child abuse, brain tumors, degenerative disorders of the brain, or unusual brain trauma. Some offices retain all brains for later review. This has begun to fall into disfavor by families who wish all the remains returned to them. In some jurisdictions, retained organs must be disclosed to families and permission sought for the disposal.

Toxicology specimens

Each toxicology laboratory will have individual requirements for specimens. It is important that the specimens be labeled with the correct labels and type of specimen, as well as sealed inside the appropriate transfer container to the lab (a box or biohazard bag) at the end of each case, and before the next case is begun to prevent confusion of specimens. It is a good time to verify that the correct labels were placed onto the specimens and that each specimen is labeled correctly. Requisitions for the laboratory may be required to be completed prior to the transfer.

DNA specimen

DNA specimens collected on FTA (fast technology for analysis) cards and in the special envelopes need to be labeled and are usually stored in the freezer. The FTA material serves as a preservative to stabilize the DNA on the card and allows them to be stored at room temperature [1]. Some offices air dry them and place them in the case file. It is important that they be completely dry before packaging or they may mold in a case file and become unusable. Labels need to be placed directly on the specimen and outside envelope for identification.

Genetic screen

Genetic screens are collected on the laboratory version of an FTA-type card. It is important they be labeled and the requisition be completely filled out or the laboratory will not complete the testing. They are usually air dried and placed into a mailing envelope without special handling necessary. Notes within the case file of the date it was mailed are helpful.

Cultures

After the specimens have been placed into their appropriate media containers for transfer to the lab and labeled, they should be stored in the refrigerator until the courier arrives to take them to the microbiology laboratory. They must be accompanied by a completed requisition outlining the specimen types and tests requested or they will not be accepted by the laboratory. They should not remain in the refrigerator for transfer to the laboratory after the workday. Transfer should occur in a biohazard bag inside a cooler with an ice pack to prevent deterioration during the courier run.

Evidence

Homicide evidence is generally transferred directly to the agency that has attended the autopsy at the end of the dissection. It is helpful to the pathologist signing over the evidence to the officer to have it orderly laid out, in the order on the chain of custody, and to have each item labeled on the paperwork with the exact working on the item's container. Each item can be verified by both parties and placed into a brown paper bag for the officer to transfer to the laboratory. Unless the medical examiner/coroner has a drying cabinet, bloody clothing items are placed into individual brown paper bags, then into a biohazard bag. This will prevent any contamination to the evidence or transfer of biohazardous material to the inside of the officer's vehicle. It should be directly transferred to the evidence handling area and checked in for refrigerated storage and drying, and to ensure a tight chain of custody.

Discard policy

Obviously all this material cannot be held indefinitely and must be sorted into those items pending litigation where they might be needed to those that are no longer needed for case evaluation. Each office will have its own policy based on

Table 5.1	Storage Periods
Item	**Time Period**
DNA cards	Indefinitely
Toxicology specimens	2 years after receipt of report
Gross formalin fixed tissues	1 year
Tissue paraffin blocks	10 years
Tissue microscopic slides	Indefinitely
Homicide specimens	5 years

local politics, case backlogs, and accreditation requirements. Homicide tissue and toxicology are usually held at least five years. Cases of unidentified remains also need to be retained longer than "usual" cases, which are generally held one year after completion. According to the National Association of Medical Examiner's Accreditation Standards the storage periods shown in Table 5.1 are recommended.

Some evidence, such as bullets and ligatures from suicides, tend to accumulate at the coroner/medical examiner office. Law enforcement rarely is interested in these items unless there is an investigative issue that arises. It is advised that a routine periodic assessment inventory of these types of evidence be performed and the investigating agency be contacted with a list of items that pertains to them. They can be informed of the type of evidence and request a disposition on each item.

All clothing and personal effects need to be released to the family or their designee, such as a funeral home, at the time or prior to the body being released. It is important that the property only be released to the person who has a right to it and many times this is the person making the funeral arrangements rather than someone who is randomly appearing at the office requesting personal effects. Most times this is best handled at the funeral home. Because families can disagree on which funeral home the body is to be released to, it is important for the death investigator to be cognizant of the next of kin available. Their rights to personal effects and designation depend on the order precedence in the state law sequence (usually spouse, adult children, parents, siblings). It is best to have the desired funeral home designation on a form signed by the appropriate designee to avoid dealing with a verbal release to the wrong funeral home.

CLOSING THE BODY

Organs are generally not retained and are returned to the body cavity for release with the body. A heavy-duty trash bag with biohazard markings is best. It needs to be heavy duty enough so when the funeral home lifts it out for embalming, it does not rupture. For this reason, any medical-care appliances such as endotracheal tubes should not be put in the organ bag.

The Y-shaped incision is closed with heavy-duty white-cotton string and a tissue needle, both of which can be obtained from funeral home supply companies.

Some offices just tack the trunk closed at intervals and others sew the cavity closed with a continuous overhand "baseball" stitch and tie off the ends when done. The latter is the most helpful and prevents leakage of cavity fluids during the body transfer to a funeral home. It is disastrous if the body bag breaks during transfer and accumulated fluids flow onto personnel. Clothing is best placed into a biohazard trash bag and closed with attached name and case labels and placed inside the body bag with the decedent. This prevents the clothing from getting separated during the body release. Valuables are generally kept separate from the clothing and body in an office safe and need to be retrieved. The body needs to be signed over to the funeral home transport person and a separate form for property, including documented valuables, needs to be signed (see the Appendix). It is important that large amounts of money be counted by the receiving personnel.

SPECIAL TECHNIQUES

The following are special techniques that can be applied.

Turning a body over from face up to face down

It may be necessary to turn a body completely over for obtaining spinal fluid or documenting numerous injuries over the back or lower extremities. This can be very difficult depending on the size of the decedent. Body mechanics will greatly assist. Put a generous amount of soap on each side of the decedent lying face up on the table. Slide the decedent to one side and extend the arm closest to the center of the table over the top of the head. Grasp the opposite shoulder and thigh to rotate the decedent toward the center. As the body is rolled, the upward arm will act as a fulcrum and pivot the decedent over face down. The arm can then be lowered and the decedent lifted by the shoulders onto a shoulder block under the chest.

Spinal fluid collection

Equipment needed for spinal fluid collection includes bactericidal soap, spinal needle (in children a vacutainer may be used), 10 cc syringe, sterile needle, and a collection tube (red-top tube without gel and no preservatives).

The easiest method is to have the decedent face down with the shoulders propped on a block and head downward, hyperextending the vertebra of the neck. It is important the head is in alignment with the spine. The base of the skull is palpated just above the posterior vertebral process and a pressure mark is made by the nail (through a glove). The area is scrubbed vigorously with the bactericidal soap and the gloves are changed. The spinal needle is attached to the syringe and inserted between the skull and vertebral body into the cisternal space around the base of the brain under the dura of the posterior fossa. During the insertion, it is important to put gentle suction on the syringe until there is a slow filling of clear to slightly bloody fluid. Cerebral spinal fluid (CSF) is generally colorless with the consistency of water. After obtaining 5–10 cc, the needle is withdrawn and changed to a regular sterile needle for insertion into the red-top tube. If possible, it is best to clean the top of the tube prior to the needle insertion to remove contaminants. It is then ready for labeling and transfer to the laboratory.

Posterior neck dissection

The purpose of this procedure is to look for fractures on the posterior portions of the vertebral bodies of the neck that are not visualized from the anterior view after the neck organs were removed. A posterior neck dissection is performed with the decedent face down in the same position as for spinal fluid collection. A vertical incision is made over the cervical spine extending into the upper thoracic spine and made in the midline. It needs to be long enough to incise the underlying muscles away from the spine to visualize the bony structures and assess the area for hemorrhage and fractures.

Anterior neck dissection

In cases of suspected strangulation, the pathologist will perform an anterior layer neck dissection. It is done after the organs have been removed from the trunk and the brain has been removed from the skull. This allows blood to drain from the neck in both directions and create a bloodless field. The diagnosis of strangulation can be made from hemorrhage in the neck muscles with or without fractures of the hyoid bone, thyroid, or tracheo-laryngeal cartilages. So, it is important that blood not pool on the muscles and create artifacts. Usually strangulation is associated with petechiae of the face or eyes, which is the clue that care needs to be taken not to dissect the skin above the clavicles. To protect the muscles at the level of the clavicles that become exposed during removal of the chest plate, a towel can be laid over the muscles to absorb any blood.

The dissection proceeds with dissection of the neck skin away from the surface of the muscles. Photographs are taken at each stage of the dissection with a ruler needed if there are areas of hemorrhage. After the muscles are exposed and photographed, each muscle will be dissected away and laid so the undersurface is viewed and documented for any hemorrhage. This will create a fanlike image of the muscles of the neck. After this documentation, the pathologist will remove the tongue and the usual neck organs. Photographs will be needed of fractures of the hyoid, thyroid cartilage, or hemorrhagic areas over the anterior spine. It is always important when removing the neck organs in routine cases to not put too much pressure on the delicate bones and create fractures.

Removal of the eyes

This procedure is done to look for periorbital and retinal (internal) hemorrhage, usually in child abuse cases. The object is to preserve the eye for confirmation of clinician documentation of retinal hemorrhages. This involves a twofold approach by removing the orbital plates from inside the skull and gently excising along the margins between the globe and the orbital bone, preserving the eyelids and the optic nerve as it enters the skull. It is then placed into a small cup of formalin, making sure to mark each eye separately with a label. The pathologist will dissect the eye after it is fixed.

Removal of the inner ears

Removal of the inner ears is done to look for an inner ear infection. It is performed by making a triangular wedge–shaped cut inside the skull over the sphenoid ridge. This can then be decalcified and reviewed microscopically.

Removal of the spine to view the spinal cord

The purpose of looking at the spinal cord is usually to confirm its integrity, which would correlate with the ability to continue moving. Other reasons to view the cord are to evaluate for subdural hemorrhage, tumors, or degenerative disorders. To view the spinal cord, it is necessary to remove the anterior vertebral bodies in a wedge shape beginning in the cervical spine of the neck and extending to the lower back. The cut is made inside the body cavity at ~45° angle to the spine. It can then be pried off using the skull key to reveal the intact dura. The dura is opened, and the spinal cord is evaluated for integrity or other abnormalities. It can be very difficult to observe the upper portion of the cervical spine where it connects with the skull. Special instruments will be needed to insert through the foramen magnum and release the spinal nerves so that a portion of the cord can be removed with the lower portion.

Removal of bullets embedded in bone

Not uncommonly, bullets need to be retrieved from thick bone. This is made more difficult if they are small caliber or are in small fragments. Obviously, the goal is to retrieve it without distorting the rifling grooves. If possible, it is helpful to have two different views of X-rays of the area, an anterior and a lateral view. The anterior view gives detail of how superior/inferior it is as well as how far left/right. The lateral view will give an idea of how front to back it is. This allows a more directed cut. Sometimes the entrance in the bone can be palpated. To avoid hitting the bullet, it is best to give the area at least a 1–2 cm rim and, using the bone saw, extricate the bone where the bullet is lodged. This can be very time consuming and trying. The skull key can be used to break the bone away from the bullet. If it is unclear if the bullet is located in the bone, it is easiest to just X-ray the fragment and, if necessary, the body.

Examination of legs for thromboemboli

Some pathologists routinely examine the lower legs as a source for thromboemboli to the lungs. The thought behind this is to identify which of the extremities is the source, especially if one had trauma and the other did not. The pathophysiology behind why a thromboembolism forms is related to stagnated blood flow due to immobilization or coagulation abnormalities. All or part of the clot formed in the leg or pelvis will become mobile then entangled in the lung vessels.

The decedent must be face down to look at the popliteal and upper leg veins. Incisions are made over the backs of both legs in the midline from the lower thigh onto the lower legs. The muscles are bisected and dissection to the vessels is done to view their lumens. Microscopic sections of the veins may be obtained.

Catheterization of the neck vessels to evaluate for a ruptured intracranial vessel

This procedure is normally considered in cases of a boxing-type injury or punch to the jaw and someone suddenly drops to the ground dead. This is a highly suggestive scenario of a lacerated vertebral artery where it crosses into the skull from the neck or along the path of the basilar artery. Internal findings show extensive subarachnoid hemorrhage over the brain, usually centered on the basilar brain. It can be very difficult to locate the tear after the brain is removed, as it may be cut during the removal process or be miniscule.

The procedure requires a vascular catheter, syringe, contrast material, and X-ray capability. It is done after the usual organs have been removed from the trunk and before the head is opened. The vascular catheter is threaded through the vertebral artery, which is located at the base of the neck as one of the branches from the subclavian artery, and tied in place to obstruct the artery from any backflow of contrast. A 20 cc syringe of intravenous contrast is then slowly injected into the artery and a series of lateral X-rays of the head are obtained to look for leakage of contrast within the skull. If uncertain of the extravasation, the catheter can be left in place and the head opened, but the skull cap not removed to support the brain. This way, the basilar brain can be observed during a repeat injection through the catheter to see any leakage from the basilar artery vasculature. A syringe of water can then be slowly injected to locate the rupture.

If the vertebral artery can't be catheterized, the carotid artery can be attempted to show a rupture through retrograde flow. Sometimes neither method works and the pathologist is left with an acute subarachnoid hemorrhage. Fixing a brain with subarachnoid hemorrhage worsens the situation because the blood becomes very stiff. The easiest method to locate vascular abnormalities, such as a berry aneurysm or vascular malformation, is to remove the arachnoid membranes and run the basilar brain under water to view the Circle of Willis. This requires time and patience so as not to tear the delicate vasculature.

Subcutaneous dissections for demonstration of subcutaneous hemorrhage

This is usually done to demonstrate the location and extent of bruises in the subcutaneous tissue that may not be well visualized from looking at the skin. Contusions are bleeding into the fat of the skin and may extend into the underlying muscle. By dissecting between these layers, this can be better visualized. Typically, it is done in child abuse cases over the anterior and posterior torso, extending onto the buttocks and legs, looking for the presence and extent of inflicted injuries. Skin biopsies can be taken from these areas for microscopic evaluation and lend information about the timeframe they occurred in.

Tongue removal with the neck organs

The tongue is removed to gain a good view of the posterior mouth, upper airway, and mouth. It is dissected to look for intramuscular hemorrhage associated with seizures, or to evaluate trauma that might be obstructing the airway.

The hazard of removing the tongue and neck organs is damage to a carotid artery, making embalming of the face more difficult. Another hazard is nicking the anterior neck skin, which creates a huge hole in an area visible in a casket, and will require repair (referred to as a buttonhole). A couple of key points of the dissection will make it easier and decrease the possibility of this occurring. To give the prosector (person doing the dissecting) plenty of visualization of the field the top horns of the Y incision can be extended to the top of the shoulder or even slightly posteriorly toward the back. An extra inch at that location will give more flexibility into the chest flap as it is stretched upward to view the base of the mandible. To prevent buttonholes, the fold should be in the retraction hand and the blade in the other hand pointed downward toward the muscle. The skin should be dissected away from the neck muscles until the submandibular salivary glands and edge of the mandible are in view. Holding the chest flap and fold in the retraction hand, the blade of the knife is inserted along the inner edge of the mandible upward into the mouth, dissecting along the inner edge of the mandible to loosen the base of the tongue. When the back angle of the jaw is reached, using scissors pointed to the inner-edge medially, the remaining muscle is cut down to the cervical spine. This is a key spot to avoid clipping the vessels that are very close by. After this, the scissors are inserted in the mouth, clipping any residual membranes and muscles holding the tongue in place. Then, by reaching into the mouth from the neck, the tongue is retracted downward so it is free and will release when the neck is dissected. Returning to the neck and using a scalpel, the right and left margins should be gently dissected, keeping the blade parallel and pointed medially along its length. This will keep the blade free of the vessels within their membranes along the lateral edge. Both sides of the neck muscles should be worked until it comes free. Care should be taken to not fracture the hyoid bone by pressing inward on the upper neck tissue. The tongue should be attached to the upper neck organs as well as the hyoid bone, epiglottis, thyroid cartilage, and tracheo-laryngeal cartilages.

Counting ribs or the spine for fractures

This seems like it should be straightforward, however, it is easy to get confused by the normal contours of the bones being obscured by blood and muscle tissue. It is easiest to locate the first rib on either side of the chest, which is located directly under the clavicle, and trace its course to the back to the spine, which is T1 (thoracic vertebra 1). This can be done consecutively along the sides of each pleural cavity to count locations of the rib fractures. **Anterior** is defined as from the anterior axillary fold extending anteriorly; **posterior** is from the posterior axillary fold extending posteriorly to the spine and lateral under the armpit. These location distinctions are important as they give an indication of how the force was applied to the chest. The intercostal spaces are named for the rib directly above the space and similar injuries to these areas are recorded.

Finding the ribs and tracing them posteriorly from T1 downward or upward will also assist in documenting a fractured spine. As a quick reminder, there are 7 cervical vertebra followed by 12 thoracic vertebra then 5 lumbar ones before the spine connects to the sacrum at the pelvis. The first through tenth ribs connect via cartilage to the sternum anteriorly leaving the eleventh and twelfth ribs floating along the posterior chest.

Airplane, train, and pipeline fatalities

The focus of this type of investigation is twofold. One is to identify and determine the cause of death of the persons who died during the accident, and two is to aid investigators to determine why the accident occurred. The focus of the latter is to identify the engineer, pilot, and crew to determine their cause of death and obtain toxicology samples. The National Transportation Safety Board (NTSB) is the regulatory agency and has a protocol for routine collection of toxicology from the pilot/engineer and the copilot/train crew (called brakemen or conductor). The kit comes in a Styrofoam packing box and is obtained directly from the NTSB prior to the autopsies. It includes a detailed explanation of all the specimens required that must be obtained during the autopsy and the specimen collection devices.

REFERENCES

[1] FTA® Technology. National Forensic Science Technology Center; 2013. Retrieved from www.nfstc.org/pdi/Subject03/pdi_s03_m04_02_d.htm. [October 2013].

[2] Schoebel P, Weiss S. Photography of Medicolegal and Forensic Autopsies. Evidence Technology Magazine 2009;7(3):10–3, 28.

CHAPTER 6
Identification

Learning Objectives

- Compare and contrast the three most common ways to confirm identity of a decedent. Include the positive and negative aspects for each method.
- Discuss the process of identification of skeletal remains by both nuclear and mitochondrial DNA. Include the family members who could supply a test sample for each.
- Illustrate by a flow diagram how you might attempt to identify an unknown decomposing body of a person who was transient and died in your jurisdiction.
- Compare the NCIC versus the NAMUS organizations for potentially identifying an unknown decedent. Discuss who may enter the data and who may view it, as well as data types entered.

Key Terms

Edentulous
Premortem
Postmortem
PCR
Mitochondria
Nucleus
CODIS
NAMUS
IAFIS
NCIC

Chapter Summary

Identification is a very important part of a death investigation because it is the initial premise upon which the remainder of the investigation follows. The wrong identity has severe repercussions and can lead to civil lawsuits and at a minimum bad press and embarrassment, if identities of two decedents are confused. Verification of a properly identified body is also important. It is good to have two people, the funeral home personnel and in turn to the family, visually confirm the identification tag on the body and obtain signatures on the release forms by both parties. There are multiple scientific modalities available to achieve a positive identification, but the key is usually finding material to connect the decedent with a known identity and then next of kin.

INTRODUCTION

Proper identification of a decedent has many implications. It ensures that the death certificate was issued on the proper person and his or her estate and affairs may be closed with certainty. In the age of extensive identity theft, it allows us to verify scientifically who the decedent is, which also will trigger the closure of various files regarding that identity, including social security benefits, outstanding warrants, FBI and state law enforcement files, bank accounts, and various estate documents. Proper identification allows the death certificate to be linked with the birth certificate to prevent unauthorized used for identity theft. This linkage is provided automatically via the 1992 Vital Statistics Act [17].

Paperwork in and around the body is a start for an investigation but it can easily be placed in the decedent's possession or previously created by the decedent as part of a new identity. More scientific means are necessary to verify the person's identity.

In addition, it is important to protect the decedent and his or her family from potential identity theft. Victimizers surf obituaries for information about funeral times to break into the residence or lift mail and credentials and create fraudulent claims against the estate [4]. When the death certificate is filed, the funeral home practice is to gather the social security number and notify the Social Security Administration Office or a family member can notify them as well. The Social Security Administration Office maintains a Death Master File that credit agencies and financial institutions can use as a resource to prevent using the decedent's credentials [3]. The Social Security Administration Office, Veteran's Administration, car or house insurance, and unions or workplaces may serve as financial resources for the family to check for death benefits to aid them in final disposition.

For identification, it obviously requires two parts, either of which can be problematic. It requires being able to obtain a piece of data from the decedent and to be able to locate a record of that type of data somewhere to compare it to. As we discuss the various methods to make identification, helpful hints will be given to deal with either issue.

FINGERPRINTS

Fingerprints are the fastest, least-expensive means to verify an identity and clear various law enforcement records (Figure 6.1). They are easily obtained and transmitted electronically either by scanning the prints in high resolution or by actually photographing the fingertips (the image has to be inverted to compare as it is a mirror image of an actual fingerprint). Portable electronic fingerprint scanners are also available to transmit the image directly to law enforcement for verification.

Integrated Automated Fingerprint Identification System

The FBI has maintained a fingerprint identification system called Integrated Automated Fingerprint Identification System (IAFIS; a.k.a. AFIS) since 1999. AFIS contains fingerprints obtained directly by the FBI, as well as those submitted by various law enforcement agencies, and contains over 56 million criminal record prints and 250 million civilian prints. It operates 24 hours a day, 365 days a year. From the time of submission for a criminal record check, results are able to be reported back to an agency usually within minutes to one hour. The rapid turnaround allows law enforcement to connect fugitives with

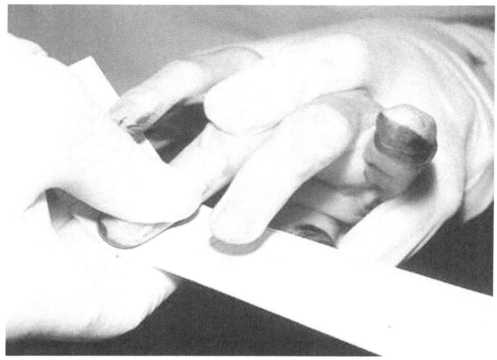

FIGURE 6.1
Fingerprinting a decedent in full rigor or following postmortem changes (e.g., decomposition, mummification, or "washerwoman" hands) can be a challenge.

the appropriate law enforcement agency. The current system is able to search for latent prints (prints left at crime scenes), as well as fingerprints associated with known persons. The system can also provide various identifying characteristics including height, weight, hair and eye color, and tattoos. It is currently unable to identify or store palm prints [6].

The next generation of identification by the FBI will be called Next Generation Identification (NGI). This will vastly expand the identification capabilities and includes biometric identification (including facial recognition), photographic documentation of tattoos and other identifying marks, and expanded fingerprint capabilities including latent and palm prints [7]. Biometrics is becoming an important parameter for another modality of identification beyond fingerprints. The study of biometrics includes iris scanning, facial recognition software, voice comparison, ear scanning, and multiple other individual characteristics, and is expanding rapidly. Unfortunately, retinal scanning technology does not appear to work for identification after death. Further research will need to be completed on all areas of biometrics and their applications to decedents.

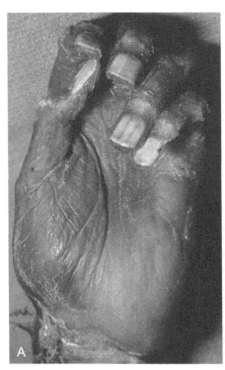
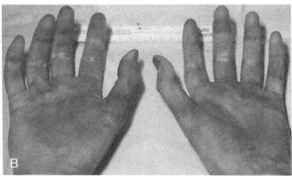

FIGURE 6.2
(A) Dried, wrinkled hands due to mummification of an unknown decedent. The hands were processed using a sodium hydroxide technique to soften and inflate the skin of the hands. (B) The fingertips after four days of this process were able to produce readable fingerprints for comparison (see appendix for procedure).

Most states contain statutes pertaining to obtaining fingerprints of the dead and forwarding them to the respective state law enforcement agency. This serves at least two purposes: to verify the identity on all decedents and clear the clutter out of the law enforcement database.

The problems with getting prints from decedents are:

- Decomposition
- Mummification
- "Washerwoman" hands
- Skeletal remains

Each of these **postmortem** changes present challenges but has potential solutions, including rehydration procedures and subcutaneous inflation by embalming fluid (Figure 6.2). The appendix has procedures that may prove helpful to restore prints on mummified or washerwoman hands. However, in some cases, prints will not be feasible and other methods for identification will be needed.

Locating prints for comparison

Prints are available in various databases for comparison. If someone has a criminal record, he or she can be located in a local law enforcement file or FBI file (**IAFIS**). Other noncriminal files of prints are available as part of criminal record checks for various government jobs. Jobs or situations that can require prints are physicians, lawyers, teachers, police, military and security jobs, corrections officers, various financial and banking institutions, applications for firearms permits and dealerships, various medical personnel, and, in some states, those seeking social welfare benefits. These may need to be accessed separately during a search.

Immigrations and Customs Enforcement (ICE), a division of U.S. Department of Homeland Security, keeps a separate database of individuals crossing the border or with customs infarctions. They accept prints in a scanned format and can search through their database as an additional resource. The United States does not require fingerprints to obtain a passport. However, a passport is linked to various photo identification items that may have a fingerprint such as a driver's license. Since August 2007, passports contain integrated chips within the back cover. The information on the chip contains the same information as the back cover with a digitalized photograph used to biometrically match the holder to the passport using facial recognition [5].

Not every state requires a fingerprint (usually thumb) as part of an application for a driver's license. At this point, California, Colorado, Georgia, and Texas retain a database as well as Honolulu County, Hawaii [1]. The lack of this information seems to have been challenged as an invasion of individual privacy laws and expansion of fingerprints on driver's licenses in many states has been struck down over the years.

Banks requiring a thumbprint for check cashing by nonaccount holders reportedly do so to deter check fraud and they do not have their own database. Their recommended practice is to scan the thumbprint on the back of the check as part of their electronic record and to serve as a natural deterrent for check fraud. If fraud occurs, the check with the print can be given to law enforcement for follow-up. It was conceived by the Texas Bankers Association, and since its inception in 1982, banks and financial institutions have seen at least a 50% reduction in check fraud [2].

Case Study

Sun Times **Article: Fingerprint for Driver's License Comes Back to Haunt Man Wanted for 1994 Shooting** For an interesting case in which driver's license fingerprinting helped identify a criminal assuming a fake identity, go to http://www.suntimes.com/news/crime/13955879-418/fingerprint-for-drivers-license-comes-back-to-haunt-man-wanted-for-1994-shooting.html.

DENTAL IDENTIFICATION

When unidentified remains are received at the death investigation office and fingerprint identification is not helpful, full body X-rays including anterior and lateral X-rays of the head can be done looking for medical-care appliances and the presence of dental restorations. In addition to the tooth amalgams, implants, root canals, and faint outlines of ceramic caps can be seen. Any of these items can be characteristic in their configuration in a particular location to make identification possible. The challenge is knowing the person had restorations done but being unable to find the **premortem** X-rays for that person to make the positive identification.

For true John/Jane Doe decedents, missing person reports can be scanned for someone missing with the physical features of height, weight, approximate age, gender, and any identifying scars or tattoos. Families or employer health plans are the best source for the location of the premortem dentist. If that person is located, it is hopeful the X-rays have not been purged or the practice dissolved and the location of records unknown. If they are located, the comparison can be relatively rapid especially if the pre- and postmortem records are digital and can be emailed to the dentist at his or her practice. He or she compares the morphology of the outlines of the restorations in a particular location to those in the premortem X-rays. Depending on the interval between the two, there may have been additional dental work done that does not appear on the premortem X-rays and the dentist may also rely on tooth root structure to add further certainty to the identification. See Figure 6.3.

Dental consultation is not helpful in cases where the person is **edentulous** and wearing dentures. Most dentures have no identifying marks in them to aid

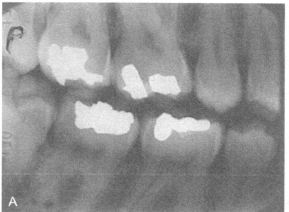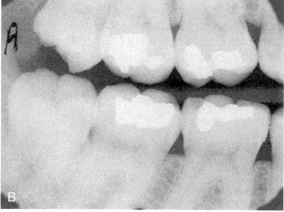

FIGURE 6.3
(A) Postmortem X-ray of the dental restorations of an unknown decedent. The investigator found a possible name of the decedent and located the dentist who provided antemortem (before death) X-rays to the forensic odontologist (B). The intricate pattern of restorations in matching teeth locations provides a positive identification.

identification, although some dental offices now have a serial number and/or the dentist's name somewhere on the dentures. The root structures are removed with the teeth, resulting in only uncharacteristic ridges along the mandible and maxilla. Rarely, the wearer may carve something in the plastic portion that characterizes the denture. Dental associations have been discussing the possibility of embedding an identifier within the denture mold as it is constructed and would resemble the serial numbers attached to medical care prostheses. However, this has not been accepted by the dentists or their association as a reasonable practice. Partial denture plates may be more characteristic and are attached to residual teeth within the mouth so dental consultation will be helpful in those cases.

An interesting comment by a forensic dentist is that they can sometimes identify other dentist's work just by observing the quality and characteristics of restorations. In poorly done restorations (as is done in poor countries) the restoration morphology may give clues to direct the investigation. All unidentified bodies need to have a dental chart and consultation done prior to the release for a county burial.

If the premortem X-rays are film, it may require the investigator to drive to get them or a delivery company to mail them overnight. It is always good advice to families who have someone who goes missing to hold onto a hairbrush or toothbrush and store it in a paper bag for possible DNA, and to gather any dental and medical records to hold onto in case the person is later found.

Sometimes the only record available is paper dental charts. These can be helpful or not depending on the quality of the recordkeeping. Sometimes errors are recorded that may cause the inability to make a positive identification or even confuse the issue more.

A circumstantial or supportive finding can be photos of the person showing a dental exposing smile. Some individuals have characteristic gaps or superimposed teeth patterns that may be characteristic and can assist investigators to search for further information to confirm a positive identification. This finding can be helpful in skeletal remains to narrow possible matches.

MEDICAL APPLIANCES

Prosthetic medical appliances like knees, hips, surgical plates, and many implants, including breast implants, have brand and serial numbers embedded on the surface. When the item is implanted the manufacturing company is notified of the name of the person and his or her demographic information, and it is filed with the surgical appliance serial number. It can be a relatively easy match between the identification on the appliance to a name and last known location by contacting the manufacturer or locating the information in a medical chart where it is also recorded. Pacemakers also have similar model and serial numbers that can be traced through the manufacturer (Figure 6.4). Whenever an embedded pacemaker is in place, even on an identified decedent, recording of

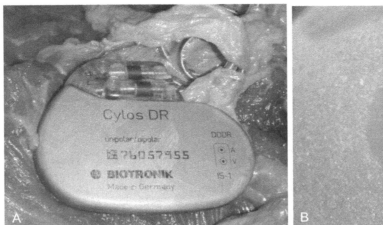
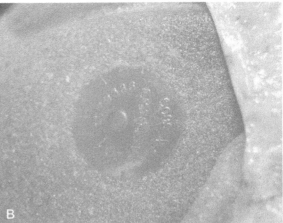

FIGURE 6.4
(A) A pacemaker with the embossed manufacturer and serial number that can be used to locate the name of the person to whom it was implanted. (B) The surface of a breast implant imprinted with the manufacturer and serial number as another example.

the information via photograph can prove useful. In newer models, pacemaker function can be verified by clinicians in the early postmortem period and may require the assistance of a cardiologist.

SKELETAL STRUCTURES

One of the most characteristic skeletal structures that is said to be as good as a fingerprint is the outline of the frontal sinuses of the skull. In the past, anterior skull X-rays were common to evaluate for head injuries as well as assessment for sinus infections. This view is rarely done today because of more advanced imaging techniques. It is important to screen bodies for prosthetic devices that can be characteristic in their positioning and provide possible manufacturing information to aid identification (Figure 6.5).

CT and MRI scans are very detailed images of bones and internal structures on cross-sections or longitudinal sections, but are not usually helpful to compare bone outlines or even internal structures. The other issue is the modality of an X-ray needs to be compared to the modality of another X-ray and most death investigator offices do not have CT or MRI technology available.

DNA

DNA is a certain way to make identification. For this reason, DNA blood samples are held on most individuals examined by most coroner/medical examiner offices. The DNA is usually isolated from nuclei within the white cells of the blood specimen and not the red cells (they do not contain nuclei), but can be retrieved from any cells containing nuclei, such as skin or muscle. Obtaining DNA from a decedent can be a challenge depending on the status of the remains.

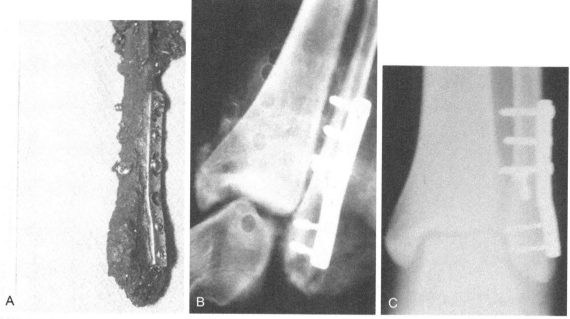

FIGURE 6.5
(A) The remains of the tibia of a decedent burned in a house fire and the metal plate is visible on the bone. (B) A postmortem X-ray obtained from the decedent to compare to (C), which is the antemortem X-ray of a potential identity. Note the placement of the screws and their position to one another, which allowed for a positive identification to be made.

Pure skeletonized remains are the most difficult because they have been subjected to environmental changes and time that causes the DNA to deteriorate and at a minimum decrease in volume. In addition, the putrefaction introduces bacterial DNA, which can overwhelm the small quantity of the unidentified person's DNA that remains during the amplification process in the laboratory.

DNA comparison is similar to dental comparison in that it can be retrieved from a decedent but the location of a match to a missing identity is not always easy. Other questions include: Has there been a chain of custody to an item from a known identity or relative's blood specimen so if a match is made it is a valid assumption? Is the DNA of a missing person in the system so a potential match is possible? Not all missing person's DNA is placed into the system or even available. Some families do not even realize the person is missing or have access to the items necessary to provide DNA to law enforcement. Missing persons can be homeless or runaways and links to known identities blurred by distance from next of kin.

To find a premortem DNA result is highly unusual unless the unidentified decedent had been convicted of a felony and it was retrieved as part of the usual law enforcement process. It's becoming increasingly helpful that most children now have DNA kit and fingerprint collection programs for parents at the children's schools. The military also maintains a DNA database on enlisted

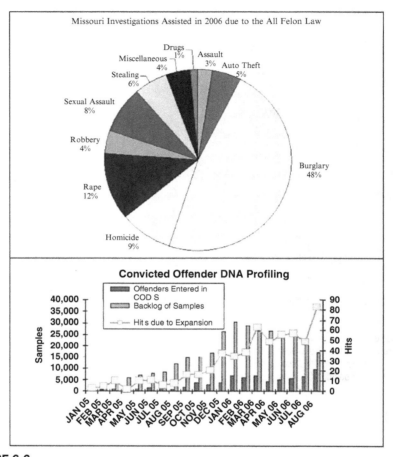

FIGURE 6.6
The state of Missouri instituted DNA procurement from all felon offenders in 2005 and submitted them to CODIS. Even with a large backlog of samples and short duration of the data input, note the drastic rise in the number of hits linking the entered DNA to other crime scenes.
Source: [16].

personnel. Each state has passed laws of convicted crimes (usually homicides, sexual assaults, burglaries, assaults) in which submission of a DNA sample is mandatory into the state's DNA database (Figure 6.6). Many states and law enforcement officials have requested to expand this sampling to other or even all convicted offenses or during any arrest, which might include a DUI. Some feel this is overstepping the boundaries of privacy and protests against this extent of sampling have been raised. The concern is not only the privacy of the arrest, but the ability of other government agencies or even private agencies to access the DNA and gain knowledge about preexisting DNA sequences for risk of diseases or other abnormalities. The extent of law enforcement and judicial reach for this material is an interesting ethical debate for solving crimes versus privacy.

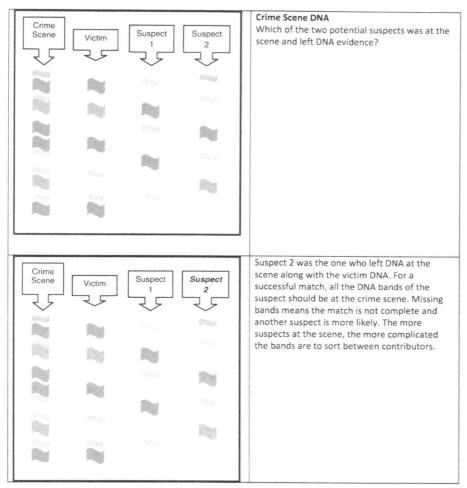

Crime Scene DNA
Which of the two potential suspects was at the scene and left DNA evidence?

Suspect 2 was the one who left DNA at the scene along with the victim DNA. For a successful match, all the DNA bands of the suspect should be at the crime scene. Missing bands means the match is not complete and another suspect is more likely. The more suspects at the scene, the more complicated the bands are to sort between contributors.

FIGURE 6.7
DNA subjected to electrophoresis with an example of comparison of recovered crime scene DNA to potential suspects and the victim.

The FBI received over 1 million profiles into the CODIS database for a total of over 9 million profiles in 2012 with over 150,000 investigated crimes aided by the information (Figure 6.7), most of which were within the state where the information was submitted [14]. The number of wrongly convicted felons who have been found innocent through the Innocence Project's postconviction DNA program is estimated at over 300 [15]. The latter is a positive bonus to the routine addition of the DNA to the database.

DNA samples from unidentified decedents can be compared to a mother and father to make identification (Figure 6.8). This can open another social issue that the reported father is not a DNA match but the mother is. Investigators have to be prepared to deal with this event in case the results come back in that fashion.

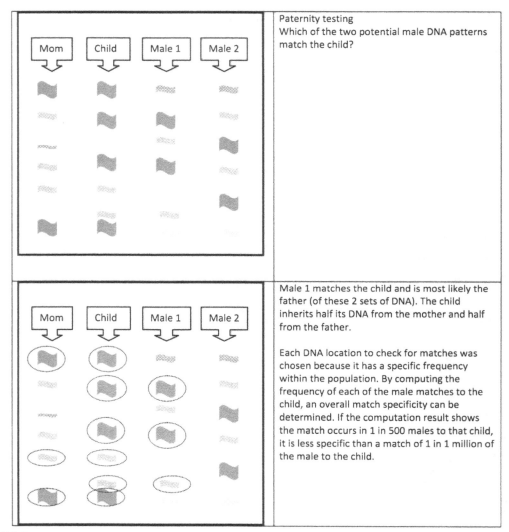

FIGURE 6.8
DNA subjected to electrophoresis as an example of paternity testing. The same type of methodology can be used to match an unknown decedent to the parents if their DNA is available.

If the father is not available, mitochondrial DNA from any family members from the maternal lineage will carry the decedent's DNA in the **mitochondria** of his or her X chromosome. Performance of mitochondrial DNA testing is more expensive than conventional nuclear DNA testing and costs between $1,000 and $1,500 per specimen. So in most cases there are at least three specimens: the unidentified and two maternal relatives.

Human DNA is largely the same among all of us and contains small repeating sequences that make each of us unique, called **polymorphisms**. It is these small repeating sequences called **short tandem repeats (STRs)** that are isolated within the laboratory and amplified by a procedure called **polymerase chain reaction (PCR)**. PCR basically acts as a copy machine making more copies of the isolated DNA. These short tandem repeats are then separated out by a process called **electrophoresis**. Each of the STRs has a particular charge reflecting its size and types of amino acid components. When they are placed onto a gel plate, these small pieces of DNA will move along the current and spread out in a particular linear pattern based on this charge. They can be identified by the various combinations of patterns of the STRs using up to 13 standard probes. Each STR has a particular statistical incidence in the population. By identifying key STRs a statistical incidence can be determined. Comparing the patterns from two individuals using statistics, a value can be computed for the match and the likelihood of this match occurring elsewhere in the random population. A match of 1 in 500 means the DNA comparison was not very unique and within every 500 persons there will be a match. A value of 1 in 1 billion is a high degree of probability that the DNA is a match and only 1 in 1 billion persons will have the same match.

Because of this amplification procedure to retrieve enough DNA to work with in a laboratory, even a small amount of contamination by another source, such as mishandling without gloves, sneezing on a sample, or bacterial contamination, can render a sample useless. For this reason, it is important not to eat, drink, spit, sneeze, or handle evidence without gloves or a mask. Mixed DNA from multiple sources can be very challenging for the laboratory to render a meaningful result. An example is a sexual assault by multiple perpetrators. During the isolation, multiple STRs will be isolated and the challenge comes from figuring out which STR belongs to which perpetrator and determining a meaningful statistical incidence.

In poorly preserved specimens or those yielding low DNA, such as dried bone or teeth, nuclear DNA will be present in small quantities and another specimen is desired. Mitochondria are small cellular organelles with each cell containing between 1 to 10,000 mitochondria and one **nucleus** (Figure 6.9). Mitochondria contain DNA inherited from our mothers (maternal DNA) and each maternal relative will have related mitochondrial DNA. Testing on these samples can yield a result that will relate the decedent to the maternal family but is not as specific as nuclear DNA because all maternal relatives will be a match. It is more expensive and time consuming so it is used only if the nuclear DNA specimens are not useable or available.

CIRCUMSTANTIAL

Circumstantial identification may be necessary in some cases where fingerprints are not available or a more scientific method is not available or financially feasible. The process will utilize the pathologist, the investigator, the resources available, and the scene findings. A 90-year-old woman found unresponsive in her secure residence may be allowed to be identified circumstantially or require

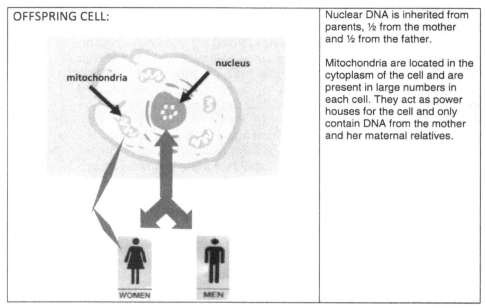

| OFFSPRING CELL: | Nuclear DNA is inherited from parents, ½ from the mother and ½ from the father.

Mitochondria are located in the cytoplasm of the cell and are present in large numbers in each cell. They act as power houses for the cell and only contain DNA from the mother and her maternal relatives. |

FIGURE 6.9
Nuclear versus mitochondrial DNA.

review of a chest or other X-ray by the physician as additional data to make identification without further consultation. In a similar but different situation, if the 90-year-old woman was found in the desert after wandering away from her home or care center, more diligence would be needed to confirm the identity.

UNIDENTIFIED

Sometimes, after searching for any and all the above categories, a decedent remains unidentified. At the time of this writing, more than 40,000 decedents in the United States remain as Jane or John Does and were buried or cremated without an identify [13]. In any single year, medical examiner/coroner offices handle over 4,000 unidentified remains, which after one year, more than 1,000 remain nameless [9]. The problem is not only the return of the remains to the families but also to follow up on crime leads and determine a final disposition of the remains. As technology advances, old cases, previously known as Does, have the technology available to identify some of them or advance the investigation. These are known as cold cases and whole squads of law enforcement have been created to assist with solving crimes related to them. These squads review available evidence and circumstances for materials that may be subjected to improved scientific methods to aid information about identity or suspected perpetrators.

PROCEDURES FOR IDENTIFYING THE BODY

It is important the body has identification tags or bracelets directly attached to prevent confusion of bodies in the morgue. The best method is for the investigator to attach this identification directly at the scene prior to the body bag being closed and sealed as part of the chain of custody. By marking the body with an identifying bracelet, the morgue personnel and pathologist can be assured the body matches the case intake information in the database and was not confused in transit. Some removal companies arrive with more than one decedent at a time and it would be easy to mix the identities if safeguards are not used. If the body is at a hospital, it is important that medical personnel begin the chain of custody by identifying the body to their medical file for the arriving investigator. A hospital identification band should be on the body prior to its removal by the transport company or investigator. A second bracelet signifying acceptance into the coroner/medical examiner office should be placed on the body in addition to the hospital identification.

Plastic identification bracelets placed on an ankle are unobtrusive, durable, and do not interfere with evidence collection from the hands. They are also hidden and funeral homes usually leave them in place for the same reason so bodies removed from the coroner/medical examiner will have a chain of custody through them to the grave. It protects all parties involved from the scene and back to the family. These bracelets can be left slightly loose to remove socks but tight enough so they do not slip off the ankle. They are marked with permanent markers so blood, water, and fluids do not remove the name. Two bracelets can be hooked together for obese decedents if necessary. It is useful if the bracelets are a different color than the ones used by the local hospitals to signify it as originating from the coroner/medical examiner. If the identity is not known, the body can be marked with "unidentified" and the case number or the address/location where he or she was found. When identification is made, the initial bracelet is not removed but instead a second bracelet is added with the identified name and case number. Toe tags are less desirable for a few reasons. Largely, they are paper and can tear and are not waterproof, allowing body fluids to imprint over the information. A tag adherent to the toes can come off, and after it is off, the identity may be in question.

A safeguard to sort out a possible confusion is to always take an identification photograph of the face at the scene as well as a cleaned face, preferably with and without its associated case number, which can be shown to a family member if needed. Good photos of tattoos, especially if they are characteristic, can also be used to differentiate bodies. Overall, photos can also be a good safeguard and backup for sorting out bodies in the morgue and comparing the photos to scenes.

Combined DNA Index System

The Combined DNA Index System (**CODIS**) is an FBI database that stores DNA profiles from multiple sources. It includes the DNA results from crime scenes (called the forensic index) and those offenders convicted of violent crimes (called the offender index). Input into the database comes from local levels that flow to state-level crime laboratories and eventually to the national level at the

FBI. This allows communication of DNA profiles across state lines for solving crimes and linking them to potential offenders.

The crime scene data that is entered has not been a subject of invasion of privacy but the volume of data has vastly increased the need for more DNA scientists and automation. The offender index also places stress on the already taxed system because of the desire for inclusion of more offenders' DNA profiles to aid in solving crimes. Offender crimes subject to mandatory collection vary from state to state as well as the rules for collection. Some of the questions that arise are: When will the collection take place, upon arrest or conviction? Before or after appeals? Who will perform the collections? Which offenses qualify for the collection? Does it require a court order? It quickly becomes complicated, and the list of offenses qualifying for collection can be very detailed. The National Institute of Justice published an article discussing some of these issues entitled "Collecting DNA from Arrestees: Implementation Lessons" with a map showing the various state differences [12].

There is no doubt that the database is helpful to linking crimes between jurisdictions, as well as being responsible for solving cold cases with few leads. It has also been responsible for freeing those wrongly convicted via a DNA match to other offenders.

National Crime Information Center

The National Crime Information Center (**NCIC**) database by the FBI has many subfiles, including types of crimes for development of statistics regarding various violent crimes, where the crime is committed and assists with targeting and fighting crimes in particular areas through resource allocation [10].

Within the NCIC is a missing person database and an unidentified person database. This information is available only to law enforcement and the data must be entered by law enforcement personnel. The intake forms for both subfile databases are quite extensive and time consuming. The concept is that comparison of the two data files may give clues to potential identification of an unidentified person so that confirmation testing can be done. The data includes usual demographic information such as height, weight, hair and eye color, tattoo descriptions, and last known location or found location. For decedents it has a modified dental chart system to be entered. It is a cumbersome system and can yield large numbers of potential matches that then need to be narrowed one by one. Probably the biggest obstacle is the inability of public and death investigator access to search for potential matches based on clothing or other information that may be with the decedent [8].

National Missing and Unidentified Persons System

Because of the obstacles with the NCIC, the National Institute of Justice (NIJ) has sponsored a parallel database that is freely open to the public to search through hundreds of cases of found decedents, called the National Missing and Unidentified Persons System (**NAMUS**). NAMUS allows families, law enforcement, and coroners/medical examiner offices to easily enter searchable fields in the missing person portion of the system and will also accept photographs to be uploaded (Figure 6.10). Coroner/medical examiner offices have similar searchable fields and allow a distinction between a public area and a hidden area for confidential information, such as X-rays, dental X-rays, and information about the circumstances of death. The NIJ has volunteers of dentists, forensic anthropologists, and forensic artists to assist. The NIJ will also perform free DNA testing of relatives or remains.

Skeletal remains can be digitally photographed and the forensic artists have software programs to render facial contours from the skull structure that can be posted. If DNA has been done it will also include that information. Photos of characteristic clothing/personal effects, such as logos on ball caps or T-shirts, eyeglasses or watches, and tattoos, can all be posted in the public section. There are groups of community volunteers who routinely screen the website and try to provide the submitting parties with potential matches they may have found. It is proving extremely useful in the quest to locate next of kin and connect them with their deceased relative.

They have recently added a section for death investigators to post identified but unclaimed decedents where next of kin was not able to be located. This should also prove useful to aid the quest of unification.

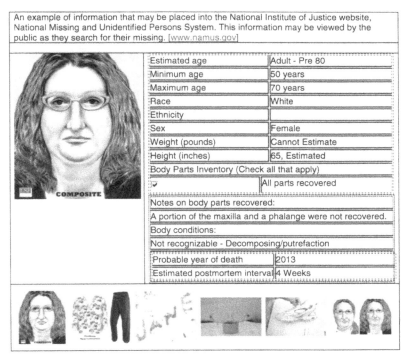

FIGURE 6.10

An example of information that may be placed into the NIJ website, National Missing and Unidentified Persons System. This information may be viewed by the public as they search for their missing person [9].

HOW TO FIND NEXT OF KIN

This can be challenging and sometimes harder than making the identification of the decedent. Cell phones can sometimes help lead to finding next of kin by looking in the contact list for "Mom," "Dad," "Aunt Polly," etc. Even if the person isn't the closest next of kin they may have information on how to reach them. If computers are on, similar contact lists may be present in email programs. Investigators can look for address books, employer identification cards, or health insurance cards. Employers may have someone listed in their files for whom to contact in case of emergency. Similar contact information may be present in hospital admission files or dental/doctor offices. Social media can also lend clues to finding next of kin. Arrest records may also list next of kin or friends who know where they may be located. Personal papers at the residence or letters may also be clues. It is important to collect any of these papers at the scene and document the collected items in the report. There may be no opportunity to return to the residence once the investigator has left the scene. Personal papers may seem like a trivial bit of information but they can be invaluable in locating next of kin. Basically, imagination and fortitude may be necessary to find them to make death notification.

HOW TO MAKE DEATH NOTIFICATION

Notification to the next of kin is not easy. It is uncomfortable because we are inflicting painful emotions on others and it also brings forth personal feelings about death and our own morbidity. Families can react differently from extreme sadness to anger and striking out.

Good practices for making notification are doing it in pairs in case the investigator needs backup due to a family member collapsing or to assist with a more aggressive encounter. As a death investigator, a good practice is to be accompanied by law enforcement at the location. If a law enforcement member is doing notification, the assist can come from the death investigator or a chaplain. Most departments have a volunteer group of chaplains for such occasions who are on call and available 24 hours a day. Similarly, law enforcement will have volunteer translators available if needed to assist with multiple different language barriers.

It is best to make notification in person. Before beginning with the bad news it is important to verify the person is related to the decedent. If the family member lives a distance away and the notification cannot be made in person, a local law enforcement agency or death investigation unit can usually assist. It may be necessary for the investigator to be on standby to answer questions directly. Phone notifications can be done, but it is good to make sure the family member has a friend or other family members nearby in case of a medical emergency.

It is best to make the notification as soon as possible after the incident and identification is confirmed. Confirmation may require a boss at a worksite, a family member, fingerprint confirmation in motor vehicle accidents, or any of the methods noted earlier. It is important that the family receive the notification prior to being told by bystanders or the press. Most offices have a policy that names are not released to the press until notification has been made. However, the press can be very resourceful in high-profile cases. In cases where the identity is not yet officially confirmed but is pretty certain, family members can be notified that someone matching, for example, Bob's description in his car and with his identification was involved in a motor vehicle accident and is dead. Once official confirmation is made, the family can be called back. The family will usually have many questions at that point and the investigator should answer the best he or she can and leave contact information.

The words used to make the notification are also important. It is important to use direct, plain language to tell the next of kin the family member is dead. Words such as "he/she passed on" or "is no longer with us" are confusing and have been shown to delay the grieving process. It is best for the investigator to be invited inside the residence and asked to sit down. A good beginning is for the investigator to state that there is bad news about the husband, wife, etc. …, Bob or Sally. It is good to mention the person's name when referring to the death rather than use the words "body" or "decedent." This intro to the news is important as it warns the family member of what is coming and also confirms the husband's or wife's name to ensure the notification is being made to the right person. It is best to pause a moment while all this sinks in.

The next line needs to include the words "dead" or "he/she died," so there is no misunderstanding about the outcome of the event [11]. An example: "Bob was driving down highway 127 when he was in a motor vehicle accident and died at the scene." The family member may ask if is certain, and this is where the degree of confirmation of identity needs to be mentioned. He or she will have other questions, such as "How did it happen?" "Where is he now?" It may be necessary to arrange transportation for him or her to a hospital or to call another family member to stay with the individual. This is where a chaplain can be very helpful as he or she will have further comforting words and have time to spend with the family member. It is best to have arrived in separate vehicles so this can transpire.

A couple of questions an investigator has to be prepared to answer are "Did they suffer?" and Why them, why today?" An appropriate response to those questions can be difficult, but in most cases, the investigator can relieve some stress by saying the injuries were extensive and it doesn't appear that he or she suffered. As for why that particular day, this is very difficult and we ponder it every day. All we know is when it is our time, there is very little that can be done to reverse it. Many times, two people can be in the same situation and only one dies and there is no logical reason why that might be true. Or the person has a long-standing chronic disease and on a particular day suddenly dies.

The next of kin also may ask if he or she can see the decedent at the morgue. Each office policy and even state laws will vary in making that determination. Most offices try to discourage visitation and would prefer family members see the decedent in better circumstances at the funeral home for their grieving process.

It is helpful to leave contact information about the investigating officer and agency, as well as for the death investigator. Many offices have developed a pamphlet of frequently asked questions to answer what happens next and what does the family need to do. The pamphlet needs to include information about personal effects, the need to select a funeral home, and the phone and address of the office. If no family members are at a residence, this information can be left at the scene in case they come to the residence after notification.

REFERENCES

[1] Fazzalaro J, Cohen R. Submission of Fingerprints for Drivers Licenses. Office of Legislative Research, Connecticut General Assembly; 2001. Reviewed from http://www.cga.ct.gov/2001/rpt/2001-R-0858.htm. [August 2013].

[2] Thumbprint Signature Program. Indiana Bankers Association. Reviewed from http://www.indianabankers.org/displaycommon.cfm?an=1&subarticlenbr=16#Whatis. [August 2013].

[3] Social Security Administration's Death Master File (DMF). National Technical Information Service, US Dept of Commerce. Reviewed from http://www.ntis.gov/products/ssa-dmf.aspx. [August 2013].

[4] ITRC Fact Sheet 117. Identity Theft and the Deceased: Prevention and Victim Tips. Identity Theft Resource Center. Reviewed from http://www.idtheftcenter.org/artman2/publish/c_guide/Fact_Sheet_117_IDENTITY_THEFT_AND_THE_DECEASED_-_PREVENTION_AND_VICTIM_TIPS.shtml. [August 2013].

[5] The U.S. Electronic Passport. Bureau of Consular Affairs, U.S. Department of State. Reviewed from http://travel.state.gov/passport/passport_2498.html. [August 2013].

[6] Integrated Automatic Fingerprint System. Federal Bureau of Investigation. Reviewed from http://www.fbi.gov/about-us/cjis/fingerprints_biometrics/iafis/iafis. [August 2013].

[7] Fingerprints & Other Biometrics: Next Generation Identification. Federal Bureau of Investigation. Reviewed from http://www.fbi.gov/about-us/cjis/fingerprints_biometrics/ngi. [August 2013].

[8] National Crime Information Center. Federal Bureau of Investigation. Reviewed from http://www.fbi.gov/about-us/cjis/ncic. [August 2013].

[9] National Missing and Unidentified Persons System. Office of Justice Programs, US Dept of Justice. Reviewed from http://www.namus.gov/. [August 2013].

[10] Strategies and Available Resources for Use in Solving Unidentified Deceased Person Cases. Florida Dept of Law Enforcement, Medical Examiner Commission. Reviewed from http://www.fdle.state.fl.us/Content/getdoc/5de72e76-be9b-4e4e-b225-ed61087bf27e/MEC-Strategies-and-Current-Available-Resources.aspx. [August 2013].

[11] "In person, In time", Recommended Procedures for Death Notification. Crime Victim Assistance Division, Iowa Department of Justice; 1992. Reviewed from http://www.nationalcops.org/downloads/in_person.pdf. [August 2013].

[12] Samuels J, et al. Collecting DNA from Arrestees: Implementation Lessons. NIJ Journal 2012;(270). National Institute of Justice, US Dept of Justice. Reviewed from https://www.ncjrs.gov/pdffiles1/nij/238484.pdf. [August 2013].

[13] Ritter N. Missing Persons and Unidentified Remains: The Nation's Silent Mass Disaster. NIJ Journal 2007;(256). National Institute of Justice, US Dept of Justice. Reviewed from http://www.nij.gov/journals/256/missing-persons.html. [August 2013].

[14] CODIS Combined DNA Index System, brochure 2012. Federal Bureau of Investigation Laboratory Services. Reviewed from http://www.fbi.gov/about-us/lab/biometric-analysis/codis/codis_brochure. [August 2013].

[15] DNA Exonerations Nationwide Fact Sheet. The Innocence Project; 2010. Retrieved from http://www.innocenceproject.org/Content/DNA_Exonerations_Nationwide.php. [August 2013].

[16] DNA Profiling. Missouri State Highway Patrol. Reviewed from http://www.mshp.dps.missouri.gov/MSHPWeb/PatrolDivisions/CLD/DNAProfiling/DNAProfiling.html. [August 2013].

[17] Taylor P (chairperson). Model state vital statistics act and regulations. Center for Diseases Control; 1992. Retrieved from www.cdc.gov/nchs/data/misc/mvsact92b.pdf. [October 2013].

CHAPTER 7
Blunt-Force Trauma

Learning Objectives

- Outline the features of the four types of blunt-force injuries.
- Illustrate the features of an incision and laceration and label the characteristic differences.
- Outline injuries that are commonly seen on a driver and those seen on a front-seat passenger.
- Recognize common injuries seen on pedestrians and contrast those with bodies dumped by the side of the road after death. Apply what you have learned about postmortem changes as well as types of injuries.
- Identify common types of evidence that may need to be recovered, as well as photographs and information that may need to be retrieved or observed in investigations of death from a traffic accident.

Key Terms
Blunt-force injury
Abrasion
Contusion
Ecchymoses
Laceration
Incision
Fracture
Undermining
Avulsion
Dicing wounds
Pillars
Pathologic fracture

Chapter Summary

It is important to recognize the characteristics of blunt-force injuries to distinguish and accurately describe report notations. Use of proper terminology ensures proper communication of the type of injury seen and how it was produced. Good documentation of patterned injuries with and without scales will allow potential impact sights to be compared to potential instruments used to create the injuries, locate a potential vehicle, or determine how the injury occurred. Toxicology specimens can be challenging to obtain in these cases but it is important information as contributing causes or for prevention and statistical purposes.

INTRODUCTION

Blunt-force trauma definitions form the basis to describe many of the injuries seen in forensics. Blunt-force injuries are very common and are seen in varying degrees on most decedents, whether from a terminal fall, a previous injury, or as the acute cause of death. It is important to learn the proper terminology so the wounds are documented accurately. A pathologist uses these descriptions to make opinions about how the injuries occurred, what instruments were used

Case Study

Police were called after an elderly gentleman was found by his wife lying on the ground in his backyard. Surrounding the head area was a small pool of blood. When an officer called it in to the office, he mentioned bruises on the hands. Upon arriving at the scene, the death investigator noted a moderately sized elderly man lying on the ground adjacent to a backyard concrete bench. The clothing was appropriately positioned and not in disarray and he was wearing slip-on shoes, one of which was lying approximately two feet from the body. A pool of blood approximately 12 in. in diameter was seen under the head area. On the right side of the head behind the ear was a 1 in. laceration. The facial area showed two black eyes but no other trauma to the mouth or lower face. The hands showed small purple-red "old age bruises" seen with thin parchment skin. No fractures were noted of the extremities and no weapons were noted nearby with blood on them.

An autopsy examination was done and showed no rib, spine, or pelvic fractures. Severe atherosclerosis (hardening of the arteries) was seen in the coronary arteries and in the aorta. Examination of the head showed the laceration with an underlying depressed fracture of the skull (i.e., the skull was actually pushed inward putting pressure on the brain). The surface of the right and left brain was covered by a layer of blood between the surface of the brain and the dura. The brain showed a bruise over the left side of the cortex and over the base of the left frontal lobes. The thin, delicate bones over the surface of the eyes were fractured.

The pathologist concluded the laceration occurred during a fall, most likely against the concrete bench, resulting in the laceration, underlying skull fracture with subdural bleeding, and contrecoup contusions of the brain. The position of the bruising on the brain on the opposite side of the laceration is a contrecoup contusion seen in fall injuries. Inflicted trauma during an assault would have resulted in bruising on the same side as the laceration and fracture.

The cause of death was certified as "blunt-force trauma of head due to fall" with a contributing cause of "atherosclerotic cardiovascular disease." The mechanism of why he fell is unknown and could be related to a poor fit of the slippers, loss of balance, or from a cardiac event.

to inflict the trauma, the position of the decedent when the injuries occurred, and whether they occurred before or after death. All these questions are asked of a pathologist during testimony, as well as by law enforcement personnel during their investigation to correlate with the interpretation of evidence retrieved at the scene. The best way to gain expertise in the interpretation of injuries is to coordinate with law enforcement findings and use the knowledge of patterned injuries in known circumstances with the application to unknown death circumstances.

DEFINITIONS

Blunt-force injuries are defined as those where a force is applied to the surface of the body or where the body comes into contact with a surface causing an injury. It can be very important to recognize various patterns created by these surfaces or forces to aid the interpretation of how an injury occurred. An example is a cylindrical item, such as a pipe, striking the body, which creates a parallel pattern of the bruise. Another important notation is the location of the injury on the body. If a bruise is on the knees, it could be interpreted as due to a fall or it could also be seen in front-seat occupants of motor vehicle accidents where the knees strike the front panel.

There are four major injuries that need to be defined within this category: abrasions, contusions, lacerations, and fractures. It is important to master the definitions of these injuries and apply them correctly to a particular injury because the definition purveys how the injury occurred. This is especially important in the distinction of a laceration (created by a blunt object) versus an incision (created by a sharp object). The interpretation and/or pattern of the injury can direct the scope of an investigation.

The mechanism of death is defined by what physiologic function failed and caused the death. In blunt-force trauma injuries it is related to shock, usually from blood loss or brain–spinal cord disruption. These result from fractured bones resulting in blood loss by tearing blood vessels, lacerating vital organs, or causing the inability to exchange oxygen.

When certifying a death related to blunt-force trauma the basic question should always be: Why is the person dead? The degree of injury should match a lethal mechanism and, if not, further investigation is needed to explain the death either at the autopsy, toxicology, or scene investigation.

Abrasion

An **abrasion** is a scrape on the skin causing a loss of the superficial layers of the skin. It is created by a force sliding across the skin or the skin sliding across a surface (Figure 7.1). An example of the first instance is a tree branch creating a scratch on someone's arm while he or she is trimming a tree. An example of the second instance is when someone slides his or her knee across a carpet creating a rug burn. Because it is a superficial injury, it is described in two dimensions: length and width. It is also described by its color: yellow-tan, red-brown, or yellow-brown. An example of an abrasion description is the following: over the left forearm is a curvilinear red-brown 5 × 0.3 cm abrasion. The description includes a location, shape, color, measurement (in two dimensions), and the type of injury.

Abrasions can be patterned or have characteristic appearances due to the objects creating them (Figures 7.2–7.4). Common examples are brush-burn abrasions, gravel imprints, and specific objects such as bumpers or grills from the front of cars or muzzle imprints from guns.

Abrasions may have directionality depending on how the force is applied. At the site of origin, the skin is superficially sheared and can be piled up or with small skin tags where the force ends. This isn't always very important, but may help the observer differentiate two types of wounds if they overlap due to multiple mechanisms of injury interplaying at the same time.

As an abrasion heals, the edge of the wound tends to dry and become heaped up. The skin margin may appear slightly increased pink or white as the pigment repairs. Abrasions may also occur postmortem due to loss of the superficial layer of skin but will appear waxy yellow and with drying will be a light red color.

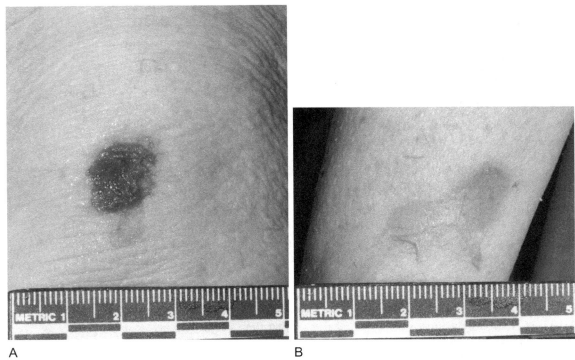

A   B

FIGURE 7.1
(A) A classic premortem abrasion with dark red-brown coloration and may be a rug burn. (B) A postmortem injury showing the waxy, smooth surface and adherent superficial skin fragment to one margin.

FIGURE 7.2
A brush-burn abrasion with large areas of superficial skin scraped from the surface. It is created by the body sliding across a surface or a surface sliding across the skin. It is commonly known as "road rash" because it is seen in accidents with pedestrians, bicyclists, and motorcyclists as the body is projected over the road surface.

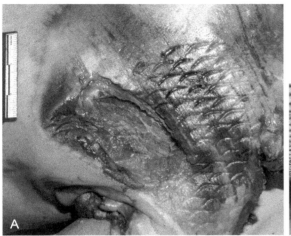

FIGURE 7.3
(A) A woven-pattern abrasion on the back of a man crushed in a grinding machine. (B) The grinding wheel with the corresponding woven pattern on the cement.

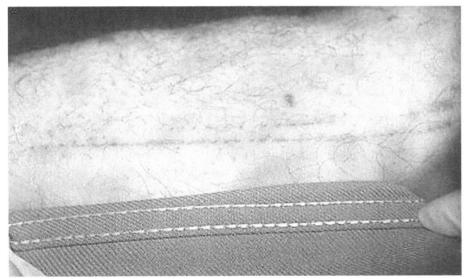

FIGURE 7.4
An interrupted-pattern abrasion on a leg that matches the stitching of the pant leg. This demonstrates why the clothing is important to receive with the body to aid the interpretation of injuries.

Contusion

A **contusion** is commonly known as a bruise. It is created by a force being applied to the skin causing rupture of the small blood vessels and bleeding into the tissue under the skin surface (Figure 7.5). The color of the contusion (bruise) can vary with its thickness, location, and how long it has been present. The colors of the bruise change due to the breakdown of the blood into its iron components and

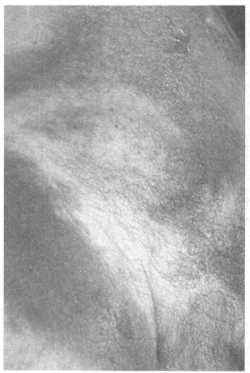

FIGURE 7.5
A recent contusion seen on an alcoholic after a therapeutic paracentesis, a procedure where a needle is inserted in the abdomen to withdraw ascites fluid. Contusions are subcutaneous collections of blood. They are more extensive with minor trauma in those people with a bleeding disorder or in alcoholics.

usually start in the red-purple range, transitioning to a green-yellow then yellow-brown coloration. How long it takes to transition can vary from one person to another, the thickness of the bruise, and its location, so it really cannot be accurately determined to a specific date or time. Dating is somewhat helpful to give a basis of injuries occurring over an extended period of time with evidence of healing of bruises. In decedents, biopsies of bruises can be performed and dated microscopically to a range of days.

Bruises may also be patterned. A classic example is that of a steering wheel or seatbelt imprint seen on the chest of a driver of a motor vehicle. Other patterns can be created by cylindrical objects such as bats, pipes, flashlights, batons, or rebar.

Bruises are three dimensional, however, it is difficult to assess the depth based on only observation of the skin surface. Most times contusions are described in two dimensions: length and width. A typical description of a contusion is as follows: over the mid-chest is an irregular, blue-purple, 5 × 4 cm contusion. The description includes the location, shape, color, size, and identifies the injury as a contusion.

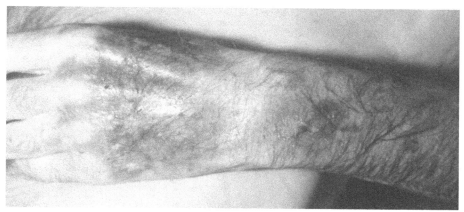

FIGURE 7.6
An ecchymoses or old-age purpura commonly seen in the elderly with minimal trauma.

Interpretation of brain contusions is helpful in distinguishing if a head injury was created by an inflicted trauma or resulted from a fall. With patterned contusions, accurate measurements, photographs with scales, or even tracings can prove useful to link injury to a suspected force that created the bruise.

It is helpful to subclassify the superficial contusions commonly seen in the elderly on the back of the arms and hands and call them **ecchymoses** (Figure 7.6). These are typically superficial and pink-brown with irregular margins, and may result in tears of the skin. As a human ages, the skin becomes thin and fragile and can result in these injuries with minimal trauma.

Laceration

Lacerations are actual tears of the skin that result when the force being applied exceeds its elastic ability to stretch, causing it to tear (Figure 7.7). Its ability to stretch depends partially on the surface the skin is covering, such a cavity like the abdomen versus the firm stretching over the skull and face. Skin over the abdomen has the ability to stretch more than skin over the skull. When a force is applied to the skin over a local area it can exceed the stretching ability and cause the skin to tear.

A laceration is characterized by irregular margins with small strands of tissue connecting the edges of the wound. The margin of the laceration will contain an abrasion or contusion. These wounds have three dimensions: length, width, and depth. An example description is as follows: on the left hip is a T-shaped 6 × 4 × 2 cm laceration with bone and muscle seen in the depths of the wound.

It is important to distinguish lacerations from sharp-force wounds because the mechanism that creates each of them is different. If the wound is a laceration, the object is some sort of blunt instrument, versus an incised wound that is created by a sharp-edged object. The distinction is made by examining the margins

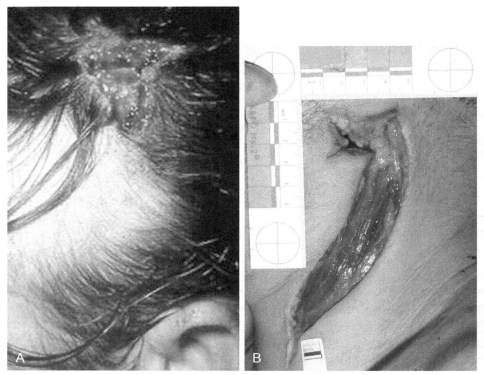

FIGURE 7.7
(A) The characteristics of a laceration with tissue bridging between the edges of the wound with irregular and abraded margins. (B) In contrast, an **incision** has smooth margins without tissue bridging or marginal abrasion.

and tissue between the edges of the wound. A laceration will have abraded margins with small pieces of tissue extending between the edges (called tissue bridging), and an incised or stab wound will have a smooth margin that extends into the depths due to the cutting by the instrument.

An **avulsion** is a subtype of laceration where the tear has created a flap of skin that is able to be lifted from the underlying muscle or bone (Figure 7.8A). Many times there will be a small shelf or beveled edge on the more pointed margin, which is the site where the injury began as the flap was created.

Another term used for lacerations is **undermining**. This description is used for skull injuries where the force is applied causing a pocket to form under the skin but it does not create a flap as seen with an avulsion (Figure 7.8B).

Fractures

The fourth term used in describing blunt-force injuries is **fractures** (Figure 7.9). The amount of force needed to fracture a bone depends on the bone, the age of the person, and the presence or absence of underlying disease affecting

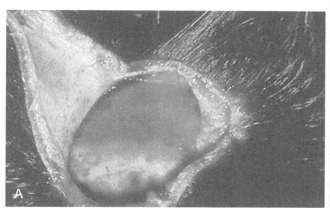 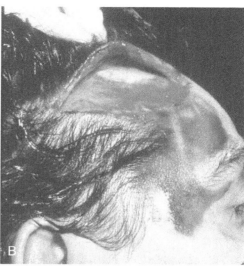

FIGURE 7.8

(A) An avulsion where a flap of skin has been sheared off, an injury most commonly located on the head where the skin is stretched tightly against the skull. (B) Depicts undermining where a segment of skin is lifted from the underlying skeletal structure forming a pocket. It is commonly seen on the skull but may also be seen on the chest, buttocks, or over the large bones of the legs.

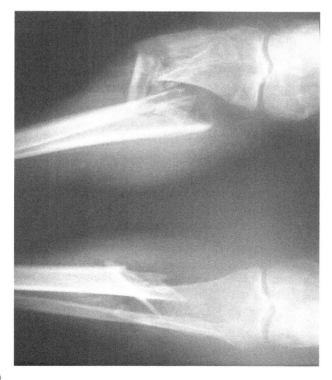

FIGURE 7.9

An X-ray of the lower legs in a pedestrian struck by a motor vehicle. Note the fractures of both legs just below knee level where the legs came in contact with the bumper of the vehicle.

the strength of the bone. Younger people have more elastic or durable bone than the elderly. A thin bone requires less force than a thicker, weight-bearing bone (e.g., rib versus femur). The presence of a bone disease, such as calcium loss (osteoporosis), infection of the bone (osteomyelitis), or a tumor that has spread to bone (metastasis), weakens the bone and allows it to fracture with minimal force that normally would not create a fracture in most people (called a **pathologic fracture**).

Fractures may be open where the bone ends extend through a skin laceration. The risk with open fractures even with prompt treatment is complications by infection, which may result in a medical amputation. Conversely, closed fractures are where the skin surface has remained intact and result in fewer complications.

Skull fractures may be linear or depressed. Linear describes a line fracture with the edges abutting against each other. Depressed is where the fractured bone is pressed inward and tears the underlying brain tissue.

A basilar skull fracture is one where the bottom, thick portion of the skull is fractured. This area is a vital region protecting the brain from the mouth/nasal area and the vital brain/respiratory centers contained in the brainstem.

The risk with fractures is the resulting tears of underlying tissues from the jagged bone margins. Life-threatening tears may occur in the heart, lungs, liver, spleen, large arteries or veins, brain, or spinal cord. The fractures may not be immediately fatal especially rib fractures, and can result in chest pain leading to poor inspiration of air and pneumonia. Tears in lung tissue can result in blood or air accumulating in the pleural cavities and poor oxygen exchange. Superficial tears of the surface membranes (capsules) of the spleen or liver can result in slow internal bleeding.

DOCUMENTATION OF INJURIES

Injuries are documented via direct visualization first with collection of any necessary trace evidence adhering to the skin followed by washing the skin surface to best outline any patterned injuries and measure them. Patterned injuries need accurate descriptions so that if a proposed weapon or surface is presented, it can be ruled in or out as the causative material.

Photographs include overalls, medium view, and close-ups with and without a scale. A medium view including the ruler is helpful so that the close-up view can have good detail and yet locate the injury on the body. If possible, it is always good to include a reference such as an ear, side of mouth or nose, a thumb, etc.

A right-angle ruler is best so that a scale is located in both dimensions of the injury. It is important to take the photo at a right angle to the plane of the injury so that there is no distortion to the wound measurements in the photo. The ruler should be placed so that one edge is parallel to the longest dimension of an injury and placed near the skin surface or level to the injury if it is a curved surface. A case number placed on one margin of the ruler is necessary for proper documentation.

Patterned injuries and toolmarks

Patterned injuries are extremely important in forensics. The patterns can be used to reconstruct the number and how the injuries occurred. Multiple accurate photographs with scales can be the best illustration to demonstrate in court and identify a suspect weapon at a later date. It may be helpful to trace a particular pattern onto clear plastic. This can be signed over to law enforcement as evidence and easily used to compare to various suspect objects with 1:1 comparison. An example is to trace patterned injuries on the skin of a hit-and-run pedestrian and compare them to the front of suspect motor vehicles. Grill injuries or particular hood ornamentation can be very characteristic.

Toolmarks can leave characteristic grooves on soft cartilage that can be matched to suspect weapons. Bone may also contain toolmarks from saw marks. These characteristic markings can be compared through expert databases of various types of cutting instruments. Because removal by medical saws creates their own toolmarks, it is important to excise a wide area around the evidentiary portion so that it is obvious to the comparing laboratory as the suspect area. It is usually preserved frozen to prevent distortion by drying or dehydration.

Coup versus contrecoup

Head injuries or blood surrounding or within the brain are common. The pattern of the skin versus the internal injuries allows for the distinction of inflicted trauma from an assault versus injuries due to fall versus bleeding due to a natural stroke. Many times the decedent is found down on the ground following an unwitnessed event.

Coup and contrecoup terminology is used when referring to head injuries. Coup injuries are defined as a force applied to one side of the head resulting in same sided brain injuries, with or without skull fractures. These injuries are consistent with inflicted trauma rather than falls. Contrecoup injuries are ones with an injury on one side of the scalp and brain injuries on the opposite side and are seen in fall injuries. This phenomenon occurs because of the way forces are transmitted through the skull and brain.

The same phenomenon does not apply to sidedness of subdural hematomas, blood accumulating between the brain and dura lining the internal skull. Subdural hematomas occur due to rupture of small veins and are not influenced by these forces. Either a fall or inflicted trauma may result in a subdural hematoma of either side of the skull.

The location of the injury on the head is also important to make the distinction between a fall versus an inflicted trauma. Classically, injuries above a hat brim are more consistent with inflicted trauma and below the hat brim more consistent with a fall. However, objects within a scene need to be evaluated for potential of inflicting the trauma. For example, some curbs or benches may result in injuries above the hat level depending on the mechanics of the fall. In interpretation of injuries, all information from the scene, autopsy, or medical findings need to be considered to make the distinction. This topic will be discussed more fully in Chapter 10.

MOTOR VEHICLE ACCIDENTS

Motor vehicle accidents are the most common cause of blunt-force injuries. Some questions that arise with them are:

- Was the person alive at the time of the accident or did the person die of an underlying natural disease?
- Were the injuries fatal instantly or did a potential delay in medical treatment affect the outcome?
- Who was the driver versus the passenger? Are the patterns of their injuries able to assist with their placement inside the vehicle? Were seatbelts in use?
- What were the underlying contributing events that may have caused the accident to occur?
- Are there underlying diseases that might contribute to the death or mortality after medical treatment? The underlying health of an individual may be used in the insurance computation of a settlement.
- Are there product or road safety concerns that need to be reported to prevent further accidents?

To answer these questions, a complete autopsy may be necessary. Documentation of the injuries via photographs and accurate descriptions of the injuries aids in the reconstruction of how the accident occurred. The collection of evidence on the surface of the body and clothing is necessary on pedestrian hit-and-run accidents to aid with linking a suspect vehicle to the decedent. An internal examination can verify the extent of injuries, underlying health and disease states, and accurate visualization of vessels for toxicology specimens. Utilizing

Case Study

Two occupants from a motor vehicle accident were discovered inside a vehicle by a passerby. One occupant was pronounced dead at the scene and transferred to the medical examiner's office. She was seated in the driver's seat with facial injuries, but investigators determined her description matched the driver's license demographics. The other occupant was alive and resuscitated. She had severe head injuries, underwent surgery, and was on life support at a local hospital. Relatives were at the bedside daily. The decedent was autopsied and released to a local funeral home where parents claimed she was not their daughter. Further investigation revealed the decedent was actually the daughter of the family sitting by the bedside and the hospitalized woman was the daughter of the family who thought their daughter was dead.

this multipronged approach leads to the most accurate determination of death for coordination with scene investigation findings.

Pertinent scene observations include seatbelt use, body position in vehicle when found, air bag deployment, type and position of the vehicle, skid marks, and witness statements about the event. With many motor vehicle deaths, bodies are deformed by their injuries and visual identification of the decedent with comparison to a driver's license photo is potentially erroneous. It is not uncommon for people to carry false identification or borrow a friend's vehicle. This makes it important to verify the identity of a battered decedent or even injured person via fingerprints, identifying scars, marks, or tattoos. Many states have thumb-prints on driver's licenses that can be used for identification. Criminal records and resulting prints may also be used to verify the identity of a decedent and release the body to the next of kin with that identity. If prints are not available, dental identification may need to be done, especially in the severely injured.

Anatomy of a vehicle

SEATBELTS

Seatbelts are described as two-, three-, or four-point restraint systems. Two-point restraints are typical lap belts where there are two attachment points to the vehicle. Three-point restraints are the lap and shoulder harness typical in modern vehicles where there are the two lap belt attachments and the third point where the shoulder harness attaches to the roof area of the vehicle. Four-point restraints are found in race cars and pilot seats of airplanes and have two shoulder attachments in addition to the two lap belt attachments.

Seatbelts were first placed into cars in the 1930s by physicians who noted the increased safety this provided during car crashes. The idea of a restraint system had been patented in 1885 by Edward Claghorn of New York and consisted of ropes and hooks to secure the person to the car. The modern-day seatbelt was the idea of a Swede, Nils Bohlin, and consisted of a three-point restraint. Manufacturers lagged in endorsing the idea, and the Volvo was one of the first to utilize restraints routinely in vehicles and they were offered as an option in some Ford and Chrysler models in the mid-1950s. In 1959, Volvo included Bohlin's idea of a three-point restraint in their vehicles. But it wasn't until 1964 that most U.S. car manufacturers placed front seat lap belts in the vehicles. In 1965, European car manufacturers followed suit and included required front lap belts. By 1965, all 50 U.S. states required cars to be equipped with front lap belts. Two years later they were required in the rear seats as well [3].

Enforcement in wearing seatbelts varies from state to state. In some states, law enforcement operates under primary enforcement, which means failure to wear a seatbelt can allow them to issue a citation based solely on the failure to wear one while driving. In other states, it falls under secondary enforcement and the officer must stop someone for some other violation, such as speeding, to issue the citation for failure to comply with the seatbelt law. Surveys from 2011 show that in primary enforcement states, 88% of people wear seatbelts, whereas in secondary enforcement states, approximately 75% wear seatbelts [1]. Proper seatbelt usage is estimated to save thousands of lives each year, especially at highway speeds.

The purpose of seatbelts is to keep the person inside the vehicle, as well as help them decelerate, decreasing injury. They are designed to stretch with the impact and allow the person to move forward in the seat, even as much as 10 in. Knowing this, it is important to comfortably sit as far from the steering wheel to safely operate the vehicle and prevent impact with the stationary portions of the vehicle. Seatbelts, like any safety equipment, may fail and proper evaluation by the traffic investigator will assist in that determination. Seatbelts are rated to withstand thousands of pounds of force. During an accident, the webbing will stretch and leave wrinkles along the area of greatest stretch, which will allow the investigator to know if the seatbelt was in use during the impact. To differentiate a torn belt versus a cut belt, the margins of the tear can be evaluated for the stretch with frayed margins versus a clean cut made during extrication [2].

CAR SEATS

Tennessee was the first state to require child car seat use in vehicles in 1978. All states require children to be restrained by a restraint system, and for children less than four years old this is a federally approved car seat. In children four to six years of age, the child can be in a restraint car seat or seatbelt, which will vary from state to state [1]. All states require, at a minimum, that all children three or younger, weighing less than 40 pounds, or less than 40 inches tall, be secured in child restraint systems while traveling in motor vehicles. Most states also specifically require that child restraint systems meet applicable Federal Motor Vehicle Safety Standards [1].

AIRBAGS

Airbags consist of a plastic bag inside the steering wheel or dashboard for front-seat occupants and were placed into vehicles in the late 1980s and early 1990s. They were designed to decrease a front-seat occupant's contact with the steering wheel, windshield, or dashboard, and in turn decrease the severity of injuries. They were found to be very effective in this endeavor and were added to side doors to decrease injuries during side impacts. Some vehicles are now equipped with head sidewall bags called curtain bags and are located at the top of doors to decrease impacts to the head. All airbags are designed to be used in conjunction with seatbelts and are not to be used alone as primary restraints.

They are deployed via sensing triggers that set off a chemical reaction that releases nitrogen gas that fills the bag like an air pillow. For the front compartment bags, the sensors are located in the front bumper and set to deploy during a front impact. Other sensors may be in the seats or seatbelt fasteners. For side compartment bags, the sensors are located in the doors. Airbags may not deploy in some impacts if the vehicle contacts the object at an angle or in such a way that the sensors are not triggered. Airbags are ejected from their storage compartment with force and can create abrasions and contusions of the upper torso and face. In the very young and old, the force is enough to cause substantial injuries or fractures. For this reason, children should ride in the seat with the airbag switched off or occupy the rear seat where they do not deploy. Infant car seats should be rear facing to prevent injury to the child.

TEMPERED GLASS AND LAMINATED WINDSHIELDS

The type of glass used in motor vehicles is designed to decrease sharp edges and cutting ability by the breaking of glass that occurs during an accident. The front glass is composed of two thin sheets of glass laminated over a piece of clear plastic. During an impact, a strike by an object will cause the glass to fracture in a radiating pattern from the site of impact, but prevents protrusion of the object through the windshield and cutting tissue. This is a site that can be useful in the collection of hair or DNA to assist with positioning of occupants or the site of impact from a pedestrian. The head is a common site of impact with the windshield and results in superficial lacerations, contusions, or abrasions located on the forehead or scalp. See Figure 7.10.

Side and rear windows are tempered glass that is designed to shatter into small ⅛ to ½ in. irregular sharp shards of glass. These pieces have the ability to superficially cut the skin but not usually to the degree of a large slicing fragment of glass. The pattern produces characteristic dicing wounds, which may assist in positioning the occupants in the vehicle. It is useful to recognize these wounds in those where the position of an occupant is known so that the knowledge can be applied to those investigations where the occupants' locations are unknown or they are ejected. It is helpful for the investigator to have cut-proof

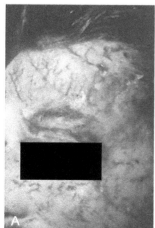 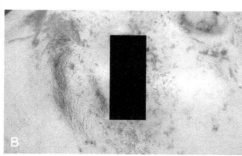 

FIGURE 7.10
(A) Classic **dicing wound** injuries appearing as small Y-shaped superficial lacerations of the skin and result from the small shards of glass projected onto the skin from the side or rear glass windows of vehicles as they shatter (C). The sidedness of the dicing wounds can assist with placement of the occupants within the vehicle as seen in this ride sided passenger (B).

gloves on underneath normal latex gloves when dealing with motor vehicle accidents. It keeps him or her from being cut on the glass or getting the small pieces embedded in the skin. They are excellent to wear under latex gloves not only for protection from cutting or sticking, but they also offer a barrier so that when the investigator has to change latex gloves multiple times at a messy scene, the gloves go on and off with ease. They also add a little bit of warmth in colder climates.

PILLARS

When reviewing accident reports certain terms will be used to describe the vehicle. **Pillars** refer to the posts supporting the roof. The A pillar is the one nearest the hood, surrounding the windshield at the front of the doors. The B pillar is the one behind the driver and front passenger doors supporting the mid-region of the roof. The C pillar is the one surrounding the rear window or rear door in a hatchback. See Figure 7.11 for a diagram.

Skid marks

Skid marks are the black marks left on the pavement when the brakes are suddenly applied and the vehicle is still moving. Law enforcement investigators can measure the length of the skid marks to the site of impact and estimate the speed

FIGURE 7.11
The locations of the pillars supporting the roof and doors of a vehicle. Accident reports received from law enforcement will reference these points as areas of impact by the occupants during a motor vehicle accident.

the vehicle was moving when the accident occurred. Obviously skid marks are harder to evaluate on the pavement due to decreased friction caused by wet, icy, or oil slippery surfaces.

A vehicle operating on the road is governed by physics and is a mass (M = vehicle) moving at a certain speed (V = velocity) and possesses kinetic energy (KE). It follows the law of kinetic energy:

$$KE = \tfrac{1}{2} MV^2$$

This means that the amount of kinetic energy it possesses is not related to the mass of the object as it is to the velocity (or speed) it is moving. With a crash, the kinetic energy is absorbed by the vehicle and the occupants and the surface it impacts. Much of the kinetic energy is absorbed by the crushing and tearing of the metal and components. Cars are designed to buckle and crush in various areas to absorb the energy. However, they do have a point where they exceed the crush points and more energy is available to create injury on the occupants. The degree of energy depends on the speed and how much dissipation can be absorbed by the object the vehicle strikes. If it is another vehicle, the vehicles will share the combined energy. If it is a stationary object like a cement wall, all the energy is absorbed by the vehicle and occupants.

Driver

It is helpful to observe the characteristic injuries seen on drivers even in single-vehicle accidents. It will help to identify them in cases where the occupants' positions are unknown. Injuries seen on ejected occupants are usually a combination of occupant- and pedestrian-type injuries.

Injuries to be noted in determining driver versus a passenger are seatbelt impressions, steering wheel impressions, airbag injuries, dashboard injuries, pedal injuries, and dicing wound injuries.

Seatbelt abrasions seen with drivers are diagonal abrasions or contusions beginning at the base of the left neck and crossing over the mid-chest to the right hip where it meets a horizontal abrasion or contusion across the pelvic area usually below the umbilicus (belly button) (Figure 7.12). This is assuming it is worn properly and the shoulder harness is not tucked under the armpit.

With the advent of airbags, steering wheel abrasions are uncommon. Airbags deploy when there is front bumper impact. They may still be seen if the airbag does not deploy either due to failure or the impact did not trigger them. The abrasions may be partial curved contusions or abrasions usually encircling the middle chest. Internal injuries include anterior and lateral rib fractures.

Even with the use of airbags and seatbelts, the occupants can move forward with the impact in addition to the intrusion of the interior compartment resulting in compression of the legs. The dashboard may put stress on the upper legs fracturing the femur, hip, and/or pelvis. The driver's feet can get entangled in the pedals causing fractures of the lower legs or ankles. Literature descriptions of pedal

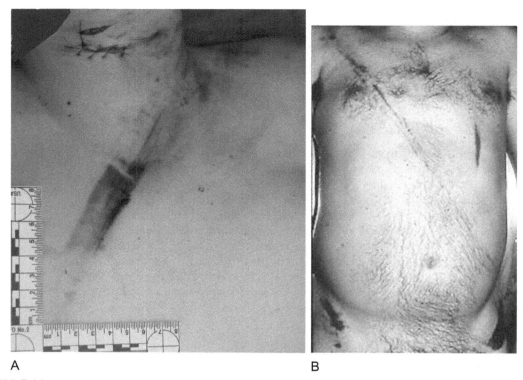

A   B

FIGURE 7.12
(A) An example of the shoulder harness pattern seen in the driver of a motor vehicle. Note the abrasion at the base of the left neck coursing diagonally across the chest toward the right hip corresponds to the belt hooking to the right of the decedent. Contrast this with (B), which shows the shoulder harness pattern of an occupant. The opposite diagonal pattern beginning at the base of the right neck coursing toward the left hip corresponds to the buckle located there. This photo also shows the lap belt imprint over the lower pelvic region.

impressions can be seen on the soles of the shoes, especially during severe braking. It is good to photograph the soles of shoes to document the presence or absence of any pedal impressions.

The impact may cause breakage of the side tempered glass with the fractured pieces striking the skin on the side closest to the glass. Most times impact on the opposite site of a compartment is too far for dense impact by glass fragments. Glass impact causes characteristic superficial small wavy lacerations and abrasions likened to chicken feet. This information is very helpful to position occupants and is noteworthy during an investigation.

Passenger/occupant

Occupants have fewer patterned injuries than drivers. Front-seat passengers may have airbag injuries if there is a front-end impact. Side window tempered glass can be seen on the right torso and face. Shoulder harness abrasions extend from the base of the right neck diagonally across the chest to the left hip where it is buckled. Due to the proximity to the dashboard, femur fractures with deformity of the thigh may be seen.

Back-seat passengers may exhibit right- or left-side dicing wounds and shoulder harness abrasions depending on their respective position in the vehicle to the breaking glass. Sometimes passengers and drivers may be unrestrained and become ejected, partially ejected, or their position jumbled within the compartment. It is important to look for any patterned injuries and dicing wounds and review the accident report to try to position them to aid in the identification of the driver. DNA collection and head hair samples may aid the accident investigator. Good photographs depicting the injuries with and without scales from above, side, and back will provide additional information and justification of findings for possible court testimony.

Compression or mechanical asphyxia

Compression of the torso or neck by collapse of the roof, front-end compression, or an upside-down vehicle with belted occupants all can impinge on the chest and the ability of a person to breathe (Figure 7.13). Autopsy examination shows a paucity of injuries and usually congestion of the head and neck.

FIGURE 7.13
A heavy object compressing the torso or upper body resulting in the inability to expand the chest and exchange air.

Petechiae within the eyes may or may not be present. The best evidence for this diagnosis is the scene photographs showing the position of the decedent within the compartment. The head and neck may also be flexed or hyperextended, further inhibiting exchange of oxygen. Scene photos can mean all the difference in these cases.

Pedestrians

When pedestrians come in direct contact with a vehicle, there may be transfer of paint, fractured plastic particles, and imprints of the vehicle onto the clothing and skin of the decedent or injured person. The scene along the path of the impact will contain a mixture of body fluids and possible materials from the vehicle. When the vehicle is examined, blood, hair and tissue from the decedent/injured can also be found in the crevices or under the vehicle [4]. During medical treatment, clothing may be cut away and left at the scene or discarded in hospitals. It is important to confiscate clothing as evidence, especially in hit-and-run accidents.

Speed at the time of impact can be estimated from skid patterns prior to impact. The speed of the vehicle, type of vehicle (high or low rise, slanted or flat hood), and height of the individual all play a role in the series of events that follow the impact. The height of the person determines his or her center of gravity. It is located near the waist in an adult, which has a higher center relative to the ground than a child does (Figure 7.14). For this reason, children are usually carried on the front of a vehicle until it slows when they fall in front of it and are then run over. Adults can be knocked down and run over at slow speeds. More commonly, an adults struck at speeds less than 35 mph will fracture his or her legs on the bumper then slide onto the hood, striking the windshield. As the vehicle slows, the person slides off the side. At faster speeds the legs are fractured and the person is lifted to the roof of the vehicle and may fly over the top to drop onto pavement. Other vehicles may then run over the injured person. In large-mass, flat-front vehicles, the adult and child will impact the front and be carried along then drop under the vehicle as it slows.

Pedestrians can also be struck by side mirrors that project outward on delivery or pickup trucks and may create only upper torso or head injuries. Other pedestrians may be struck only by a vehicle's front edge and have isolated one-sided injuries depending on which way he or she was facing at the time of impact. These glancing blows can result in fatal injuries depending on how the pedestrians are impacted and ejected to the side. Injuries not only can occur from the impact with the vehicle but also by the impact of the person with the ground.

Injuries peculiar to pedestrians are leg bumper injuries and grill injuries (Figure 7.15). Bumper injuries occur when the car bumper impacts usually the lower leg. The height of this fracture is important because it is the height of the front end of the vehicle at the time of impact and needs to be measured at the time of autopsy (Figure 7.9). It is measured from the sole of the foot to the mid-portion of the lower-leg deformity. Other important measurements

Pedestrian struck at lower speeds. Bumper injuries will correspond to the height of the bumper at the time of impact. Note the bumper dips downward with braking. After the initial impact, the person strikes the head on the hood or windshield and with braking, slides off the side of the hood onto the pavement.

Pedestrian struck at higher speeds. Here the pedestrian will be struck by the front of the vehicle but is swept upward to strike the roof and land behind the vehicle or be swept over the top entirely to land behind.

FIGURE 7.14
Diagram of impact of a car with a pedestrian [5].

are any patterned injuries on the torso, buttocks, or backs of the legs. In living victims, the height is difficult to obtain. The height of the front end of a vehicle decreases when the brakes are applied and can corroborate or dispute the statement given. The bumper height will vary from vehicle to vehicle and needs to be documented in the investigative report while at the resting state.

Collection of evidence

Toxicology for alcohol determination as well as prescription and illicit drugs is useful to obtain on all traffic victims. This is especially important if the positioning of each of the occupants is unknown and the identity of the driver is

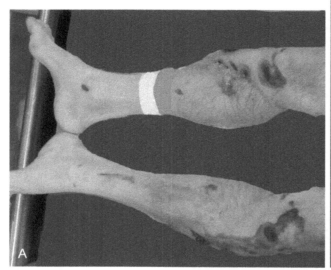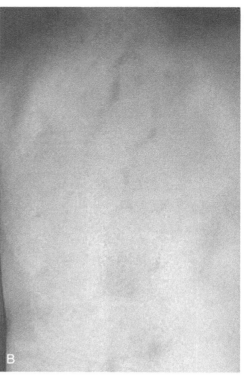

FIGURE 7.15
(A) Typical bumper fractures of the legs seen in pedestrians struck by a motor vehicle. The injuries may occur on one or both legs during an impact. (B) A patterned contusion over the back of a decedent that corresponds to the tire imprint as the decedent was run over by a motor vehicle.

questioned. This information is used for prosecution and civil litigation for factors influencing outcome of injuries or the cause of the accident. Underlying diseases and health of decedents is also important to document because civil settlements are based on life expectancy and lifetime earnings. Pain and suffering are also factored in, and those who die instantly usually receive less than those who live for an interval with a period of potential awareness. For these reasons, a complete autopsy will aid retrieval of specimens to ensure accurate information is used to form an opinion.

The best specimens for toxicology are obtained from the femoral artery/vein of the groin and vitreous specimens. Femoral specimens are preferable to subclavian or chest specimens because they can be contaminated with gastric contents resulting in false elevations of measured values. It is not uncommon for the diaphragms and stomach/esophagus to rupture spilling freshly ingested food into a pleural cavity. When drawing subclavian or heart specimens it is easy to get the needle into the cavity contaminating the blood with ingested alcohol rather than metabolized alcohol that might be present. If someone goes to a party, drinks a beer, and immediately drives with a fatal traffic accident, the freshly ingested single beer would likely have a blood alcohol of less than 0.02 mg/dl in the blood, which would be under the legal limit. But if collected from a contaminated pleural cavity, the specimen would be over the legal limit of 0.08 mg/dl, and the person erroneously determined to be driving under the influence.

A verification test of blood alcohol is usually determined by doing a vitreous (ocular) fluid level. Since it is protected from the body cavities and contamination factors, it is a useful adjunct to a blood alcohol test. The value determined in the vitreous runs slightly higher (1.2× higher) than blood and also lags behind a blood value. So a value of 1 mg/dl in blood is equal to 1.2 mg/dl in vitreous, and the person is said to be at a steady state where ingested quantity is equal to excretion. As the person quits drinking, the blood value will drop and the vitreous value will remain slightly higher, lagging behind in its excretion.

Besides toxicology, other surface evidence may be useful to an investigation. Surface evidence is most important in pedestrian impacts because the materials can link the injured to a particular vehicle. Paint chips, glass fragments, car parts, and patterned imprints can all be useful in the investigation (Figure 7.16). Databases exist for comparison of these articles of trace evidence and can aid the identification of the suspect vehicle. Small pieces of plastic from headlamps may contain portions of the VIN number to further narrow the suspect pool and need to be collected as evidence. When the list is obtained, each car can be inspected

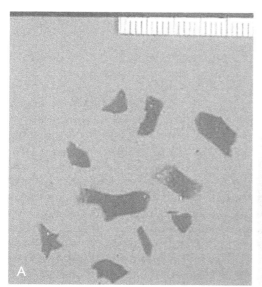

FIGURE 7.16
(A) Paint chips collected from the clothing and wounds on a pedestrian motor vehicle accident. The red color corresponds to the outward color of the vehicle and the gray corresponds to the underlying primer coat near the metal. (B) A microscopic examination of a paint chip showing the layers of paint on a vehicle [6].

for damage corresponding to the victim's injuries. Suspect vehicles can then be impounded and inspected for decedent tissue or DNA in vehicle crevices.

Clothing may have imprints of front ends of vehicles and so it should be removed without cutting and photographed front and back. Investigators may wish to impound the clothing and, if so, it should be packaged separately in brown paper bags then signed over with a chain of custody. Photographic documentation of injuries is imperative in pedestrian accidents. In hit-and-run accidents it may prove useful to trace patterned grill or bumper injuries using a clear plastic sheet over the patterned area and tracing with a permanent marking pen. The top/bottom and right/left should be documented so it can be coordinated with any photographs. The tracing can be useful to law enforcement investigators in looking for a matching vehicle.

Work and farm related

Work- and farm-related blunt-force injuries usually involve a piece of machinery, electrical malfunction, or natural disease. It is important to determine a site of risk to prevent injury to other workers. Occupational safety is usually involved in the investigation if it occurs in a workplace. It is important to document the type of clothing and if the person was wearing proper standard apparel. Clothing may become entangled in machinery and it is important to photograph it on the decedent, as well as spread out for documentation of the front and back. Gloves, helmets, and safety shoes are also important to note. Safety harness use, proper attachment to the person, and the stationary object also need to be noted or inquired about. An autopsy examination will add information about an underlying natural disease that may have contributed to the cause, as well as full toxicology to answer a question of impairment.

Trains

Train accidents usually involve two types of deaths: ones in which the person is within a vehicle and one involving a pedestrian. There are rare mass disaster train derailments which follow a mass disaster protocol of locating the engineer and conductor of the train to determine their cause of death and toxicology status to aid determining how they influence the cause of a derailment. Because of the mass, the resulting injuries are usually quite extensive whether within a vehicle or a pedestrian. Train investigations usually include train investigators who will assist in relaying information from the engineer and conductor. Most passenger and freight trains are now equipped with front-end cameras with real-time videos that can be reviewed, corroborating the engineer's account and also providing important information about the train's speed, whistle, and position of the victim or vehicle. It is very helpful in determining the manner of death and whether the victim dies as a result of accident, suicide, or homicide. Review of the video can greatly assist in this determination. The train engineers can give an estimate for approximately how long it takes to stop the train and how far it goes before it comes to a complete stop. The investigator needs to inquire how many train cars are attached and the approximate weight the train is pulling. There is some urgency to the investigation because the trains are usually stopped in both directions while the investigation is being conducted.

Death certification and report writing

Information needed for proper completion of the death certificates includes the date and time of the accident, the place of the accident (highway/road, farm field, residence, etc.), and the circumstances surrounding the death, the time of death pronouncement, or the time law enforcement arrived at the scene on cases where death was obvious. Pertinent circumstances that need to be communicated directly at the time of death include the position within the vehicle (driver, passenger, ejected occupant, pedestrian), seatbelt use, presence or absence of skid marks, estimated speed, weather conditions at the time of the accident, and evidence of possible impairment (liquor bottles or drug paraphernalia). Some cases may even require certain product model numbers to relate to the Product Safety Commission (helmets, vehicle or machinery models, safety equipment in use). In the case of farm or train accidents, information about how the decedent was behaving before the accident and details of how he or she was found are relevant to certifying the cause and manner of death. All of this information is needed by vital statistics and eventually forms part of the national statistics for accident prevention.

It is possible to achieve suicide via a motor vehicle. Contents of the vehicle should be searched for potential suicide notes. The absence of braking with resultant skid marks can be a clue, as well as veering purposefully into oncoming traffic. Semi-tractor trailers as a target are commonly used in this method and drivers of the rigs can relay useful information about how the driver was acting prior to the impact. Many times a suicide manner is difficult to prove to a certainty and they may be ruled undetermined or accidental depending on the toxicology and the opinion of the pathologist.

Death prior to the impact and a resulting natural cause of death is also possible. In these cases, the individual will have few to no external injuries and an internal examination will show an absence of lacerations, fractures, or internal bleeding that would occur if death were caused by a motor vehicle. There may be findings of coronary artery disease, stroke, or other natural diseases that can impair operation of a motor vehicle. It is important to rule out a high neck spine fracture because these injuries can result from "whiplash" at impact with minimal internal findings. The latter manner of death would be accidental. Compression asphyxia should also be considered in cases with minimal to no internal injuries.

Homicide is also important to rule out. Decedents, even those apparently severely injured, found along the side of the road or those lying on train tracks are not necessarily dead by what would seem the obvious cause. It is important to note all scene information and make sure it is consistent with the suspected cause. A pedestrian struck by a motor vehicle should have lower-leg fractures versus a person beaten then dumped by the side of the road. It is important to look for gunshot wounds in those with severe head wounds. X-rays may be a useful adjunct for that purpose.

Literature review

Numerous case studies in the literature exist with photos of various patterned injuries that continue to change as new instruments evolve. Much of the older literature regarding traffic accidents is useful even today. New safety measures have been instituted with side and front airbags, improved side-rail design, and retraction of the motor downward to prevent intrusion into the compartment.

Probably the biggest area of research is the amount of force needed to create various lethal injuries. This is a common question in court but is difficult to answer due to the variations of the human body and its interaction with the force that was applied. Much of the research has been done either with simulator models of the human body or animals. Neither of these are true representations of the decedent to answer the question accurately.

REFERENCES

[1] National Highway Traffic Safety Administration. Summary of Vehicle Occupant Protection Laws. 10th ed; 2011. Retrieved from http://www.nhtsa.gov/staticfiles/nti/pdf/811648.pdf. [August 2013].

[2] Virginia Commonwealth University. Tips and Crash Investigation. Transportation Safety Training Center. Retrieved from http://www.vcu.edu/cppweb/tstc/tips. [August 2013].

[3] History of Seatbelts in the US. Bisnar|Chase Personal Injury Attorneys. Retrieved from http://www.bestattorney.com/defective-seatbelts/history.html. [August 2013].

[4] Lucas J. Forensic Investigation: Motor Vehicle Accidents and Motor Vehicle-Pedestrian Accidents. Medscape; 2012. Retrieved from http://emedicine.medscape.com/article/1765532-overview#a30. [August 2013].

[5] Spitz WU. Essential Postmortem Findings in the Traffic Accident Victim. Arch Pathol 1970, Dec.90(5):451–7.

[6] Paint. Missouri State Highway Patrol. Retrieved from http://www.mshp.dps.missouri.gov/MSHPWeb/PatrolDivisions/CLD/TraceEvidence/paint.html. [August 2013].

CHAPTER 8
Gunshot Wounds

Learning Objectives

- As an investigator, you arrive at a homicide scene of a gunshot victim and the detective asks you to obtain a fingerprint for identification. Apply what you know about the various types of evidence that may need to be retrieved and discuss how you think this might affect further evidence gathering.
- Outline the types of photographs you as an investigator would need to obtain when responding to a gunshot wound suicide death.
- Apply what you have learned about gunshot wound deaths and list the information about the gun or bullets that the pathologist will ask the investigator and needs to be included in the report. Discuss why this information may be needed to plan for the examination.
- Contrast the scene features of a homicide gunshot victim to those of a suicide victim.
- Analyze and list the features of a gunshot victim that should not be included in an investigator's report.

Key Terms
Caliber
Gauge
Wadding
Bullet
Casing
Cylinder
Magazine
Gunshot residue
Kinetic energy

Chapter Summary

Gunshot wound investigations can be very detailed requiring notation of multiple pieces of evidence and evaluation of this evidence with witness statements. It is best to consider suggestive statements of accident, suicide, or homicide as only one piece of the puzzle and evaluate the body's relationship to the location the gun was found, trajectory, and pathologist's range of fire estimation to make the best judgment for manner of death. It is important to include the type and caliber of weapon within the report so the pathologist can utilize this information during the examination. Photographic documentation of the scene is invaluable and should include the usual overall photos from multiple perspectives of the decedent and the relationship to the gun if present. Mid-range and close-up photos of visible injuries and clothing are also important. Surroundings rooms, vehicle compartments, or involved areas are also useful in the scene reconstruction of shooter versus victim, or if self-inflicted. After the body is removed, photographic documentation of the surface the body was resting on is also needed. Consultation from homicide detectives, pathologist response, or blood-spatter experts can be useful to direct the investigation.

INTRODUCTION

To talk about gunshot wounds requires basic knowledge about the general types of guns and terminology used to describe the various parts that compose them. There are three main categories of guns: handguns, rifles, and shotguns. The basic premise of all guns is the discharge of a projectile down a tube (barrel) using a controlled explosion created by gunpowder. In this chapter we will discuss the various types of guns, ammunition used, the wounds created, range of fire, evidence collection, scene documentation, and how the scene information is used to determine manner of death.

TERMINOLOGY

- *Handgun:* A handheld weapon that varies from low to high velocity depending on the capability of that gun's barrel diameter corresponding to **caliber**, barrel length, and type of ammunition used.
- *Rifle:* A high-velocity weapon utilizing larger amounts of gunpowder and a longer barrel to achieve greater accuracy, as well as more complete burning of the powder and of which the barrel diameter is described by caliber.
- *Shotgun:* A high-velocity weapon that utilizes shot shells rather than bullets as projectiles and is usually described by **gauge** rather than caliber.
- *Barrel:* The tube that gives the projectile directionality and allows the gun to achieve its maximum velocity.
- *Cartridge:* The complete "bullet" that contains the true lead bullet on the tip, with or without an overlying jacket, and a **casing**, which holds the gunpowder, primer, and bullet in alignment.
- *Bullet:* The lead portion of the cartridge that leaves the end of the barrel (muzzle) when the gun is fired.
- *Casing:* The spent portion made of a cartridge that is discarded after firing. It is usually made of brass or steel and remains in the **cylinder** of revolvers or can be ejected to the side in semi-automatic weapons.
- *Projectile:* A generic term used to describe anything exiting a weapon. In wounds created by guns it is typically the lead bullet, but in some weapons, such as a dart gun or handmade ammunition, it made be atypical.
- *Shotgun shell:* A term used to describe the equivalent of a cartridge but used only in a shotgun. Contains the lead shot as well as the gunpowder, **wadding**, and primer. When all the contents are expended it is called a shot case.
- *Shot:* The round balls composing the lead portion of a shotgun shell. These can vary in size from 9.14 mm to 1.3 mm. In general, the larger the number the smaller the size of the ball. As an example, 0 or 00 size is much larger than 7 size shot. Smaller shot is influenced more by aerodynamics and air friction and flies accurately a shorter distance than larger, heavier shot. In summary, the smaller the number on the shot, the larger the diameter and the fewer number of shot per shotgun shell.

- *Wadding:* A disc composed of cork or cardboard used to separate the shot from the gunpowder and creates a more efficient explosion by containing the gas in the gunpowder area of the shot shell.
- *Power piston:* A plastic form of wadding that lines the inside of the shotgun shell and serves the same purpose as the cardboard discs. In addition, it is designed to keep the shot together, creating more accuracy at the target and less fouling of the barrel by less contact with the lead.
- *Gunpowder:* The material that creates the power behind propelling the **bullet** from the gun. There are three main types: cylinder, ball, and flake. Ball powder is smaller and more aerodynamic, allowing it to penetrate clothing and other intermediate targets much easier than flake powder, which has a greater surface area. Cylinder powder has intermediate properties.
- *Primer:* A volatile explosive material that comes in contact with the firing pin and precipitates the ignition of the gunpowder explosion.
- *Perforation versus penetration:* Perforation describes a wound that enters an organ and passes through it. Penetration describes an entrance of a wound into an organ or body cavity and usually no exit. These terms tend to be used interchangeably.
- *Rifling:* The spiraled tooling inside the barrel of a rifle or handgun that puts a spin on the bullet projectile and is gun specific. The gun barrel is created from a tube of steel that is then bored out to a machine to create these characteristic grooves which will vary in spacing and depth. Most guns have a right-twisting spiral as viewed from the shooter's perspective looking down the barrel. The exception are handguns manufactured by Colt which are left twist.
- *Lands:* The raised portions of the rifling inside the barrel of a gun that create markings on the soft lead bullet as it travels down the barrel (Figure 8.1). These markings are gun specific and allow a projectile to be matched to a particular rifled weapon.
- *Grooves:* The depressed areas inside the gun barrel of a handgun or rifle that create the bullet markings on the projectile and allow guns to be matched to the recovered projectile (see Figure 8.1).
- *Caliber:* The diameter measurement inside the barrel between two lands and is measured in millimeters for most weapons.
- *Gauge:* Reflects the diameter of the barrel of a shotgun and is determined by the number of lead balls that can fit in the diameter of the shotgun barrel that equal 1 pound. In the instance of a 12-gauge shotgun, the barrel diameter is 0.73 mm and it would require 12 balls of that diameter to equal 1 pound.
- *Choke:* A mechanism on a shotgun that is used to prevent scatter of the pellets. They come in different degrees from modified cylinder to variants of modified to full choke. According to DiMaio, they do not affect the pattern distribution of shotgun pellets seen in ranges of fire less than 10 ft [1].
- *Firing pin:* The portion of the trigger that strikes the primer at the base of the bullet causing ignition of the gunpowder. The firing pin is located on the tip of the hammer inside the firing chamber. The pattern created on the bullet casing base can also be characteristic and add information about the specific weapon.

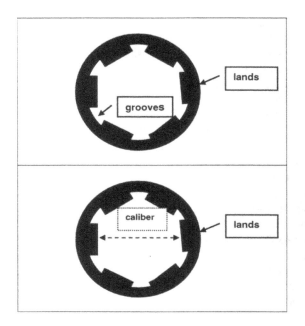

FIGURE 8.1
Lands form the raised portions inside the barrel of a handgun or rifle. Between the lands are valleys called grooves. Each gun has a characteristic land and groove pattern creating the rifling on a bullet as it travels down the barrel. It is this rifling that allows a bullet to be matched to a particular weapon.

- *Centerfire:* The primer being located in the center portion at the base of the bullet casing.
- *Rimfire:* The primer being located in a circular rim at the periphery of the base of the bullet casing.
- *Ejector:* Each gun needs a method to extrude the expended bullet casing/cartridge and move the next active bullet into firing position. This can be done manually in bolt- or lever-action rifles or by sliding the racking mechanism on a shotgun. In semi-automatic handguns and rifles, the mechanism is automatically done after firing with the ejection of the casings either right or left depending on the particular weapon. In revolvers, the bullet casing remains within the cylinder but the cylinder rotates whenever the hammer or trigger are pulled during the firing action.
- *Trigger:* The mechanism that fires the bullet from the chamber in all guns. Pulling it toward the handgrip will cause the trigger to be cocked and ready for release to fire the bullet.
- *Stock:* The wooden or plastic portion of a rifle or shotgun used to steady the gun against the shoulder during firing.
- *Handgrip:* The handle portion of a handgun used to encircle the base of the gun for the hands to steady it for firing.

TYPES AND ANATOMY OF GUNS

There are three main categories of guns: handguns, rifles, and shotguns. Handguns differ from rifles in the barrel length, which affords more efficient burning of gunpowder and in most cases a higher velocity to the bullet projectile. Shotguns differ largely in the anatomy of the projectile used.

Other terminology used to discuss guns is the velocity of the weapon, which largely determines the **kinetic energy** released into the target and the damage created by the surrounding shock waves by this release. Handguns generally have lower velocities in the range of 800 to 1,400 ft/sec. Rifles impart velocities of 1,100 to 3,300 ft/sec with centerfire having higher velocities than rimfire ones. Shotguns are intermediary but generally in the 1,100 to 1,200 ft/sec range.

The amount of energy released and damage created follows the standard kinetic energy formula of general physics:

$$KE = \tfrac{1}{2} MV^2$$

where M corresponds to the mass of the bullet (in turn related to the caliber of the weapon) and V corresponds to the velocity of the bullet, which is squared. The formula reads: *The kinetic energy released is equal to one-half the product of the mass of the bullet multiplied by the velocity squared*. This means that the mass of the bullet is not the largest determining factor in the amount of damage. The kinetic energy is largely related to the velocity achieved. So a high-velocity weapon has more destructive energy than a low-velocity weapon. The formula shows the importance of small increases in velocity have more effect on the amount of kinetic energy than increasing the amount of mass.

The velocity is largely dependent on the amount of gunpowder resulting in a greater explosion. The efficiency of the explosion is influenced by the length of the barrel. The mass of the bullet may not change the amount of kinetic energy as significantly as changing the velocity does, but after a point, only so much gunpowder can be used and the next item to be increased is the mass. As the velocity of the weapon increases in high-powered rifles it becomes necessary to use jacketed ammunition otherwise the velocity may melt the bullet inside the gun and cause it to damage the gun. By placing a hard metal over the lead it protects it and has the added benefit of creating a secondary projectile that can separate into another path. The real damage from the gunshot, however, is not just the immediate path of the bullet but the damage it produces in a temporary cavity around it as the kinetic energy is released.

The main parts of a revolver are the hammer, trigger, cylinder, cylinder latch, grip, and barrel and extractor rod. A revolver can hold five or six bullets in the cylinder and is loaded or unloaded by pressing the cylinder latch (Figure 8.2). The cylinder will rotate outward and used or unused bullets are removed by pressing the extractor rod into the cylinder. The gun can be reloaded; then the cylinder is rotated back into place and is ready to fire again. Many modern revolvers are able to be fired without first pulling the hammer back, which is referred to as

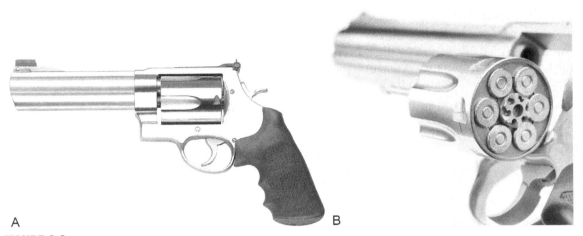

FIGURE 8.2
(A) A typical revolver. (B) The cylinder containing a maximum of six bullets that has been rotated outward to reload or empty.

double action, meaning that pulling the trigger back also cocks the hammer and in the second motion will fire the projectile. The bullet then exits down the barrel, which usually is usually 2 to 8 in. long. The longer the barrel, the more accurate the bullet is able to be on its target depending on the skill of the marksman. The expended cartridge will remain under the hammer until the trigger is pulled once again. This allows an investigator to faintly mark the cylinder with a pen then disengage and rotate the cylinder out to establish the number of expended bullets and their positions within the cylinder, as well as their relationship to the firing pin. It is important to document this information photographically and within the body of the report. There are two main manufacturers of revolvers: Smith & Wesson and Colt. Modern Smith & Wesson revolver *cylinders* rotate to the left (counterclockwise) and have a right-hand twist to the *rifling*. Colt revolvers have cylinders that rotate to the right (clockwise) and have a left-hand twist to the rifling [2]. The rifling notation on a recovered bullet is an important one and can help identify the manufacturer of the suspect weapon without having to wait for the crime lab.

The components of a semi-automatic handgun are similar to a revolver with the biggest difference being the bullet reloading mechanism (Figure 8.3). The components of a semi-automatic handgun include the hammer, trigger, **magazine**, slide, grip, and barrel. The magazines vary in the capacity of bullets they can hold and may depend on state gun control laws. Some states have been known to restrict magazines to as few as seven bullets. The magazine slides into and snaps into the base of the handgrip. To rack a bullet into the chamber requires the slide mechanism to be pulled back toward the handgrip. The magazine contains a spring in the base to move bullets automatically into the firing chamber as they are spent or during the racking of the slide. During the firing process, the gun uses some of the spent energy to move the slide toward the grip, which mechanically discharges the spent cartridge out the side of the barrel, allowing

FIGURE 8.3
(A) A semi-automatic handgun with the magazine ejected from the handgrip of the weapon. With the magazine out of the weapon, it may still not be safe to handle until any live rounds are ejected from the chamber and it has been cleared (B).

the next bullet to move into place by the spring-loaded mechanism. The slide moves automatically after each trigger pull until the magazine is empty.

It is important before examining a weapon at the scene to make sure the firing chamber is empty prior to extensive examination. The magazine is first removed, then the slide is manually racked toward the grip to eject any bullets in the firing chamber. It is important to keep fingers off the trigger and the muzzle away from surrounding people to prevent injury from an accidental discharge. This is called making the gun safe and all examination of weapons needs to follow the protocol of ensuring that all bullets have been removed from the firing chamber prior to packaging, photographing, or examination. Gun etiquette includes packaging and handing from one person to another with the open firing chamber visible.

Rifles are also bored weapons, meaning they impart rifling on the bullet projectiles. The components of a rifle are the barrel, trigger, stock, firing chamber, bolt or lever action (some are semi-automatic as well), and magazine within the stock. Bolt-action rifles are the most common and are seen in hunting rifles. The bolt is a hand-rotating mechanism that moves the next bullet from the storage magazine into the firing position within the chamber. Lever action is the type seen in BB or pellet guns as well as in TV westerns. These involve a lever near the trigger that ejects a cartridge or, in the case of BB guns, loads the next bullet into place. There are semi-automatic rifles such as AK47 and machine guns that utilize mechanisms similar to semi-automatic handguns to load bullets into the firing chamber from a magazine. Magazines vary in size on these weapons and can hold many more bullets than the semi-automatic handgun.

Shotguns are composed of a single or double barrel (side by side or over and under) and a stock, which also contains the magazine, trigger, and a pump-action mechanism. They are smooth bored and contain no rifling. They fire by placing a cartridge into the firing chamber and can also be loaded with cartridges from the magazine that can be racked into the chamber by sliding the pump mechanism. The gun is fired from the shoulder by pulling the trigger. Reloading is accomplished by racking back the pump mechanism on the barrel, which ejects the spent cartridge and loads the next cartridge. Some shotguns are breakaway and each shell cartridge must be hand loaded into the firing chamber.

ANATOMY OF BULLETS AND PROJECTILES

Bullet cartridges fired from a rifled weapon are uniformly composed of a lead bullet, gunpowder, primer, and bullet casing to hold it all together (Figure 8.4). Upon the hammer firing pin coming in contact with the primer (either centerfire or rimfire), the gunpowder ignites, causing the controlled explosion and separation of the bullet from the casing. As the bullet exits the barrel, burned and

FIGURE 8.4
(A) Cross-section of a projectile with the lead bullet at the top of the photo and the casing at the bottom, which contains the gunpowder. (B) Various caliber bullet projectiles from rifle (left) to handgun (right).

unburned gunpowder and hot gases including carbon monoxide are expelled into the surrounding environment. The degree of efficiency of this burning will depend on the length of the barrel. The barrel's length, its distance from the victim, and the amount and type of gunpowder in the casing will determine how much is seen on the skin and clothing of the victim.

Handgun bullets vary in design from jacketed to unjacketed lead bullets, as well as design differences described as hollow points or fully jacketed. Jackets describe a surface coating over the lead usually composed of copper, brass, or lightweight steel, and occasionally plastic material. The jacket serves to protect the inside of the barrel from damage at higher velocities and will separate from the lead portion upon impact, creating a secondary projectile and increasing the damage rendered. Rifling from the inside of the barrel will be seen on the jacket rather than the lead portion so it is important to locate that portion when doing scene or autopsy retrieval. The jacket is less dense than the lead portion of the bullet when viewed on X-ray but is still visible.

Rifle cartridges are similar to handgun ones but are largely jacketed ammunition due to the high velocity. The majority of cartridges are larger than handgun ammunition (except .22 caliber) and contain a larger amount of gunpowder. Due to the high velocity and design, rifle projectiles shatter upon impact into small fragments. This makes gun comparison by rifling to residual fragments very difficult. Screening X-rays will show small dusty particles of lead along the trajectory path, described as the "snowstorm effect." The long tube of the rifle also allows nearly complete combustion of the gunpowder, and gunpowder deposition near wounds or clothing is minimal to nearly absent even in contact or near-contact distances. Because of the high velocity, tissue destruction is extensive. Depending on the distance of the shot, the wound may appear as a typical wound with a small to moderate entrance containing a marginal abrasion with extensive release of the energy causing huge gaping exit wounds. See Figure 8.5 for examples.

Shotgun cartridges are composed of a plastic or paper cylinder containing multiple pellet projectiles, separated from the gunpowder in the base by a second piece of plastic called a power piston, or by circular cardboard/cork/felt wadding, gunpowder, primer, and brass base (Figure 8.6). When fired, the pellets and wadding/power piston are expelled from the cartridge down the barrel of the shotgun. Because the inside of the shotgun is smooth bore, no markings are made on the wadding, power piston, or pellets. Each pellet has the ability to penetrate the body and cause internal damage. The smaller the diameter of the pellet, the larger the number inside the cartridge and vice versa. Large pellets, namely 00 buckshot, utilize eight individual pellets inside a cartridge and each are about the size of a 9-mm bullet. Shotguns are extremely lethal as one shot of a cartridge with 00 buckshot is equivalent to eight shots from a handgun. The small pellets are commonly referred to as birdshot because they are frequently used in bird hunting. The scattering of the small pellets over a distant shot allows the hunter to bring down small birds in a single shot. These X-ray opaque shot

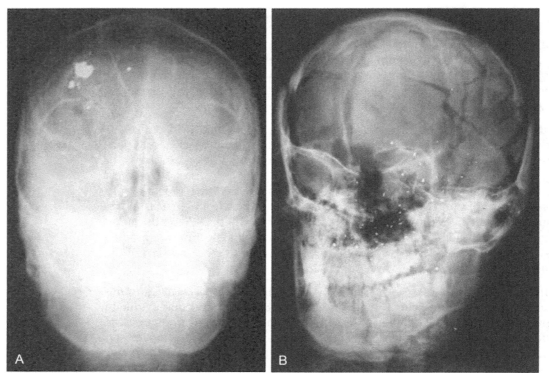

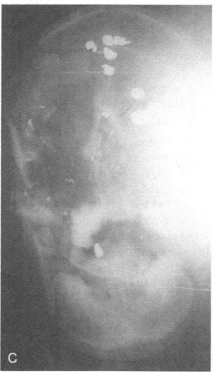

FIGURE 8.5

(A) X-ray showing a single bullet within the skull that appears as a radio-dense irregular object. (B) X-ray of a rifle wound that has only fine small bullet fragments visible that are nearly impossible to recover. This is the classic "snowstorm effect" seen with rifle wounds. (C) X-ray of a shotgun wound of the head with buckshot pellets.

FIGURE 8.6
(A) A shotgun cartridge loaded with buckshot. It also demonstrates the empty casing that is the portion that may be recovered at a scene. (B) In contrast, a cartridge loaded with birdshot. Note the much smaller size of the shot pellets and larger number of them that are contained within the cartridge.

pellets are easily seen on X-ray, however, the plastic or cardboard wadding is not visualized. The wadding or plastic piston will give an indication of the gauge of the shotgun based on its diameter and the pellets need to be recovered whenever possible. In small birdshot pellet wounds, the pellets are difficult to locate and representative samples can be obtained and the whole number seen on X-ray is not necessary. In fewer pellet numbers such as 00 buckshot, all the projectiles from the victim should be recovered.

ENTRANCE VERSUS EXIT

All entrance wounds have one thing in common: a marginal abrasion (Figure 8.7). When a gun is shot the bullet projectile contacts the skin and scrapes off the margins of the wound as it enters. If the wound is nearly straight on, the abrasion around the margin will be concentric. If the bullet enters at an angle the wound will be oval with the scraping portion being along the margin toward the muzzle of the gun. As the angle to the body surface gets shallower, the bullet can actually graze across the surface, tearing the skin, and may or may not enter the body. In graze wounds the margins will be lacerated with small pointed margins pointing in the direction from which the bullet came (Figure 8.8). The shelf abrasion on the margin will also be in the direction the bullet enters.

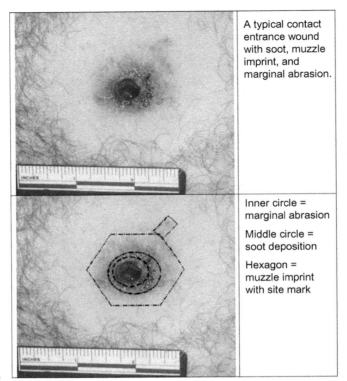

A typical contact entrance wound with soot, muzzle imprint, and marginal abrasion.

Inner circle = marginal abrasion

Middle circle = soot deposition

Hexagon = muzzle imprint with site mark

FIGURE 8.7
Contact gunshot wound showing marginal abrasion, soot deposition and a faint muzzle imprint.

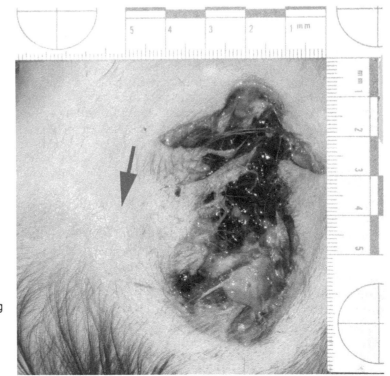

FIGURE 8.8
A graze wound creates a long laceration because the bullet is skimming along the surface of the body. The top (superior) margin has a crescent marginal abrasion with multiple pointed edges along the margin pointing from the direction from which the bullet came. The arrow in the photo depicts the direction of bullet travel.

An exit wound can appear round, or as a small or large laceration, or as a small slit in the skin (Figure 8.9). There is common belief that the largest wound is usually the entrance, which is untrue. The size of the wound is not related to entrance or exit. Exit wounds are characterized by the absence of a marginal abrasion rather than size. Usually no soot is able to reach an exit wound.

Occasionally there will be an abrasion near or somewhat surrounding the exit wound. This abrasion usually looks atypical from the usual marginal abrasion or other marginal abrasions associated with other gunshot wounds seen on the body. It is helpful to count the number of projectiles seen on X-ray and compare them to the number of typical entrance wounds seen on the body. This comparison may assist the investigator or pathologist in making the distinction that the funny-looking wound is actually an exit wound. The location where it is located may also assist in making the distinction. These funny-looking abrasions are usually located in an area of elastic (bra, waistband of pants, or underwear), band of a hat, back brace, etc., or in the area resting against the floor, wall, or chair back, and are called shored exit wounds (Figure 8.10). Examination of the clothing may also assist to look for outward tears, but usually they are soaked by blood and very difficult to assess and aid in this determination.

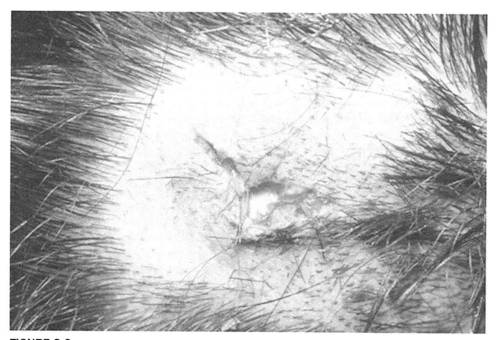

FIGURE 8.9
A laceration and typical appearance of an exit wound. They can vary greatly in size depending on the velocity of the weapon and release of kinetic energy.

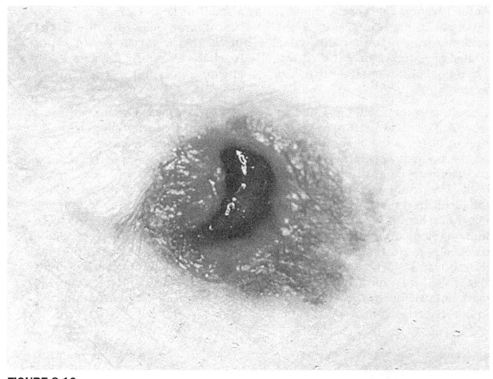

FIGURE 8.10
A shored exit wound. Note the central laceration surrounded by a wide slightly irregular abrasion. The entrance wound was a classic wound with soot and the decedent was sitting in a recliner when he shot himself. The bullet was recovered in the back of the chair.

RANGE OF FIRE

As the gun is fired, burned and unburned gunpowder and hot gases exit the muzzle (Figure 8.11). The distance the end of the barrel is from the victim as well as any objects between the two, and the type of gun, ammunition, and gunpowder will determine whether the gunpowder gets deposited on the skin or clothing. The further the distance, the less likely it will come in contact with either. Wounds are usually described in terms of hard contact, near contact, intermediate, distant, or indeterminate.

HANDGUN AND RIFLE WOUNDS

In hard-contact wounds the gun is firmly against the body and causes all the outpouring of the muzzle to enter the wound. On the torso this means the hot gases, including carbon monoxide from the burning gunpowder, enter the subcutaneous tissue and muscle causing a bright-red discoloration of the muscle (Figure 8.12). This is called the carboxyhemoglobin effect. The gunpowder residue is deposited within the depths of the wound and burning may be seen

FIGURE 8.11
A gun firing showing the flame, smoke, bullet, and gunpowder exiting the muzzle of the gun. It is the distance of the muzzle to the skin that will result in the pattern of the wound and the distribution of soot [5].

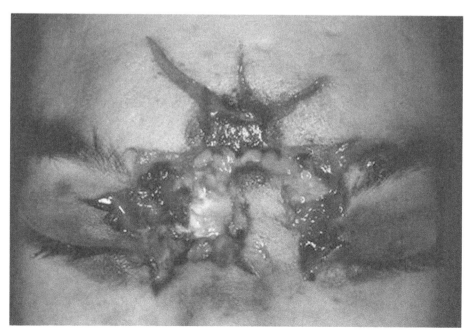

FIGURE 8.12
A hard-contact wound of the head with the central entrance wound containing a marginal abrasion, soot, and searing on the margins of the wound, and distortion by a large stellate tear. The tearing is caused by the gun discharging in contact with the skin and the hot gases escaping into the tissue between the skin and the skull.

along the wound margins. In handgun wounds the marginal abrasion will be seen with a full or partial muzzle imprint and stellate tears are evident on head wounds. Rifle wounds will show a marginal abrasion, but due to the large velocity, there may be extensive tissue destruction and it is more difficult to identify. Soot deposition can get deposited onto the surface of the skull or even the underlying dura membrane in a gunshot wound of the head.

In near-contact wounds, the distance from the muzzle to the skin can vary from nearly in contact (Figure 8.13) to a couple of inches away. In this scenario, the gases have the ability to diffuse from the end of the weapon and there will be less tissue destruction than hard contact. The marginal abrasion will be apparent but a muzzle imprint will be absent. Soot deposition will be apparent around the margin of the wound and be small to quite apparent depending on the weapon (Figure 8.14). Soot is greasy, black material but can easily be washed from the surface, so it should be evaluated prior to the body being cleansed. Soap should be avoided when cleansing the areas near gunshot wounds so as not to remove the soot and it can be captured photographically.

Intermediate wounds are ones extending usually from 12 in. to arm's length from the muzzle of the weapon. Because of the increased distance, the gases and much of the gunpowder have the ability to burn or diffuse. However, some gunpowder may reach the skin and burn into the surface causing powder tattooing (a.k.a. stippling), which appears as pin-dot red abrasions on the skin at the margin of the wound (Figure 8.15). The closer the muzzle is to the skin, the denser the

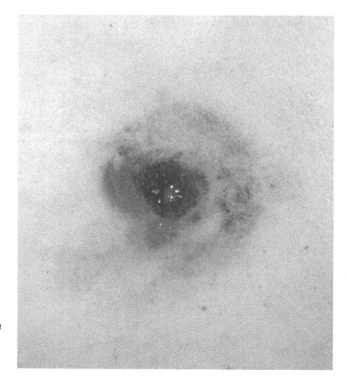

FIGURE 8.13
A loose contact wound with soot deposition on the skin surrounding the entrance wound and a partial muzzle abrasion on one margin.

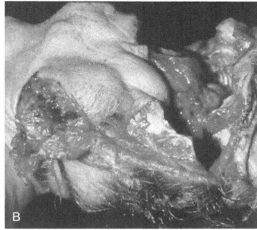

FIGURE 8.14
(A) A near-contact wound of a rifle showing only a very small amount of soot deposition due to the efficiency of the longer barrel. It does show the typical marginal abrasion characterizing it as an entrance wound. (B) The corresponding exit wound with the massive release of kinetic energy causing severe destruction of the head.

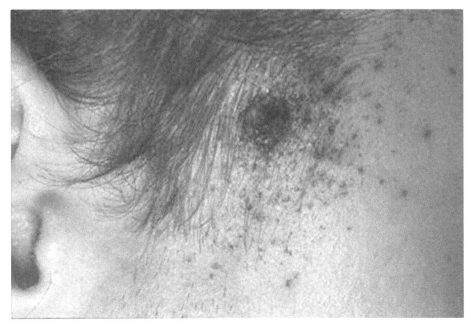

FIGURE 8.15
An intermediate range wound with stippling, also known as powder tattooing. It represents small particles of gunpowder seared onto the skin creating the punctate red-brown abrasions. Many times the particles of gunpowder can be seen in the depths of the wound. The separation of the stippling from the margin of the wound was created by the hairline of the decedent, which prevented the gunpowder from reaching the skin. Clothing may also create the same type of barrier.

tattooing, and it may be mixed with soot. As the distance increases, the tattooing becomes lighter and more scattered. Because tattooing is embedded in the skin it does not wash off readily, and if necessary, small particles can be retrieved using the pointed edge of a clean scalpel and collecting them onto a filter paper.

It is important for the prosecutor to measure length and width of the densest area where the tattooing is present, disregarding outliers, and to photograph this with the usual right-angle bite-mark ruler. If the gun is recovered, the range of fire can be estimated by reproducing the pattern of stippling by test-firing the weapon in the laboratory onto white cloth.

Distant wounds are those where the end of the gun is far enough away for neither the gases nor the gunpowder to reach the victim and it will show only the entrance wound with its marginal abrasion and absence of soot or stippling. Indeterminate-range wounds describe entrance wounds where the skin shows a marginal abrasion with the absence of soot or stippling. It has the same appearance as a distant wound but there is an intermediate target that may have precluded the presence of either soot or stippling being deposited and visualized on the skin (Figure 8.16). A typical scenario for an intermediate target is clothing, a car door/window, or house door/window that is between the muzzle and

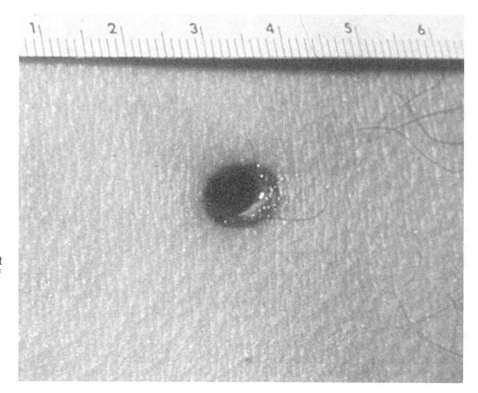

FIGURE 8.16
An entrance wound with the typical marginal abrasion but lacking soot or stippling. The range of fire is indeterminate and can represent a distant wound or one where the soot or stippling was unable to reach the wound because of clothing or some other intermediate target.

the victim, causing the gunpowder to be deposited elsewhere or filtered out prior to reaching the skin.

Clothing typically does not distort the bullet path to a significant degree unless it is a bulletproof vest or other substantial item. Gunfire through a car/house door or window will distort the pathway and cause the bullet to begin to tumble, resulting in an atypical entrance wound and marginal abrasion. The wound appears wider and irregular and is usually surrounded by other small irregular abrasions created by secondary projectiles from the doors or windows themselves. Depending on the scene investigation, it may aid determining the order of particular wounds. For example, if someone is initially shot through a door window creating the atypical wound and the window is shattered, no longer forming a barrier, or the door is opened, the wounds that follow will have their typical marginal abrasion and lack of secondary projectiles.

Gunshot wounds to the head have particular characteristics that gunshot wounds in other locations do not have. The skin of the head is stretched tightly over the skull. In hard-contact wounds, the hot gases have only the area between the skin and skull to escape into and may exceed the stretching ability of the skin. This can cause it to tear into large stellate (starlike) lacerations with a central entrance wound containing a marginal abrasion. In near-contact wounds, this may not occur to the same extent because of the ability of the gas to escape. Typical soot deposition patterns previously described will be the same depending on the range of fire. The skull also has unique capabilities due to its particular anatomy of being formed as an inner and outer table (layer). With an entrance gunshot wound to the head, it will enter the skull as a punched-out appearance externally with a wider chipped margin internally. This process is called internal beveling and denotes the entrance site. As the bullet exits the skull, the opposite occurs with the punched-out area internally and chipped margin externally (called external beveling). This unique property confirms the directionality in those wounds with soft tissue and skin overlying them, as well as forms a method to determine the entrance and directionality of a gunshot wound even on skeletal remains. See Figure 8.17 for examples.

Gunshot wounds to the ears, nose, scrotum, hands, and feet will appear different than gunshot wounds to other locations. Skin stretched over cartilage on the nose and ears tears more like a laceration and the presence of a marginal abrasion is more difficult to assess. Calloused hands and feet also have similar atypical appearances. The scrotum contains loose skin with multiple folds and will not have the usual marginal abrasion seen in other locations. Skin folds due to obesity or breasts in a bra can also create unusual wounds with partial marginal abrasions/soot/stippling on one fold and the entrance on another fold inches away, but when the gun was fired the two margins were in close proximity.

Gunshot wounds in decomposed bodies are very difficult to locate especially if they are purging fluids obscuring blood pooling on the adjacent floor or ground.

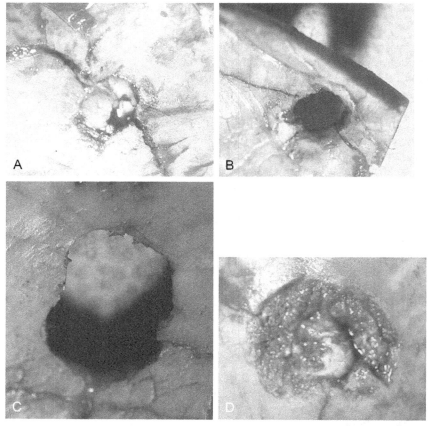

FIGURE 8.17
These photographs depict beveling of the skull and can aid in the determination of the direction of fire. The beveling is created by the unique anatomy of the skull, which is formed by an inner and outer table. (A) The entrance wound on the external portion of the skull with soot deposition around the edge. (B) The corresponding internal beveling on the internal table on the other side of the entrance wound. (C) The bullet then passes through the brain tissue and approaches the internal table on the other side of the skull where its exit appears punched out internally. (D) The external beveling seen on the other side of the skull as the bullet passes outward then through the skin.

Maggot activity can further complicate identification of wounds. Surrounding scene findings or investigative information such as a missing wallet or vehicle, an empty wallet lying on a bed, bloody footprints, or an unsecure residence should all heighten the suspicion for foul play. X-rays of decomposed bodies are recommended to prevent missing bullets and their associated wounds.

Severely obese people and small-caliber wounds, especially .22- and .25-caliber, tend to have very small entrance wounds that can seal closed with very little surrounding blood. These wounds usually measure less than ¼ in. in diameter and may be hidden in body creases. Small droplets of blood on clothing or holes in clothing may be the only clue that can be confirmed with X-rays.

SHOTGUN WOUNDS

The appearance of a shotgun wound is going to change dramatically depending on the distance the muzzle is from the skin. In contact wounds the entrance will range in diameter from ~¾ in. to 1 in., and contain a smooth contoured marginal abrasion and absence of pellets around the margin to the wound because all the discharge has entered the wound (Figure 8.18). Soot can usually be seen in the depths although in a minimal amount.

As the muzzle increases in distance, the wound will enlarge reaching up to ~1 in. to 1¼ in. in diameter, and continue to have a marginal abrasion but gain small scalloped margins along the internal border. This is created as the pellets begin to disperse and is commonly called a cookie-cutter margin. The spreading of the pellets begins about 3–4 ft from the muzzle of the gun.

As the muzzle gets further away, the shot pellets disperse more widely and begin to form satellite entrance wounds around the main entrance wound (Figure 8.19). The major wound will become less distinct and is jagged along the margins. The pattern of the main spread of pellets is important to document via vertical and horizontal measurements, as well as photographically with a right-angle ruler. This pattern can be reproduced in the crime lab to give an estimate of range of fire.

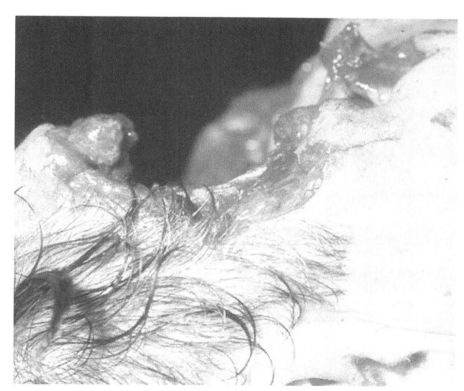

FIGURE 8.18
A contact shotgun wound to the head showing the wide marginal abrasion on the residual skin margin and minimal soot deposition. Note the severe destruction of the cranium.

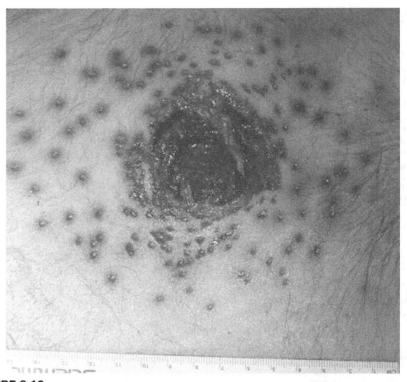

FIGURE 8.19
A distant shotgun wound with a large central laceration from the large number of birdshot pellets entering the wound, and a peripheral ring of multiple pellet wounds showing they have started to separate. Measurement of the width and length distribution of the peripheral pellets aids in the determination of the range of fire by the firearms division of the crime laboratory if the weapon is recovered.

The wadding will also play a role in the wound appearance and assist with determining range (Figure 8.20). The power piston has a unique quality after it is fired as it goes through transition from a tube to the cup opening into three or four petals, then the petals will bend back onto the base of the cup. At close range, the wadding will enter the wound along with the pellets and in the plastic form will not create any distortion to the wound. At 1–3 ft from the muzzle, the petals have begun to open and will create rectangular abrasions in a cross pattern on the margin of the wound. Shotguns with .410-gauge utilize power pistons with only three petals. Those cartridges using the cardboard variety will show no distortion to the margin of the wound until a further distance when they start to float to the side where they create small irregular to semi-oval abrasions. This usually occurs at distances greater than 5 ft. Otherwise, the wadding tends to enter the wound in distances less than 5 ft.

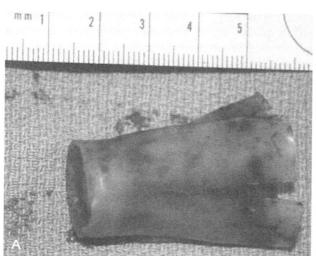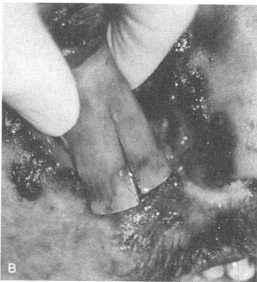

FIGURE 8.20
(A) The plastic wadding from a shotgun wound that contains four plastic petals. (B) The corresponding wound with the margin of the wound containing a rectangular abrasion due to the margins of the petals starting to open, which can aid the estimation of the range of fire.

According to DiMaio, sawing off the shotgun to aid concealment or the presence of choke has not been shown to alter these range estimations until the distance is greater than 10 ft from the muzzle to the victim [1].

TEST-FIRING THE WEAPON

If the weapon is found, the best determination of range is to fire it in the laboratory setting and create various soot/stippling patterns at known distances using the same gun and ammunition. The patterns are usually performed onto white cloth or ceiling tiles so they can be compared to residue photographed on the skin/clothing to estimate the range of fire more accurately. This description needs a preface to court testimony that the estimate given by the witness is only an estimate and that the best determination is done by the above procedure.

REPORT DOCUMENTATION

Gunshot wounds are documented describing the size of the wounds measuring the diameter of the wound, presence or absence of a marginal abrasion, and soot or stippling. The general location of the wound is described then measured either from the sole of the foot or the top of the head. If the wound(s) is/are on the side of the head, the ear canal can form a useful landmark and document a trajectory path. The best location of the measurement depends on the scenario. If the person was thought to be standing, the sole of the foot would be most helpful to reconstruct the scene, especially if there is an exit wound and alignment with the trajectory of its recovery is going to be used, or if the site of recovery is still in question. If the person is sitting in a car or on a piece of furniture, an additional measurement from the base of the buttocks may be useful for the pathologist to document. Also noted is right or left of midline with the midline being defined as a line drawn down the center of the body from the nose to the navel or down the spine.

Next is a description of the path of the bullet and what it passes through, including soft tissue and bone landmarks.

This is followed by a site of recovery or exit wound description. Exit wounds are easy to measure at the outset of an autopsy, but sites of recovery have to wait until the bullet is located. Measurements sometimes get overlooked or are not easily obtained because of their location, but they should be attempted if possible. This aids the documentation of the trajectory, and more information about the degree of upward or downward movement of the bullet as well as the side-to-side movement. For the most part, larger-caliber bullet trajectory is in a straight line and it is the body or body parts that are distorted to create that trajectory in relation to the muzzle of the gun. The positioning of the two parties cannot be determined by the trajectory, rather only that the muzzle had to be on the side of the entrance; what the two parties were doing at the time of the shooting is unknown except to witnesses. The abilities of the person after he or she was shot are hard to say to any certainty unless a bullet involves the spinal cord or extensive destruction within the brain. Cases of injured with severe wounds of the heart, lungs, major vessels, and liver have been known to run city blocks because of residual oxygen reaching the brain to maintain consciousness. The location the body is found may not indicate where the initial confrontation occurred.

Also of note is the need to qualify within the report and remind the jury during testimony that the numbers associated with multiple gunshot wounds are done for clerical reasons only and do not signify or imply the order in which they occur. For later testimony, it is best to be organized about assigning these numbers and is helpful to start at the head and work down the neck, torso, and extremities systematically. Some people assign numbers to each entrance and exit. Others assign numbers to the entrance wounds and letters to the exit wounds. Either way, it is helpful to denote the number/letter after the initial set of clean photos with/without scale next to the wound and in the report. When the photos get presented at court it is much easier to sort out a particular one with this added documentation. Many times the photos are taken out of context or order in their presentation and it can be very easy to become confused. It also allows attorneys and juries to align your report with the photos.

A body diagram with the gunshot wounds numbered corresponding to their respective entrance and exit wounds is also very useful to include as part of the report. Many times photos can be excluded due to their prejudicial nature of the trauma and the wounds become difficult to explain to a lay jury without this assistance.

The following is an example of a gunshot wound description for an autopsy report:

Gunshot wound

Entrance wound: There is an entrance wound on the left upper chest measuring 45 in. from the sole of the left foot and 6 in. left of midline. The ¼ × ¼ in. wound is surrounded by a concentric marginal abrasion without soot or stippling.

Path of the wound: The bullet enters the chest through the left fourth intercostal space, passes through the left upper lobe of lung, aorta, and is recovered in the right middle lobe of lung.

Site of recovery: A 1 × 1 × 0.6 cm lead bullet is recovered in the right middle lobe of lung at approximately 40 in. from the sole of the left foot and 3 in. right of midline. The bullet is collected and labeled as "bullet, right lung." The path of the wound is left to right, downward, and slightly front to back.

When describing trajectories or wound descriptions, it is from the decedent's point of view and his or her right or left, front or back rather than the observer's perspective.

EVIDENCE COLLECTION

Gunshot wound cases present their own set of special evidence collection. It is important that the terminology used in the autopsy report to describe a particular piece of evidence corresponds to the wording on the container and the chain of custody so there is no confusion. It is also helpful to include photographic documentation of each piece of evidence with a patient label, the specific notation, the date and time collected, as well as a two-dimensional (bite-mark) ruler in the photo. Each piece of evidence should have its own notation on the chain of custody and be signed over from the person retrieving the evidence usually to a law enforcement representative. He or she can then transmit the evidence to the evidence locker/crime lab for evaluation and sign it over to them for storage. A chain of custody should reflect the fewest number of handlers of the evidence as possible to ensure that it was handled promptly to its storage or laboratory destination.

Bullets are never collected using metal instruments as popularly seen on TV. This has the hazard of creating artifact striations or distorting the ones present. Typically they are collected using fingers (wearing latex gloves) and placed in plastic containers or paper envelopes after being photographed. It is best not to wash them as the surface may contain trace debris such as pavement from ricochet wounds or fragments of clothing that may aid the investigation. To prevent cross-contamination within the morgue, they should only be placed on clean towels or filter papers that can also be included in the packaging to prevent damage/absorb surface blood. They are wrapped, labeled, and sealed with the seal initialed, dated, and timed.

Paper and plastic wadding and shotgun pellets are similarly handled as bullets. It is important to measure the diameter of the plastic or paper wadding, whichever is recovered, and include a ruler in the photo of these items.

GUNSHOT RESIDUE

The usual evidentiary procedure for a decedent with gunshot wounds is to transport the decedent with brown paper bags secured over the hands. This assists the evaluation of the hands during autopsy and prevents blood from contaminating the hands as it accumulates within the bag. One of the pieces of evidence first obtained after removing the bag is to acquire materials for a **gunshot residue** (GSR) kit (Figures 8.21 and 8.22). Gunshot residue is not needed in all cases and is usually worthless if the decedent lives for a period of time in the hospital or the hands have been extensively handled. If it is going to be obtained it is most useful in the immediate period after the shooting occurred and can be obtained from the victim as well as suspects. It needs to be understood, however, that gunshot residue can be easily transferred from handling the weapon, touching the decedent in areas that have residue on them, or transferred to the decedent if he or she is in a closed space where a gun was fired. Interpretation of the results can be challenging.

Gunshot residue testing is performed using scanning electron microscopy to look for the typical round spheres of gunpowder and testing for the by-products of expended gunpowder/primer materials of lead, barium, and antimony via

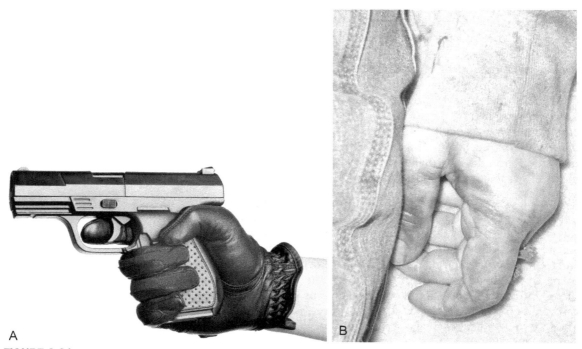

A

B

FIGURE 8.21

(A) The typical grip used to handle a weapon. When it is fired the residue will be deposited on the top part of the hand closest to the firing mechanism. (B) The hand of the decedent with adherent soot deposition on the hand after firing a weapon.

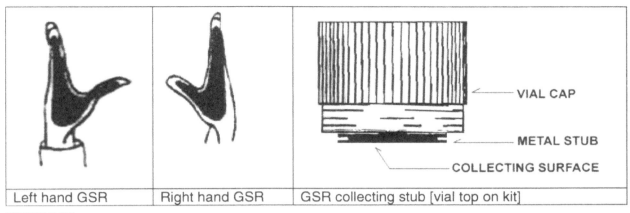

| Left hand GSR | Right hand GSR | GSR collecting stub [vial top on kit] |

FIGURE 8.22
The stub type of gunshot residue (GSR) collection techniques. One edge of the stub is the lid to the vial and the other edge is sticky to pick up any adherent particles. It should only be handled with gloves. Each kit comes with two marked stubs/vials, one for the left hand and one for the right hand. Using the correct stub, it is blotted over the thumb, web of the thumb, and onto the first finger in the area where residue would be deposited following use of the gun or in the area of gunfire [4].

flameless atomic absorption with coupled plasma spectrophotometry. Both must be positive to a significant level to call it a positive test [3]. Before beginning the collection, it is important to wear a clean set of gloves and not touch the decedent in any areas except the hands. The hands of the decedent should not be handled prior to obtaining the test so as not to smear the particles from one area to the testing site.

Gunshot residue kits are of two types. One is a set of metal buttons containing adhesive and secured in a plastic vial. The other type is a cotton swab with clear nitric acid liquid in a vial accompanying the kit. The liquid is used to moisten the swab and swipe the swab along the suspected areas of each hand. It is important to verify or mark each hand vial separately with the appropriate right-hand and left-hand designation. A neutral may accompany the kit and it is to be opened and set on the clean counter while performing the test collection. This allows a background check of the environment to rule out a false-positive result. The swabs (or buttons) are swiped or dabbed along the surface of the forefinger, web of the thumb, and the thumb in areas where blowback from the gunpowder may come to rest if the person were holding a gun in the shooting position (Figures 8.21 and 8.22). For many years gunshot residue testing was not done because the interpretation is difficult and may lead to false accusations by the uninformed, and naïve interpretation of the results. Many times the kit is obtained on homicide or suicide cases to appease defense attorneys or the public that all was done to answer their questions rather than aid the scientific evaluation of the course of events during a shooting.

DNA AND FINGERPRINTS

Decedent DNA sampling onto an FTA card or filter paper can be immensely helpful in reconstructing a scene and blood spatter, especially in cases of multiple decedents or the possibility of the perpetrator leaving blood or other DNA material at the scene. Fingerprints of the decedent are equally useful for this reason as a known exhibit to rule out those from the other unknowns either on surfaces or a potential weapon. Fingerprints can also be used to confirm the identity of the decedent if prints are available in a known database by local law enforcement, FBI, Homeland Security, or Customs (ICE). By entering the confirmed identity of the deceased into the system, it allows the database to reflect current data and to close outstanding warrants.

ESSENTIAL SCENE DOCUMENTATION

The scene investigation findings can be very important in determining the manner of death especially in the single gunshot wound scenario. Some of the items to photograph and make note of in the report is the body position, location of the weapon in relation to the body, position of casings, bullet holes in walls or ceilings, and blood spatter in relationship to the body. Also critical to the evaluation is witness statements and if they match what the scene is demonstrating to the investigator.

Upon arrival, overall views of the body in relation to its surroundings from the corners of the room or at least three or four circumferential views of the scene are standard. If there are areas of the site where the gun safe, ammunition, or gun bag were kept or found those are also photo worthy. Photos of any medications, alcohol use, or notes are also useful. The body position needs to be photographed with note of the weapon in position to it. Include overall, medium, and close-up views of the weapon in the position it was found in if possible. Sometimes it has been moved by emergency medical personnel or law enforcement in an attempt at medical intervention. If that is the case, photograph the gun as it is being made safe for storage. Be sure to include the serial number, position of expended cartridges in the cylinder of a revolver, or the presence of live rounds in the chamber of a semi-automatic.

Location of expended casings should also be noted because it gives an indication of the weapon in relation to the proposed trajectory. It is helpful to take medium and close-up photos of the hands prior to covering them with paper bags to demonstrate any soot deposition or blood spatter. Medium and close-up photos of visible wounds or external clothing is also helpful. After the body is moved, blood can continue to saturate clothing and make the visibility of soot deposition difficult. As the body is being rolled to be placed into the body bag, this is a good time to quickly photograph the back and the amount of blood on the floor under the decedent. Prior to leaving, it is good to take an overall shot of the site where the body was positioned.

Blood spatter is usually projected in the area around the gunshot wound site and tissue with blood can extend across the room, car, or outside location. Blood spatter from gunshot wounds shows a high-velocity fine mist appearance. Larger round to oval blood droplets are low velocity and are not due to the gunshot wound itself unless the victim was able to move around after the shooting occurred. Blood oozing from the wound tends to follow the path of gravity and streak downwards from the site. An aberrant pattern in relation to the current position of the body and the dried blood may indicate the body was moved prior to the investigator's arrival.

Casings from a semi-automatic gun largely eject to the right. Because they are cylinders they may roll or bounce and become somewhat difficult to locate, especially if others have entered the scene. These need to be handled carefully so as not to smear any fingerprints that might be adherent to the surface. The easiest way to pick them up is to use a pen or pencil and insert it inside the casing to lift it into the proper envelope/bag.

Expended bullets outdoors, especially if they are small caliber, are very difficult to locate. Lead is not usually detected with even sensitive metal detectors, but they may be useful to locate casings. Inside a residence, expended bullets are easier to locate in ceilings, doors, or walls. It may be necessary to cut sections of drywall or wood away to retrieve them and it may be easiest to transmit the section to the laboratory for retrieval rather than risk damage to the striations. It may require dismantling surfaces to retrieve them, so having tools accessible in the response vehicle is a good idea. Expended bullets are best collected and placed in small envelopes or plastic containers. Wrapping in paper ensures they do not protrude through the envelope and become contaminated, allows absorption of blood, and pads the surface of the soft lead from damage during storage.

The report should also include the make, serial number, and caliber of the weapon, as well as the number of spent and unspent cartridges in the gun or scene. In multiple gunshot wounds, it is helpful to provide that information to the pathologist prior to autopsy. If multiple weapons are involved, the exact weapon may not be known but generalities of rifle versus handgun or shotgun are useful pieces of information for them.

All items collected from a scene need to be logged into a chain of custody by the collecting investigator and signed over to the property clerk at the evidence storage facility. Many times items directly on the surface of the body are transported with it to be collected at autopsy. It can be signed over at that time by the pathologist to the law enforcement investigator with other articles of evidence. It is helpful if the appearance of the body at the scene is disturbed as little as possible until evaluated by the pathologist. This means no wiping or washing of the wound, removal of clothing, or probing of wounds. Obviously, some disturbance will occur during resuscitative efforts, but it is helpful if emergency personnel can preserve evidence such as holes in clothing or make incisions, vascular attempts, and the like at sites away from wounds.

SUICIDE VERSUS ACCIDENT VERSUS HOMICIDE

The determination of the manner of death in a shooting depends on many factors in addition to the trajectory and estimation of the range of fire and number of gunshot wounds. It is possible to commit suicide with multiple self-inflicted gunshot wounds as well as walk around after nonlethal injuries creating a bloody scene. It is important to keep an open mind when evaluating gunshot wound scenes and evaluate each piece of the puzzle to come to the best determination. When in doubt, treat it as a homicide investigation until the information can be best evaluated by autopsy, toxicology, and witness statements.

Witness accounts may lend information about the recent state of mind of the decedent including health, social, or financial concerns, as well as knowledge of safe gun operation and gun storage. Information that the gun is normally in a gun safe or gun bag implies that certain purposeful actions needed to be undertaken to utilize it on oneself or fire accidentally. The more knowledge one has, the less likely the shooting occurred accidentally. Recent breakups with significant others, loss of job or home, depression including use of antidepressants, or excessive alcohol use all factor into the decision. Notes left at the scene are helpful but may not be totally indicative of a particular action or even when the person was writing the note. Helpful photographs of scene information, such as putting out keys, wills, and personal papers, are useful to indicate purposeful action against oneself. It is always good to take each piece of information systematically, but keep an open mind as families can alter scenes in attempts to make a suicide appear as accidents or homicides or vice versa. Motives for either can be financial, including insurance policies or inheritances. If something is not adding up, follow the instinct to hold the scene if possible until the pathologist can view the body or further information can be obtained from other witnesses or family members. Toxicology results may be necessary to confirm or deny their statements and add information about state of mind.

Russian roulette provides its own challenges as to manner of death. Russian roulette involves the use of a revolver in which a single cartridge is placed into the cylinder with the other chambers filled with empty casings. The cylinder is then spun so the location of the active cartridge is unknown. It may then be passed around or held by a single individual while pulling the trigger at oneself. If it does not fire a bullet, it will be spun again and passed or held usually to the head and fired. Eventually odds prevail and the gun goes off. This scenario commonly occurs during alcohol and/or drug use. Some would call this shooting an accident because of the muddled state of mind by the alcohol use. However, most pathologists call it suicide from the point of view that a person knows that pointing a gun to one's head and pulling the trigger can result in a lethal outcome. The willingness to perform the act is interpreted as a willingness to die and purposefully take one's life. Most are called suicide or occasionally undetermined manner of death.

Case Study

A 30-year-old male was found shot in the hallway of his residence after neighbors called 911 with complaints of shots fired. Upon arrival, police found the young male lying on his back with a 9-mm gun lying beside him. The door to the residence was open. The death investigator was called to the scene and noted gunshot wounds of the left clavicle and one to the right upper back. Abundant blood was present on the clothing where the body was lying in a pool of blood. The door did not have evidence of breakage or being forced open. His wallet was lying on the table in the hallway and the house was in order. Brown paper bags were secured over the hands and he was transported to the morgue for examination.

Head, chest, and abdomen X-rays were performed through the unopened body bag by morgue personnel. No bullets were visible on X-ray. Examination of clothing by the pathologist showed no gross soot on the shirt in the front or back. The shirt was torn near the left clavicle in a slit pattern with frayed threads evident on the outside of the shirt. Examination of the left clavicle wound showed a laceration without surrounding soot or stippling. The right upper back wound showed an oval marginal abrasion with the abrasion located at the 3 o'clock position and fine dusty stippling on the right shoulder in an area of 3 × 3 inches. Internal findings included a trajectory through both lungs and the left subclavian artery with 750 ml of blood in each pleural cavity. The pathologist certified the cause of death as "gunshot wound of chest" and manner as a homicide. The range of the wound was intermediate (arm's length, depending on the caliber of weapon) and the trajectory was right to left, back to front, and nearly horizontal.

MULTIPLE GUNSHOT WOUNDS

Multiple gunshot wound homicides can be very time consuming, especially the search for small-caliber bullets or the sheer number of wounds. It is best to approach these cases with full-body X-rays and have the X-rays available at the autopsy during the search for retrieval of the bullets and the trajectory. Bullets may cross paths and become very confusing.

Some pointers that may help to speed up retrieval of multiple bullets and sort out the trajectories include utilizing an autopsy diagram to draw the location of each entrance and exit wound with an assigned number or letter. Photographing the body with these designations marked on the skin adjacent to the wounds by a black felt marker will greatly aid dictation, transmission of information to law enforcement, and also be useful for later testimony. As a mentor mentioned, it is rare that internal examination will tell you which wound is entrance or which is an exit. The internal examination allows the investigator to link entrances to exits and delineate their path through the body. But the entrance and exit need to be decided to at least a high probability prior to opening the cavities. A chart to record the standard measurements for these types of cases can be found in the Appendix. This ensures systematic recording of each wound easier and dictating the report later. An assistant to record information on the chart is invaluable.

It is also very difficult to link entrance wounds and paths of multiple gunshot wounds with the organs removed from the body. It is best to try to link these up while the organs are within the cavity in their anatomical positions and, if at all possible, to note the trajectory paths during each layer of dissection from the skin and muscle to the bony landmarks to internal organs and paths through them. The initial autopsy has one chance at making certain determinations that can never be retrieved after certain alterations are made so the primary prosecutor has the best view to record this data.

Another useful trick is making a paper copy of the digital X-ray so that as each bullet is recovered its designation can be noted on the paper and the focus can turn to the unretrieved bullets. With more than a couple of bullets in a particular body area, it can quickly get confusing. Yellow sticky notes can even be used to obscure the ones found, further highlighting the ones still needing to be retrieved.

If possible, it greatly assists law enforcement, lawyers, and the lay public if trajectory rods are used to delineate the path from entrance to exit while the decedent is in the customary anatomic position. It should be noted that rods should never be inserted into the body prior to its being opened as they can create a new trajectory path. It is also very difficult with intersecting trajectories to determine the proper trajectory with each wound without viewing the internal organ pathways. Bony landmarks will be helpful in guiding the metal or wooden rods and are best utilized at the end of the autopsy after the bullets are retrieved and trajectories understood.

REFERENCES

[1] DiMaio V. Gunshot Wounds. New York: Elsevier; 1985.

[2] DiMaio V, Dana S. Handbook of Forensic Pathology. Boca Raton, FL: Taylor & Francis; 2007.

[3] Trimpe M. FBI Law Enforcement Bulletin: the Current Status of GSR examinations. The Federal Bureau of Investigation; 2011. Retrieved from http://www.fbi.gov/stats-services/publications/law-enforcement-bulletin/may_2011/The%20Current%20Status%20of%20GSR%20Examinations. [August 2013].

[4] GSR Collection. Instructions for Collecting Gunshot Residue (GSR) kit. Texas Department of Public Safety Crime Laboratory; 2010. Retrieved from http://www.txdps.state.tx.us/internetforms/Forms/LAB-17A.pdf. [August 2013].

[5] Gun Firing. Gunshot Residue. Missouri State Highway Patrol. Retrieved from http://www.mshp.dps.missouri.gov/MSHPWeb/PatrolDivisions/CLD/TraceEvidence/gunshotResidue.html. [August 2013].

CHAPTER 9
Sharp-Force Injuries

Learning Objectives

- Compare three features that distinguish hesitation wounds from defense wounds.
- Identify three features that characterize hesitation wounds.
- List the characteristics of a stab wound, incised wound, and laceration.

Key Terms
Exsanguination
Hesitation wound
Incision
Laceration
Stab wound
Defense wound

Chapter Summary

Sharp-force injuries are time consuming to examine, usually because they are in large numbers requiring meticulous measurements and documentation of each wound. This is hypothesized to result from the inability of these wounds to immediately incapacitate the victim. Unless the stab wound is to the head or spine, the decedent has the ability to continue to breathe and move, causing blood spatter, and usually resulting in death due to blood loss. Delayed complications from stab wound victims who survive can include pneumonia, wound infection, peritonitis, or brain death due to hypoxia.

Investigation techniques important to stab wounds include photographs of blood spatter in relation to the decedent and patterned hand, foot, or shoe prints. The position of the decedent at the scene is also important to document, as well as his or her physical proximity to a suspect knife, all knife holders/drawers, knives in dishwashers, etc. Attempts at clean up or containment of blood should also be noted.

It is important to secure the clothes of both the victim and on any suspects where it is important to look for transfer of blood or other evidence. It is useful to lay out the clothing on a clean papered surface to document these items for posterity.

Sharp-force injuries resulting from suicide are largely based on scene investigation findings and mental health history. Families and previous medical records can prove invaluable in making the distinction regarding manner of death.

INTRODUCTION

Sharp-force injuries are ones caused by knives or other cutting instruments or materials. This category of injuries includes chopping wounds and glass wounds. This chapter will begin with a discussion of the parts of a knife and the documentation needed to record the injuries and rule in or out various knives as the potential weapon. Various evidence procedures as well as the mechanisms of death will also be discussed.

ANATOMY OF A KNIFE

Most knives have a single cutting edge and a dull edge. An occasional knife will have a double cutting edge and create slightly different appearing wounds. The injuries knives create can vary in their dimensions, which may assist differentiating one weapon from another as being more consistent with the injuries on a body. To communicate accurately, some basic terminology of a knife needs to be understood (Figure 9.1).

- *Blade:* The blade is the cutting portion of a knife and is tapered to a point, through a belly (mid) region before connecting to the handle. The length of a knife is measured from the tip to the beginning of the handle.
- *Spine:* The spine is the dull edge of the blade of the knife. This edge is the portion that gives the knife thickness as compared to the tapered cutting edge.
- *Ricasso:* At the handle portion of the blade is a blunt, thicker portion called the ricasso that gives the blade strength at the junction. If the blade enters to this level it will give the wound a squared-off margin.
- *Guard or "hilt":* A feature not seen in every knife is a guard, occasionally referred to as a hilt, which is derived from its counterpart in a sword. It is a dull piece of metal that projects at right angles from the handle and blade and serves as a protective device preventing the hand from sliding down onto the blade during use.

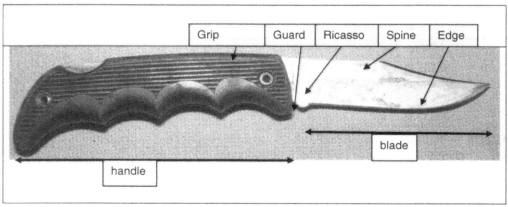

FIGURE 9.1
Depicts the terminology used to describe various parts of a knife [1].

- *Handle:* The handle forms the grip area of the knife. It can be smooth or rough in texture, and contain a handhold grip or not. It may contain fingerprints if the surface has not been smeared or if the surface is not rough.
- *Butt:* The butt of a knife refers to the base of the handle opposite the tip. It may not leave sharp-force injuries but can be used as a blunt weapon leaving blunt-force injuries.

Each portion of the blade can leave particular characteristics to narrow the potential pool of weapons that may have created particular **stab wounds**. This forms the basis of the necessary documentation that needs to be recorded during autopsy. DNA testing in and around the handle for areas of blood transfer is usually sought, as well as fingerprints on the surface or handle.

AUTOPSY DOCUMENTATION

Sharp-force injuries are a general category to include all injuries created by a sharp edge. The wounds have smooth margins and lack bridging tissue between the margins. Within this category are stab wounds and incised wounds (Figure 9.2). Stab wounds are deeper than they are long, and incised wounds are commonly known as slashing injuries or **incisions** (surgical incisions can be an example) and measure longer than they are deep.

It is important to review the distinction between **lacerations** and sharp-force injuries. Lacerations contain abraded margins, have small strands of tissue extending between the edges of the wound, and tend to have irregular margins. This distinction and correct terminology is very important because a laceration is associated with blunt impacts, not knives. Sharp-force injuries have smooth margins, lack tissue bridging, and are not typically surrounded by contusions or abrasions. This distinction is important to aid the search for the correct weapon.

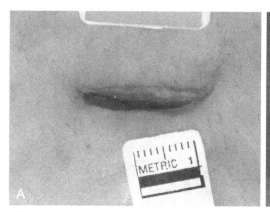 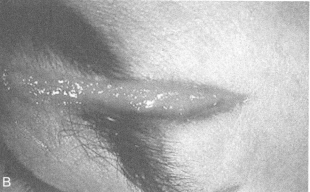

FIGURE 9.2
(A) A stab wound that enters the trunk of a decedent. (B) An incision is longer than it is deep, forming a slashing injury.

MEASUREMENTS

Sharp-force injury wounds are measured in three dimensions: length, width, and depth. The length of the wound is created by the cutting margin of the blade and depends on not only the specific knife but also how far it was inserted. As a knife is inserted and withdrawn, the edge of the wound is cut. The wound can actually be much longer than the width of the blade because of this cutting motion (Figure 9.3). The width of the wound corresponds to the thickness of the blade. A single-edged blade will have a square margin corresponding to the dull edge of the blade. The cutting edge will correspond to the acute angle portion of the wound. The length of the wound will vary due to the cutting as the blade is inserted or withdrawn. The depth of the wound is only a rough estimate of the length of the blade due to compression of the body as a knife is inserted and will also depend on how deeply the knife is placed.

The width and length of the wound is best estimated by reapproximating the edges of the stab wound (Figure 9.4). The margins gape apart due to

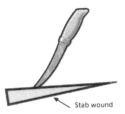

Stab wound

FIGURE 9.3
Diagram of a stab wound.

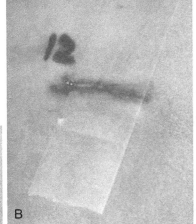

FIGURE 9.4
(A) The measurement of the dull edge of the knife that corresponds to the width of the wound when the edges have been reapproximated. (B) The edges of a stab wound reapproximated and held in place with tape to demonstrate the width of the wound.

the inherent elasticity of the skin called Langer's lines. While the wound is reapproximated, it is useful to characterize the angles of the wounds to determine if the wound is single or double edged. It is important to evaluate each of the wounds for potential abrasions created by the handle or guard of the knife. It is useful to look at multiple wounds to get a sense of the type of weapon used by comparing one to another, as well as to determine if the wounds appear to be caused by a single weapon or different ones.

The square margin of a wound is created by the spine of the blade and the acute angle is created by the cutting edge. If the blade has been inserted all the way to the handle and a ricasso is present, both margins may appear square. These characteristics should be noted in the description of each wound along with the dimensions and approximate location on the body.

The depth of the wound is an approximation and is done while the decedent is lying on his or her back in the anatomic position and the organs are located mostly posterior. Obviously, most people are not in this position when the incident occurs. However, this is the standard that has been adopted by pathologists for documenting all injuries. Wounds should not be deeply probed with a large instrument or finger until the wound track can be identified internally. A thin delicate probe can be used to get a depth from the skin to the surface of the cavities and identify a general direction of the wound path. It can be very difficult to line up wound paths after the surface skin has been reflected due to the elasticity and also the disturbance of the anatomy. Gathering the depth data is best done before the organs have been removed or moved around during the initial inspection.

An example of a stab wound description is as follows:

> Stab wound #1: There is a stab wound of the right upper chest measuring 71 in. from the sole of the right foot and 3 in. right of the midline. With reapproximation, the wound measures 2 in. long × 1/8 in. wide with a square margin superiorly and acute angle inferiorly. The wound passes into the chest through the right anterior second rib, incising the right upper lobe of the lung and ascending aorta. The path of the wound is right to left, downward, and slightly front to back. The estimated depth of penetration is 4 in.

Incised wounds are commonly known as slashing injuries or cuts. They are longer than deep but can also be life threatening when overlying major blood vessels. The location of these injuries can assist with the manner of death or add information about how the injuries occurred. When incised wounds are present on the anterior wrists, antecubital fossae, and isolated neck, a question of self-intent may be raised. Self-inflicted wounds may contain surrounding superficial wounds looking like curved abrasions on the arms, neck, abdomen, or legs. These are called **hesitation wounds** and are thought to be a test of the weapon and ability to inflict the final incision to end life. The wound depths need to be evaluated to note major blood vessel involvement. Many times the vessels retract

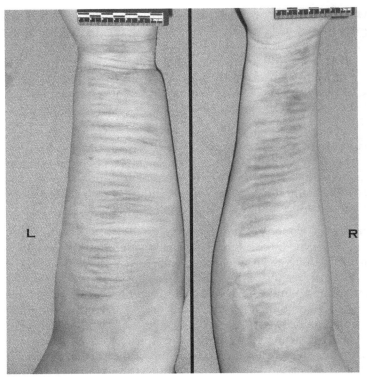

FIGURE 9.5
Numerous healed self-inflicted cutting injuries of both forearms.

under the muscle upon cutting and make this challenging. Scenes of self-inflicted incised wounds can be very bloody and need to be evaluated carefully so as not to miss a homicide incident.

Serrated blades are sometimes used and the depth of the wound will show no distinction from a smooth-edged knife. An indication that one was used is seen at the margin of a wound where fine, curved parallel abrasions may appear that correspond to the distance between the teeth of the serration.

Healed self-inflicted cutting scars can be seen on decedents and may reflect an underlying psychiatric issue pertinent to death (Figure 9.5). These are best documented photographically. Previous medical records documenting suicidal ideation, antidepressant use, or psychiatric illness are useful to determine a manner of death if the cause is related to drug intoxication rather than a cutting injury.

If the incised wounds are located on the backs of the arms or on the legs, they are consistent with defensive wounds as the injured is trying to ward off an attack. This is an important thing to note, as it means a person was conscious at the time of at least some of the inflicted sharp-force injuries. This is commonly brought up in court testimony.

COLLECTION OF EVIDENCE

The importance of collecting a knife is not only to preserve the evidence of the object itself but also the evidence that may be adhering to it, and to protect anyone from injury during its transport and storage. For this reason a sturdy box is useful (Figure 9.6). Companies actually make knife storage boxes but if none are available, a clean pizza box or gun or rifle box can be used. If all else fails, the knife can be placed into a large brown paper bag then a large box until it can be properly stored. Not only does the blade need to be protected but also the handle. Fingerprints may be retrievable. Even on blades that appear clean, the handle can be removed and blood located in the grooves of the handle or between the handle and the metal insertion into it, and can be used to link the knife to the victim.

Occasionally, the scene of the crime has been cleaned prior to it being located. Because sharp-force injuries are usually bloody, blood can become entrapped in tiles, baseboards near floors, behind door knobs, and in various other cracks. The amount of blood needed for a match is very small due to DNA technology. Location of the crime is important to determine a link between a suspect and the victim, as well as to establish law enforcement jurisdiction for investigation. Usually, the location of the crime determines who will prosecute unless they waive the jurisdiction to the one that contains the body. For comparison purposes, it is important to obtain a known DNA sample of each victim to link to a possible crime site or weapon.

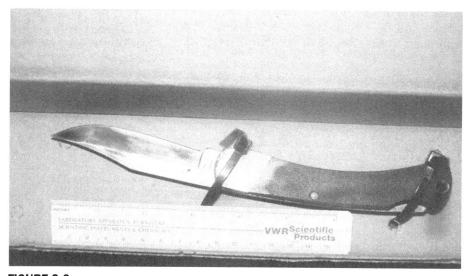

FIGURE 9.6
A knife should be secured for safe transport and handled as little as possible before it is processed by the laboratory. Special transport boxes are available that secure a knife in place and prevent injury by the blade.

Sometimes the knife has been left in the decedent either by their own hand or by a perpetrator. The knife should not be removed prior to its location being examined by a physician (in the alive or dead victim). The grip area needs to be protected from smudging of prints and can be covered by a brown paper bag and secured in place by tape or string at the bottom of the bag. This allows adequate photography to be done and the knife handled in a clean environment to preserve prints and trace evidence adherent to the knife. It is usually not difficult to remove or dislodge the knife, and it should be handled in areas not usually gripped, such as the butt of the knife, sparing the handle as much as possible. It is then placed into a flat box and secured for evaluation by the laboratory.

Documentation of the clothing includes laying out each item and demonstrating the knife injuries through the surfaces if present. Many times the clothing is very bloody and these areas are difficult to visualize. It is useful to have white filter paper available to lay under the clothing defects and also to utilize pointers to show them more clearly. The clothing needs to be adequately dried in a clothing dryer prior to long-term storage in sealed brown paper bags that are then usually placed into bankers boxes. After photographing, the items can be placed into brown paper bags for short-term storage and transferred to the drying room. It may take a few days to adequately dry saturated clothing, and the interior of the drying cabinet is lined on the bottom by absorbent paper to contain draining blood from the clothing.

HESITATION WOUNDS

In self-inflicted injuries from sharp force, the decedent or injured person may have scattered superficial wounds appearing like scratches. They may be located at the margin of a major incised wound or located elsewhere on the body. Common locations are the wrists, forearms, abdomen, or neck (Figure 9.7). It is thought to be a testing of the sharpness of the blade and how much pain is

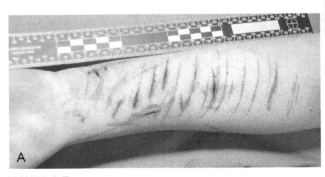
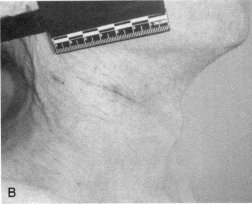

FIGURE 9.7
Two common locations for hesitation wounds to be located: superficial abrasions/incised wounds on (A) the forearm and (B) side of the neck.

associated with the cutting prior to a fatal wound being inflicted. The locations, as well as the number of superficial wounds, help distinguish these wounds from **defense wounds**, or those inflicted by another party.

DEFENSE WOUNDS

Defense wounds are those stab or incised wounds inflicted by another person on the victim and are characterized by being located on the arms or legs as they are being used to ward off knife blows. They are usually on the backs (posterior) of the arms, on the backs of the hands, or on the palms if the knife is grabbed (Figure 9.8). They may be located on the lower legs as they are raised to keep someone away from the vital head, neck, or torso areas.

SURGICAL INCISIONS

Surgical incisions have the same appearance as many stab wounds and the mechanism by which they are created is the same. It is important that medical personnel adequately document any changes made to the skin during resuscitation attempts and place them in the medical record (Figure 9.9). After death, all medical care appliances including chest tubes and thoracotomy sites need to be left intact. If at all possible, any medical intervention should avoid sites of previous stab or gunshot wound injury so that a forensic pathologist can adequately evaluate wounds in the event of the patient's death. If a wound is altered in some fashion, it is advisable to photograph it prior to alteration if at all possible and, at a minimum, document the description in the medical record. Otherwise,

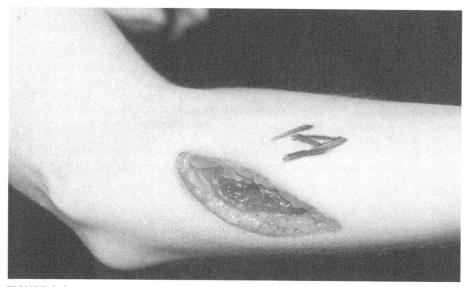

FIGURE 9.8
A defense wound of the arm. They are also commonly seen on the posterior arms and hands as the arms are used to ward off the knife or the knife is grabbed by the hands.

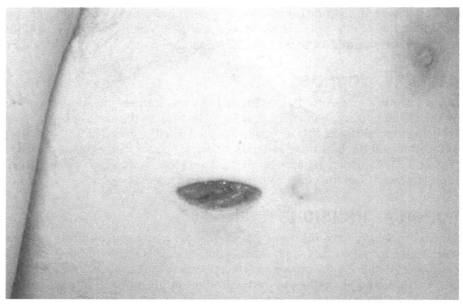

FIGURE 9.9
An incision made by medical personnel to insert a chest tube into the side of the chest. It is important for medical personnel to document resuscitative attempts such as this and leave medical care items in place to differentiate these efforts from homicidal injuries.

Case Study

The office received a call regarding a decedent found dead on the bed of his residence. Upon arriving, the investigator noted a thin, middle-age male dressed in pajama bottoms lying on the bed with a cooking pot beside the bed on a newspaper. An outstretched arm was extended over the top of the pot, which contained about 500 ml of coagulated blood. The house was secure upon the officer's arrival and he had been called by the son of the decedent during a welfare check. Antidepressant medications were on the kitchen counter and multiple personal papers were lying orderly on the kitchen table, including a life insurance policy and driver's license. The son related that his father had lost his job approximately six months previously and was in jeopardy of losing his home due to financial difficulties. Examination of the body showed a deep incision of the right wrist including the area of the vessels to the hand. Superficial cuts were seen over the right antecubital fossa and to the right neck. A bloody kitchen knife was lying on the bed beside the decedent.

it is nearly impossible for the forensic pathologist to testify about the origin of these wounds and may require the clinician to appear in court testimony.

OTHER INSTRUMENTS

Knives are the most common instrument inflicting sharp-force injuries and vary in length, width, serrated or smooth, and single or double edge. Measuring and characterizing the various sizes of the wounds may lend some ability to rule in or out various blades. It should be remembered that when a knife is thrust to its deepest length, it may measure slightly longer than the blade length due to compression of the skin, fat, and body cavities. If a knife is presented to the pathologist for evaluation, it is helpful to make a rough diagram of its appearance and provide measurements within the file and for later testimony.

Other instruments causing sharp-force injuries include machetes, scissors, ice picks, forks, etc. These types of instruments will result in different patterns of the wounds from the usual and typical knife wounds in that they may be paired, appear more as punctures, or, in the case of a machete, have chop-wound qualities or even both entrance and exit wounds if it is thrust through the body. See example in Figure 9.10.

Chopping wounds from hatchets, swords, and axes will show qualities of both sharp and blunt impact depending on the sharpness of the cutting edge. The margins of the wound will be abraded due to the thickness of the instrument, and the destruction of bone will be more severe due to the greater energy dispersed in the wound. Gaping wounds of muscle, bone, and skin will be apparent.

Glass wounds, especially laminated windshields and house windows, can also lead to an abraded sharp-force injury due to the thickness of the glass and its blunt margins. The depths of the wound will show sharp margins of muscle

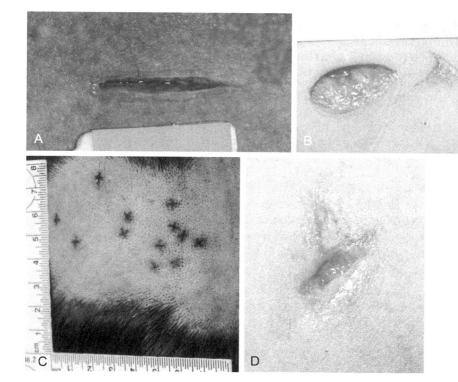

FIGURE 9.10
(A) A stab wound from a single-edged knife that shows the square margin (left) created by the dull edge of the knife and the acute angle (right) created by the cutting edge. (B) The wound's margins gape due to the elastic fibers of the skin (called Langer's lines). This photo also contains a patterned abrasion adjacent to the wound created by the guard of the knife. (C) Patterned stab wounds created by a Phillips-head screwdriver. (D) A stab wound from a flat-head screwdriver.

and vessels. Glass injuries can occur in the armpit or mid-arms if a window is broken, and cut edges injure the arm as it is reached or thrust through. An occasional case is an intoxicated individual who cannot find his or her keys to the residence and attempts to break a window to gain entrance, but results in gaping sharp-force injuries and dying outside the window.

MANNER OF DEATH

Most commonly, the manner of death from sharp-force injuries is either suicide or homicide. Occasionally, accidental deaths may result from unusual circumstances. The investigative information is the key to determining the manner and the presence or absence of hesitation-type wounds. The latter must only be one part in the distinction because some perpetrators inflict superficial wounds to coerce a victim to tell them information or to facilitate cooperation. Suicide notes, evidence of preparation to prevent a mess such as pots to catch draining blood, protective sheets or towels, and history of depression all support a diagnosis of suicidal intent. Someone found outside, blood trails through the crime scene, lack of depression, wider distribution, and the numbers of wounds all support a diagnosis of homicide. In either instance the weapon may be nearby or not. Pots of water, bathtubs of water, or watery blood in the sinks should also be evaluated. Some individuals commit suicide in bathtubs of water so the vessels will dilate and they will bleed faster and also so as not to make a mess. Other times bloody residue can mean the perpetrator cleaned blood off him- or herself or the weapon prior to leaving. Many times the person will have multiple and quite numerous sharp-force injuries and documentation of each wound can be quite laborious. A chart is in the Appendix to assist with recording the various measurements in an orderly fashion.

The usual mechanism of death is blood loss (**exsanguination**), which takes some period of time. The period of time someone survives even from fatal wounds depends on many factors. The number of fatal wounds, which organs are involved, and the underlying health and age of the decedent all play a role in the rate someone dies or collapses. Some victims have been known to run city blocks or even slowly deteriorate in front of witnesses. Since death is not immediate with stab wounds, the number of wounds inflicted by a perpetrator usually increase as the victim keeps moving or fighting during the confrontation. Depending on the size and location of the wounds with exposure of vessels outside of the body cavities will result in how much blood is present at the scene. Arterial blood spatter can be seen as periodic arcs of fine blood spray. Venous bleeding tends to be seen as a pattern of falling droplets.

A rare but occasional mechanism of death is an air embolus. This occurs in arterial stab wounds where the artery is exposed to the air. As blood is attempting to be pumped through the arterial wound incision, air is mixed with the blood causing a "gap" in circulation. Exactly how this causes death is speculation. The appearance of air in the vasculature is very difficult to see grossly or microscopically unless it is a large bolus and may not be appreciated at autopsy.

Another mechanism by which stab wounds can cause death is via compromise of the airway either by a wound directly to the tracheobronchial tree within the mouth or blood draining into the airway from other wounds. This can be sometimes seen as aspirated blood into the more peripheral areas of the lungs. Obstruction of the airway may also be seen as coughed blood onto walls or surroundings.

Delayed deaths from stab wounds can result from the sequelae of blood loss resulting in hypoxic brain injuries (loss of oxygen to the brain and resulting brain death) and infectious complications either via pneumonia, peritonitis (infection within the abdominal cavity), or within the stab wound itself. I have seen at least one death of necrotizing fasciitis (severe sloughing and infection of the skin and muscle) due to a sutured stab wound by a food-contaminated knife. The wound later became infected and inadequately treated, resulting in death.

Examination of a suspect/perpetrator should include photos of the arms and hands to demonstrate any injuries during the confrontation. This person may also have palmar injuries where the hand slipped down from the handle onto the cutting edge during the wielding of the knife. Suspect clothing is also important to document for spatter and droplets from the victim. Bottoms of shoes can be especially important for matching of a sole tread to any track areas at the scene, and also to document the presence or absence of blood. Victim DNA may be recovered from any of these items. It is important to look for discarded clothing in trash bins, burn piles, laundry hampers, or dumpsters. Some items may be located in the washer in an attempt to obscure the evidence. If bleach has been used on areas of spatter, DNA retrieval can be difficult, but consultation from the crime lab may be helpful.

Suicide by sharp-force injury is more common in countries where guns are regulated. They can appear as dramatic injuries with large gaping incised wounds of the neck or as multiple incisions over the arms and wrists. Occasionally they are single stab wounds to the chest or abdomen but are usually multiple. Hesitation wounds or healed areas of self-inflicted cuts are helpful to distinguish suicide over homicidal injuries. Suicidal neck wounds may show an upward deviation to one margin as the knife is drawn across by the opposite hand, and can be deep with visualization of the trachea and multiple sawed cuts over the anterior spine in the depths. Suicidal arm wounds are usually multiple and can be placed vertically or horizontally over large vascular sites. Rarely, hesitation wounds have been seen on the legs or backs of the knees.

Suicidal wounds of the abdomen are rarely seen but may show the adjacent superficial wounds and a deep penetrating wound with or without the knife still in place. Similarly, suicidal stab wounds of the head are seen and usually have the knife still in the skull. Stab wounds of the chest can be single or multiple and, in one instance of multiple stab wounds, a depressed man was witnessed to place the knife on his chest, and ram the knife into the chest multiple times by running into a wall, removing it, and repeating the process.

REFERENCE

[1] Fisher J. Knife Anatomy, Parts, Names, Components, Definitions, Terms. Jay Fisher-World Class Knifemaker; 2013. Retrieved from www.jayfisher.com/Knife_Anatomy_Parts_Names_Definitions.htm#Knife_Anatomy_1. [August 2013].

CHAPTER 10
Sudden Death in Adults

Learning Objectives

- The pathologist hands you, the investigator, a death certificate stating the decedent died of a myocardial infarction due to coronary artery thrombosis. It is the investigator's job to call the family with the cause of death after autopsies are completed. Apply what you have learned about this cause of death and sketch the key features in layman's terms to explain it to the family over the phone.
- List three common causes of death on a death certificate submitted for cremation that would require further investigation and why.
- Review the list of reportable deaths for your state. Formulate three standard general questions you need to routinely ask a physician reporting a death from a hospital to determine if you should take coroner/medical examiner jurisdiction of the decedent or let him or her sign the death certificate.
- A death occurs in a heavy-equipment construction site and you, the investigator, need to respond to the scene to evaluate and photograph. What three items of personal safety gear would you make sure are in the response vehicle before leaving the office?

Key Terms
Atrophy
Proximal
Distal
Aneurysm
Cardiac valve
Myocardium
Alveolus
Thrombus
Embolus
Jaundice
Epi-
Sub-
Hypo-
Hyper-

Chapter Summary

This chapter discusses numerous common natural causes of death that may be seen in the coroner/medical examiner office. Many of these natural diseases also are impacted by drug use or may occur in a work environment. It requires investigative input to make the distinction of a natural death from an unnatural one in many circumstances. Drug levels are helpful but require interpretation in light of the decedent's underlying renal and liver function, as well as a specimen type and underlying pathological diseases. Also discussed are environmental causes of death with investigative documentation that can assist to make the diagnoses.

INTRODUCTION

Sudden death in adults can range from a natural disease such as a heart attack or can be related to drugs or an environmental incident causing sudden collapse. In this chapter we will discuss common natural diseases that can cause sudden death, as well as environmental and drug-related causes that may contribute to or directly cause death.

NATURAL CAUSES OF DEATH

This is a huge category of pathological processes. Only the most common causes will be discussed here. To keep organized, it is easiest to divide this section into organ systems. A quick review of the anatomy and physiology is also given for each organ system.

Cardiovascular

ANATOMY AND PHYSIOLOGY

The heart is divided into four chambers: right atrium, right ventricle, left atrium, and left ventricle. Each chamber is separated by a valve that controls the flow of blood through the heart based on its beating contractions. The tricuspid valve is located between the right atrium and right ventricle, and the pulmonic valve controls the blood flow out of the right heart into the pulmonary arteries. Blood flows through the pulmonary arteries into the right and left lungs. Oxygenated blood returns to the heart via the pulmonary veins. It enters the left atrium and passes into the left ventricle through the mitral valve. Blood flows out of the left ventricle through the aortic valve into the aorta and general venous circulation where it takes the oxygenated blood to the muscles and tissues. Oxygen reaches the cells of the tissues via capillaries and exchanges it for carbon dioxide. Deoxygenated blood returns to the heart via veins from the extremities and tissues into the right atrium. See Figure 10.1.

The aorta is the large vessel lying over the spine carrying oxygenated blood from the heart throughout the body. It is especially prone to acceleration/deceleration injuries from traffic accidents at the ligamentum arteriosum in the arch of the aorta within the chest. This area serves as a fetal structure that closes at birth, but is a weak attachment point for the heart. With sudden stopping, such as in a motor vehicle accident, the heart will act as a pendulum continuing forward with the momentum. This point of attachment is the common site of large lacerations and bleeding into the chest.

In the **distal** region (near the pelvis), the aorta divides into the right and left iliac arteries. These vessels then form the right and left femoral arteries in the groin to supply oxygen to the legs. The return from the legs enters into the right and left femoral veins to the right and left iliac veins then the inferior vena cava (Figure 10.2).

Blood also enters the inferior vena cava from the gastrointestinal tract where nutrients and swallowed medications are absorbed from the small intestine. Blood flows through the liver where nutrients are metabolized and by-products are prepared for excretion. Medications that were absorbed from the intestine are metabolized into active compounds or converted into inactive compounds. This phenomenon is called first-pass metabolism and it is important for the interpretation of toxicology results and the collection of specimens for toxicology. If the

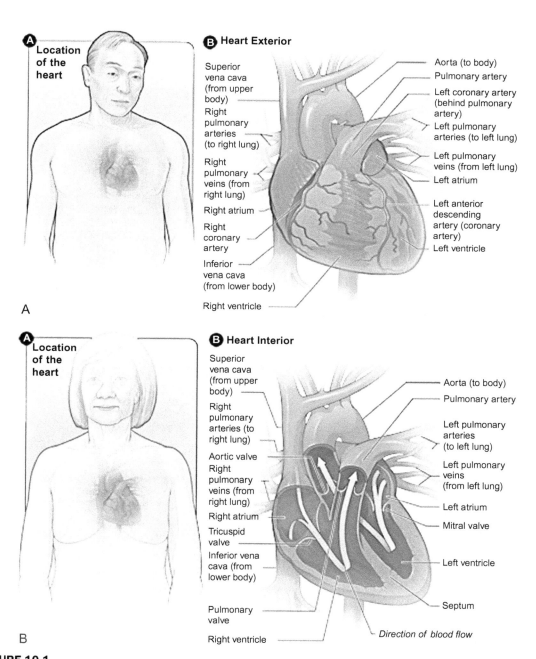

FIGURE 10.1
The (A) exterior and (B) interior heart anatomy, as well as the blood flow through the heart chambers and vessels.

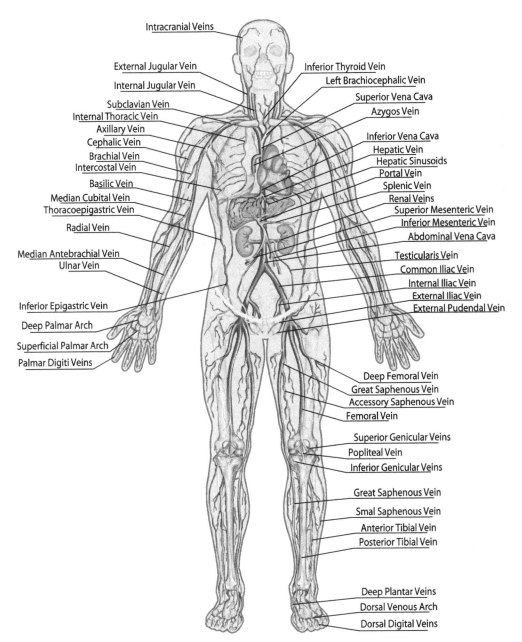

Intracranial Veins

External Jugular Vein
Internal Jugular Vein
Subclavian Vein
Internal Thoracic Vein
Axillary Vein
Cephalic Vein
Brachial Vein
Intercostal Vein
Basilic Vein
Median Cubital Vein
Thoracoepigastric Vein
Radial Vein
Median Antebrachial Vein
Ulnar Vein
Inferior Epigastric Vein
Deep Palmar Arch
Superficial Palmar Arch
Palmar Digiti Veins

Inferior Thyroid Vein
Left Brachiocephalic Vein
Superior Vena Cava
Azygos Vein
Inferior Vena Cava
Hepatic Vein
Hepatic Sinusoids
Portal Vein
Splenic Vein
Renal Veins
Superior Mesenteric Vein
Inferior Mesenteric Vein
Abdominal Vena Cava
Testicularis Vein
Common Iliac Vein
Internal Iliac Vein
External Iliac Vein
External Pudendal Vein

Deep Femoral Vein
Great Saphenous Vein
Accessory Saphenous Vein
Femoral Vein

Superior Genicular Veins
Popliteal Vein
Inferior Genicular Veins

Great Saphenous Vein
Smal Saphenous Vein
Anterior Tibial Vein
Posterior Tibial Vein

Deep Plantar Veins
Dorsal Venous Arch
Dorsal Digital Veins

FIGURE 10.2
The circulatory system. Note the locations of the subclavian vein and femoral veins, which are common sites of toxicology specimen collections. It is helpful to note their locations in relationship to easily palpable bone landmarks for orientation on a decedent.

specimen is obtained from the inferior vena cava prior to passing through the liver or from the heart, quantitative results may be skewed from the actual systemic value obtained from a peripheral specimen. This first-pass metabolic phenomenon is the reason for obtaining femoral blood for toxicology testing.

The heart muscle is supplied by oxygenated blood through the coronary arteries, which originate in the aorta just above the aortic valve. The right coronary artery supplies the anterior, lateral, and posterior right ventricle. The left main coronary artery originates from the aorta just above the aortic valve then almost immediately divides into the left anterior descending coronary artery, which supplies the anterior and lateral left ventricle, and into the left circumflex coronary artery, which supplies the lateral and posterior left ventricle. These vessels are very small caliber and easily blocked by clots or cholesterol deposits (Figure 10.3).

The heart beats synchronously to perform as an efficient pump. The beats are controlled by an electrical current that originates in the right atrium and spreads throughout the right and left ventricles. The current is recorded by an electrocardiogram (ECG), and in the majority of the living, is called normal sinus rhythm (NSR). With decreased oxygen to the heart cells, they can become

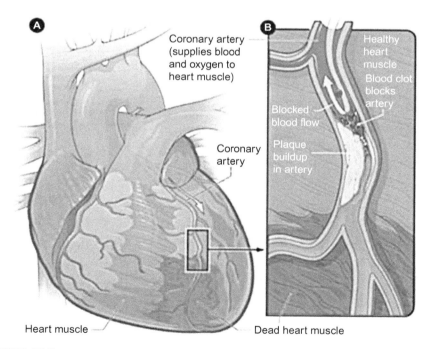

FIGURE 10.3
Graphic depiction of what happens during a myocardial infarction, or heart attack. The coronary artery becomes narrowed either by atherosclerosis or coronary artery spasm resulting in blood clotting and further obscuring the lumen. The loss of blood flow becomes critical to the heart cells (**myocardium**), and with lack of prolonged oxygen, they die, resulting in failure of the cardiac pump.

irritable and the electrical pattern becomes disturbed, resulting in rhythms that can be rapidly fatal (e.g., ventricular tachycardia or ventricular fibrillation). Because it is an electrical phenomenon, there are no anatomic findings at autopsy to confirm an arrhythmia. However, the underlying pathology may be present to precipitate one and that can be documented.

ATHEROSCLEROSIS OR ARTERIOSCLEROTIC CARDIOVASCULAR DISEASE

The most common cause of death in the modern world is blockage of the coronary artery vessels of the heart or arterial vessels in the body by cholesterol and fatty deposits. This process is called atherosclerosis, arteriosclerotic cardiovascular disease (ASCVD), or hardening of the arteries (Figure 10.4). It involves deposition

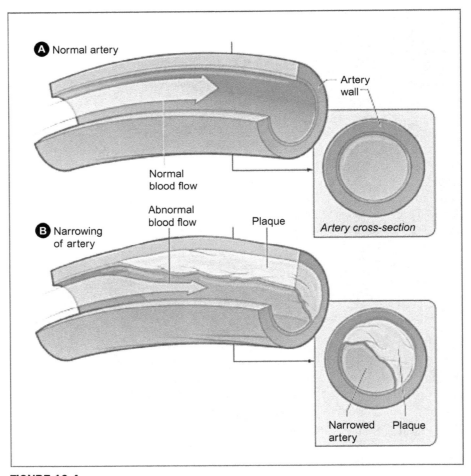

FIGURE 10.4
Atherosclerosis of an arterial wall. The deposit is composed of inflammation, fibrin, fatty deposits, and eventually calcium, causing the inner lumen to narrow. Small blood clots become adherent and may totally occlude blood flow downstream.

of the fatty material along the inner wall of the vessel. This invites inflammation and breakdown of the underlying arterial wall with resulting **aneurysm** formation (bulging of the arterial wall due to weakness of the muscular component), and further accumulation of lipid blocking the lumen or blood clot adhering to the damaged wall with total blockage of blood flow (thrombosis). Blockage of oxygenated blood to an organ causes the cells of that organ to die (called an infarct or necrosis). Heart attacks are called myocardial infarction in medical terminology. The blockage of a coronary artery by a clot (usually adherent to an atherosclerotic plaque) (Figure 10.3) is called coronary artery thrombosis and can be a cause of sudden death due to abnormal heart arrhythmias. Risk factors for atherosclerosis include obesity, poor diet, diabetes, and family history.

Atherosclerosis can also result in blockage of blood flow to the legs resulting in peripheral vascular disease. Signs of this include brown discoloration of the skin on the lower legs and loss of hair. In the distal aorta near the branches to the legs, atherosclerosis can cause an abdominal aortic aneurysm (AAA) to form, which can suddenly rupture causing death by internal bleeding. An aortic aneurysm can be surgically treated to prevent rupture by placing a clothlike vascular graft reinforcement within the lumen. Similar graft material can be used to repair blockage to the femoral arteries in peripheral vascular disease (Figure 10.5).

Atherosclerosis of the heart is treated by stent placement (small tubes of metal mesh) placed within the coronary arteries. This usually requires dilation of the coronary vessel (coronary angioplasty) during cardiac catheterization, a procedure performed using a large intravenous catheter inserted in the groin. This dilation is somewhat risky because the coronary artery may burst, causing bleeding inside the pericardial sac, and sudden death or bleeding. Bleeding may also occur from the groin insertion site. Another treatment for cardiac atherosclerosis is coronary artery bypass graft surgery (CABG), where a length of vein is surgically removed from the leg then attached to the aorta and sutured distal to a coronary artery blockage (bypassing the blockage) to allow oxygenated blood to reach the heart cells. Lack of oxygen to the myocardial cells causes chest pain, referred to as angina, many times treated with nitroglycerin tablets that dilate the coronary arteries, allowing blood to flow around a blockage. See Figure 10.6 for examples of procedures.

VALVULAR HEART DISEASE

The valves may become narrowed by aging, from a disease like rheumatic heart disease, or because they were congenitally malformed, resulting in valvular stenosis. This process may occur in any of the valves but is most common in the mitral or aortic valves. Narrowing of the valve causes more workload for the heart to get blood past the narrowing. Valves may also become incompetent from other disease processes. Incompetence occurs when the edges do not close completely, resulting in backflow of blood during cardiac pumping. This backflow is called regurgitation and can lead to heart failure because of the constant inefficiency of the outflow process. Heart failure results in blood backing up in all the organs trying to return venous blood to the heart. The result is blood and

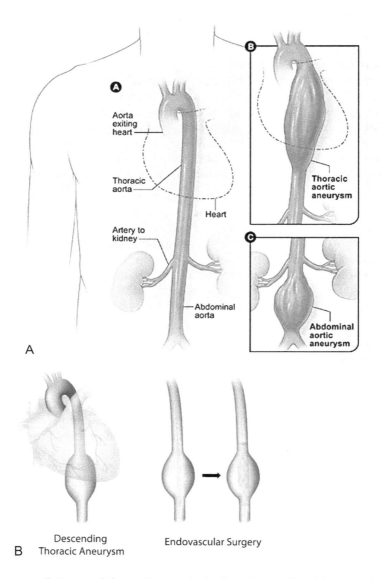

FIGURE 10.5

(A) The two forms of aneurysms that commonly form in the aorta due to atherosclerosis. The bulging outward occurs due to the inner pressure on the weakened arterial wall. The size of the aneurysm becomes critical after a maximum dimension of 6 cm, and is at high risk of rupture into the abdominal cavity causing sudden death. (B) These are repaired by vascular graft material within the lumen. http://www.nhlbi.nih.gov/health/health-topics/topics/arm/types.html

fluid accumulating in the lungs, which eventually causes blood to accumulate in the liver, and fluid in the extremities, which is seen as swelling of the ankles (peripheral edema). Valves can be repaired during open-heart surgery similar to CABG procedures.

HYPERTENSION

High blood pressure puts increased stress on the heart and strain on the vessels due to increased workload (Figure 10.7). If not controlled by medication, this causes the heart to enlarge and outgrow its blood supply. The myocardium becomes irritable and is prone to an arrhythmia and infarction. Increased

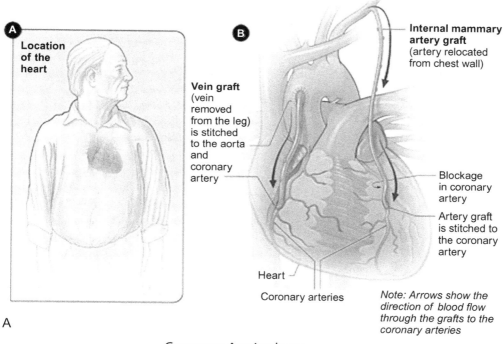

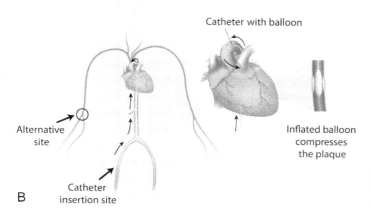

FIGURE 10.6
Depictions of the various cardiovascular procedures that are commonly performed [12].

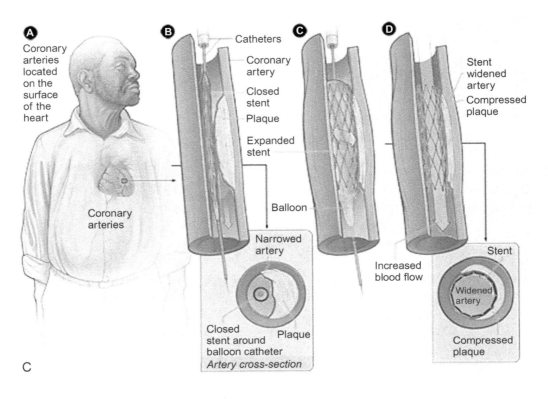

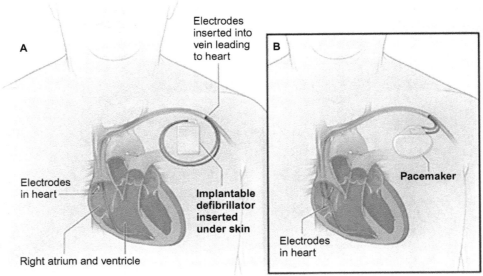

FIGURE 10.6, cont'd

Main complications of hypertension

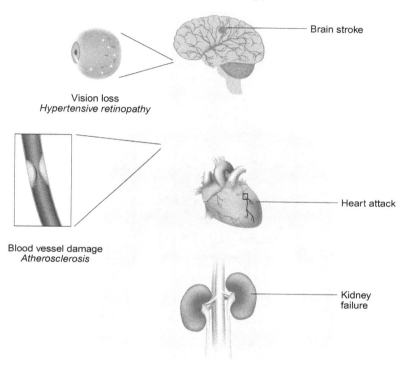

FIGURE 10.7

Hypertension (high blood pressure) is a systemic disease. The elevated arterial pressure puts an increased workload on the heart, kidneys, and vessel walls, and is a risk factor for renal disease, myocardial infarction, and strokes [12].

blood pressure can also lead to ruptured vessels, resulting in strokes or bleeding internally from ruptured aneurysms. Elevated blood pressure also causes damage to kidneys and can decrease renal function for excretion of waste from the blood.

MYOCARDITIS AND BACTERIAL ENDOCARDITIS

The heart is susceptible to viral and bacterial infections. The most common bacteria result from intravenous drug use or as sequelae of Streptococcus infection resulting in rheumatic fever. Symptoms of myocarditis are vague and include generalized muscle aches, mild shortness of breath, and, possibly, intermittent fever. If the cause of the fever or source of the infection is not well documented, it may be necessary to take jurisdiction of the case to aid the public health department to trace exposed contacts.

Bacterial endocarditis is inflammation and bacterial growth on the **cardiac valves** causing their destruction (Figure 10.8). The risk factor for this disease is intravenous

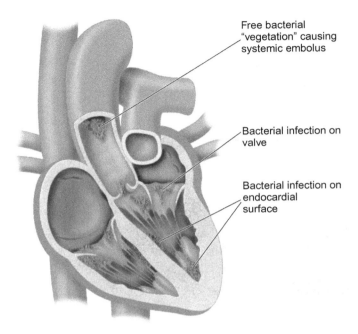

Free bacterial "vegetation" causing systemic embolus

Bacterial infection on valve

Bacterial infection on endocardial surface

FIGURE 10.8
Bacterial endocarditis is composed of bacterial colonies growing on the surface of the heart valves and destroying their surface. The bacterial colonies are friable and may break off, causing colonies to grow in distant organs, as well as occlude blood flow with necrosis. Risk factors are intravenous drug use, long-term intravenous therapy, and dental procedures [12].

drug use with dirty needles. It is occasionally seen in hospitalized patients requiring long-term intravenous therapy. If the person has an underlying history of rheumatic heart disease or structurally abnormal valves, the risk of contracting endocarditis is even greater, and may occur following a dental cleaning. Bacteria within the blood settle on the surface of the valve followed by the body's inflammatory response, which basically dissolves the valve. The patient presents with severe respiratory distress due to fluid accumulation in the body, a new onset heart murmur, and poor heart function. It is associated with a high morbidity and mortality.

DISSECTION OF THE AORTA

Dissection of the aorta may occur in young or older adults. It is more common in patients with a history of hypertension because of the added stress it places on the aorta. It is also seen in a genetic disorder of young males with Marfan's Syndrome, a connective tissue disorder. A dissection occurs when intravascular blood enters the wall of the aorta and separates the layers until it ruptures into a body cavity and exsanguination occurs. Occasionally, it may rupture back into the lumen of the aorta and the patient will live until further bleeding occurs from the weakened wall. The tear most commonly begins in the arch of the aorta and extends distally into the thoracic region. Occasionally, it will also dissect **proximally** and around the coronary arteries, causing sudden occlusion of them or rupture into the pericardial sac. It can similarly extend into the carotid arteries and result in a stroke. Symptoms include pain in the back between the shoulder blades prior to the collapse.

CARDIOMYOPATHY

Cardiomyopathy is a group of diseases of the heart muscle cells causing the heart to assume an enlarged or dilated chamber size, resulting in decreased pumping efficiency and heart failure (Figure 10.9). A dilated cardiomyopathy is related to chronic alcohol use. Other types are restrictive cardiomyopathy, where deposits of material are present within the myocardium, causing poor contractile function. Hypertrophic cardiomyopathy is an extremely large heart, two to three times the normal size, with resulting susceptibility to arrhythmias. Except for alcohol-related cardiomyopathy, these can have a genetic predisposition and follow-up by surviving family members with a cardiologist is recommended.

FIGURE 10.9
Contrasts the changes of hypertrophic cardiomyopathy with dilated cardiomyopathy and their appearance to a normal-size heart. Some of the etiologies of the cardiomyopathies are family related and follow-up with a cardiologist is advised [12].

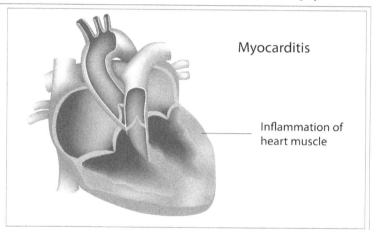

Heart Muscle Diseases

Myocarditis

Inflammation of heart muscle

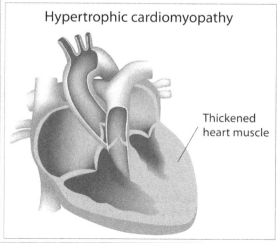

Hypertrophic cardiomyopathy

Thickened heart muscle

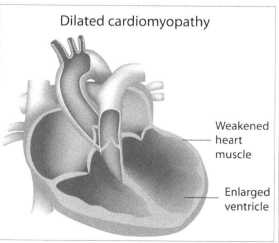

Dilated cardiomyopathy

Weakened heart muscle

Enlarged ventricle

Respiratory

ANATOMY AND PHYSIOLOGY

The main function of the lungs is the exchange of oxygen and carbon dioxide for efficient healthy cell functions (Figure 10.10). The air enters the respiratory system via the mouth or nose and flows past the epiglottis and vocal cords to enter the trachea. The lower airway divides into the right and left main stem bronchi, then bronchioles, and, finally, the **alveoli**. It is within the alveoli where the capillaries of the blood are in very close proximity to the inhaled oxygenated air and the

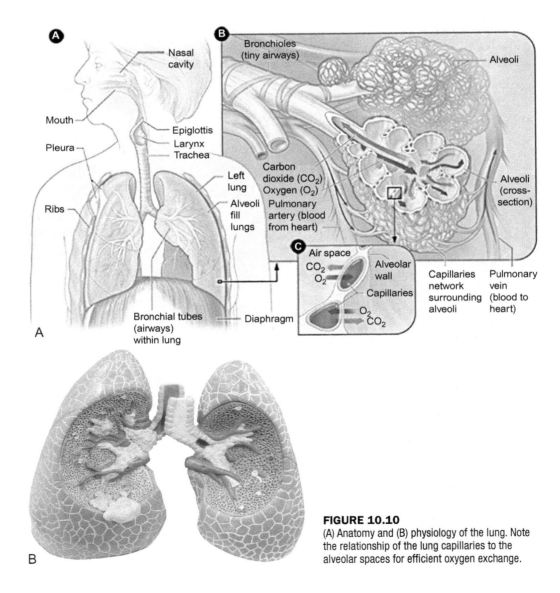

FIGURE 10.10
(A) Anatomy and (B) physiology of the lung. Note the relationship of the lung capillaries to the alveolar spaces for efficient oxygen exchange.

waste carbon dioxide can diffuse from the blood into the alveoli for exhalation. The lung alveoli look very similar to a sponge with the small outlines formed by the capillary walls. Spaced throughout the lung tissue (parenchyma) are small bronchioles that convey the air to and from the alveoli from the larger airways. The more alveoli, the greater ability the oxygen/carbon dioxide exchange, because of the increased surface area the gases come into contact with the blood supply.

Deoxygenated blood enters the lungs via the pulmonary arteries and oxygenated blood returns to the left heart via the pulmonary veins. These large vessels along with the main stem bronchi are located in the hilum of each lung. The right lung has three lobes (right upper, middle, and lower) and the left lung two lobes (left upper and left lower). The easy way to remember this is that the heart occupies the left lung cavity and needs to have fewer lobes than the right.

Because of the close interrelationship of the heart and lungs, heart disease results in lung disease and vice versa. Pulmonary edema (fluid on the lungs) is a common secondary symptom of heart disease (Figure 10.11). Disease states can exist at any level of the respiratory anatomy and result in decreased oxygenation of the blood. Blockage of the posterior mouth or upper airway will cause an inability for the gases to enter and leave the lungs. An example of this is a bolus of food. The smaller airways may become blocked by mucous, swelling by inflammation, or food. Oxygen exchange can become inhibited at the alveolar level by inflammation, fluid, or disease. An example would be pneumonia or cancer. If blood flow is decreased to the lungs or the number of red cells carrying the oxygen is decreased (anemia or blood loss), oxygen-carrying capacity to the body will decrease. Examples of decreased blood flow would include a pulmonary **embolus** where a clot is blocking the vessel or hemorrhage from trauma.

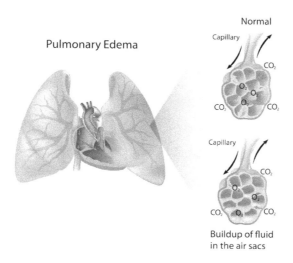

FIGURE 10.11

Pulmonary edema decreases the efficiency of oxygen exchange because the alveoli are filled with watery fluid. The origin of the fluid is commonly heart failure with inefficient pumping or fluid overload due to renal or liver disease.

CHRONIC OBSTRUCTIVE PULMONARY DISEASE

Chronic obstructive pulmonary disease (COPD) is a pathology term describing both emphysema and chronic bronchitis (Figure 10.12). It is a disease process usually resulting from smoking, which causes enlargement of the airspaces (emphysema) and/or excess mucus production with inflammation of the bronchi (chronic bronchitis). Both result in decreased ability to exchange oxygen and the patient experiences shortness of breath, as well as being prone to pneumonia and increased risk of cancer.

PNEUMONIA

Pneumonia is an infection within the lungs that can be acquired by breathing in the infectious organism, spreading to the lungs during a septic event from another primary source, or inhaling food or saliva (Figure 10.13). Whatever the origin, all result in the alveolar air spaces becoming blocked by inflammation,

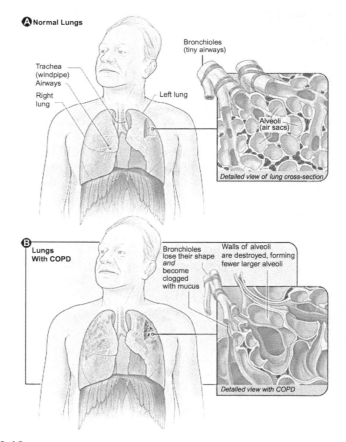

FIGURE 10.12
Describes the changes associated with COPD. The destruction of alveoli (emphysema) and abundant bronchial mucous (chronic bronchitis) decreases the efficiency of oxygen exchange and can eventually make the person oxygen dependent and eventually is terminal.

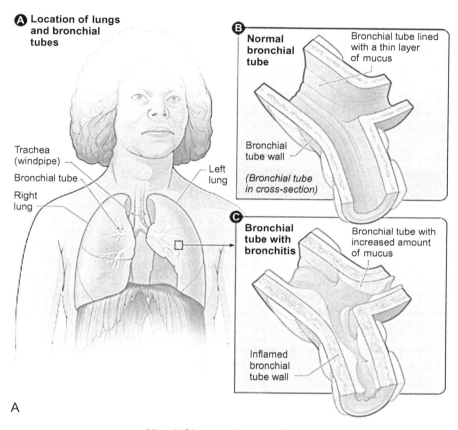

Ⓐ Location of lungs and bronchial tubes

Trachea (windpipe)

Bronchial tube

Right lung

Left lung

Ⓑ **Normal bronchial tube**

Bronchial tube lined with a thin layer of mucus

Bronchial tube wall

(Bronchial tube in cross-section)

Ⓒ **Bronchial tube with bronchitis**

Bronchial tube with increased amount of mucus

Inflamed bronchial tube wall

A

Alveoli Changes in Lung Diseases

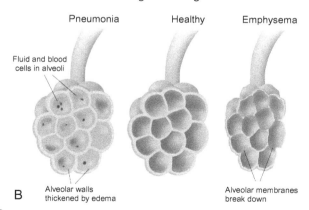

Pneumonia   Healthy   Emphysema

Fluid and blood cells in alveoli

Alveolar walls thickened by edema

Alveolar membranes break down

B

FIGURE 10.13
(A) Bronchitis may also occur in patients without COPD and is an infection of the bronchi with abundant mucous resulting in coughing and shortness of breath, usually with fever. (B) Pneumonia is the spread of infection into the lung alveoli where the bacteria or viruses cause an inflammatory response. Both result in decreased efficiency of oxygen exchange and shortness of breath. Pneumonia is a common cause of death, either primary or as a complication of some other disease process.

mucus, and debris with decreased oxygenation of the blood. Pneumonia is a common complication of traumatic injuries, such as falls resulting in fractured ribs or hips, as a result of assaults or motor vehicle accidents. It can rapidly cause death in or outside the hospital. Whenever a primary diagnosis of pneumonia is the only cause on a death certificate, it should be evaluated by the investigator and be further investigated for any non-natural risk factor that would result in the death being certified as an accident, homicide, or suicide. The death certificate may come to the investigator's attention via the health department vital records, funeral home, or as an authorization for cremation. Prior to permits being given for burial or cremation, the information will need to be determined either via speaking with the treating physician or obtaining medical records.

PULMONARY THROMBOEMBOLISM

A pulmonary thromboembolism is a blood clot that has lodged in the pulmonary arteries, causing obstruction to the outflow of deoxygenated blood from the heart to the lungs. The mechanism of death is sudden right-sided heart failure (Figure 10.14). A pulmonary **thrombus** is one that forms directly within the pulmonary artery rather than travel there. A pulmonary embolus is one that forms elsewhere, becomes dislodged, and travels to the lungs where it becomes an obstruction. The distinction is difficult and usually the term pulmonary thromboembolism is used to describe either origin of the clot.

The importance for the death investigator is the underlying cause of why such a clot should form. Risk factors for thromboemboli include obesity, immobility, and trauma. The trauma may be minimal or massive resulting in bed rest. Other causes of immobility can be recent surgery, especially of an extremity, which would

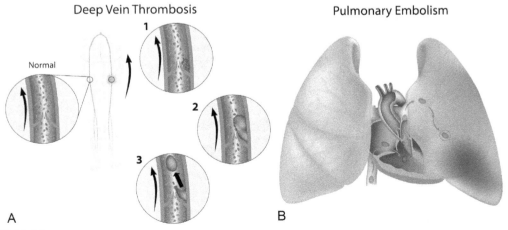

FIGURE 10.14
Pulmonary thromboembolism is a result of blood clots blocking the pulmonary arterial blood flow from the heart into the lungs (B). The clots usually originate in the legs (thrombophlebitis) or the pelvis and migrate to the lungs (A). The lungs are able to inhale and exhale, but the exchange of gases at the alveoli is inhibiting without constant blood flow. The person presents with sudden onset of shortness of breath and chest pain. Risk factors are patients who are bedridden from trauma, those with a clotting disorder, immobile patients, or those with poor leg circulation.

make it reportable in some state law statutes. Pulmonary thromboemboli can also be sporadic, with no underlying trauma, but have familial clotting factors that increase the risk. This diagnosis is suspected by clinicians when a patient presents with sudden onset of shortness of breath, decreased oxygen concentration in the blood, and sudden collapse. Tests done by clinicians to make this diagnosis include a ventilation perfusion scan (a positive test is one where there is ventilation but no perfusion of the lung, called a VQ mismatch) or Doppler studies of lower extremities to determine the presence of vascular clots. The importance for an investigator is to recognize that this diagnosis may have resulted from trauma and will usually require evaluation by the pathologist to determine the cause and manner of death. Many times this results in an autopsy to confirm the presence of the pulmonary thromboembolism and may require dissection of the extremities to determine the site of origin. Sometimes the entire clot has moved to the lungs and no longer resides within the legs; other sources of these clots include the pelvis or pelvic organs. Occasionally, a vascular catheter or nidus will be present within the pulmonary artery causing the clot to form directly under the same set of risk factors.

PULMONARY HYPERTENSION

Pulmonary hypertension is high blood pressure isolated only to the lungs and is caused by cardiac disease or by abnormalities of the pulmonary arteries. It can progress to eventual heart failure and death. It is not usually a reportable case to a death investigation department unless there is a therapeutic misadventure in its treatment that causes death (Figure 10.15).

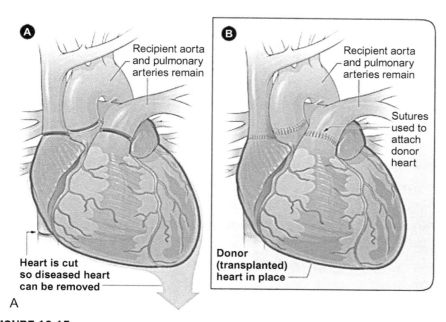

FIGURE 10.15
Transplantation of the heart, lungs, or heart–lung transplant together are not uncommon and may be the only treatment available for some patients. (A) The incisions made by the transplant team to remove a heart and insert in a recipient.

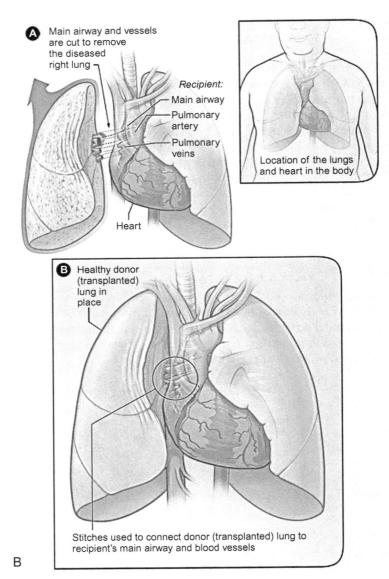

A Main airway and vessels are cut to remove the diseased right lung

Recipient:
Main airway
Pulmonary artery
Pulmonary veins

Location of the lungs and heart in the body

Heart

B Healthy donor (transplanted) lung in place

Stitches used to connect donor (transplanted) lung to recipient's main airway and blood vessels

B

FIGURE 10.15, cont'd
(B) The incisions made to recover and implant lungs for transplantation. It is helpful to understand these procedures when donor teams are requesting organs from decedents falling under the jurisdiction of the death investigator.

Liver

ANATOMY AND PHYSIOLOGY

The liver is an important organ to detoxify chemicals and medications; assist with metabolism of fats, sugars, and proteins to basic building blocks; and aid digestion via bile secretions. It is an extremely vascular organ and sensitive to low blood flow in periods of shock, but has regenerative properties to heal itself to some extent. If toxic materials accumulate within the liver or it is frequently exposed to abuse, it will fail or scar, decreasing its efficiency, which can lead to death. Signs of liver failure or disease are yellow discoloration of the skin or whites of the eyes (**jaundice**), accumulation of liquid in the abdominal cavity (ascites), and swelling of the feet and hands (edema). Because blood returning to the heart from the lower torso and gut must filter through the liver first, scarring can cause increased pressure in the venous system, resulting in enlargement of small vessels within the esophagus and stomach (varices) that can easily bleed, sometimes massively, resulting in death.

CIRRHOSIS

The scarring that forms in the liver is called cirrhosis and many times results from alcoholism, hepatitis B or C, or abnormal accumulation of minerals such as copper. Cirrhotic patients who die at home are usually reported to the death investigator because the scene can show large areas of blood loss. The cirrhosis inhibits drug excretion and routine medications can accumulate causing death by drug intoxication or combined with alcohol use. The scarring also causes increased pressure to develop in the portal vein and backup of blood into the esophageal and splenic veins. The esophageal veins can become greatly dilated causing rupture and massive bleeding via vomiting or from the rectum (Figure 10.16).

Liver failure occurs when the liver has shut down and is no longer able to keep up with the body's needs. The liver may be necrotic or cirrhotic. The decedent turns bright yellow and may require dialysis if the cause is thought to be reversible. Causes of liver failure include acetaminophen overdose, extended periods of low blood pressure, hemorrhage, or end-stage cirrhosis from alcohol use or hepatitis. When this type of case comes to the attention of the death investigator, it will need questioning as to the underlying etiology of the failure to determine if it falls within the jurisdiction of the office. Many times, the initial event occurred some days prior, and admission blood specimens may be needed from the hospital laboratory to evaluate a drug screen.

Easy bruisability is frequently seen in those with liver disease because the liver is the site of production of the blood-clotting factors. With cirrhosis and other diseases of the liver, production of these proteins will be lacking. Some of the factors require vitamin K to produce them, and in the past, vitamin K was commonly given to cirrhotic patients who were bleeding in an attempt to correct the deficit. Minimal trauma, even medically induced, can result in huge contusions or oozing from wounds. This bleeding can also extend to minimal brain trauma resulting in intracranial hemorrhage from a minor fall. The fall can be remote from the time of death or recent. Any bruising about the head or chest should alert the investigator to have the body further evaluated by the forensic pathologist.

Not all those with cirrhosis have jaundice of the skin or eyes. Other disease states that can affect coagulation include fatty change within the liver, which is also seen in alcoholics, chronic hepatitis, or an inherited condition due to lack of a particular coagulation factor. The liver is a common site of metastatic tumors

Liver, Gallbladder, Pancreas and Bile Passage

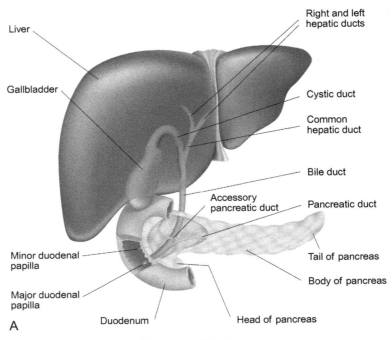

A

Esophageal Varices

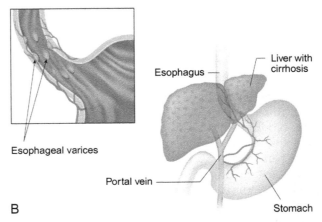

B

FIGURE 10.16
(A) Relationship of the liver to the stomach, pancreas, and blood flow to esophagus. With cirrhosis of the liver, the scarring causes increased venous pressure and blood backs up into the portal vein system, resulting in an enlarged spleen and enlarged veins in the esophagus called varices (B). The varices may rupture causing massive internal bleeding and death.

to spread from the primary origin within the bowel, pancreas, lung, ovary, or breast, and may also exhibit jaundice.

HEPATITIS

There are multiple kinds of hepatitis, but A, B, and C are the most common. Hepatitis A is contracted by fecal oral contamination, usually of food by someone who has the disease. It is a relatively short-lived illness with jaundice and a low-grade fever, but communicable. Long-term disease and chronic carrier states are not seen in hepatitis A. The person may feel sick with these low-grade symptoms, but will recover without treatment. The importance in making the diagnosis is to prevent the spread of the disease and distinguish it from other types of hepatitis or causes of jaundice.

Hepatitis B and C are caused by different viruses than A and are both associated with acute and chronic liver disease. They are acquired through intravenous drug use or exposure to body fluids, either via blood or sexual contact. Hepatitis B and C are associated with chronic hepatitis and cirrhosis, which can lead to liver failure. Hepatitis B has immunizations available to prevent transmission but hepatitis C does not. Either hepatitis B or C may remain only as an acute disease without progressing to a chronic state, but C commonly does become chronic. All types of hepatitis are reportable to the health department for tracing contacts to prevent further transmission.

LACERATION

The capsule of the liver is tense and easily lacerated by direct blows or compression of the overlying ribs, which is commonly seen in motor vehicle accidents. Occasionally CPR during resuscitation can lacerate the liver as well because of the compression of the ribs. Since the liver is very vascular, a laceration can lead to internal bleeding. In the postmortem state, blood may ooze from a superficial laceration, but is usually a lower quantity than that seen in motor vehicle accidents.

Gastrointestinal tract

ANATOMY AND PHYSIOLOGY

The gastrointestinal tract includes the esophagus, stomach, and small and large intestines. Food enters the mouth where chewing decreases the size of the food particles to be swallowed. The tongue moves the food to the back of the mouth where the epiglottis closes over the airway protecting it from inhalation. The food passes down the esophagus to the stomach where it is mixed with acid and further decreased in size for better absorption. It passes through the pyloric valve into the duodenum where pancreatic digestive enzymes are added. The small intestine is the site of absorption of the food nutrients and drugs taken orally. The first part of the intestine is called the jejunum followed by the ileum. By the time the food reaches the lower ileum, it is still a thick liquid, and passes through the ileocecal valve into the ascending colon, followed by the transverse colon, then the descending colon and rectum. The large bowel is the site of water reabsorption and does not absorb nutrients. See Figure 10.17.

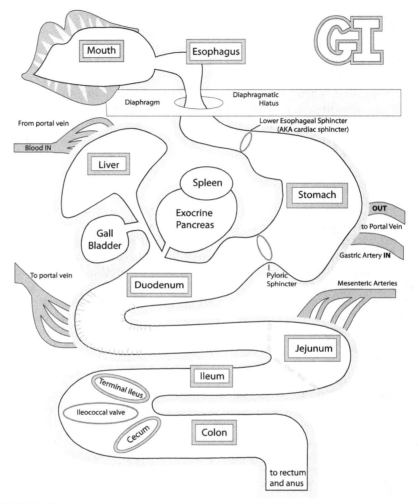

FIGURE 10.17
Outlines the relationship of the gastrointestinal tract to the liver and absorption of nutrients. It is important to understand the relationship of the blood flow from the small intestine to the liver. Orally ingested medications are absorbed into the blood from the small intestine and many undergo metabolic changes in the liver to active or inactive compounds. This is the first-pass phenomenon. The blood then goes to the heart before becoming systemic. If toxicology specimens are retrieved in the blood from the heart or the blood from the gut, the quantitative values may not be representative of systemic values and be artificially high.

BLEEDING

Bleeding may occur anywhere within the tubular system but most commonly from the esophagus, stomach, or duodenum. Causes of bleeding from the esophagus are most commonly dilated veins (varices) from a cirrhotic liver. The veins become greatly distended with cirrhosis and even the process of eating may erode off the surface epithelium, exposing the vein to rupture and massive bleeding.

Bleeding may also occur from gastric erosions over a large surface area. This type of bleeding is less dramatic but can also be a result of chronic alcohol use.

Gastric or duodenal ulcers are craters that form in the lining of the stomach/duodenum that can erode downward into an artery or vein causing massive bleeding. They may also perforate through the stomach or intestinal wall, leaking gastric acid and food into the sterile peritoneal cavity, resulting in peritonitis. After a ruptured esophagus, stomach, intestine, or appendix, peritonitis will rapidly occur and the situation is life threatening unless the rupture is repaired.

An obstruction of the bowel may also cause peritonitis. It can be a twisted bowel, some internal blockage such as a tumor or polyp, foreign material, or an incarcerated hernia where the bowel is pinched in the hernia sac. Sudden death may follow if not medically treated. Signs of blockage include distended abdomen without decomposition, early decomposition changes over the abdomen even in the early postmortem period, and, if bleeding has occurred, dark, tarry feces on the buttocks or clothing.

Occasionally abdominal aortic aneurysms may erode into the lumen of the intestines and cause massive bleeding out the anus. Most of these cases might not be a death investigation case, other than they die suddenly at home with large areas of blood that concerns detectives, or the person is without a treating physician.

Endocrine abnormalities
ANATOMY AND PHYSIOLOGY OF THE PANCREAS
The pancreas is the site of manufacture of multiple digestive enzymes and insulin for the metabolism of sugars (glucose). The digestive enzymes enter the duodenum along with bile through the common bile duct. This duct can become blocked by gallstones and cause the enzymes to be released into the pancreatic tissue resulting in self-digestion of the tissue. The intestines have checks and balances to prevent this, but tissues such as the pancreas and peritoneum do not, which causes pancreatitis and peritonitis. Pancreatitis can also occur in alcoholics without a blockage by gallstones. Long-term pancreatitis can cause a loss of digestive enzymes and insulin, the other product of the pancreas. Insulin is necessary to usher glucose into the cells where it can be used by the metabolic machinery for energy production. Without insulin, glucose remains in the bloodstream and is able to reach high levels, resulting in diabetes mellitus.

DIABETES MELLITUS
Diabetes mellitus takes two forms: type I (insulin dependent) and type II (medication dependent). The pathology is the same in both types, and the only variation is how quickly the glucose can get out of control (Figure 10.18). In type I it can be very rapid within a few hours, and type II usually is a more chronic elevation. However, both can result in a condition called diabetic ketoacidosis.

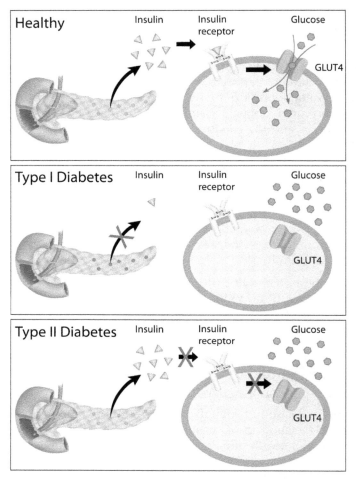

FIGURE 10.18
Contrasts the cellular differences of type I and type II diabetes. Insulin is produced by the islet cells of the pancreas and is necessary for glucose to enter cells where it is utilized for energy production. In type I the pancreatic islet cells are destroyed and there is not enough insulin to escort the glucose into the cell. In type II, the body is able to produce insulin but in decreased amounts for the demand, and the cell receptors are resistant to it so the glucose is not able to enter the cell. Both types I and II result in elevated blood glucose.

Because insulin is needed for glucose to enter the cell for the metabolic machinery, if glucose is not available to it, the machinery goes to its backup plan. It begins to inefficiently metabolize fats and proteins within the cell to generate energy. This creates products called ketones and acids, which alter the body's delicate acid-base balance. Electrolyte abnormalities will develop and be seen predominately as rising potassium in the blood. This can reach lethal levels with cardiac arrest.

Testing for glucose levels is easily done by diabetics using a home glucometer and adjusting insulin levels to prevent the acidosis. The same testing can be done in decedents, but on vitreous looking for the elevated glucose. Diabetic ketoacidosis is usually suggested with postmortem vitreous glucose values greater than 400 mg/dl. Testing for ketones is easily done using urine dipsticks and looking for the excreted ketones and excreted glucose when it reaches very high levels. These products are associated with the early symptoms of diabetes, which are increased thirst and frequent urination.

Too much insulin and low blood glucose can also result in a lethal outcome. This occurs if the person takes the insulin but doesn't eat or takes too much insulin in relationship to the intake of food. Blood glucose needs to be above 60 for the brain cells to maintain consciousness. This is why paramedics give a bolus of glucose upon finding someone unconscious. If the unconsciousness is due to low glucose, the patient can have rapid reversal of symptoms. Postmortem, a low glucose is impossible to diagnose because the vitreous glucose normally begins to drop immediately upon death, and if already at a low level to begin with, it will be 0 at a postmortem reading. However, if the premortem glucose was 800 mg/dl, testing will show it to still be elevated postmortem, depending on the estimated interval between death and testing.

Diabetes is a risk factor for other diseases that can result in sudden death, including atherosclerotic cardiovascular disease, peripheral neuropathy resulting in injuries to feet and hands, ulcers of the legs and feet from poor circulation, impaired vision, cardiac disease, and strokes. In type I any small infection can precipitate ketoacidosis.

ANATOMY AND PHYSIOLOGY OF THE THYROID GLAND

The thyroid gland is responsible for how rapidly metabolic machinery works in the body. It tends to equilibrate cell machinery over days to weeks rather than making minute-to-minute changes. Thyroid gland diseases rarely cause sudden death.

ANATOMY AND PHYSIOLOGY OF THE PITUITARY

The pituitary, in conjunction with the hypothalamus in the brain, controls the thyroid, adrenal, and growth hormones, as well as the production of eggs or sperm by the ovaries and testes, respectively. It also secretes an antidiuretic hormone, controlling the water balance of the kidneys by increasing water reabsorption, and making the urine more concentrated.

Diabetes insipidus is a disease commonly confused with diabetes mellitus. However, it is a totally different disease caused by an abnormality in the antidiuretic hormone system within the pituitary, or within the kidneys, where the hormone acts. This abnormality results in large quantities of water being excreted and excess urination. Therefore, the relationship to the symptoms of early diabetes mellitus are increased thirst (polydypsia) and increased urination (called polyuria). The blood sugar in diabetes insipidus is normal and there is no risk for ketoacidosis.

Renal abnormalities

ANATOMY AND PHYSIOLOGY OF THE KIDNEYS

The kidneys are the filtering machine of the body and sort out the by-products of cellular metabolism that are no longer useful from the ones needed to maintain homeostasis (balance) of the cell processes. The kidneys excrete harmful products of protein metabolism, and yet retain a level of blood protein that is healthy for water balance (Figure 10.19). They also maintain electrolyte balance by excreting any excess materials not needed, such as excess salt, calcium, or potassium that may be ingested. Some useful products are normally reabsorbed, including glucose. A disease affecting the kidneys will affect this delicate balance of filtering, which can create electrolyte abnormalities resulting in disturbance of water balance or cardiac arrhythmias. Renal failure is the term used to describe this electrolyte abnormality due to damage to the filtering mechanism of the kidneys. The kidneys also dispose of protein waste, which is monitored by blood tests for urea and creatinine values. Renal failure can be acute or slow in onset, termed chronic. Acute failure can occur with sudden blood loss damaging the microscopic structures responsible for the filtration, called glomeruli. Chronic renal failure results from diseases such as diabetes mellitus or atherosclerosis.

Nervous system

ANATOMY AND PHYSIOLOGY OF THE BRAIN AND SPINAL CORD

The brain is responsible for conscious thoughts, control of movement through the spinal cordand primitive nonconscious things such as respiration, cardiac activity, swallowing, and movement of food through the gastrointestinal tract (Figure 10.20). It is possible to lose large areas of the cortex where consciousness resides and still maintain respiratory and cardiac functions. This is declared as brain death. The brain works much like an electrical circuit with the "wires" between different areas insulated from cross-communication by a material called glial tissue. The neurons are the main cellular structures with the wires formed by delicate strands of neural tissue extending from them. To consciously move the arm, it requires a group of these wires to form a tract and extend from the brain to the spinal cord and eventually to the arm. Disruption anywhere along this tract can impair the conscious movement. The spinal cord is composed of thousands of the wires forming tracts extending from the brain to all body functions, including the organs and muscles. Branches off the spinal cord occur at all levels. Disruption of the spinal cord in the neck affects all functions below the neck—movement of the arms and legs—with the possibility of respiration affected, depending on the level of the transection. In contrast, a disruption in the lower spinal cord at the waist will only affect the legs and bladder function with cardiac and respiratory activity intact.

The nervous system includes the brain, spinal cord and its coverings, and skull. Any of these layers may become involved by disease processes. From the outer

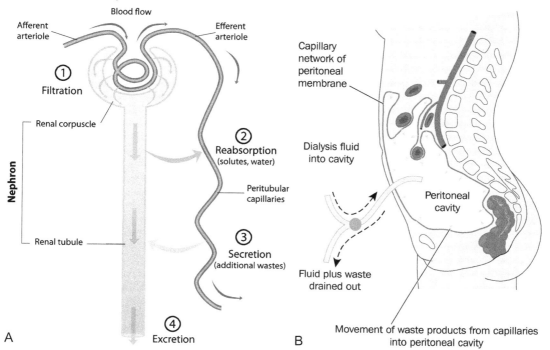

Basic steps in urine formation

Blood flow

Afferent arteriole

Efferent arteriole

① Filtration

Renal corpuscle

Nephron

Renal tubule

② Reabsorption (solutes, water)

Peritubular capillaries

③ Secretion (additional wastes)

④ Excretion

A

Continuous ambulatory peritoneal dialysis

Capillary network of peritoneal membrane

Dialysis fluid into cavity

Peritoneal cavity

Fluid plus waste drained out

Movement of waste products from capillaries into peritoneal cavity

B

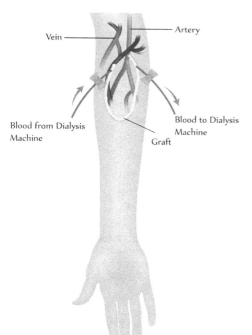

Vein

Artery

Blood from Dialysis Machine

Blood to Dialysis Machine

Graft

C

FIGURE 10.19
(A) The efficiency of the microstructures within the kidney called glomeruli and tubules. Their job is to filter the blood and rid the body of excess water, minerals, electrolytes, and other by-products to maintain a steady-state balance. (B) If the kidneys fail, these materials accumulate and can cause death. Treatment is via peritoneal or (C) hemodialysis, which operates as artificial kidneys.

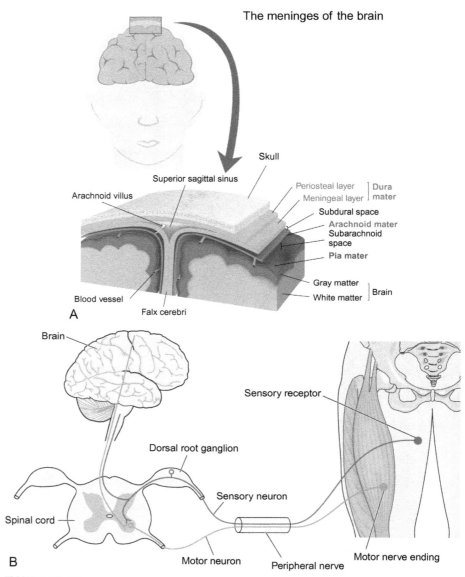

The meninges of the brain

Skull

Superior sagittal sinus

Arachnoid villus

Periosteal layer] Dura
Meningeal layer] mater

Subdural space

Arachnoid mater
Subarachnoid space

Pia mater

Gray matter] Brain
White matter

Blood vessel

Falx cerebri

A

Brain

Sensory receptor

Dorsal root ganglion

Sensory neuron

Spinal cord

Motor neuron

Peripheral nerve

Motor nerve ending

B

FIGURE 10.20
(A) The relationship of the dura to the brain and skull. Note the subdural and epidural spaces, which are sites of potential hematomas. (B) The relationship of the brain to coordination of movement. Single nerve fibers extend from the brain to the lower portions of the spinal cord, then to the muscles. Interruption of the tract in its course from the brain, spinal cord, or nerve fibers to the muscle can affect the ability to control movement.

table of the skull inward, the layers progress from bone, to dura, then to brain or spinal cord tissue. Between the nervous tissue and the dura is a potential space called the subdural space (**sub-**, meaning below). Between the dura and the skull is a small potential space called the epidural space (**epi-**, meaning above).

A filmy layer of nearly clear membrane lies directly on the brain called the arachnoid with a potential space called the subarachnoid space. Trauma is the most common cause of pathology within the nervous system and can manifest as bleeding in any of the potential spaces or even into the brain or spinal cord tissues themselves.

INTRACRANIAL HEMORRHAGE

This is a general term that encompasses different pathologies and describes any type of bleeding within the skull. When seen on a death certificate not issued by the coroner/medical examiner, it requires further investigation to define which of the pathologies it is, and to determine if it is an unnatural death. This will require the admission medical records including the emergency personnel report, admission history and physical, as well as CT/MRI scan reports. Depending on this information, it may require the body to be brought to the office for examination. Sometimes it can be very difficult from the history to differentiate whether a coexistent pathology resulted in a fall or the fall resulted in the pathology. Examination of the brain by the pathologist may be necessary to sort out the findings.

Intracerebral hemorrhage usually refers to a stroke (Figure 10.21). A stroke results from a blockage of blood flow to an area of the brain by a clot and results in necrosis (cell death). It can also result from a ruptured capillary vessel, with bleeding into the brain tissue, causing swelling and cell death. Risk factors for a stroke include hypertension and atherosclerotic cardiovascular disease and all the risk factors that have been mentioned for either of those.

Subdural hemorrhages are blood accumulations between the dura membrane and the surface of the brain. The origin of this blood is ruptured veins that extend across this space and is caused by acceleration/deceleration injuries. Bleeding occurs more commonly if the brain is **atrophied** (shrunken, usually due to aging or disease), which stretches these veins. Subdural hemorrhages commonly occur in alcohol-related deaths, as well as the elderly, and can occur from a standing height or even minimal trauma, leaving few surface skin features of the underlying hemorrhage. It can present with symptoms of slowly decreasing consciousness with or without an episode of witnessed trauma. It is easily diagnosed by internal examination of the skull or a clinical CT/MRI scan. Occasionally an intracerebral hemorrhage can rupture through the cortex and extend into the subdural space. Examination of the inner skin surface (called the galea) may also aid the differentiation by locating a contusion not previously seen externally. Skull fractures not previously appreciated may also be identified with an internal exam and corroborate an accidental manner of death.

Contusions of the brain are actual bruises to the brain tissue. They typically occur on the tips of the brain or in areas directly underlying blows to the skull. They are usually focal contusions involving only the surface of the cortex and

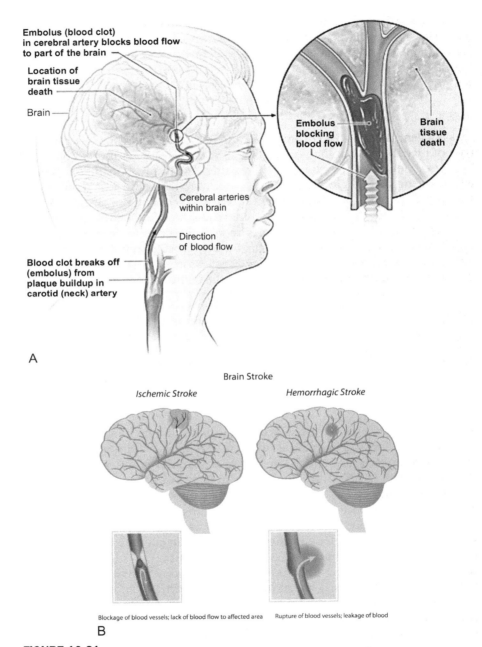

Embolus (blood clot) in cerebral artery blocks blood flow to part of the brain

Location of brain tissue death

Brain

Embolus blocking blood flow

Brain tissue death

Cerebral arteries within brain

Direction of blood flow

Blood clot breaks off (embolus) from plaque buildup in carotid (neck) artery

A

Brain Stroke

Ischemic Stroke

Hemorrhagic Stroke

Blockage of blood vessels; lack of blood flow to affected area

Rupture of blood vessels; leakage of blood

B

FIGURE 10.21
The difference between an ischemic and hemorrhagic stroke. A stroke results from lack of oxygen to the brain tissue resulting in cell death (necrosis). In ischemic strokes (figure B on the left) the stroke is due to a blockage of the blood flow by atherosclerosis or a clot causing the brain to die. In hemorrhagic strokes (figure B on the right) blood vessels rupture, causing bleeding into the brain as well as disrupting oxygen supply. A hemorrhagic stroke can rupture into the subdural space and result from natural disease, which may need to be distinguished from a subdural hematoma due to trauma.

not the deeper white matter seen with strokes. Contusions can heal and result in yellow tan scars that can become seizure foci.

Coup contusion is the term used to describe bruises directly underlying an inflicted injury or blow to the skull (Figure 10.22). The force is transmitted directly to the brain parenchyma causing rupture of the surface blood vessels. A small overlying subarachnoid hemorrhage may also be present. In these injuries, the brain injury will be in the same location as the skin injury, plus/minus a skull fracture. Homicidal manner needs to be excluded with these injuries.

Contrecoup contusions are injuries that occur on the opposite site of the skin injury and are due to a fall injury. As the person falls and strikes their head on the ground, the bruise will be created on the skin. The force of the fall is transmitted to the brain tissue, which strikes the opposite internal portion of the skull creating the brain contusion. Occasionally, a small contusion will also be seen on the side of the fall, but the majority of the hemorrhage will be opposite. A skull fracture may result from the fall and will be located on the side contacting the ground. These types of brain injuries have an accidental manner of death. All things need to be considered from the scene, however. It is possible to get a contrecoup contusion from a fall after someone is struck on the head and received a coup contusion.

Subarachnoid hemorrhages are ones within the delicate membranes covering the surface of the brain parenchyma. These do not cause death by volume accumulation like subdural hemorrhages, but by the presence of blood creating irritability of the electrical system. This is thought to affect the respiratory/cardiac centers. The etiology can be an underlying natural disorder or an inflicted injury by a blow to the lower face causing a rupture of a vertebral artery. Natural causes of death include a ruptured Berry aneurysm or a ruptured arteriovenous malformation (AVM). Occasionally strokes may extend into the subarachnoid space. A Berry aneurysm is a sacular area of one of the arteries at the base of the brain caused by a weakness of the arterial muscular wall. Ruptures of aneurysms or AVMs can be precipitated during spells of elevated blood pressure or rupture spontaneously. Either may have symptoms of headaches and occasionally seizures. Berry aneurysms may run in families and survivor follow-up for screening is recommended. See Figure 10.23.

Epidural hemorrhages are arterial bleeds located between the dura and the skull with resulting pressure on the brain. The arterial bleeding originates from a skull fracture lacerating a communicating artery lining the internal skull. These bleeds occur rapidly with sudden deterioration in consciousness. If the skull fracture communicates externally through the skin, the epidural hemorrhage will be minimal due to drainage. The distinction of the epidural hemorrhage from a subdural one is important for defining the etiology of the fracture and the underlying manner associated with it.

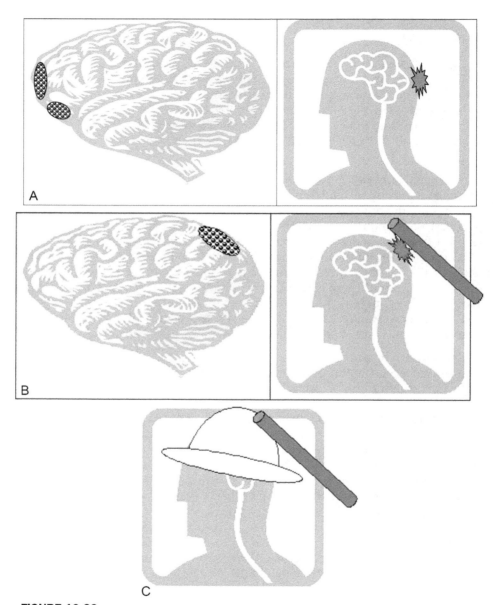

FIGURE 10.22
(A) A contrecoup contusion where the fall results in external trauma on one side of the skull and brain injuries on the opposite side. (B) A coup contusion where the injury site is on the same side and many times underlying the site of impact, and is due to inflicted trauma from a weapon. Injuries below the hat brim suggest accidental origin and those above the hat brim (C) suggest nonaccidental origin. Investigation of how the injury occurred is very useful to make the distinction.

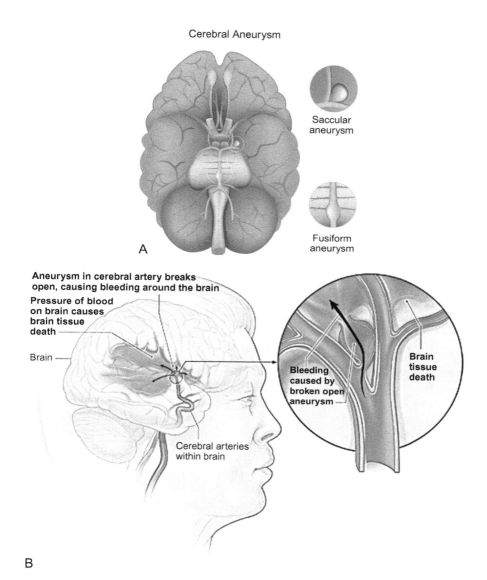

Cerebral Aneurysm

Saccular aneurysm

Fusiform aneurysm

A

Aneurysm in cerebral artery breaks open, causing bleeding around the brain

Pressure of blood on brain causes brain tissue death

Brain

Bleeding caused by broken open aneurysm

Brain tissue death

Cerebral arteries within brain

B

FIGURE 10.23
Common locations of small aneurysms that occur in the brain. Their thin walls may rupture resulting in subarachnoid hemorrhage and sudden death.

Seizures are a result of a disturbance of the brain's electrical system causing irregularities with symptoms of altered awareness of the surroundings, possibly a movement disturbance, and loss of bowel or bladder control. Some patients with seizures have a previous history of trauma and others have no known trauma but have experienced seizures for many years (idiopathic seizures). It is possible to die of a seizure disorder. The underlying mechanism causing death is not clear since death is not always a result of aspiration of food or continuous seizures (called status epilepticus). Patients with chronic seizures may not be compliant with medications or have breakthrough poorly controlled seizures, even on medications. Toxicology will add information about the decedent's medication compliance. The diagnosis is made by excluding other causes of death and finding low levels of seizure medication. Occasionally the levels will be therapeutic, but may have the history of breakthrough seizures. There are usually no brain findings in the idiopathic type. Hemorrhage within the tongue is occasionally seen, but not diagnostic of a seizure disorder, as any mechanism resulting in the tongue being between the teeth will result in the muscular bleeding. Old brain injuries can be an etiology for a seizure disorder, and if documented to a previous injury, can result in an accidental or homicidal manner. Idiopathic seizures have a natural manner. It is important to identify the type of seizure medication and perform a medication count for information about compliance. It may be difficult to locate information about a remote injury and the family may be the best source to locate the medical record documentation.

Seizures can also be a symptom associated with other disease states such as drug intoxication or a brain neoplasm. Witnesses may describe a seizure as part of a terminal event but their presence does not necessarily indicate a seizure disorder.

MENTAL ILLNESS AND SUDDEN DEATH

Those with mental illness diagnoses have a myriad of potential causes of death and many will need to be examined and evaluated by the coroner/medical examiner office. The mental illness can precipitate an overdose of medication, either intentionally or accidentally. Other suicide methods, including cutting, gunshot wounds, hangings, etc., may have an underlying psychological history.

In cases of no obvious causes of death in a mentally ill person, underlying natural disease may have precipitated death, such as pneumonia or sepsis. Ingestion of foreign substances can cause bowel obstruction or perforation, or even death due to ingestion of materials contaminated by botulism organisms from dirt or other foreign materials.

Many of the psychiatric medications, namely the tricyclic antidepressants and the antipsychotics, affect the thermoregulatory centers of the brain [7]. Mentally ill patients taking their medications are prone to hyperthermia and sudden collapse in hot environments. The drug levels can be therapeutic values and there are no diagnostic signs at autopsy. Scene findings will include elevated body temperature, which may be difficult to assess in a homeless person found outside in a hot environment. The diagnosis will then become one of excluding other causes.

DELAYED DEATHS DUE TO BRAIN INJURIES

This category includes multiple etiologies of brain injuries, including birth injuries, delayed traffic injuries, delayed gunshot wounds, and basically any hypoxic injury. Many of these patients become confined to care centers or are wards of the state. The reason for the underlying brain injury may be buried in medical records that deal with the multiple chronic natural illnesses resulting from the brain injury. These include aspiration pneumonia, urinary tract infections with sepsis, decubitus ulcers, contractures, seizures, or even failure to thrive. Many times a patient's body structure is distorted, making it difficult to place into body bags. It may be necessary to wrap him or her in a plastic shroud and sheet.

The challenge is to determine the underlying etiology of the brain injury and determine if it falls within the jurisdiction of the coroner/medical examiner to issue a death certificate, or if it is a natural cause of death, allowing the attending physician to sign the certificate. There may be issues of care the person received, necessitating at least a scene response to evaluate the condition of the surroundings and body to make the best decision. Photo documentation is advised to communicate the findings to the forensic pathologist or an investigating agency. Adult protective services may have been involved in the death, and communication can be initiated with them, as well as the appropriate law enforcement division, if necessary.

NEOPLASMS

Patients dying of known previously diagnosed tumors are not usually within the jurisdiction of the death investigator unless they die at home and the physician is not available or hospice arrangements have not been made. Occasionally unknown neoplasms are diagnosed by a forensic pathologist. Some may be massive necrotic neoplasms of the face or breast with large ulcerations not previously treated. Other times the findings may be more subtle, with only internal masses that have usually spread (metastasized) from the initial (primary) site. One question many families has is whether the tumor in the decedent puts them or the decedent's offspring at risk for similar malignancy. The best response is to have the family seek evaluation by their family physician after they have received a copy of the autopsy report. The physician can use this information to best decide how to proceed and counsel them medically.

Some neoplasms may have a link to previous employment and families are requesting autopsies for pathologic diagnosis to receive compensation. It will depend on state law and individual office policy whether these fall under the coroner/medical examiner jurisdiction. An example is mesothelioma, which is commonly associated with asbestos exposure. Employment history where this exposure occurs includes plumbing, ship building, and construction. The development of the neoplasm occurs many years after the exposure, and an exposure does not necessarily result in development of a neoplasm.

Neoplasms of the brain can be either primary (they originate solely within the brain and rarely spread elsewhere) or a metastatic spread from a primary neoplasm elsewhere. Common neoplasms that spread to the brain are breast, lung cancers, or melanoma. In either benign or malignant lesions, the neoplasms can put pressure on various locations of the brain and result in personality, behavior, or movement disorders; seizures; or decreased levels of consciousness as the disease progresses. Primary brain tumors include glioblastomas, astrocytomas, meningiomas, pituitary adenomas, or spinal cord ependymomas.

Some neoplasms present with obstruction of the kidney or bowel with abdominal distention, weight loss, or even bile duct obstruction, resulting in jaundice or severe pain due to pancreatitis. Some neoplasms and metastatic disease to lymph nodes cause obstruction of the ureters and the onset of renal failure.

Hospice patients and those with previous do not resuscitate (DNR) directives may die at home and come to the attention of the death investigator if the paperwork was not completed or the physician is not available to sign the death certificate. There may also be allegations of overmedication by a caregiver as an assisted suicide. In some states, assisted suicide is legal but in the majority it is not. These cases will need to be evaluated on a case-by-case basis by consultation with the forensic pathologist.

Infectious disease

State health departments publish a list of reportable diseases requiring follow-up for exposed contacts, preventive treatment, and prevention of widespread epidemics, such as the one for California shown in Figure 10.24. They also do reporting to the Center for Disease Control in Atlanta where nationwide trends are evaluated. For epidemiological purposes, they may require blood or other frozen preserved tissue biopsy material to perform identifying procedures. Hospital laboratories usually notify health departments of an organism identified from the list, however, as a death investigator it is also a good idea to confirm notification for the pathologist. They may request this tissue, which can be coordinated through the pathologist.

Epidemiological studies are important to prevent an outbreak of a disease from spreading through the community, state, nationally, or even internationally. A study locates vectors carrying the disease and treats or eradicates them to prevent spread. It also allows coordination of proper treatment regimes for exposed family members, medical personnel, and those who have contracted the disease.

Establishing a cause of death due to an infectious disease involves culturing various fluids and tissues in a microbiology lab to determine the infectious agent. This means the necessary biological materials must be acquired during the autopsy procedure, placed into the appropriate transport container required by the laboratory, and promptly transported to the lab for proper procedure and handling. The laboratory can have standards requiring that it be processed within a necessary time so prompt attention is required. It can take up to five days for results to be obtained in routine bacterial or viral cultures, and up to six weeks in fungal or tuberculosis cultures.

Many patients who die of an infectious disease may show minimal or no external findings on examination. The one clue is they tend to decompose more quickly than what the environment or circumstances would predict. There may be vague history of not feeling well, cough, and possible fever. There may be publicized outbreaks in the community. To prevent transmission to the investigator

Title 17, California Code of Regulations (CCR) §2500, §2593, §2641.5-2643.20, and §2800-2812 Reportable Diseases and Conditions*

§ 2500. REPORTING TO THE LOCAL HEALTH AUTHORITY.

- **§ 2500(b)** It shall be the duty of every health care provider, knowing of or in attendance on a case or suspected case of any of the diseases or condition listed below, to report to the local health officer for the jurdiction where the patient resides. Where no health care provider is in attendance, any individual having knowledge of a person who is suspected to be suffering from one of the diseases or conditions listed below may make such a report to the local health officer for the jurisdiction where the patient resides.
- **§ 2500(c)** The administrator of each health facility, clinic, or other setting where more than one health care provider may know of a case, a suspected case or an outbreak of disease within the facility shall establish and be responsible for administrative procedures to assure that reports are made to the local officer.
- **§ 2500(a)(14)** "Health care provider" means a physician and surgeon, a veterinarian, a podiatrist, a nurse practitioner, a physician assistant, a registered nurse, a nurse midwife, a school nurse, an infection control practitioner, a medical examiner, a coroner, or a dentist.

URGENCY REPORTING REQUIREMENTS [17 CCR §2500(h)(i)]

⊘ ! = Report immediately by telephone (designated by a ◆ in regulations).

† = Report immediately by telephone when two or more cases or suspected cases of foodborne disease from separate households are suspected to have the same source of illness (designated by a ● in regulations).

FAX ⊘ ✉ = Report by electronic transmission (including FAX), telephone, or mail within one working day of identification (designated by a + in regulations).

= All other diseases/conditions should be reported by electronic transmission (including FAX), telephone, or mail within seven calendar days of identification.

REPORTABLE COMMUNICABLE DISEASES §2500(j)(1)

Acquired Immune Deficiency Syndrome (AIDS)
(HIV infection only: see "Human Immunodeficiency Virus")
FAX ⊘ ✉ Amebiasis
Anaplasmosis/Ehrlichiosis
⊘ ! Anthrax, human or animal
FAX ⊘ ✉ Babesiosis
⊘ ! Botulism (Infant, Foodborne, Wound, Other)
Brucellosis, animal (except infections due to *Brucella canis*)
⊘ ! Brucellosis, human
FAX ⊘ ✉ Campylobacteriosis
Chancroid
FAX ⊘ ✉ Chickenpox (Varicella) (only hospitalizations and deaths)
Chlamydia trachomatis infections, including lymphogranuloma venereum (LGV)
⊘ ! Cholera
⊘ ! Ciguatera Fish Poisoning
Coccidioidomycosis
Creutzfeldt-Jakob Disease (CJD) and other Transmissible Spongiform Encephalopathies (TSE)
FAX ⊘ ✉ Cryptosporidiosis
Cyclosporiasis
Cysticercosis or taeniasis
⊘ ! Dengue
⊘ ! Diphtheria
⊘ ! Domoic Acid Poisoning (Amnesic Shellfish Poisoning)
FAX ⊘ ✉ Encephalitis, Specify Etiology: Viral, Bacterial, Fungal, Parasitic
⊘ ! *Escherichia coli*: shiga toxin producing (STEC) including *E. coli* O157
† FAX ⊘ ✉ Foodborne Disease
Giardiasis
Gonococcal Infections
FAX ⊘ ✉ *Haemophilus influenzae*, invasive disease (report an incident of less than 15 years of age)
⊘ ! Hantavirus Infections
⊘ ! Hemolytic Uremic Syndrome
FAX ⊘ ✉ Hepatitis A, acute infection
Hepatitis B (specify acute case or chronic)
Hepatitis C (specify acute case or chronic)
Hepatitis D (Delta) (specify acute case or chronic)
Hepatitis E, acute infection
Influenza, deaths in laboratory-confirmed cases for age 0-64 years
⊘ ! Influenza, novel strains (human)
Legionellosis
Leprosy (Hansen Disease)
Leptospirosis
FAX ⊘ ✉ Listeriosis
Lyme Disease
FAX ⊘ ✉ Malaria
⊘ ! Measles (Rubeola)
FAX ⊘ ✉ Meningitis, Specify Etiology: Viral, Bacterial, Fungal, Parasitic
⊘ ! Meningococcal Infections
Mumps
⊘ ! Paralytic Shellfish Poisoning
Pelvic Inflammatory Disease (PID)
FAX ⊘ ✉ Pertussis (Whooping Cough)
⊘ ! Plague, human or animal
FAX ⊘ ✉ Poliovirus Infection
FAX ⊘ ✉ Psittacosis

FAX ⊘ ✉ Q Fever
⊘ ! Rabies, human or animal
FAX ⊘ ✉ Relapsing Fever
Rickettsial Diseases (non-Rocky Mountain Spotted Fever), including Typhus and Typhus-like Illnesses
Rocky Mountain Spotted Fever
Rubella (German Measles)
Rubella Syndrome, Congenital
FAX ⊘ ✉ Salmonellosis (Other than Typhoid Fever)
⊘ ! Scombroid Fish Poisoning
⊘ ! Severe Acute Respiratory Syndrome (SARS)
⊘ ! Shiga toxin (detected in feces)
FAX ⊘ ✉ Shigellosis
⊘ ! Smallpox (Variola)
FAX ⊘ ✉ *Staphylococcus aureus* infection (only a case resulting in death or admission to an intensive care unit of a person who has not been hospitalized or had surgery, dialysis, or residency in a long-term care facility in the past year, and did not have an indwelling catheter or percutaneous medical device at the time of culture)
FAX ⊘ ✉ Streptococcal Infections (Outbreaks of Any Type and Individual Cases in Food Handlers and Dairy Workers Only)
FAX ⊘ ✉ Syphilis
Tetanus
Toxic Shock Syndrome
FAX ⊘ ✉ Trichinosis
FAX ⊘ ✉ Tuberculosis
Tularemia, animal
⊘ ! Tularemia, human
FAX ⊘ ✉ Typhoid Fever, Cases and Carriers
FAX ⊘ ✉ Vibrio Infections
⊘ ! Viral Hemorrhagic Fevers, human or animal (e.g., Crimean-Congo, Ebola, Lassa, and Marburg viruses)
FAX ⊘ ✉ West Nile virus (WNV) Infection
⊘ ! Yellow Fever
FAX ⊘ ✉ Yersiniosis
⊘ ! OCCURRENCE of ANY UNUSUAL DISEASE
⊘ ! OUTBREAKS of ANY DISEASE (Including diseases not listed in **§ 2500**). Specify if institutional and/or open community.

HIV REPORTING BY HEALTH CARE PROVIDERS § 2641.5-2643.20

Human Immunodeficiency Virus (HIV) infection is reportable by traceable mail or person-to-person transfer within seven calendar days by completion of the HIV/AIDS Case Report form (CDPH 8641A) available from the local health department. For completing HIV-specific reporting requirements, see Title 17, CCR, § 2641.5-2643.20 and http://www.cdph.ca.gov/programs/aids/Pages/OAHIVReporting.aspx

REPORTABLE NONCOMMUNICABLE DISEASES AND CONDITIONS §2800-2812 and §2593(b)

Disorders Characterized by Lapses of Consciousness (§2800-2812)
Pesticide-related illness or injury (known or suspected cases)**
Cancer, including benign and borderline brain tumors (except (1) basal and squamous skin cancer unless occurring on genitalia, and (2) carcinoma in-situ and CIN III of the Cervix) (§2593)***

LOCALLY REPORTABLE DISEASES (If Applicable):

---

* This form is designed for health care providers to report those diseases mandated by Title 17, California Code of Regulations (CCR). Failure to report is a misdemeanor (Health & Safety Code §120295) and is a citable offense under the Medical Board of California Citation and Fine Program (Title 16, CCR, §1364.10 and 1364.11).
** Failure to report is a citable offense and subject to civil penalty ($250) (Health and Safety Code §105200).
*** The Confidential Physician Cancer Reporting Form may also be used. See Physician Reporting Requirements for Cancer Reporting in CA at: www.ccrcal.org.
CDPH 110a (revised 10/03/2011)

FIGURE 10.24

A list of reportable diseases for the state of California [13]. Each state will have its own list and can be found on the public health website.

or morgue staff, it is always advisable to utilize a mask, gloves, and personal protective equipment as outlined in office policy. Because microorganisms can adhere to surfaces, it is best to not place personal effects, medication vials, etc. directly on the office desk, but to contain them within plastic/paper bags. The scene response bag may need to be cleaned after being carried into this type of environment.

Fractures

Fractures commonly result from trauma, but in some instances the amount of force imposed is minimal. Either mechanism can result in a fracture that shortens a patient's life due to complications. Common complications of fractures are pneumonia, urinary tract infections, decubitus ulcers (bedsores), or sepsis (bacteria within the bloodstream). Pathological fractures result when bones involved by metastatic neoplasms have weakened the bone structure by the replacement with cancer cells. Osteoporosis is the loss of calcium and bone structure usually seen in older females. The bones weaken to the point that the body weight itself may cause compression fractures especially of the vertebra. Hip or arm fractures may also result from either type of pathology. Fractures in these underlying diseases may result from suddenly sitting, turning in bed, etc., and are not ruled accidental in origin rather usually certified as a natural manner of death.

Environmental

Environmental deaths are largely based on scene photographs, scene investigation, and the lack of an anatomical cause of death. There may be contributing information obtained from toxicology that places the person at risk within the environment, such as acute alcohol or drug intoxication.

Disorders of body temperature

Normal body temperature is 95–100°F (~35–38°C) measured via a core body temperature (rectal). Normal body temperature is needed for cell functions and metabolism to proceed at a normal rate. If the core (internal) body temperature decreases, cell functions slow, and eventually deplete their oxygen storage and restoration capabilities. Lowering body temperature during transplantation and cardiac surgery is used therapeutically to decrease the rate of metabolism and cell processes.

HYPOTHERMIA

Hypothermia is defined as a core body temperature below 95°F or 35°C [15]. Prolonged exposure to cold will be lethal and is commonly seen in alcoholics in snowy environments. The rate this occurs depends on the environmental temperature including the wind chill factor, degree of skin exposure, body habitus, and the presence of clothing. If the body or clothing is wet, the rate heat evaporates from the skin will increase, lowering core temperature more rapidly. The very young, the elderly, and thin individuals usually have less body mass and fat, and are more susceptible to environmental temperatures. Symptoms of hypothermia include confusion and disorientation, which can be compounded by alcohol and drug use. As the hypothermic state continues, the person experiences a period of vasodilation and flushing, causing him or her to shed clothing even though he or she may be extremely hypothermic. This is referred to as paradoxical undressing, meaning a person undresses when he or she should be putting more clothing on. Cases of acutely intoxicated individuals being found in the snow at the bottom of the steps to their residence are not uncommon. There may be a surrounding trail of their possessions as they made their way to shelter. The degree of intoxication may be a moderate level of 0.2 to 0.3 mg/dl, which is not uncommonly seen in chronic alcoholics.

It should also be noted that resuscitative attempts of individuals, especially the young, found in extremely cold water may result in successful return to consciousness with few long-term complications. This is because the sudden drop in body temperature is similar to those simulated in the hospital environment during surgery. Children have been known to survive being submerged in icy waters up to 20 minutes.

Frostbite is freezing of the skin, which occurs at −40°F [7]. Skin exposed to temperatures or wind chill at this temperature is subject to freezing within a few minutes depending on circulation, dampness, and clothing factors. The nose, cheeks, fingers, and toes are most prone. Symptoms include tingling, numbness, and paleness, followed by redness and blistering. The final stage is permanent skin damage and necrosis, which appears red-black in prone areas (the person has to live for it to become apparent). Frostbite is an initial symptom of extreme cold exposure that will progress to death if shelter is not sought immediately.

Autopsy findings in hypothermia are minimal and not diagnostic. Usually it is determined by the absence of trauma, such as a body found frozen or extremely cold in a cold environment. Peculiar brown hemorrhagic spotlike hemorrhages can be seen in the gastric mucosa and are called Wischnewski ulcers, but are not diagnostic. Bright-red discoloration of livor is also seen in cold exposure and is commonly seen in bodies stored in refrigeration overnight. Areas lying in contact with the snow or ground may have a pinkish red discoloration or yellow parchment skin slippage.

Investigative materials needed to make the diagnosis are weather and wind chill readings from the time of the decedent's exposure. If the person was inside the residence, notations of the thermostat reading and functionality of the heat and power sources are factors that need to be documented. Observations of food frozen on the counter or frozen pipes are also good to note and photograph. If the death occurred in a vehicle, the presence of gas and notation of the ignition are important findings. In the far north, some persons rely totally on wood heat so these findings may not be totally indicative of the cause of death but secondary to another cause of death. In those cases, carbon monoxide poisoning should be considered in the differential of a person with bright-red livor and found frozen inside the residence or vehicle.

HYPERTHERMIA

Hyperthermia is defined as a core body temperature above 100°F (~38–40 °C) [14]. Fever is also defined as a temperature greater than 100°F but the mechanism creating a fever is internal derangement of the fever center by bacterial toxins, viruses, or other pyrogens that reset the body thermostat to a higher level. Hyperthermia is caused by environmental temperatures causing the body heat regulation system to be unable to compensate and the normal heat loss mechanisms are exceeded causing the internal body temperature to rise. This results in increasing cell metabolism that adds to body heat production, depleting reserves, and finally succumbing to cell death.

Heat-related illnesses fall into a continuum to death by hyperthermia if not remedied. This continuum includes heat cramps, heat exhaustion, and heat stroke. Heat cramps are the mildest and are symptoms of muscle cramps due to lack of salt and water. If there is continued exposure to heat with no replacement of salt and water, it will progress to heat exhaustion with symptoms of headache, nausea, weakness, and pale moist skin. If not treated with fluids, it will progress to heat stroke, which includes absence of sweating, hot skin, and elevated body temperature. Heat stroke can be fatal. Due to the inability to establish physical symptoms except elevated body temperature at death, these deaths are included in the general category of hyperthermia.

Autopsy findings of individuals exposed to extreme heat generally show advanced decomposition. There are no specific findings associated with hyperthermia. The autopsy is done to document the extent of underlying pathology to rule out a cause of death that occurred with secondary decomposition versus death due to environmental heat exposure. Decomposed bodies also present challenges in obtaining toxicology, including vitreous. If vitreous is available, a sodium, creatinine, and urea can be done by the laboratory to evaluate the degree of dehydration, which would contribute findings to the diagnosis of hyperthermia.

Investigative documentation of the house and body temperature can also be helpful. Infrared thermometers can be extremely useful to assist with this. Many times first responders open the doors and windows of closed environments and this distorts air temperature readings. Infrared readings of the walls, floor, or area under the body can be done with this equipment. They can be obtained from local hardware stores relatively inexpensively. The position of the body needs to be photographed, as well as cooling mechanisms such as fans and air conditioners and power to them. If the power was discontinued, it is important to note the date that was done, and by whom, as it may prove to be a civil liability. Examination of the refrigerator food contents with their expiration dates may give an indication of the postmortem interval. In some cases of recluses or lack of family, there can be a long interval between the time of death and the decedent's discovery. Again, weather conditions are easily researched from the Internet and form an important part of the investigative report in hyperthermic deaths.

The cause of death in temperature-related deaths is usually accidental. Occasionally they are natural deaths with the heat as a contributing factor. The degree of this interaction between natural and accidental is a difficult assessment and largely rests with the pathologist weighing the degree of natural disease against the environmental exposure. Toxicology can play an extremely important role in making the diagnosis both from knowing the alcohol and drug levels to the degree of dehydration.

Tricyclic antidepressants affect the thermoregulatory center of the brain and persons taking these medications are at increased risk for hyperthermia. Illicit drugs that increase the body metabolism, such as amphetamines and cocaine, also pose an increased risk [8].

Malignant hyperthermia is a rare condition where a patient under or shortly after anesthesia experiences a sudden increase in body temperature that may be fatal if not treated promptly. It has genetic predisposition and occurs in response to halothane or succinylcholine used during surgery. In some states this may become a death investigation case falling under the auspice of sudden death under anesthesia or surgery. It is important to obtain anesthesia, surgical, and nursing notes from the period around the incident and during surgery. An autopsy will show a dry surgical site and knowledge of the notes will describe the course of events. There is a genetic and muscle biopsy test available to make the diagnosis in other family members to prevent a fatal outcome for them, and this should prompt the investigator to encourage them to seek genetic counseling [1].

WORKPLACE CAUSES OF DEATH

Workplace injuries are common and range from moving vehicle or equipment injuries to fires and electrical injuries (Figure 10.25). Approaching a scene in a work environment requires the investigator to be vigilant to hazards toward him- or herself and other rescue workers. It is important to prevent further injuries to other workers as they return to work, or even to the public. Puncture-proof shoes or boots and use of safety equipment in hardhat areas are important to prevent self-injury. Situational awareness as the investigator approaches the decedent cannot be overstressed.

Electrocution can be a subtle finding that is easily missed depending on the voltage of the electrical line. In high voltage, the damage can be quite dramatic and approach that of lightning injuries. Workers on high-voltage power lines can actually have their clothes charred or thrown off the body. A hot power line can be a hazard to approaching rescue workers and the death investigator. Depending on the voltage, the current can arc to nearby objects. Downed power lines can also occur during motor vehicle accidents, which in the dark are difficult to see.

If the decedent was in the process of using power tools in the area of power lines, electrical boxes, or in a shop, or near a pool of water with electricity, then electrocution should be considered. Signs of potential electrocution include

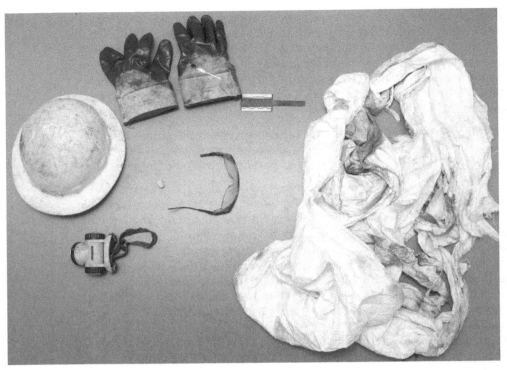

FIGURE 10.25
The clothing received from a worker who died on duty. It is important to note serial numbers and photograph safety equipment from multiple angles to document their integrity or sites where they may have failed.

burned clothing; subtle findings of raised, chalky, slightly burned callous areas of the hands or feet; or no findings if the person was in a pool of water. Small burn areas may be located on clothes, hands, or the soles of the shoes or boots. Typically, the electrical charge enters the hands, travels across the torso, and exits the feet where the person was grounded (Figure 10.26). It is the transfer of the charge across the heart that results in a lethal cardiac arrhythmia and death.

Understanding electrocution injuries requires some basic knowledge of electricity and flow of current. Electricity is the flow of charged particles usually from a positively charged source to a negatively charged one. Current applies this principle to the flow of the particles along a conductive material like a wire and the intensity is measured in amperage. There are two kinds of current—direct current (DC) and alternating current (AC)—that refers to how current is flowing over time. Direct current is one where the flow is constant over time in one direction with a classic example of a battery providing power to a car or flashlight. Alternating current is one where the flow waxes and wanes over time much like a wave in the ocean and is the common type seen in house current. Amperage is the amount of current flow and is the most important factor in electrocutions.

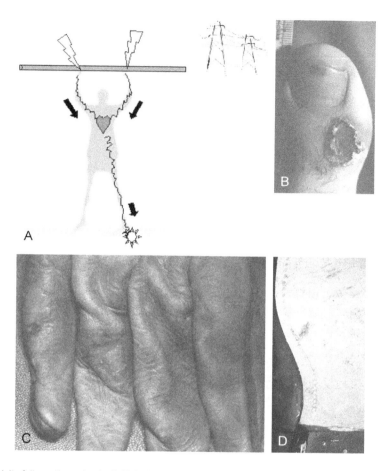

FIGURE 10.26
(A) The pathway electricity follows through a body if the line is touched by a hand. (B) An electrical burn. Clues that the death may be electrically related are downed power lines, extension cords especially near water, open power boxes, or recent electrical work done on a residence. Examination may show burns on the hands or gloves from the wires (C) and exit burns on the soles of the shoes (D).

Voltage is the measure of the force of the current. The third factor involved is the amount of resistance to the conduction of the electricity.

The skin has the greatest resistance to the flow of current in a body. If the skin is dry it has a high degree of resistance. However, if the skin is wet the current flows easily. The ability of current to pass through the remainder of the body is related to our high content of water. It tends to flow from the point of contact with the wire through the body and exit where the body touches the ground. Generally, it follows the most efficient and shortest path. This is the reason high-voltage workers can work on power lines. There is no risk of electrocution if they are not grounded. However, if a malfunction occurs and they suddenly are grounded through their bucket, then electrocution will occur.

Low-amperage wounds (i.e., less than 1 A) crossing the path of the heart cause death by ventricular fibrillation, which leaves no anatomic finding when viewed during autopsy. The only sign may be the small burns from arcing of the wire at the entrance or the charred burn at the exit wound. Higher-amperage wounds (i.e., greater than 1 A) can cause death via the burns themselves in addition to the fibrillation.

Lightning

Lightning deaths occur in persons working or doing recreational activities outdoors. Being located near electrical lines or water is a risk factor for a strike to occur. The strike usually occurs onto an object extending into the air and is transmitted onto the person nearby. Fishing poles, flag poles, metal buildings, etc. are all subject to strikes. The injuries are very similar to high-voltage electrical injuries with clothes burning and being ripped from the body (Figure 10.27). Death is from cardiac and respiratory arrest due to sudden depolarization of the heart by the current from the lightning bolt. When in a thunderstorm, the most secure place to seek shelter is inside a vehicle because it is grounded and will protect those inside from arcing [9].

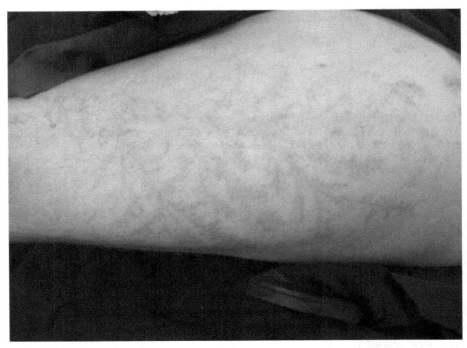

FIGURE 10.27
Lightning injury. The pink arborization is a classic lightning injury, sometimes referred to as a Lichtenberg figure. (Used with permission from Dr. John Hunsaker. Photo credit: Daryl Hodge.)

Burns and explosions

Fires can take many forms, from slow-burning smoldering ones with extensive smoke, to sudden explosions. Either form can be lethal. With a higher concentration of oxygen, the fire burns more efficiently, creating more heat. In a closed environment such as a building, the fire consumes the internal oxygen and produces a rising level of noxious gases, largely carbon monoxide. Contents may also be burning and plastics, foam, other synthetic fabrics, and rubber produce cyanide as a by-product, which can also build up and be inhaled. Cyanide can be more lethal than carbon monoxide [2,3,4]. Sudden explosive fires, such as exploding gas tanks on vehicles that result in a compartment fire, occur so suddenly that death results from inhalation of superheated gases rather than living for a period of time and inhaling the carbon monoxide or the cyanide by-products (Figure 10.28).

Blunt force and crushing injuries

These are the most common injuries encountered in the workplace. They can occur from falls from a height, entanglement of clothing in rollers and belts, objects swinging or falling on the worker, or being run over or crushed by moving machinery. The injuries are similar and described like motor vehicle injuries with

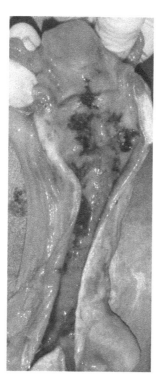

FIGURE 10.28
Soot in the trachea and lower airway due to smoke inhalation. Carbon monoxide or cyanide from the burning materials are usually greatly elevated and may cause the muscle, blood, and livor to appear unusually bright red.

contusions, abrasions, and lacerations being the key terms. The worksite safety officer and Occupational Safety and Health Agency (OSHA) need to be notified of any workplace fatalities so they may conduct an investigation to prevent further injuries to other workers. They can provide investigative data regarding faulty electrical materials and dysfunction of safety equipment or machinery.

It is important to photograph the presence of the body as it was found, if possible, and any suspected items that might have caused the injuries. If the injuries are patterned and a suspected area of the tool or machinery is suspected of causing it, photographic documentation is important, if not a hazard to the investigator. Particular attention is needed for tread marks, and presence of safety equipment including boots, gloves, helmets, and coveralls. Any harnesses or other items that may have safety issues also need to be photographed on and off the body. OSHA may wish to obtain these items for further inspection and a transfer with a chain of custody will be needed.

Autopsy photographs need to include overall, medium, and close-up views of any patterned injuries with and without scales. Toxicology is important to evaluate impairment as a contributing factor for the injury to occur. Sedatives, alcohol, or drug use can impair reaction time as well as attentiveness to detail.

Cave-ins can be hazardous to an investigator and the presence of trained rescue response workers can assist with the body recovery and photography if needed. It is important to be aware of the worksite hazards and follow experts' direction at the site while still preserving and documenting the evidence if possible.

Because worksites can be a location of homicides, inflicted blunt-force injuries should always be considered while evaluating the scene. Blunt objects lying nearby should be observed for blood and tissue. The injuries on the body should be consistent with the degree of suspected force that created them. An example is a body thought to be a fall to the floor from standing height should not have crushing head injuries, unless some object inflicted them. It could be an object on a chain or an object impacted on the head by a person. It is very difficult to determine if someone was pushed off a building versus falling, but careful scene documentation, including measurements from the edge of the building and estimates of the height of the fall, will be helpful if further investigation of that scenario is warranted by witness statements. These types of measurements can be obtained by new electronic instruments used by law enforcement, construction personnel, or even surveyors. Handheld models can be purchased and are something to keep on the wish list for documentation of these scenes, as well as traffic accidents, mass fatalities, and train deaths.

DRUG AND ALCOHOL CAUSES OF DEATH
Drug intoxication

Interpretation of drug levels need to take into account the underlying health of the person, the types of drugs, the values reported, the sample site the value was determined from, and the presence of underlying liver or renal disease. The values

FIGURE 10.29
(A) A small example of the pills that may be present at a scene and require the investigator to seize them as evidence. They are routinely counted and documented on a log prior to destruction. (B) The scene of an alcoholic with numerous liquor bottles, which can be stored by some in the hundreds within a residence.

can be artificially elevated by poor specimen type or storage, abnormal drug excretion, or a phenomenon called postmortem redistribution. The latter term refers to release of a drug from its site of action inside a cell of an organ back into the blood after death. Quantification is typically performed on blood and, depending on the site of collection, can be greatly altered in its value. A site where it commonly occurs is the heart, lungs, and liver. Types of drugs prone to redistribution are the antidepressants, amphetamines, and digoxin [10] (Figure 10.29). In cases of altered liver or renal disease, the patients usually must take lower dosages of medications because of their impaired metabolism and excretion. Parent and metabolic products may accumulate in the blood with the appearance of a possible suicide when the value may be related to an underlying natural disease process. Mental health information and family history may assist in making the distinction.

Alcohol related

Alcohol values are relatively straightforward in their determination in the laboratory via gas chromatography. In all states acute alcohol intoxication is determined at 0.08 g of alcohol/100 ml of blood or higher. The value can be artificially lowered by infusion of intravenous fluids from resuscitative efforts or passage of time. An improperly drawn specimen via a blind stick from a pleural cavity can give an artificially elevated value by contamination from the esophagus or stomach contents. To prevent misinterpretation of values, the vitreous alcohol analysis is usually performed as a parallel evaluation of the blood alcohol. The vitreous alcohol normally lags behind the blood value and is protected from dilution by intravenous fluids. It normally runs approximately 1.2 times higher than a blood alcohol, so a conversion factor is needed to convert to a blood value. How people act during acute alcohol intoxication is widely variable and can range from aggressive to passive.

A Caveat for the Medical Witness: Advice Regarding Testimony about Alcohol Intoxication

Excerpt from The Pathology of Homicide *by Dr. Lester Adelson*

Given equal degrees of tolerance and health, most persons respond more or less similarly to ethanol insofar as their physical abilities and capacities are concerned. Thus, the pathologist can state authoritatively that a sufficiently elevated blood-alcohol level hampers proper muscular coordination, interferes with the ability to judge distance correctly, increases reaction time, impairs visual and auditory acuity, and leads to deterioration in insight, judgment, and critical faculties.

On the other hand, the emotional and personality responses of a specific person after he had consumed more than a "little" alcohol can be prognosticated in guarded fashion only on the basis of *repeated* previous observations of this conduct and comportment under similar conditions. Even then, one must remember that the same person *can* react differently to the same exogenous factors (i.e., amount of alcohol, type of occasion and company) as a result of differences in endogenous conditions, such as mood and emotional status.

Thus, the physician *cannot* state positively, solely on the basis of a specific blood-alcohol concentration, that the subject was mean, combative, and hostile, *or* that he was affable, pleasant, and affectionate.

Source: Adelson, L. (1974). *The Pathology of Homicide.* Springfield, IL: Charles C. Thomas, p. 896 [11].

Other alcohols may be identified while searching for ethanol, the common alcohol found in beer, wine, and other liquor. Methanol is a solvent and sometimes used as a pesticide that can be ingested. It is fatal in small volumes and can be detected during an alcohol screen. It may also be an ingredient in embalming fluids, which can contaminate vitreous fluid determinations.

Ethylene glycol is a sweet-tasting liquid forming a large component of antifreeze. If ingested, it can give feelings of euphoria similar to ethanol intoxication but can be lethal if ingested in a quantity of at least 3–4 oz. It may be seen as an accidental poisoning in alcoholics or as a means of homicidal or suicidal poisoning.

Isopropyl alcohol, commonly known as rubbing alcohol, may also be lethal if ingested in large quantities and will give symptoms of inebriation as well as potential coma. It is not as lethal as ethylene glycol or methanol. It is more commonly seen on toxicology lab reports in conjunction with ketones consistent with a chronic alcoholic ketoacidosis picture where the body is breaking down fats and proteins because of distorted insulin use in alcoholics.

Prescription medications

Every medication is a potential poison in a large enough quantity. Over-the-counter medications are justified as such because they have a very wide margin of safety and it requires large amounts of them to become intoxicated or for lethal levels to be achieved. Prescription medications are regulated because they have lower margins of safety and, to prevent access, they require a doctor's prescription to obtain them. Which category a medication is placed into is determined by premarketing testing used by the Food and Drug Administration (FDA).

The Drug Enforcement Agency (DEA) classifies all narcotics and determines their level of safety and regulates physicians who prescribe them. Narcotic prescriptions require a DEA number issued to a physician for it to be filled by a pharmacy. The number allows the DEA to monitor physician prescription practices.

Individual pharmacies or even pharmacy chains can provide lists of prescribed medications for a patient that were filled at their establishment and will include the name of the drug, date filled, amount, and prescribing physician. This information can be helpful in sorting out manner and for locating medical records.

Some of the common drugs encountered that are commonly lethal are cardiac medications, antidepressants, pain medications, and antipsychotics. These classes of drugs cause death by inhibiting respiration or disrupting cardiac activity. Combining these drugs can have additive effects that can be further accentuated by the addition of alcohol or illicit drug use. Each drug may be in a therapeutic or sublethal range, but when in combination, they may cause death. In many cases of drug intoxication they become another class of deaths where the diagnosis is one of exclusion. Scene findings of open pill containers, spilled pills, and mental history can all play a part in sorting out the many factors needed to determine the cause and manner. The testing laboratory usually provides some direction as to interpretation of the reported value. There are also multiple resources available in a toxicology text for interpretation of data for individual postmortem drug levels.

Illicit drug use

Illegal drug use has multiple complications including the social issues of addiction, which can lead to criminal activity or impaired judgment, placing the person at risk for homicides or accidental causes of death. Other risks include natural diseases such as hepatitis or bacterial endocarditis from injections, or talc lung from injecting drugs "cut" with talc as part of the processing. Drug use also poses risks to fetuses and children.

COCAINE

Cocaine is a derivative of coca leaves, a plant that is native to South America, then imported via drug traffickers. It comes in two forms: a powder that can be inhaled or injected, or a rock called "crack" that can be smoked. Its physiologic effects on the body are increased blood pressure and heart rate due to its properties of vasoconstriction. It may cause periods of paranoid psychoses or delirium that are not necessarily associated with a particular drug level. It can precipitate cardiac arrest, especially in those with underlying cardiac disease and intracranial hemorrhage, due to its vasoconstrictive properties.

OPIUM

Opium is derived from the opium poppy that is native to many parts of the world, as well as being able to be grown in the United States. It is harvested from the pod that forms after the petals have fallen away. The internal sap of the pod is collected and dried. This sap is the precursor to heroin, morphine, codeine, and oxycodone. It has legal medicinal uses, as well as being available via the black market in any of these forms. Heroin is available as a brown or white powder that can be smoked or inhaled or injected, known as mainlining, which is the most potent method of use. In this form it can also be found as impure black tar, which is a black rock material that is melted and injected. Morphine is the derivative form detected in the laboratory and is the same compound detected if it originates from a hospital source. The illicit form may contain detectable by-products that were used to cut the heroin or contain a metabolic form called acetylmorphine. Codeine and oxycodone are common prescription medications that patients can become addicted to. Combined use with alcohol or over use with other prescription medications can be lethal.

Methadone is a synthetic opioid used to treat opiate-addicted patients because of its long duration of action. It is synthesized in medical pharmacy laboratories for prescription use for detoxification and slow withdrawal of narcotics to relieve patient symptoms of withdrawal. It can be given in oral form or injected, and usually requires the patient to receive his or her dose at intervals from a methadone clinic. It has pain-relieving benefits similar to morphine and can be used for chronic pain relief as well. It too can be abused, and if prescribed in oral form, can be overingested, leading to overdose.

METHAMPHETAMINE

Methamphetamine (meth) is a manufactured material in homegrown labs. These labs pose a particular hazard to the investigator and the community. They contain multiple volatile, explosive, and corrosive hazards with harmful by-products. Full protective equipment use, including an air pack, will be necessary to investigate these scenes. Hazmat units usually survey the scene and make it safe of explosives prior to the investigator being admitted. The body may have hazardous chemicals on the skin requiring multiple body bags and the use of a chemical-resistant outer layer. Heavy-duty chemical-resistant gloves may be necessary to handle the decedent and any evidence that needs to be removed. The Environmental Protection Agency (EPA) has published a manual on cleanup and handling of contaminated scenes within a meth lab [5].

Because of these toxic issues, children raised in these environments and suddenly found unresponsive or deceased need to be evaluated for ingestion or inhalation of these toxic chemicals.

The National Alliance for Drug Endangered Children has authored a flow diagram of medical evaluation of children exposed to a drug lab environment, as well as their symptoms, which would prove useful in evaluating a decedent within the same environment [6].

DESIGNER DRUGS

New drugs are being synthesized continuously and, because of the way they are manufactured, are able to stay ahead of laws and enforceability by law enforcement. One example is bath salts, a designer drug derived from a plant, Catha edulis, grown in Africa and the Arabian Peninsula where it is known as khat. The plant derivatives are modified chemically to form synthetic cathinones. These will be seen in a toxicology screen as MDPV, mephedrone, and methylone, but are not routinely detected on testing and must be requested from referral labs. They have stimulant properties similar to cocaine and amphetamines but include hallucinations and cravings similar to LSD. Deaths have been linked to its use via repeated highs, cutting, paranoia, and leaping off buildings. It affects the brain's neurotransmitters and stimulates the cardiovascular system, causing sudden death from cardiac arrest or edema within the brain. The term bath salts has no relationship to how this drug is produced, but packaging is marked with that label to avoid detection by law enforcement. It is also known as insect repellant and plant food and the package marked "not suitable for consumption." It is relatively cheap and used via smoking, injecting, or snorting, and comes in powder, pill, or tablet form.

Synthetic marijuana is marketed in foil packages marked "Spice," "Incense," or "Puff Puff." It is derived from herbs and sprayed with chemicals to mimic the active ingredients in marijuana. Since it does not have the compounds found in cannabis, it will not give a positive drug screen for THC, the active component. The effects are similar to cannabis but include paranoia that may be long lasting or even precipitate a psychotic breakdown and death. Drug screens for synthetic cannabis are difficult because manufacturers change the chemical structure to avoid law enforcement detection. The testing targets the synthetic cannabinoid structure used in the manufacture of the chemicals but must be specifically requested from a reference laboratory.

Basic principles of toxicology testing

ELECTROLYTES

Electrolytes on decedents usually include testing for sodium, chloride, creatinine, urea, and glucose. In the living, these tests can be done on the blood. However, with death, the mechanisms that keep these items in balance inside and out of the cell are disrupted and the blood testing results in artificially elevated or distorted results if tested. The best example is potassium levels. In the living, this value is tightly regulated by the body to a normal range of 3.5–5 mEq/L circulating in the blood but is much higher inside the body's cells. With death, the cell membrane is no longer regulated and the high content inside the cell diffuses out into the blood, causing blood values to increase to values that, if interpreted, would be lethal.

The other elements noted above have similar issues with their pre- and post-mortem values if performed on blood specimens. For this reason, vitreous (fluid removed from the eye) is the specimen of choice. This specimen has a lower cell concentration and is not subjected to these same rapid changes seen within blood specimens. Even so, the potassium will slowly rise and bacteria within the fluid will slowly lower the glucose value. The sodium, urea, and creatinine will remain relatively steady and be used to assess for dehydration. Extremely elevated glucose values seen with diabetics in lethal ketoacidosis will lower but remain higher than normal for the postmortem interval. For a quick bedside interpretation, a diabetic glucometer can be used for a quantified estimate of the glucose value in the vitreous and can be done quickly upon admission to the morgue. In the same fashion, a dipstick of the diabetic urine can reveal the presence of ketones.

ENZYME-LINKED IMMUNABSORBENT ASSAY (ELISA)

This method utilizes antibodies that produce a color change to determine the presence of a substance and a positive result. Urine drug screening by this methodology is cost effective and useful for presumptive identification of drugs or their by-products. It utilizes antibodies similar to the ones we have in our blood to fight infection. These molecules have particular chemical structures much like a jigsaw puzzle piece. The drug for which it is a match will fit directly into the piece exactly, and after doing so, will emit a change of color at a particular wavelength that can be detected by the instrument. This is an inexpensive and rapid method to screen for particular broad classes of drugs and the test is considered a qualitative test. To confirm the identity and quantify the amount of the drug, further testing can then be done by more sophisticated instrumentation. If the screen is negative, further time-consuming testing can be avoided. A positive result in this method must be confirmed by another methodology because the antibody match is not specific. In some cases, the antibody puzzle piece can fit in a similar drug antigen piece, not exactly, but enough so that the emission of light can occur and turn the result positive when it is actually negative. This is called cross-reactivity. These cross-reactive antigens create a false-positive result. All laboratory tests have an innate level of false-positive and false-negative results attached to them. The key to a good analysis method is to minimize both, and yet gather the true positives in the largest percentage. For these reasons, most laboratories confirm positive test results and quantify the amount via gas chromatography–mass spectrometry. See Figure 10.30 for examples.

GAS CHROMATOGRAPHY–MASS SPECTROMETRY (GC-MS) OR LIQUID CHROMATOGRAPHY–MASS SPECTROMETRY

These two methods are used by most laboratories to confirm the identification of a drug or substance by its chemical structure (Figure 10.31). The testing is performed by comparing the multiple chemical structures in a specimen to a library of known structures and the instrument is able to give an accurate quantification. Specimens are usually performed in duplicate to confirm values before reporting a result. Major law decisions may be made by these test results, and the values need to have the best validity and reproducibility as possible by the laboratory.

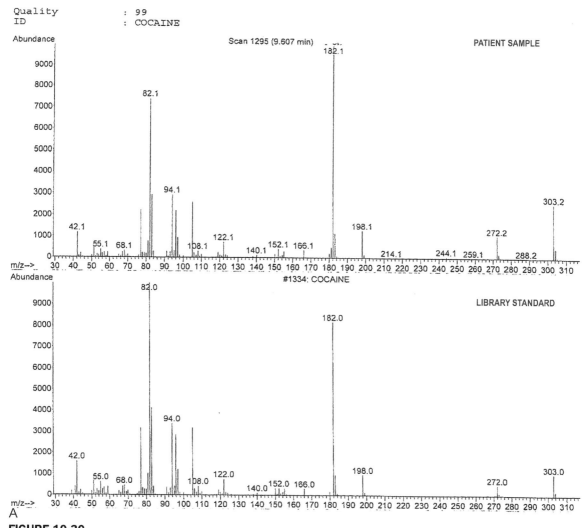

FIGURE 10.30
(A) Sample results of a specimen submitted for confirmation of a drug screen. Here you see the instrument emission pattern of the unknown (the top pattern) matches the library pattern of cocaine (seen in the lower pattern).

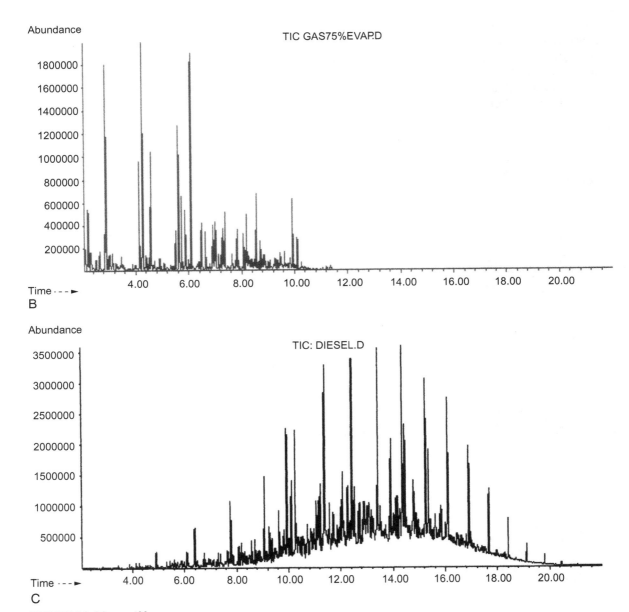

FIGURE 10.30, cont'd

(B, C) Specimens submitted for volatiles. The patterns match those of the library patterns of gasoline and diesel. This information can be useful in arson determinations and is done on the air that accumulates the fumes within an airtight container (called headspace analysis). Clothing or other items to be submitted for this testing are usually placed in new paint cans and sealed. The air is extracted through a pinhole made in the lid and injected into the instrument.

Courtesy of Dr. Craig Chatterton

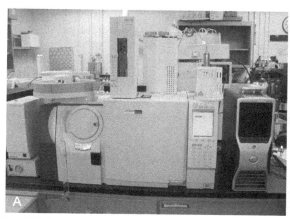

FIGURE 10.31
(A) Gas chromatography–mass spectrophotometer. (B) Liquid chromatography–mass spectrophotometer. Both instruments are used in toxicology testing.

REFERENCES

[1] Metterlein T, et al. In-vitro Contracture Testing for Susceptibility to Malignant Hyperthermia: Can Halothane be Replaced? Eur J Anaesthesiol 2011;28(4):251–5. doi:10.1097/EJA.0b013e32833ed06c. Retrieved from http://www.ncbi.nlm.nih.gov/pubmed/20827211, http://www.ncbi.nlm.nih.gov/pubmed/15114203. [August 2013].

[2] Rochford R. Hydrogen Cyanide: New Concerns for Firefighting and Medical Tactics. Fire Engineering, PBI Performance Products, Inc e-newsletter; 2009. Reviewed from http://www.fireengineering.com/articles/2009/06/hydrogen-cyanide-new-concerns-for-firefighting-and-medical-tactics.html. [August 2013].

[3] Cyanide Compounds. Technology Transfer Network - Air Toxics Web site. 74-90-8, United State Environmental Protection Agency; 2009. Reviewed, from http://www.epa.gov/ttnatw01/hlthef/cyanide.html. [August 2013].

[4] An introduction to Indoor Air Quality (IAQ): Carbon Monoxide (CO). Environmental Protection Agency; 2013. Reviewed from http://www.epa.gov/iaq/co.html. [August 2013].

[5] Environmental Protection Agency. Guidelines for methamphetamine lab cleanup. Retrieved from http://www.epa.gov/osweroe1/meth_lab_guidelines.pdf.

[6] National Guidelines for Medical Evaluation of Children Found in Drug Labs. National Alliance for Drug Endangered Children; 2013. Reviewed from http://www.nationaldec.org/user_files/18918.pdf. [August 2013].

[7] Thurlow D. The Weather Notebook, 40 Below; 2001. Reviewed from http://www.weathernotebook.org/transcripts/2001/02/07.html. [August 2013].

[8] Rampulla J. Hyperthermia & Heat Stroke: Heat-Related Conditions. Healthcare of Homeless Persons; 2012. Reviewed from http://www.nhchc.org/wp-content/uploads/2012/02/Hyperthermia.pdf. [August 2013].

[9] Cooper M. Lightning Injuries. Medscape Reference; 2012. Reviewed from http://emedicine.medscape.com/article/770642-overview#aw2aab6b2b2. [August 2013].

[10] Yarema MC, Becker CE. Key Concepts in Postmortem Drug Redistribution. Clin Toxicol (Phila) 2005;43(4):235–41. Reviewed from http://www.ncbi.nlm.nih.gov/pubmed/16035199. [August 2013].

[11] Adelson L. The Pathology of Homicide. Springfield, IL: Charles C. Thomas; 1974.

[12] Heart and Vascular Diseases Health Topics. National Institute of Health: National Heart, Lung and Blood Institute; 2013. Reviewed from http://www.nhlbi.nih.gov. [August 2013].

[13] Reportable Infectious Diseases for California. California Department of Public Health; 2011. Retrieved from http://www.cdph.ca.gov/HealthInfo/Documents/Reportable_Diseases_Conditions.pdf. [August 2013].

[14] Bouchama A, Knochel J. Heat Stroke (Review article). N Engl J Med 2002;346:1978–88. doi:10.1056/NEJMra011089. Reviewed from http://www.nejm.org/doi/full/10.1056/NEJMra011089. [August 2013].

[15] Brown D, et al. Accidental Hypothermia (Review article). N Engl J Med 2012;367:1930–8. doi:10.1056/NEJMra1114208. Reviewed from http://www.nejm.org/doi/full/10.1056/NEJMra1114208. [October 2013].

CHAPTER 11
Sudden Death in Children

Learning Objectives

- A baby with no external evidence of trauma is dead in a local hospital emergency department. You, as the investigator, respond to the hospital to examine the child and meet with the family. Outline three common questions you would expect the family to ask and potential answers to those questions.
- Outline at least five specific materials the pathologist may need to complete a baby autopsy.
- A call comes to the office that a baby is dead at home in a very remote location from the office. An officer is on the line asking for help to photograph the decedent in the residence. Outline at least five key photographs that will be essential for him or her to take and forward to the office.
- A doctor is calling to report the death of a baby in the operating room for surgical correction of transposition of the great vessels. You, as the investigator, take the call and need to determine if the case falls under the jurisdiction of the office. Outline three key questions you will need to ask to make that determination.

Key Terms

Babygram
Co-sleeping
Skeletal survey
Cyanotic
Meconium
Hematoidin
Fetus
Neonate
Infant

Chapter Summary

This chapter discusses the various common natural diseases causing deaths in infants and children, as well as nonaccidental trauma and specific issues related to fetal deaths. Autopsy procedures for children are usually modified to answer specific questions to determine cause and manner of death. Investigations require attention to detail to assist the pathologist to make the best determination.

INTRODUCTION

Sudden death in children requires methodical observation, photographs, and systematic questioning of the caretaker(s) to establish the series of events that led to the child's death. Subtle findings can be the key to the determination of the cause and manner of death (Figure 11.1). The process to determine a cause

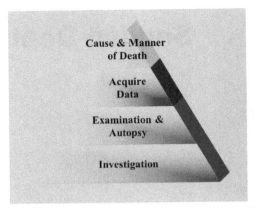

FIGURE 11.1
Depicts how each level of information is needed to determine the cause and manner of death.

of death is a multistep approach in gathering the necessary information for the pathologist to come to the best conclusion.

INVESTIGATION TECHNIQUES

Depending on the scenario, many times the child has been removed from the site of death during resuscitative efforts, and will be pronounced dead at a hospital. The hospital generally notifies law enforcement, but if they have not done so, it should be done. The local agency will have resources available to check for previous involvement at the residence by law enforcement and child protective services (CPS). Also, entry into a residence by death investigator personnel may not be possible without a search warrant or advisable without law enforcement participation, especially in cases of suspected inflicted injuries.

Each state has an infant death protocol checklist that needs to be completed. The Appendix has examples of the death investigation checklists from Arizona and California. These checklists allow uniform information documentation to ensure that all aspects of the investigation are reviewed with the caretakers. It begins with the usual demographics of the family, caretakers, and child, including dates of birth, addresses, and occupations. It is important to establish the time the child was found and time he or she was last noted to be alive and to determine what occurred in between. The interview covers feeding habits including types of formula, how it is mixed, solid foods, and when the child last ate; recent illnesses; birth history; past medical history including immunizations; doctor, urgent care, and hospital visits; illnesses in the residence; sleep habits; observation of the sleep environment; and where the child was found unresponsive.

Examination of the crib should begin with photographing it as it is first observed followed by examining the underlying layers of bedding. Toys or other objects in the crib should be examined for possible leakage of stuffing contents. Details of small or soft foreign objects within the crib should be noted. Thermostat settings

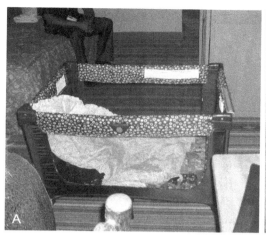

FIGURE 11.2
Examples of scene reenactment where a doll is used to recreate the course of events immediately before and after the child was found unresponsive. It may generate useful information concerning the airway or position within the sleep environment that cannot be discovered at autopsy.

in the house, as well as the location the child was found, also are noted. Particular questioning should be centered to the time period when the child was last seen alive and details regarding how, where, why, and by whom he or she was found.

Near the conclusion of the interview, it is recommended that a scene reenactment be performed if the family is willing to participate (Figure 11.2). This process involves using a small doll or even a stuffed animal that may be present at the scene. The caretaker who placed the **infant** in its sleep environment repositions the doll in that position with attention to detail for location of the arms, airway, and face up, face down, or on his or her side. The caretaker who found the infant then positions the infant how he or she was found with similar documentation. Photographs are taken during each stage of the reenactment for review by the pathologist. Notation is made of emesis or other food material in the sleep environment. An investigator should also document the softness of the surface the child was resting against. Children can typically raise their head at two months old and roll over at approximately four months, sit at six months, crawl at nine months, and walk at one year. Prior to four months, they may not be able to maintain a clear airway from fluffy or pillow-type surfaces that can partially obscure their airway. The ability to raise the head at two months may allow them to reposition but not maintain the airway for a prolonged period. The fluffy surface may also bunch around the airway, obscuring it. These milestones are approximations, and if a child is born prematurely or has a developmental disorder, he or she will be delayed in acquiring them.

In some instances, the caretakers will report the infant was **co-sleeping** with adults and/or other children. The same type of information needs to be documented as to last known positions of the parties while the child was alive, followed by the position he or she was found. Risk factors for co-sleeping include obesity (breasts obscuring the airway of the infant breast feeding); drug or alcohol use, which may further hamper the caretaker's awareness of the surroundings or deepen his or her sleep; and multiple people in the bed.

AUTOPSY PROCEDURE

Many times only preliminary information is available to the pathologist at the time of autopsy. The initial scene information just described may be only partially completed. It may take time to contact the treating pediatrician or obtain hospital records. For this reason, the autopsy examination is more extensive than for adults.

The usual procedure is to perform a total body X-ray (**babygram**), including anterior and lateral views of the head, and at a minimum screening X-rays of the extremities and ribs (Figure 11.3). Any questionable areas may need coned-down views to better visualize the contours of the bones and joints looking for subtle or healing fractures. All fractures are of concern, especially if they were not previously documented by hospital personnel. Fractures are evaluated by the extent and location, as well as the caretaker's explanation of how they happened. Mismatches are clues that further investigation is needed. This may require high-resolution X-rays and evaluation by pediatric radiologists, which may only be available at a hospital

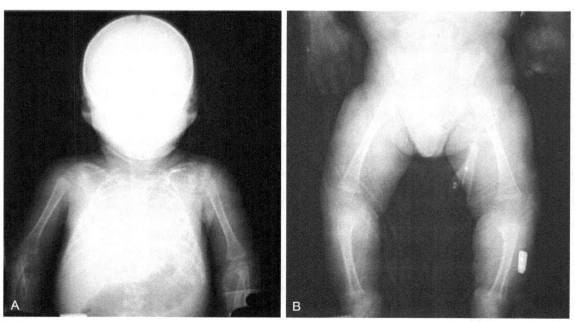

FIGURE 11.3
Typical babygram X-rays that are done during the course of an infant death investigation. They assist with screening for acute and healing skeletal fractures. If the child was evaluated at the hospital, the technology is of higher quality and the results reviewed by a radiologist. Evaluation of those studies may also prove useful.

radiology department. Findings of acute fractures are seen as small chips off corners of joints or as curved lines through the skull, or long bones of the upper or lower extremities. Healing fractures appear as raised irregular areas along the margins of the normal bones and need to be differentiated from a tumor. Findings on MRI scans include blood within the cranial cavity or evidence of swelling. Hospitals also have the ability to perform **skeletal surveys** where the body of a child can be screened for both acute and healing injuries and the X-rays read by the radiologist. These are extremely helpful in aiding the distinction between accidental and nonaccidental trauma. Reports of all the X-rays are important for the pathologist to have available for review, including copies of the hospital X-rays.

The external examination, X-rays, and scene information will direct the pathologist as to what needs to be done next. Overall photographs, including the usual medium and close-up photos with and without a scale, of any injuries are documented. It is important to photographically document the child with all medical treatment in place so any artifacts can later be explained if needed. External examination also needs to include an accurate weight after all medical appliances are removed. Body length is confirmed. Other measurements taken include head, chest, and abdominal circumferences, and crown (top of head) to rump (to base of buttocks fold) length. Circumferences are best done with a flexible tape measure without stretch. A head circumference is measured around the head like a hatband at the mid-forehead encircling the widest part of the back of the head. Chest circumference is measured around the chest at the nipples level. Abdominal circumference is measured around the abdomen at the navel level. Crown to rump length is done from the top of the level head to the bottom crease of the buttocks. Crown to heel length is done from the top of the level head to the sole of a foot without crossing over the torso. All are recorded in inches or centimeters, whichever is standard protocol of the office. (Photographic descriptions of baby measurements can be found in the Appendix.)

If the child's death appears accidental (e.g., motor vehicle or drowning) without suspected inflicted trauma, a standard autopsy without special studies can be done. The purpose is solely to establish a cause of death and rule out aberrant traumatic findings that might otherwise be missed.

If the child's death appears in the range of natural or unknown death but not traumatic, it follows the state protocol and includes cultures and genetic screening, and a full autopsy including biopsies for microscopic review by the pathologist. Cultures from a pediatric autopsy include obtaining a nasopharyngeal swab culture for viral pathogens. This is done by inserting a special nylon-tipped swab in the nostril and, upon removal, placing in special red liquid media called Hank's medium (normally supplied by the public health laboratory). The vial needs to have the decedent's name, date and time collected, and identify it as a nasopharyngeal swab. A requisition form needs to accompany the specimen to the laboratory and include the demographic identification, physician and contact information, specimen type, date and time collected, and test ordered. The specimen needs to be delivered to the viral laboratory within a couple of hours after it is obtained, and definitely before the end of the workday.

Bacterial cultures include spinal fluid, blood, and lung cultures. The same procedure used for viral cultures is used to label each specimen and completion of a bacterial culture requisition form. Spinal fluid can be obtained from either of two locations. One method is via the lumbar region of the lower back where it is performed in the living. The child is positioned in a fetal position, which widens the space between vertebral bodies and assists with the passage of the needle into the space. Another method to obtain the fluid is to position the child face down with the head draped over the side of an autopsy block, which will separate the vertebral body spaces for entry of the needle. The needle is passed into the cisterna magna located at the base of the skull where it joins the spine. In either location, it is important to clean the skin thoroughly with soap to remove skin contaminants. (Special autopsy procedures relevant to infants can be found in the Appendix.)

Blood cultures are obtained from heart blood. To decrease contamination, it is best to obtain the blood from the aorta or pulmonary artery, furthest from the intestinal bacteria. Three to 10 ml of blood is placed into a transfer media bottle(s) obtained from the microbiology laboratory. The rubber stopper is covered by a plastic lid and the surface is sterile if not previously opened or handled.

Lung cultures are obtained by using a microbiology swab that has a transfer media in the tube. A slit is made in the lung tissue and the swab is placed into the slit opening then replaced into the tube for transfer to the laboratory. Some pathologists sear the surface of the lungs or the cardiac vessels prior to obtaining the lung and bacterial cultures. These surfaces are sterile unless they have been touched by gloved hands, so the searing may not be necessary if the cultures are obtained promptly upon opening the chest cavity and pericardium.

Full toxicology sampling is performed next with retrieval of blood, urine if present, and bile. The pathologist will usually retain liver and brain tissue as needed for additional submission. Genetic screening consists of a commercially available filter paper requisition, upon which small samples of blood are placed, and then air-dried before mailing back to the commercial laboratory. These screens are not as comprehensive as the initial neonatal screen, but they do check for the common diseases that can cause death after the first few days of life.

The autopsy routinely includes an evaluation of the large vessels entering and leaving the heart to establish a congenital heart defect. This is best done if the heart and lungs are removed together to confirm proper vascular connections. The remaining organs can be removed organ by organ if attention is paid to their proper anatomic relationships. Gastric contents need to be retained for possible toxicology testing. The bowel contents need to be noted.

The head is examined next with photos of any scalp injuries documented. The exterior skull is evaluated for fractures and expanded sutures. In the first two to four weeks of life the skull is extremely malleable and may be opened by cutting through the sutures and opened "eggshell fashion." After the skull is further calcified it is best to use the typical saw pattern and remove the skull cap. There should be an absence of blood over the surface or extreme swelling. It is helpful to photograph the brain prior to removal followed by the internal skull. The dura needs to be removed from the basilar skull and the cranium to verify the absence of fractures. After the brain is examined and there is an absence of blood, the vitreous fluid may be obtained for toxicology. In children this can be a very small quantity and the testing limited to sodium, creatinine, and urea (all on one panel in the laboratory), or if a higher priority is on the glucose, that can be done instead. Some pathologists retain and fix all children's brains to cut later. In this instance, a container of formalin will be needed, and each department has a procedure on how it will be suspended, cut, and for final disposition of the remains.

The neck, removal of the tongue, and evaluation of the posterior pharynx is very important to look for obstruction by objects, food, and evaluate the palate and tonsils. The airway is evaluated as well as the neck muscles to verify a lack of hemorrhage that might be present suggesting an asphyxial death.

The cavity is then dried to evaluate the inner surfaces of the ribs to look for fractures. The spine and pelvis are similarly evaluated. The spine can be removed for better evaluation of the spinal cord. This is made by making cuts through the anterior vertebral bodies in a linear fashion using the bone saw at a 45° angle to the side of the vertebral bodies. The cut is extended from the neck to the lumbar region and can be lifted off, exposing the underlying dura and spinal cord.

In nonaccidental trauma cases, the dissection becomes a bit more intense because there are questions concerning the ages of any visible injuries. Skin biopsies are taken of these areas for microscopic evaluation. If possible, the face and hands should be spared so the family may have a visitation after the autopsy. Generally, the autopsy begins with a skin dissection only and the muscle layers are left intact. This allows evaluation and documentation of any hidden injuries that might appear externally on the skin surface. This technique also can be repeated down the back and buttocks. It is especially important to perform a skin dissection if the child is dark skinned, which makes visualization of injuries more difficult than in pale-skinned children.

Other special procedures in nonaccidental trauma are the forfeiture of vitreous fluid, so the eyes are removed instead for evaluation of intraocular hemorrhage, which may be associated with head injuries among other causes. The inner ears may also be sampled looking for inner-ear infections. Any sites of rib or long-bone fractures are removed, photographed, possibly X-rayed, and sampled microscopically for dating of the fracture.

FOOD

The type of food the child last ate, the amount of formula, and the time of the last feeding are all important to the evaluation of cause of death and confirming caretaker accounts of what has transpired. This can take a critical turn if the child appears undernourished. It becomes imperative to inquire exactly how the formula was mixed, the volumes the infant was consuming, and how often the feedings were occurring, as well as any natural or solid foods that were being attempted. If the child is older, the kinds of foods he or she was served, amounts, frequency, and documentation of unusual feeding practices may be in order. Observations of other children in the household may also hold clues for the etiology of the undernourished decedent. Questioning should also center on the quantity and types of stools, how often diapers are changed, etc.

Any hospital admissions or evaluations by physicians or other healthcare workers need to be obtained for the pathologist to review. Birth records and genetic screenings need to be obtained for any congenital issues that might contribute to poor weight gain, also known as failure to thrive. A detailed growth chart is necessary to evaluate these children. Weight and height measurements can be found in emergency room records and records of visiting nurses and pediatrician offices. Growth charts depict multiple curved lines upward over time with the age of the child plotted on the x axis and the weight on the y axis. The curves are divided into percentiles ranging from 5% to 95%. These graphs normally show progressive weight gain in a curvilinear fashion falling no lower than the initial percentile curve on the graph established at birth. For example, if a premature infant's initial weight and height measurements place him at the 5% curve, his first checkup at two weeks should show growth at least at the level of the 5% curve, if not above. If it is level or dropping, feeding practices need to be explored and the child followed more closely. By plotting each of these weights over time, and including the one obtained at the time of the autopsy, it can give further indication of progression or lack of progression. If the weight varies over time with different caretakers or hospital admissions, then feeding practices by the caretaker(s) need to be questioned further. Postmortem electrolytes are also important for the evaluation of an undernourished infant or child.

FOREIGN OBJECTS

Children commonly put things in their mouths or other orifices that may obstruct the airway, create a nidus of infection, or perforate the gastrointestinal tract. An example is swallowing a toothpick that punctures the stomach or bowel causing peritonitis. Common airway obstructions are caused by coins, hot dogs, pieces of toys, candy, or items of food they are not able to reduce to a smaller bolus for swallowing. The item becomes lodged at the back of the tongue at the opening to both the trachea and the esophagus. This vulnerable location can result in the inability to swallow the item or cough and dislodge it. Coughing requires enough air behind the blockage to exhale during the cough. This is the reason a finger sweep of the mouth is used to dislodge any blockage freeing the airway. The Heimlich maneuver in adults is one where a bear hug is done to the mid-abdomen with a thrust in the upper abdomen to dislodge the obstruction. In babies, the Heimlich is performed face down supporting the head in the hand with a swift blow between the shoulder blades. Symptoms of a blockage are the inability to talk or cry with raspy breathing and a panicked look of the face.

ILLNESS

Probably the most common symptoms related by caregivers is the child was experiencing a stuffy nose, slightly decreased appetite, was fussier than usual, but sometimes they relate no change in behavior or activity. The symptoms may be mild or nonspecific and may even have been passed as teething or just the beginning of a cold. The interval between symptoms and death may be very short because children can succumb to bacterial infections and sepsis rapidly. Fever is difficult for many parents to assess and a temperature may not have been taken. If other family members have been recently ill, the probability of the death being related to an infection is much higher.

MEDICAL HISTORY

Infectious diseases are also more common in children who have not been immunized. Some families resist immunizations and relate that they feel they cause disease and death. The risk from not being immunized is much higher than the risk of being immunized, and all facets of modern medical care continue to recommend them on a scheduled basis. Immunization history and locations they were obtained should also be a part of the investigative report. It also may reflect on the parents' attentiveness to the needs of the children with routine evaluations by medical personnel. Immunizations are available free or at little cost at local health departments. County hospitals also have indigent health clinics for routine care, as well as emergency departments for sick children if finances are an issue.

Birth and prenatal history is important because it can give an indication of possible exposure in utero to toxins, drugs, or alcohol, which may affect organ formation and result in congenital anomalies, or symptoms of drug withdrawal. Alcohol use in utero can lead to fetal alcohol syndrome, a disease characterized by hyperactivity, behavior and cognitive disorders, and structural abnormalities of the heart, kidneys, and characteristic facial abnormalities. The amount of alcohol that can be ingested without injury to the **fetus** is unknown [1]. Fetuses who succumb in utero, or infants who die and the mother is found to be under the influence of drugs or alcohol, are usually reported to the coroner/medical examiner investigator. Generally, the case is accepted if the infant is of the age of viability as established by state law. It is difficult for charges to be brought about in this situation, but documentation and confirmation of the drug use can have repercussions for the care of other children living in the household and allow social services to take a more active role in the family dynamics.

Drug use in pregnancy is similar to alcohol use and is associated with cognitive, behavior, and seizure disorders, and withdrawal complications including death and structural abnormalities of organs. Death can occur in utero and lead to a miscarriage. Many times the mother presents due to lack of movement of the fetus, bleeding, or a spontaneous abortion. Drug screens are routinely checked and, if positive, law enforcement may be notified, especially if it occurs late in the pregnancy. If the child has been dead for a few days, the fetus/infant will be macerated, which is a form of decomposition. It is difficult to obtain blood in these cases to perform toxicology. **Meconium** is a great sample for testing and is nearly always available. Meconium is the thick, dark, tarry stool that a child expels in the early days of life. It accumulates in the fetal digestive tract during development through ingestion of amniotic fluid containing by-products of development and reflects the close proximity of fetal and maternal circulation intercommunication. The meconium begins forming about 12–15 weeks in the pregnancy and testing will reflect drug use through the last four to five months of the pregnancy. Head hair samples can also be evaluated and a qualitative result of positive or negative for illicit drugs can be reliably performed. In some states, law requires mandatory meconium testing on all infants. In others, it is done only if there is a positive maternal drug screen at birth or during the pregnancy.

Infants may survive pregnancy and the early newborn period but exhibit any number of symptoms, including seizures, brain disorders, and structural abnormalities of the heart or other organs, which will vary to some extent with the drug used [2]. Marijuana use during pregnancy can also result in learning disorders and behavior problems. Cigarette smoking and drug or alcohol use in pregnancy can result in a higher risk for sudden infant death. Since meconium is only present in the infant's system for the first week after being born, historical information from records will be needed. If acutely exposed to illicit or prescription medications, it will show in routine samples of blood or other tissues. Head hair can also be a useful specimen to retain as it will reflect a longer period of exposure.

Breast feeding will also transfer drugs to the infant. Nearly all drugs have the ability to be excreted into the milk and may exhibit symptoms in the infant. Drugs such as methadone will cross into the milk but may also have some calming effects on an opioid-addicted infant as well as to prevent withdrawal. The problem occurs if the amount in the infant is too high and causes respiratory suppression. **Neonates** and fetuses have less efficient drug metabolic pathways of the liver or renal excretion of drugs than adults. This decreased efficiency lasts at least the first couple of months of an infant's life and is more prolonged in premature infants. The result is the inability to rid an infant's body of the continued ingestion of drugs and may reach toxic levels depending on the dosage and the pharmacologic properties of the drug [3,4].

NATURAL DISEASE
Infections and sepsis

Bacterial organisms causing infant and child sepsis vary with the age of the child. In the neonatal period, *E. coli*, Streptococcal organisms, and Hemophilus influenza organisms predominate. Older infants are more prone to *Staphylococcus aureus*, *Neisseria meningitidis*, Klebsiella, Pseudomonas, and Streptococcus species [6]. Depending on the immunization status, other organisms may be encountered. Some organisms operate through their actual presence in a tissue and cause inflammation. Children will have the typical symptoms including fever, cough, mucus, elevated white blood cell count, etc., as seen with pneumonia. Other organisms operate through production of a toxin that is released by the organism into the tissue and causes rapid death by hypotension and shock with little chance of the body to mount a brisk inflammatory response. Some infants are slow to mount an inflammatory response and an organism can quickly overpower the compensatory mechanisms of the infant, leading to septic shock. See Figure 11.4 for an example of changes associated with meningitis.

If treated with antibiotics in the emergency room, postmortem cultures will most likely be negative for growth due to the antibiotics inhibiting their growth in the laboratory. It is important the hospital laboratory complete any culture specimens received to establish the identity of the organism. Some hospitals routinely cancel testing upon death and discard the specimens. Prompt attention is needed to inquire about the types of labs ordered and

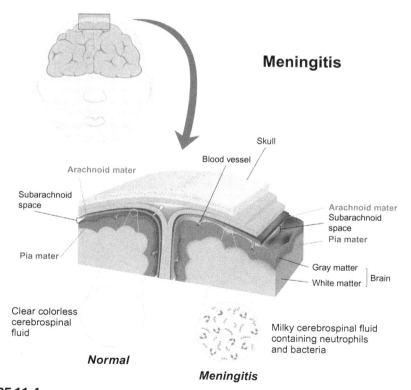

Meningitis

Skull

Blood vessel

Arachnoid mater

Subarachnoid space

Arachnoid mater
Subarachnoid space
Pia mater

Pia mater

Gray matter
White matter } Brain

Clear colorless cerebrospinal fluid

Milky cerebrospinal fluid containing neutrophils and bacteria

Normal

Meningitis

FIGURE 11.4
The changes associated with meningitis, which is usually a bacterial infection of the meninges within the brain. Meningitis can be rapidly fatal and family members may need to be treated.

speak to the laboratory directly and request continuation of the testing for the pathologist and/or the specimens so that the pathologist can send them for testing.

Cardiac

Structural abnormalities of the heart and great vessels are a reflection of fetal circulation. Because the lungs are not aerated in utero, blood flow to them is bypassed by a connection from the pulmonary artery to the aorta. This connection is called the ductus arteriosus and normally closes during the first week of life. Nutrients enter the fetus through the umbilical vein, which connects to the vasculature near the liver to be delivered to the heart and circulated. Blood returns via the umbilical arteries through the placenta to the maternal circulation.

CONGENITAL HEART DISEASE

This term describes any one of various structural abnormalities of the heart. They can range from a simple atrial septal defect that is an opening between the two atrial chambers and is easily repaired (Figure 11.5). They can also be complex transpositions of all the vessels with abnormal blood flow patterns, which can be lethal or life threatening. These abnormalities occur during the early fetal life at approximately 8–12 weeks gestation (called the period of embryogenesis) when the fetal development of internal organs is at its peak. After the organs are formed, the remainder of pregnancy is basically a continuation of building on this framework.

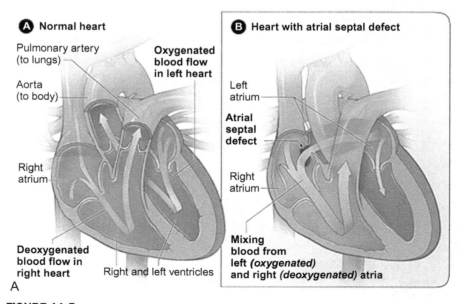

FIGURE 11.5
(A) An atrial septal defect, which is a communicating opening between the two atria and is not a life-threatening heart defect.

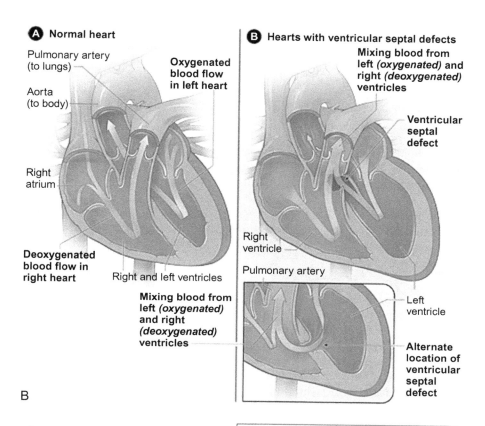

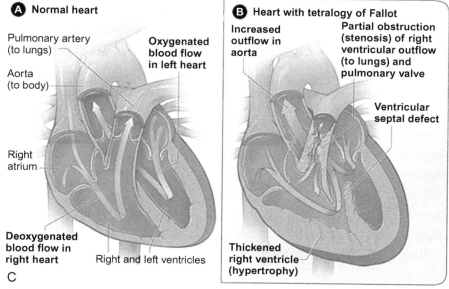

FIGURE 11.5, cont'd
(B) A ventricular septal defect, which is an opening between the two ventricles. Depending on the size this can be more serious because of the shunting of blood from the left side of the heart to the right ventricle.
(C) A defect called Tetralogy of Fallot, a cyanotic congenital heart abnormality composed of four major defects.

The heart is formed into its adult four chambers with vascular connections via a series of twisting and folding of the cardiac tubular structure. It is during this twisting and folding that the major congenital heart abnormalities occur. Smaller abnormalities such as the atrial or ventricular defects occur due to lack of growth of various membranes later in development or due to blood flow abnormalities. Some of these flow abnormalities are a result of persistent fetal circulation and retention of the structures to bypass blood from the lungs (patent ductus arteriosus, or PDA). These flow abnormalities may exist due to structural abnormalities making them necessary to sustain life. If the circulations of oxygenated and deoxygenated blood are mixed it results in a **cyanotic** (blue baby) heart disease, and is more critical than those infants who can maintain normal oxygen status.

Occasionally these diagnoses are missed during the routine assessment of infants prior to discharge from the hospital or even by pediatricians in the outpatient setting. Clues include poor feeding, decreased growth and development, and respiratory difficulties. Other times, the case may come to the attention of the death investigator after a failed surgery and mandatory reporting of operating room deaths. In these cases, it is important to gain some insight into the severity of the abnormality, as well as if anything unexpected happened during the surgical procedure (e.g., laceration of a major vessel unexpectedly or malfunction of bypass machine) to contribute to the death requiring it to be assessed by the pathologist. Many times because it is a natural disease, it can be certified by the clinician. On the other hand, if there are issues concerning the quality of homecare or potential inflicted trauma, it needs to be admitted to the office for further evaluation.

VIRAL MYOCARDITIS

Viral myocarditis is the result of a virus infecting the heart resulting in inflammatory cells responding and causing muscle cell damage. This can be a focal abnormality or involve a large portion of the heart. Death is related to the amount of heart muscle damaged and the cell damage, causing a fatal arrhythmia and sudden death. Symptoms include shortness of breath due to pulmonary edema, chest pain or epigastric pain, and malaise (flulike symptoms). Organisms that are the most common causes include influenza, adenovirus, Coxsackie virus, Cytomegalovirus, and Mycoplasma. Other infectious organisms including parasites (toxoplasmosis) or fungi may also cause a myocarditis. Underlying immunosuppression is not necessary to acquire myocarditis but is more common among patients with low white blood cell counts. It is more common in older children and young adults or the immunosuppressed of any age.

RHEUMATIC HEART DISEASE

Rheumatic heart disease results as an immunologic response to a previous group A beta hemolytic Streptococcal infection. The person may relate a severe sore throat, usually within the previous month to six weeks, which was not treated with antibiotics. A low percentage of these cases (<1%) develop rheumatic fever and, of those, about 40% develop cardiac complications called rheumatic heart disease. This is an autoimmune disease where the body attacks the heart muscle and surface cells destroy the myocardium and damage the valves. Acute rheumatic heart disease may cause death from irritation of the conduction system with fatal arrhythmia. More commonly there are sequelae many years later of valvular heart disease resulting in the need for surgical valve replacement.

Respiratory

Pneumonia is a common cause of death in children of all ages, especially if they have an underlying disease such as brain damage, severe seizures, cardiac disease, or underlying respiratory diseases such as cystic fibrosis. Commonly bacterial in origin, it causes filling of the alveolar air spaces by acute inflammation (pus) that inhibits diffusion of oxygen through the airspaces into the alveolar capillaries for distribution to the remainder of the body. It can be community acquired from inhalation or as a result of aspiration of food. It can also be a symptom of spread from another site through the bloodstream or it can spread from the lungs into the bloodstream creating septic shock. Pneumonia in children can be rapidly fatal via sepsis and may not have large infiltrates in the lungs due to the septic shock and death before the body can respond with inflammatory cells.

Viral pneumonia may also result in severe respiratory symptoms. The location of the pathology is different with the inflammatory response occurring in the alveolar walls increasing the diffusion properties into the capillaries, or from swelling and inflammation of the small parenchymal bronchioles. The body responds with proteinaceous and fibrin deposition within the alveolar, which also affects the oxygen saturation. The viral infection can become complicated by a secondary bacterial infection that overwhelms the host and is lethal.

ASTHMA

Asthma is an acute airway obstructive disorder caused by an environmental trigger, for example, allergies or cold air. This results in an inflammatory response by eosinophils, which also cause a mast cell response (Figure 11.6). This combined inflammation causes the release of histamine, which further increases the inflammatory response with mucus secretion and bronchoconstriction, sending the breathing into a downward spiral. The mucus within the airways allows air to enter into the alveoli, but during attempts to exhale, the narrowed bronchi collapse inward and are blocked by the mucus. This causes air to be present within the lungs but unable to get out. Eventually no further air can enter, and as the oxygen is depleted in the alveoli, the patient becomes short of breath. This will get progressively worse without treatment until the child collapses into respiratory arrest. The treatment is epinephrine products to dilate the bronchi and allow exchange of air. As air reenters the alveoli, enough pressure beyond the obstruction will enable coughing to dislodge the mucus plugs.

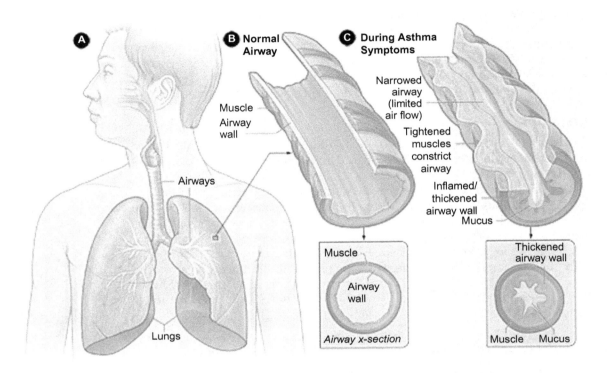

FIGURE 11.6
Shows the changes associated with asthma. The narrowed bronchioles cause shortness of breath with wheezing or coughing symptoms.

CYSTIC FIBROSIS

Cystic fibrosis is an inherited disease in which the child lacks an enzyme product that results in abnormally thick mucus and pancreatic secretions (Figure 11.7). This causes frequent lung infections and poor digestive functions with bowel obstructions and pancreatitis. This diagnosis is not usually a reportable case to a death investigator unless there is an underlying issue with medical care or abuse.

Case Study

A 10-year-old girl with a history of asthma requiring frequent use of an inhaler and emergency room visits for exacerbations went home for lunch, which was without incident. She was late returning to school and arrived short of breath and wheezing when she suddenly collapsed. Resuscitative efforts described stiff lungs after intubation. Autopsy findings showed hyperexpanded lungs that met in the midline over the heart and were very fluffy upon palpation. Sectioning of the lungs showed numerous mucus plugs throughout the parenchyma and collapse of the fluffy parenchyma upon dissection. Microscopic evaluation showed the typical findings of the small bronchi with intraluminal mucus strands, as well as surrounding mast cells and eosinophils in large numbers (not normally seen). The cause of death was certified as acute asthma, and manner of death as natural.

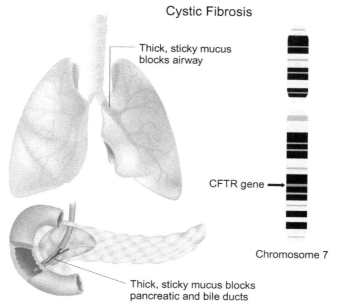

Cystic Fibrosis

Thick, sticky mucus blocks airway

CFTR gene →

Chromosome 7

Thick, sticky mucus blocks pancreatic and bile ducts

FIGURE 11.7
Cystic fibrosis is a disease characterized by thick mucus that plugs the airways and pancreas.

Neuromuscular disorders

Down's syndrome is an inherited disorder composed of an additional X chromosome and is frequently called Trisomy 21. The result is varying degrees of mental retardation with those who may function at basic jobs to those with severe deficits and are wards of the state. These individuals may also have underlying cardiac disease that makes them susceptible to sudden cardiac death. In later years, those with Down's may exhibit early onset dementia and require care in a facility. Whether the case is within the jurisdiction of the coroner/medical examiner will vary with the circumstances surrounding the death and will need to be decided on a case-by-case basis.

Hydrocephalus is swelling of the brain's ventricular spinal fluid compartment. This accumulation of fluid expands outward, compressing the cortex and white matter against the skull, which damages it. If not treated early, the child may have irreversible brain damage. Treatment is relatively easily completed by threading a vascular-sized catheter from the ventricular system in the brain, through the subcutaneous tissue of the neck, and draining excess fluid into the peritoneum. This is called a ventriculo-peritoneal shunt (VP shunt). The diameter of the catheter is small and may become clogged with sudden onset of repeat hydrocephalus and deterioration of consciousness.

Occasionally, hydrocephalus will present in the differential diagnosis of head injuries in a child due to a sudden onset in increased head circumference. The cause of hydrocephalus is a blockage in the spinal fluid flow dynamics and can result from a cyst, congenital abnormality, or tumor. An autopsy examination will rule out a traumatic origin and may require assistance from a neuropathologist for the underlying natural cause.

Cerebral palsy is a cognitive, behavioral, and neuromuscular disorder as a result of hypoxic-ischemic injury in utero or as a result of prematurity. The degree of brain injury varies on the degree of injury and varies from severely debilitated children who are vegetative, to those with various learning disorders. An investigator may become involved in these cases due to living conditions or because of a medical issue that required it to be reported.

Metabolic disorders

The most common metabolic disorders are screened for at birth and submitted to the state health agency. Typically these results can be found in the pediatrician's records. Occasionally they will need to be obtained from the screening agency. The initial screening is done for common diseases determined by each state [5].

Diabetes mellitus commonly presents in children and young adults. It is typically type I diabetes and the first symptom can be diabetic ketoacidosis. The initial diagnosis may be at the time of death. The child will have been experiencing the typical symptoms of polyuria, polydypsia, and feelings of lack of energy, but may not have sought medical treatment.

Fatty acid oxidative disorders are inherited diseases due to lack of an enzyme in the metabolic breakdown of fats. This results in accumulation of the fats in the liver and can cause death. The accumulation of by-products can require a period of time and the diagnosis missed on the initial newborn screening. It is one of the causes of death screened for in the sudden death of an infant. When the diagnosis is made, families should be offered genetic counseling. Dietary restrictions in some metabolic pathways may prevent further symptoms and death.

Neoplasms

Occasionally undiagnosed neoplasms may cause death in children. These can range from brain tumors, leukemias, bone/soft tissue tumors, or solid tumors of the internal organs. Children with previously documented neoplasms are rarely seen in a coroner/medical examiner investigation, unless there were issues with them receiving medical care. Cases of holistic medicine use or refusal of care based on religious grounds have occasionally received widespread press and may fall under the jurisdiction of a coroner if documentation of the disease is needed.

Acquired diseases

Ingestion of poisons/medications is always a concern in sudden death of children. Toddlers especially may find pills on the floor or within reach or on counters. Because some items can appear as candy to a child or due to their oral fixation at that age, they can ingest them and parents not know. Part of a scene assessment is noting the location of parent's medications and cabinet locks for securing cleaning products and insecticides. The diagnosis may not be suspected until evaluation of gastric contents or the results of toxicology are known. If it is prescription medication, especially sedatives, parent-assisted ingestion should be considered. The easiest way to give this medication to kids is through a bottle, therefore confiscation of a bottle and its contents should be done as part of all infant death scenes. Bottles need to be secured in an upright position so they do not leak during transit. It is important to only handle the outside of the bottle with gloves, as it may become important to fingerprint the bottle to determine who last fed the infant. Another source of contamination can be a dried formula container that can also serve as a drug stash. Small quantities spilled within the milk powder can be enough to severely affect an infant. Inspection of milk containers and the preparation of formula can be an extremely important part of a death scene investigation.

Anaphylaxis is a severe allergic response to an ingested food, bee stings, or even skin surface application of an irritant. In anaphylaxis, the first instance the child or adult is exposed to the allergic material will result only in a relatively mild response of the body. However, it is this initial introduction that creates a memory in the body for a severely heightened response at the next exposure, which can be lethal prior to emergency response. If the severe allergy is known, it can be treated by immediate injection of epinephrine, which can be carried as an epi-pen. Because these cases are sudden, unexpected, and generally accidental in nature, they are reported and certified by the coroner/medical examiner office. Important scene documentation includes the person's statements just prior to their collapse, as well as findings by emergency response teams and witness statements about the course of events. They may document that the child was stung by a bee or consumed peanuts or shellfish, common anaphylactic agents.

Anaphylaxis is modulated by the body through mast cells and immunoglobin E found in particular white cells. The latter value can be quantified if needed. Autopsy findings can include sites of a bee sting or possible food in the stomach, swelling of the airway including the epiglottis, or mucous plugs within the small bronchi, similar to what is seen in an acute asthma attack. It is a good practice for the investigator to review the food and areas surrounding the child who dies to see if they contain the items that they are allergic to.

Case Study

An 8-year-old girl with known allergies to peanuts went to a week-long summer camp away from home. Counselors and nurses were aware of the allergy. During dinner she took a bite of a chocolate crispy treat containing peanuts. She immediately discarded the bite but almost immediately began having symptoms of anaphylaxis. She had no epi-pen with her and she died before resuscitative efforts could support her.

Public health notifications

In pediatric infectious diseases it is extremely important to notify the public health department of the organism identified to prophylactically treat other family members or children in the home or school to prevent an outbreak. Even though these people may be asymptomatic, they may be in a period where the organism is quiescent but can produce disease if certain environmental and body parameters are present. The health department can trace contacts and provide surveillance and public announcements if needed to prevent further deaths. The local health department will perform the notifications to the Center for Disease Control (CDC), which follows national trends. Either department may request frozen tissue or blood to perform subtype species analysis for epidemiological studies and further characterize the pathogen. Since there are no diagnostic findings always notable at the time of autopsy in infectious diseases, it might be prudent to routinely hold frozen tissue biopsies on key organs such as the heart, lungs, brain, and liver in case it is requested. These frozen samples may also be useful for genetic analysis of inherited diseases. Formalin-fixed tissue biopsies that are routinely held are usually unsuitable for either purpose.

Congenital and genetic counseling

In deaths related to an underlying genetic disease, it is useful to have pediatric counselors or genetic counselors available to families to answer their questions regarding familial risk factors and for future pregnancies. Some diseases have easily obtained laboratory tests available to screen the family members for the disease. In metabolic diseases they may be treated by dietary restrictions. A list of counselors can be very helpful for suggestions over the phone or may be included in a referral letter citing the cause of death as genetically related.

NONACCIDENTAL TRAUMA

Patterned injuries are one of the keys to evaluating inflicted trauma. Patterned abrasions matching belts, flyswatters, electrical cords, etc. help distinguish a nonaccidental cause of death from accidental injuries. Varying ages of injuries, locations, patterns, and internal findings are all used to make the diagnosis. When observing a child dead in the emergency department or at a residence, it is important to evaluate the skin surfaces and look for trauma, but especially patterned injuries. The object responsible for the injuries may be located nearby or discarded in trash bins as a means to hide the evidence. It is also good to note the caretaker history about how the child came to be in medical care and if the story is plausible with the degree of injury. This usually requires investigation at the site of injury and careful recording of carpet padding, wall trauma, toys, or whatever else might have resulted in the injuries noted by medical personnel.

Markings from belts are flexible and may only partially match along curved body surfaces as they wrap across the skin. The pattern on a belt, such as weaving, stitching, snaps, or the buckle, may be imprinted as contusions or abrasions. The width of the injury will nearly match the width of that portion of a belt and will help to narrow the confiscated items as evidence. Electrical cords leave thin, narrow, parallel abrasions/contusions with a central parallel line corresponding to the central trough on the cord. Plugs may also create partial or full imprints.

Cable cords create curved abrasions and contusions matching the diameter of the cord, which may be formed into a loop. Toys such as swords, bubble wands, tent poles, etc. all can be used as instruments for punishment and may leave characteristic imprints on the skin. The objects used for punishment many times are nearby and may not even be obscured as they are used frequently.

Irons and hair curling irons may also leave patterned burns. Immersion of hands, feet, or buttocks in hot water will leave water-level burns as a ring in a glove- or sock-type pattern. In immersion of the buttocks into hot water, the line will appear around the seat area of the buttocks. If the story is the child got into a bath without assistance, then it is not consistent, as the feet should also contain similar burn injuries at a depth of the water. It is important to document hot water temperature and length of time for the water to reach the highest temperature from the suspected faucet. If the immersion was in a bath tub, the time it takes to fill the tub and reach a scalding temperature is also important to note.

Genitalia are also areas that need to be carefully evaluated for trauma. Many times the period of risk is near the time of potty training, and sitting on the toilet for long periods may leave ulcers on the skin or burns may be inflicted to the genitalia as punishment for wet clothing. Sexual assault may also be a motive, so careful photography of the genitalia at the time of autopsy is good documentation for later questions. If trauma is present, penile and vaginal DNA swabs need to be obtained.

Severe spankings or a "whooping" may result in bruising of the buttocks with severe subcutaneous bruising into the fat within the buttocks. In dark-skinned children and in children with a thick layer of fat, this can be difficult to see. A subcutaneous dissection of the skin over the back and buttocks can demonstrate the extent of hemorrhage and assist visualization of patterns not seen well on the surface skin. Other gray-brown discolorations can be seen on the lower sacrum and are called Mongolian spots. They are not contusions, and when incised, the underlying skin will be normal without hemorrhage.

Sometimes hand or finger marks can be seen across the back, arms, or face. In acute injuries, DNA swabs may be considered to link the possible suspect with the patterned injury. It is important that all of the injuries be documented with and without rulers in the photographs and good measurements of the size of these patterned injuries be documented by the pathologist for the potential ability to match the injury to the person or an object. See Figure 11.8 for examples.

Contusions anywhere on the abdomen, but especially near the umbilicus, are highly suspicious for inflicted trauma until proven otherwise. The thin layer of fat and abdominal muscles of infants and children are not sufficiently strong enough to withstand a fist or kick to the surface without resulting in internal damage (see Figure 11.8B). This can result in lacerations of the liver or spleen and internal

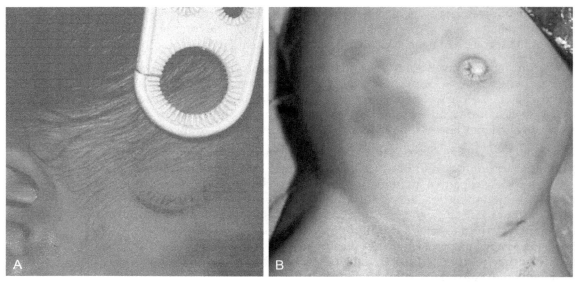

FIGURE 11.8
(A) Patterned abrasion on the scalp and the corresponding toy was found nearby. The scalp and torso contained multiple similar abrasions. (B) A large contusion of the abdomen. Internally there may be extensive hemorrhage from a lacerated liver or there may be a ruptured small bowel with peritonitis. A young child has thin abdominal fat and not fully developed abdominal muscles to withstand a blow to the abdomen.

bleeding. The mid-abdomen is particularly vulnerable to a punch as the force forces the duodenum–proximal jejunum and pancreas against the spine causing it to lacerate. The bleeding may be minimal but the loss of integrity of the lumen of the bowel or the leakage of digestive enzymes into the sterile peritoneal cavity rapidly leads to peritonitis and death if not immediately surgically repaired.

Other clues to suspected nonaccidental trauma are the distribution of contusions over the body (Figure 11.9). Bruises over bony prominences such as the knees, elbows, chin, and forehead can be associated with falls, especially in active kids or toddlers learning to walk. They would not be expected in a bedridden child, one confined to a wheelchair, or immobile infants. So the distribution of injuries needs to be assessed with the developmental milestones as well as the mobility of the child. Areas of great concern are protected areas not exposed to normal childhood bumps and scrapes, such as between the shoulder blades and the neck, lower back, abdomen, chest, cheeks, or forearms. Other areas such as the frenulum, the small piece of membrane that attaches the lips to the gums, should be an area not usually associated with accidents but may be torn with slaps across the mouth or forceful feeding or even aggressive intubation. Loss of teeth or gum lacerations should also be assessed carefully with regard to the offered mechanism of how it happened for plausibility, as well as visual assessment of other obvious injuries in conjunction with it. See Figures 11.10 and 11.11.

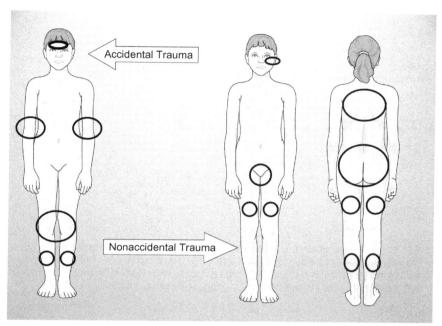

FIGURE 11.9
Classic distribution differences of accidental versus nonaccidental injuries. It is important to correlate the scenario with the pattern, extent, and distribution of injuries to make the best assessment of how the injury may have occurred.

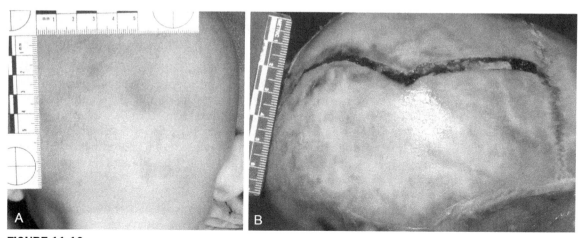

FIGURE 11.10
(A) Faint contusion of the scalp; when reflected there is a large linear skull fracture (B).

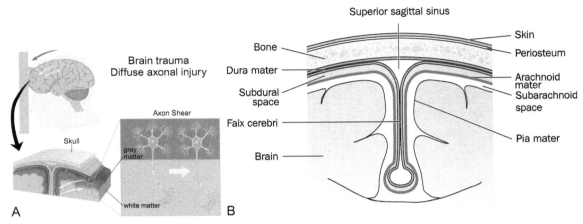

FIGURE 11.11
(A) A diffuse axonal injury is basically a shearing of the neuron extensions from the body of the neuron cell. This occurs during acceleration/deceleration injuries and may not show gross bleeding or obvious abnormalities on autopsy. The finding is a microscopic one. Fatal head injuries in infants and children may result in bleeding within the brain tissue (contusion), subarchnoid or subdural hemorrhages. (B) A review of the anatomy of the location of those injuries in their respective layers of brain tissues.

Extent and duration of injuries

Common court questions are: When did the fatal inflicted injury happen? Is this a single or repeated injury over time? Would earlier medical treatment have resulted in a different outcome? These questions are difficult to answer with current scientific methods available to forensics. A good general response to the medical therapy question is the sooner medical treatment is sought in care of trauma, the outcome is usually better. In some cases the injuries are so extensive that medical treatment probably would not have changed the outcome. Earlier social intervention prior to the fatal trauma would have improved the outcome.

When the injuries happen is also a very difficult question to answer. At best, it can be estimated within a range of days, not hours or a specific time unless it was a witnessed event. The estimates are made via skin biopsies and biopsies of injured sites, such as a ruptured bowel, subdural hematoma, or sampling of fractures. As hemoglobin in bruises breaks down, it releases the cellular iron that is absorbed by macrophages. Special microscopic staining procedures can demonstrate the presence of these macrophages. As the iron changes its configuration it develops a different morphology and can be seen as yellow pigment on slides called **hematoidin**. This can also be noted grossly on skin bruises as the green-yellow coloration they assume with healing. This all occurs over a continuum with the hematoidin appearing at approximately 4–5 days and the hematoidin at 8–10 days after injury. This is not an exact science and, depending on the depth and extent of a bruise, it may take slightly longer or shorter. Multiple studies have determined that gross appearance of bruises is not a good indicator of age of the injuries and dating them via observation is not valid [8].

Dating of fractures is also variable because the underlying nutrition of the child and continuous injury over the site causing repeated fractures and hemorrhages all distort the healing and making an exact determination of the injury date difficult.

CHILDREN LEFT IN VEHICLES

There has been a bit of press over the past few years regarding children left in their car seats while caretakers went shopping, or forgotten in the backseat when the caretaker arrived at work and had not dropped off the child at daycare. Even though the temperatures outside a vehicle may only be 80°F, the temperatures inside a vehicle parked in the sun can reach over 120°F in 60 minutes if the windows are closed. This is due to the radiant energy being absorbed into the dashboard, seats, and other objects, then heating the compartment via conduction and convective currents [7]. The trunk has also been utilized to contain children while parents go shopping, go to a friend's house or bar, or go to work. Temperatures inside the trunk may also become similarly excessive.

Scene investigation of this type of death is similar to other heat-related deaths. Core body temperature or infrared temperature of the child and compartment are important scene findings. Also document if the child was restrained in a car seat as well as efforts of the child to escape, if any. Also the presence of liquids or food left for the child (or children) is important to photograph and document. Even though in some instances this is seen as an accidental death, in other jurisdictions it has been successfully prosecuted as child abuse or neglect and associated with prison sentences. Children left in a hot car may be showing early decomposition changes and will continue to rapidly decompose even though they are refrigerated at the morgue. It is important to photograph a child as completely as possible for the pathologist to review for possible additional injuries. Electrolytes, full toxicology, and stomach contents will be important documentation to note and substantiate that hyperthermia was the cause of death.

FETUSES AND HOME BIRTHS

Intrauterine demise occasionally comes to the attention of the investigator if there was maternal trauma from a motor vehicle accident or assault, demise while in prison or as a ward of the state, or maternal drug use. The autopsy is done to determine fetal gestational age and to note congenital or placental abnormalities for a cause of death. For this determination, the placenta will need to be obtained for examination by the forensic pathologist. Many times the hospitals discard the placentas, so prompt attention will be required.

Home births, sometimes in the toilet, or discarded infants in an attempt to hide the birth will need to be examined by the forensic pathologist. If it can be found, the placenta needs to be collected as well. All items surrounding the birth or infant are also needed and should be photographed as found at the scene. Questions asked by law enforcement include whether it was a live birth, age of viability, how long the fetus/infant lived, if it was a live birth, etc. These can be very complicated, especially if the infant was buried or is decomposed. DNA of the fetus may be helpful to link parentage and should be held on the fetus/infant.

Skeletal remains of infants can be minimal or appear as partial bones due to the large amount of cartilage present. Recovery of child and infant skeletal remains can be challenging and experienced anthropology consultation may be needed.

SUDDEN DEATH WITH NO CAUSE IDENTIFIED

Not uncommonly, observed findings aggregated in the evaluation of an infant or child death may not clearly point to a single cause or even a single manner of death (Figure 11.12). Sometimes there may be findings of a microorganism only present in one culture and not others, or the organism identified may be either a pathogen or a contaminant, or the scene may have included co-sleeping. There may be no way to differentiate the exact cause resulting in an "undetermined" cause and manner. Other times a head injury may have been caused either accidentally or by inflicted homicide, or just plain poor judgment on the part of the caregiver. Failure to seek medical therapy may play into the determination or it may be unable to be determined exactly how the injury occurred. In this case the cause of death is relatively obvious—blunt-force trauma of the head—but the manner uncertain and therefore called undetermined.

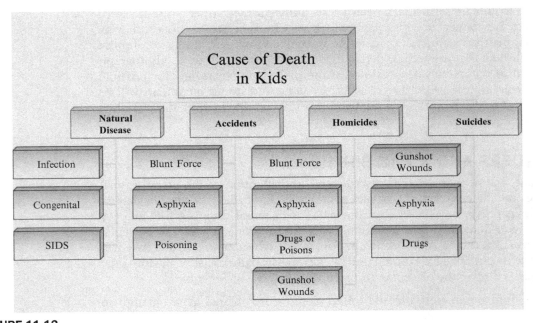

FIGURE 11.12
Diagram of the broad causes of death that fall within the four major manners of death. SIDS (Sudden Infant Death Syndrome) is now known as SUID (Sudden Unexplained Infant Death) and may be ruled undetermined or natural manner of death depending on the investigation and pathologist viewpoint.

There is obviously pressure to make decisions by attorneys, families, and law enforcement, but it must also be remembered that the science and forensic judgment may only support a certain level of certainty. The bottom line is "do no harm" and call only what you can support and defend. Many times the greatest punishment may already have been rendered with the loss of one's child.

REFERENCES

[1] Fetal Alcohol Spectrum Disorders. Centers for Disease Control and Prevention, National Center on Birth Defects and Developmental Disabilities, Division of Birth Defects and Developmental Disabilities; 2011. Retrieved from http://www.cdc.gov/NCBDDD/fasd/facts.html. [August 2013].

[2] Illegal Drug Use and Pregnancy. John Hopkins University, Health Library. Retrieved from http://www.hopkinsmedicine.org/healthlibrary/conditions/adult/pregnancy_and_childbirth/illegal_drug_use_and_pregnancy_85,P01208/. [August 2013].

[3] Choonara I. Drug Metabolism in the Neonate. J Arab Neonatal Forum 2005;2:1–4. Retrieved from http://www.fmhs.uaeu.ac.ae/neonatal/iss003/p1.pdf. [August 2013].

[4] Gardiner S. Drug Safety in Lactation. Medsafe, New Zealand Medicines and Medical Devices Safety Authority, Publications; 2001. Retrieved from http://www.medsafe.govt.nz/profs/puarticles/lactation.htm. [August 2013].

[5] About Newborn Screening: Conditions Screened by State. Baby's First Test; 2013. Retrieved from http://www.babysfirsttest.org/newborn-screening/states. [August 2013].

[6] Santhanam S. et al. Pediatric Sepsis. Medscape; 2013. Retrieved from http://emedicine.medscape.com/article/972559-overview#aw2aab6b2b3. [August 2013].

[7] Heat: A Major Killer. National Weather Service, Office of Climate, Water, and Weather Services; 2013. Retrieved from http://www.nws.noaa.gov/os/heat/index.shtml. [August 2013].

[8] Vanezis P. Interpreting Bruises at Necropsy. J Clin Pathol 2001;54:348–55.

CHAPTER 12

Asphyxia

Learning Objectives

- Compare and contrast the ligature furrow of a suicidal hanging to a homicidal ligature. List two key features for each.
- Differentiate petechiae from Tardieu spots and include their locations and underlying causes.
- A call comes to the office for the investigator to respond to a man dead at a residence. Upon entering the scene, the house is noted to be full of piles of empty liquor bottles and you are directed to the bathroom. There you note a man lying over the edge of the tub empty of water. Outline three key questions and five photographs that are needed to properly investigate the scene.

Key Terms

Anoxia
Hypoxia
Asphyxia
Positional asphyxia
Compression asphyxia
Strangle
Choke hold/blood choke/sleeper hold
Tardieu spots
Adipocere
Carbon monoxide
Cyanide

Chapter Summary

This chapter discusses multiple methods resulting in hypoxia and potentially life-threatening events. Hangings are most commonly suicide but also require vigilance by the investigator to not overlook ligature strangulation. Manual strangulations and choke hold-type injuries can be subtle and have few external findings. Asphyxial deaths due to noxious gases require vigilance for safety, as well as documentation to provide the information to determine which gas was present in the environment that caused the death. Inhalation injuries are very difficult to document through toxicology and have few autopsy findings, so the cause of death largely depends on scene information. Photographic and written information will greatly assist a forensic pathologist with these differential diagnoses.

INTRODUCTION

Asphyxia results when a process causes a lack of oxygen to the brain, unconsciousness, and death. **Anoxia** is the total lack of oxygen, and **hypoxia** is a decreased level of oxygen to the brain and vital organs. Common causes of asphyxia include hanging, strangulation, drowning, or mechanical causes like compression of the chest or **positional asphyxia**. An extended period of hypoxia can result in brain death.

A 39-year-old man was the single occupant and driver in a motor vehicle accident. According to officers and witnesses, the car was traveling at a high rate of speed when the man lost control of it on an area of wet pavement, flipped the car, and crashed it upside down into a light pole. Upon arrival he was found trapped and pinned in the vehicle, strapped into the driver's seat. The roof of the vehicle had collapsed down to the level of the steering wheel. The decedent was pinned between the seat and steering wheel with his head flexed toward his chest and the roof pushing onto his back. The jaws of life were used to open the compartment. Pry bars were needed to extricate him from the position he was in. Examination at the scene and by the pathologist showed no fractures of the torso or extremities. His face was intensely congested and the sclera mildly hemorrhagic. An autopsy examination showed no fractures or internal injuries. The brain, neck, and spine were free of injury. The cause of death was certified as compression asphyxia due to motor vehicle accident, and the manner of death as accidental.

HANGING

Hanging is a combination of a ligature around the neck and the body in a position of either partial or full suspension. It does not require the body to have the ligature tight and totally compressing the neck, falling from a height (like a judicial hanging), nor free suspension. It can occur in any position by something encircling the neck and the person leaning forward. Children can accidently become entangled in window blind strings or crib toys hanging from the edge of the crib railing, or they can become wedged between pieces of furniture while in suspension.

Hanging with a noose can occur in a sitting, standing, kneeling, or full suspension position. The ligature can be fashioned from a rope, curtain, tow strap, shoestring, sheet or shirt, belt, electrical cords, necklace, posey restraint, or even a pacifier string. The knots forming the ligature range from a simple overhand knot to a full hangman's noose. The classic hangman's noose is used by some but a simple sliding overhand-type knot is more common. A hangman's noose was actually a scientific phenomenon with the number of coils depending on the weight of the condemned, as well as the type of the rope to be used. The weight of the condemned was also used to calculate the distance of the drop through the trapdoor to prevent decapitation. The position of the knot behind the ears aided the fracture of the cervical spine.

Fractures of the neck in suicidal hangings are rarely seen, as most are done from a short-distance fall. Petechiae are also rarely seen. An internal examination will show a compression area of the tissues but rarely any hemorrhage or fractures of the hyoid or thyroid cartilage.

Sometimes one ligature fails and will be hanging in a nearby location while a different one is found on the body. It is important to note where the items may have originated, especially if the hanging occurs in prison. Prisoners usually do not have access to shoestrings or belts and may fashion a noose from bed sheet strips hung from an overlying bunk. The same findings need to be observed if the decedent is a patient in a psychiatric ward. Usually these patients are relieved of belts and shoestrings especially if they are on suicide watch. Those who wish to commit suicide can be quite focused and creative in achieving their goal. Depressed prisoners and patients need close observation if they are suddenly having improved positive feelings, because it may indicate a resolve to perform the final act rather than true progress toward recovery. Drug intoxication may be a part of the findings in a toxicology test.

The mechanism of death is usually compression of the blood flow to or from the head, rather than obstruction of the airway or fracture of the spinal column (Figure 12.1). This is usually a reflection of physics. The head alone weighs about 10 lbs. The amount of force required to obstruct venous flow (blood flowing from the head) is approximately 7 lbs and the amount to obstruct arterial flow to the brain is approximately 11 lbs. This is because the walls of arteries contain a thick muscular layer that is lacking a vein. The trachea supporting the airway is even stronger due to its presence of cartilage and requires approximately 20 lbs of pressure to collapse it. A fracture of the spine will require a larger degree of force, and usually one with acceleration/deceleration, such as the drop that occurs in a judicial hanging.

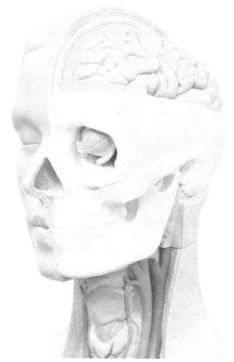

FIGURE 12.1
Human throat including veins, bones, and organs.

As the noose tightens around the neck, it will first obstruct the jugular veins followed by the arteries. With unconsciousness, the head will collapse and contribute to the obstruction of blood flow by further placing weight on the neck. Depending on how the force and noose are applied will result in the presence or absence of petechiae. Petechiae within the eyes are created by the rupture of capillaries. One way to think of this is by compression of the venous return to the heart and continued arterial blood flow into the brain, causing increased pressure on the small vessels, which finally rupture, creating the petechiae.

Externally, a typical suicidal hanging furrow abrasion shows upward deviation to one or both ears or the back of the head depending on the knot placement (Figure 12.2). The furrow should match the suspected ligature in pattern and dimension. In some areas, the furrow may be wider than the ligature due to sliding upward as the suspension is occurring.

Ligature as evidence

If the decedent is obviously dead, there is no need to remove the ligature around the neck, and it should be left in place for examination by the forensic pathologist. If it has been removed, it should be placed into an evidence envelope, sealed, and submitted with the body for examination. Many of the ligatures will fray when they are cut. When multiple loops are used, it can be difficult to reapproximate the ligature for later duplication and examination.

Remember, each piece of evidence should be retained so that it can be reproduced as the original whenever necessary. The easiest way to do this with a ligature is to use wide masking tape or duct tape and take a length approximately 6 in. long. Slide this under the binding with the sticky side toward the loop of the ligature then fold over the tape so that it forms a sealed edge with a small

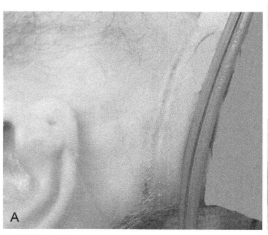

FIGURE 12.2
(A) Ligature abrasion showing upward deviation, and (A & B) ligature abrasion patterns.

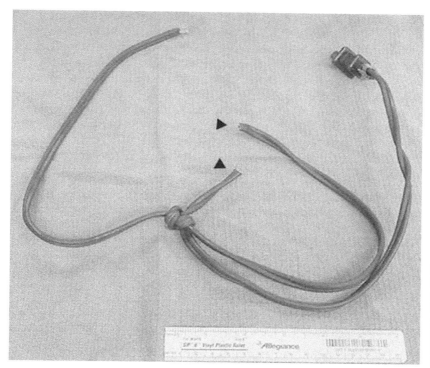

FIGURE 12.3
Ligature removed from a hanging victim. Note how the ligature is removed from the neck away from the site of the knot so that the knot is preserved as evidence.

tab extending from the margin. Cut through the middle of the tape and the loops of the ligature so that each cut edge has an adherent length of doubled-over tape. For each area of the ligature with its own separate loop, such as the one securing it to the fixed beam and the one surrounding the neck, each tab can be marked "A," "B," etc. to differentiate the connections. This technique also works on homicide cases for bindings at wrists, ankles, or body wraps. The area where ligatures are cut should be distant from any knots so they are preserved (Figure 12.3). Knots should not be unwrapped as a means to remove the ligature. Sometimes tape will not stick and strings on either side of the cut will suffice.

SEXUAL ASPHYXIA

Some hanging scenes will appear very different from the moment an investigator enters them. These are sexual asphyxia scenes where there may be an intricate asphyxia mechanism with pulleys, bondage mechanisms, or even a simple noose. These are nearly always males who may be dressed in woman's clothing or underwear. Cross-dressing and pornography seem to be a part of the fantasy that occurs. Sex toys may be lying about as well. Drug use may or may not be a part of the scenario. It is written that asphyxia and oxygen deprivation heightens sexual gratitude, therefore the reason some individuals participate in the behavior.

The bondage and asphyxial apparatus is associated with escape mechanisms, such as keys or releases for ropes, which may still be clutched in the hands or dropped on the floor out of reach. The problem usually arises due to the loss of consciousness and being physically unable to release the mechanism or some miscalculation about the release. Either results in the asphyxia going too far, total loss of consciousness with further oxygen deprivation, and death. If a noose mechanism is used it usually has some type of padding like a towel or scarf between the noose and the skin to protect the person's neck. The penis is many times exposed or the underwear is disarranged. High heels, bras, pantyhose, bows, leather outfits, or items encircling the penis are commonly seen.

Sometimes individuals suddenly collapse during masturbation or sexual relations. The increased heart rate and blood pressure can precipitate a cardiac event with arrythmias or even a ruptured aneurysm. The risk for cardiac events is increased with a history of cardiac disease and drugs for erectile dysfunction. They are contraindicated but may be used anyway and should be inquired about during investigation in to the medical history when death occurs in this situation. It is not uncommon for a sex partner to not be aware that the decedent is taking erectile dysfunction drugs. Sex toys or hand-carved items may be lying next to or attached to someone collapsed with underwear and pants in disarray. There might be a computer with pornography displayed or signs of drug use. It is a good practice for the investigator to eject a DVD from the TV or computer, in the presence of law enforcement, to document pornographic movies.

A female dying during sexual intercourse is less common than a male dying. If the female is young, and especially if she is, or has recently been pregnant, oral sex with inflation of the vagina by air can cause an air embolus to enter the vascular area of the placental surface. This is a very rare occurrence, but questions concerning the activities during the sexual relations may need to be asked during the investigation.

Case Study

A 55-year-old man with a history of coronary artery bypass surgery was found sitting in pajamas in a chair at a desk in his residence. The family related they came home and found him in that position. He had recently been complaining of back pain and increased chest pain, usually relieved by nitroglycerin. The investigator at the scene noted no trauma and there was a mid-sternotomy scar on the chest consistent with the history of a bypass graft surgery. The only unusual finding was a plastic dry cleaning bag attached to the big toe and threaded up through the pajama bottoms. Also noted was a disposable plastic glove on one hand. When the investigator inquired from the family about the bag on the toe they said it was not unusual and he rigged this bag to help with his back pain. Upon admission to the office and removing the clothing for examination, it was noted the plastic bag was fashioned into a strip, tied around the big toe on one end and encircling the testes on the other, forming a tight bondage. Review of the scene photographs showed a computer on the desk where the decedent was sitting. Postmortem toxicology was positive for moderate levels of cocaine use. The death was certified as atherosclerotic cardiovascular disease with the contributing factor cocaine use. The combination of drugs with the heart disease and probable masturbation led to a significant cardiac event.

SUICIDE NOTES

Many suicide deaths are not accompanied by suicide notes. It is estimated they are found in 40% of suicide deaths and are seen more commonly left by females than males. The presence or absence of a note is not always helpful as many are wandering, reminiscent memories that may be open to interpretation. Others, however, may spell out last wishes or give good-byes to family members or friends. Some are vengeful. Whatever their content, their location can be important, and they need to be recovered as evidence. It is best to place a note inside a clear plastic envelope. This allows the note to be photocopied or scanned and easily shared with other agencies, plus it contains body fluids and retains any fingerprints on the surface should that prove necessary to test.

STRANGULATION

Homicidal strangulation may occur from a ligature or by arms or hands. The term **strangle** is defined as to choke to death by compressing the throat with something (e.g., a hand or rope). Some people commonly use "strangulation" for all ligature deaths and others reserve it for homicidal-type injuries.

Homicidal ligature strangulations externally vary from suicidal hangings by their position of the ligature furrow (Figure 12.4). Homicidal ones have a horizontal pattern partially or fully encircling the neck and lack the upward deviation to the

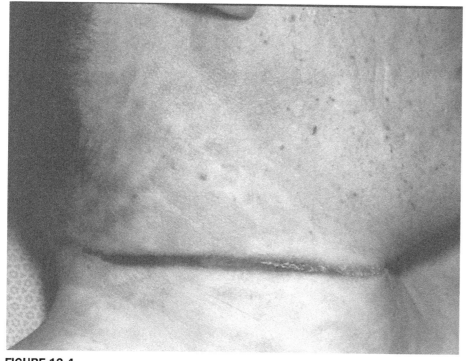

FIGURE 12.4
Ligature furrow from a homicidal ligature strangulation. Notice the horizontal pattern with absence of upward deviation toward the ears or chin seen in suicidal hangings.

side or back of the head seen in suicidal hangings. The ligature may be removed by the perpetrator and no longer with the body when it is found, so accurate dimensions of the furrow may help to narrow the suspect weapon. A crossover point or garrotte may also be used to tighten the ligature and leave a secondary pattern. Common homicidal ligatures are wires, ropes, leather bands, or clothing items such as pantyhose, underwear, socks, or shirts.

Manual strangulation involves using the arms or hands. This type of injury can leave obvious, faint, or no injuries to the external neck (Figure 12.5). Occasionally

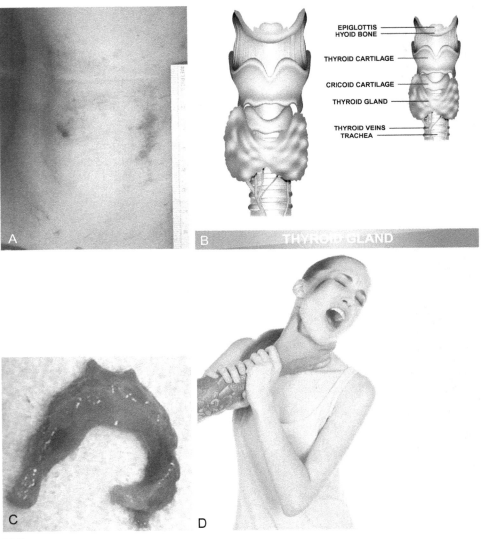

FIGURE 12.5
(A) Finger impressions on anterior neck from a manual strangulation. (B) Anatomy of the neck showing the relationships of the thyroid cartilage (Adam's apple) and the superior hyoid bone. Either may be fractured in manual strangulation. (C) Fractured hyoid bone: note the angulation of the curved bone on the right as well as the bilateral hemorrhage at typical sites of fracture. (D) Depiction of manual strangulation.

the pattern will duplicate outlines of fingers. Petechiae may be florid, minimal, or absent. Circumstances of how the body is found may be the biggest clue that this diagnosis may be possible. This should be considered as a potential cause in dumped bodies, female decedents, lover quarrels in residences, bodies in alleys, or bodies found out in the open with no obvious injuries. The decedent may be found dressed or naked, but note should be made of any necklaces or clothing bands at the neck by good photographs at the scene. The diagnosis is made by finding hemorrhage of the anterior and/or lateral muscles of the neck. Because the muscles are easily bathed in blood early in the autopsy, this can obscure this finding, therefore the neck is usually examined last to create a bloodless field.

CHOKE HOLDS

Choke holds previously were used by law enforcement to subdue a suspect. The mechanism of application is usually from the rear of the suspect with the upper arm on one side of the neck and the forearm on the other with the crook of the elbow at the front of the neck (Figure 12.6). By application of one hand on the other and compressing the arm inward, it puts pressure on both carotid arteries and jugular veins, causing the subject to collapse. The practice is no longer used by law enforcement because it resulted in a number of deaths either by prolonged application or fractures of the airway.

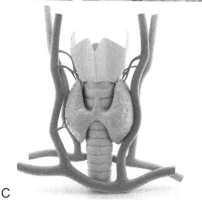

FIGURE 12.6
(A) Young boys performing a choke hold. (B) The choke hold is a commonly used move in wrestling and cage fighting. (C) Depiction of jugular veins and carotid arteries and their relationship to the trachea and areas of potential compression.

Choke holds have seen a resurgence in popularity with cage fighting and are easily seen on TV and the Internet. These tactics are also taught in the military. The terms **blood choke** or **sleeper hold** are sometimes used to describe it as well. The findings in a death associated with these can be subtle and only have focal hemorrhage in the strap muscles of the neck, or they can have fractures of the hyoid bone or even the midline thyroid cartilage.

MECHANICAL ASPHYXIA

Mechanical asphyxia includes both compression asphyxia and positional asphyxia. **Compression asphyxia** results when some mechanical device compresses the chest or abdomen, inhibiting movement of the diaphragm and lack of oxygen–carbon dioxide gas exchange. Common causes include motor vehicle accidents where the occupant is compressed between the steering wheel and the seat, or industrial accidents where the decedent's torso may become entrapped in the machinery or between two vehicles. The findings include abrasions or compression areas seen on the skin and intense congestion, petechiae (Figure 12.7A,B), or hemorrhagic spots above the compressed area. Hemorrhages may be seen in the sclera (white portions of the eye) and face. The way to envision the physiology is a garden hose with the water on being run over by a vehicle. The hose portion between the faucet and the tire will expand and eventually

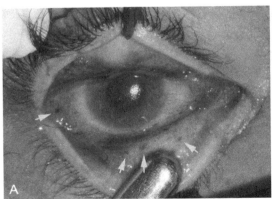

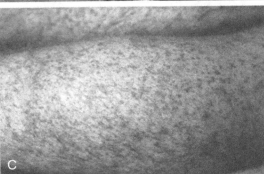

FIGURE 12.7
(A & B) Petechiae in the upper and lower conjunctivae of the eyelids as well as on the sclerae (white portion of the eyeball). (C) Tardieu spots seen in areas of dependent livor and commonly seen in lower extremities of hanging victims.

rupture. In the case of compression asphyxia, the ruptures are seen in the capillaries rupturing and creating the small hemorrhages on the skin, called **Tardieu spots** (Figure 12.7C). These spots are not diagnostic of compression asphyxia and only indicate increased vascular pressure with resultant rupture. Tardieu spots can also be seen in the lower legs and feet of a fully suspended hanging victim or in an extremity lying over the arm of a chair.

Positional asphyxia is more subtle and where the position of the body itself causes the impairment of oxygen exchange (Figure 12.8). Note the difficulty in taking deep breaths if your head is flexed with the chin near the chest or if the head is tilted far back. Either direction decreases the ability to exchange oxygen. Another method to produce impaired oxygen exchange by position is if the weight of the body is largely resting on the diaphragm, such as being in an upside-down position. A person's natural instinct is to remove him- or herself from this position if he or she is not in some way impaired.

Examples of impairment include alcohol, drugs, senility, or entrapment by obesity or weakness of the legs or arms. Common examples resulting in positional asphyxia are alcoholics falling off the toilet and becoming entrapped between the toilet and the wall, reaching for something behind a washer or refrigerator and becoming entrapped, or being suspended upside down in a motor vehicle accident with the roof collapsed onto the occupants. An autopsy examination may show minimal to no findings. The key to the diagnosis is awareness by the scene investigator and photographs of the decedent showing the compressed head-to-chest or hyperextension position. Toxicology may give additional clues by revealing acute alcohol or drug intoxication. A medical history investigation can include impaired mobility through use of a cane or even wheelchair. It's not uncommon for a nursing home patient to partially fall out of a chair or wheelchair and becoming asphyxiated by the strap used to hold him or her in the chair.

DROWNING

Drowning is a common situation where a body is found in water but has no diagnostic findings at autopsy. This is referred to as a diagnosis of exclusion, which means other diseases have been excluded as the cause of death, and the only finding is the decedent found within a water environment. It is possible to commit suicide by drowning oneself, as well as to drown in a very shallow amount of water. Older textbooks discuss finding hemorrhaging in the middle ears, water in the sinus cavities, or heavy lungs as those associated with drowning. However, many times these findings are negative, or, even if present, the significance is unknown because they can be seen in other causes of death. After death, water can passively gain entrance to the sinuses, hemorrhage of the ear canals can be seen in other causes of death unrelated to drowning, and heavy lungs are nonspecific. Light, fluffy lungs are also seen in drowning cases and thought to represent a period of spasm of the epiglottis preventing water from entering the lung tissue.

Inhalation

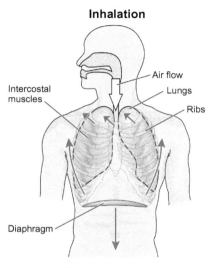

Intercostal muscles

Air flow

Lungs

Ribs

Diaphragm

Air flows into lungs due to increased lung volume following contraction of diaphragm and intercostal muscles

A

Exhalation

Air expelled from lungs due to relaxation of diaphragm and intercostal muscles

Compromised inhalation with lung trauma

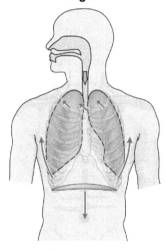

When trauma to the lung occurs, and intrathoracic pressure is increased, lung expansion becomes compromised

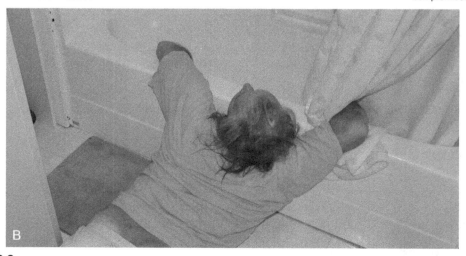

B

FIGURE 12.8

(A) Diagram depicting normal breathing and the effects of lung trauma as well as the role of the diaphragm and intercostal muscles in moving air into and out of the chest. (B) Positional asphyxia where extension of the neck and head posteriorly as well as weight on the chest prevents proper respiratory chest expansion for exchange of oxygen/carbon monoxide.

Diatoms are small microscopic particles found in bodies of water and historically have been related to the diagnosis of drowning when found in quantities within the lung tissue. This too is not thought to be diagnostically significant. Salt concentrations in blood were also thought to be significant in seawater drownings. This too has not been found to be diagnostically significant.

Scene findings important to establish are witness accounts describing the course of events as to how the person came to be in the water. Information about ability to swim, environmental conditions (ice, darkness, from shore or a boat, while crossing an ice surface), alcohol use, etc. are all useful. Examination of the decedent may show swimming attire, street clothes, or heavy outdoor clothing.

Suicide may also be a motive in unwitnessed events. Some can be quite dramatic with cinder blocks attached to the feet and the hands bound. It is important to treat these cases as a possible homicide until further background information can be obtained.

Artifacts associated with drowning include washerwoman effect of the hands and feet. This appears as washed-out wrinkling of the hands and feet similar to that seen in living persons. The skin is very fragile and easily damaged so it needs to be protected during transit since fingerprints may be needed for identification. The extensive wrinkling is challenging and patience is required to get good fingerprints. This may require subcutaneous injection by water, formalin, or a tissue builder (used by funeral homes in embalming) to remove the wrinkling. Blotting and wrapping the hands in towels also helps to remove some of the water. See the Appendix for a method for obtaining fingerprints from washerwoman hands.

Body submersion is associated with delayed decomposition but it depends on the water temperature for how quickly a body will precede through the decomposition stages. Initially, the body sinks as water fills the cavities and clothing. As subcutaneous gas formation begins with putrefaction, the body will rise to the surface and assumes the "dead man float" position. This is best described as face down with the hands, face, and legs curved downward into the water, and the lower back at the surface. This position explains fish and crustacean postmortem activity of the distal extremities as they rake along the bottom of a river. Other injuries that can occur are propeller injuries. These are difficult to assess if they occur pre- or postmortem as the blood leaches from the wounds. The lack of blood and vital reaction can make them very pale to visual inspection for making the distinction of them occurring after death or being the cause of death. The length of time for a body to surface will vary with the amount of air in the lungs and body fat, how much clothing the person is wearing, water temperature, and if the person becomes entrapped within rock crevices or underwater obstructions and currents.

Submersion in ice water can preserve a body for many years. The body acquires a special type of decomposition called **adipocere** where the fatty portions become saponified and partially calcified. Adipocere can appear as a damp cheese-like texture to a crumbly dried plaster texture. I can relate a case of a snowmobiler crossing a partially frozen lake that collapsed and the body remains were recovered six years later with an intact torso and organs. The exposed areas showed skeletal exposure with usual decompositional slippage. The areas of preservation were the ones protected from direct exposure by a heavy layer of clothing. The adipocere was very dry and crumbly, requiring a saw to enter the torso cavity.

NOXIOUS GASES

Carbon monoxide

Carbon monoxide is a tasteless, odorless, colorless gas, which means someone can be exposed and not realize he or she is in an environment of increased concentration. Smokers inhale carbon monoxide with levels up to 7–10%. Carbon monoxide preferentially binds to hemoglobin in blood, causing displacement of oxygen from the red cells and resulting in tissue deprivation of oxygen. The tissues most affected by high levels of carbon monoxide are ones with high oxygen demand: the brain and heart. Levels are measured as a percentage of the total hemoglobin in the blood.

Neurologic symptoms of carbon monoxide exposure are progressive confusion, disorientation, and eventually coma with death. Cardiac symptoms include progressive exercise intolerance, shortness of breath, chest pain, cardiac arrythmias, and collapse. Fatal levels are usually encountered greater than 35% up to 70% depending on the underlying health of the individual and length of exposure. Children have a higher metabolic rate and are more susceptible than adults. There have been reported cases of sudden deaths in infants thought to be "crib death" only to have the adults in the house succumb to carbon monoxide poisoning within days after. It is an important consideration in any environment where there is vehicle exhaust in a closed environment, or a wood-burning stove, furnace, or fire item is in use.

Suicide via carbon monoxide poisoning commonly involves either the exhaust being attached to the vehicle compartment by a hose, an obstruction within the tail pipe exhaust system, or the vehicle running inside a closed space. See Figure 12.9.

Other methods are charcoal barbecue grills ignited in a closed space such as a vehicle or small room. To increase the concentration capability, the suicidal

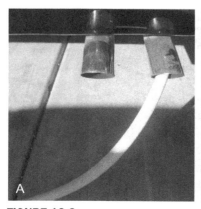  

FIGURE 12.9
(A) Car exhaust showing hose connecting to interior compartment. (B) Noting the amount of fuel registering on the car dash is an important investigation notation as well as (C) the position of the keys in the ignition and whether the car was found in the 'on' or 'off' position.

person will utilize tape, towels, or plastic along door or window openings. When a vehicle is used, it is important to note the position of the key in the ignition, amount of gas in the tank, and body position inside the car. It is helpful to look for receipts for charcoal briquettes, grill, hose, or tape items used during the process. Because of the heat generated from the car exhaust and the grill, many of these decedents will be decomposed or have extensive skin slippage. There may also be a component of drug intoxication that may account for a lower than expected carbon monoxide level.

Cyanide

Cyanide is colorless but does exhibit an odor of burned or bitter almonds detectable by 60–80% of the population. The remaining 20–40% do not have the genetic trait and cannot smell it. Cyanide can be inhaled or ingested and is lethal in high concentrations within 10 minutes and estimated to be 35 times more toxic than carbon monoxide [2]. It acts upon cellular metabolic pathways (electron transport system) by irreversibly binding to the iron within the body and inhibiting an enzyme called cytochrome C. This system is important in the utilization of oxygen within a cell and formation of ATP, the cellular energy packets needed for cell functions. Like carbon monoxide, it affects high metabolic organs (brain and heart) most and has similar symptoms of disorientation, chest pain, and sudden collapse. This binding can be very rapid with sudden death, and is the basis of cyanide ingestion portrayed in spy novels.

Cyanide has no common household uses but may be present in the environment in low levels from car exhaust. Industrial uses include fumigation, electroplating, and metal ore harvesting. Both carbon monoxide and cyanide exhibit bright red livor. It has a history of being used in the execution chamber and, in those situations, the concentration is very high, requiring the surface of the body to be hosed down prior to transport to decrease exposure to investigative personnel.

Hydrogen cyanide is also a component formed in burning plastics and manmade materials, and may be a cofinding to carbon monoxide in those succumbing in a house or factory fire.

Hydrogen sulfide

Hydrogen sulfide gas has shown an increasing trend as a method of suicide. Internet how-to postings have been linked to heightened awareness by the public, as well as the easy availability of materials to create it. The websites encourage proposed enlistees to post a note on the door or window to warn responders to beware of the toxic hydrogen sulfide gas. Other warning signs to note are empty buckets or chemical bottles seen through a car or door window. At that point, hazmat needs to respond to deal with the situation and prevent injury to others.

The online recipes actually direct the user in a step-by-step process of mixing the materials, as well as provide the signs and party-hosting suggestions. The chemicals used to make the hydrogen sulfide are easy to find and include toilet and bathroom cleaners (the acid portion) combined with bath salts, pesticides, or detergents (the base portion) [4].

CAVES, FREEZERS, TANKER CAR, OR SILO ASPHYXIA

Deaths in closed environments are hazards to investigators until they are understood. It is important in these situations that all safeguards be utilized to protect the safety of rescue and investigative personnel, as well as to prevent further injuries after the decedent is removed. Unlike a noxious gas, these environments can kill a person by a lack of oxygen in the environment causing an immediate anoxia with rapid collapse. In tanker cars, there may be nitrogen gas present; its presence alone is not lethal because it is present in the air we breathe where it is mixed with oxygen. In a tanker car, it is a closed environment and pure nitrogen may be used to empty the car rendering the environment oxygen deprived [1]. Typically, it is a repair worker who enters the tanker to repair something and suddenly collapses. Other workers may enter in an attempt to render aid and also succumb.

Typically our environment contains 20% oxygen and 78% nitrogen [1]. As concentrations of oxygen decrease, it causes increased work for the heart, which responds by an increasing heart rate and the lungs compensate by increasing the respiratory rate. If the oxygen concentration continues to decrease, the person becomes confused and disoriented, eventually collapsing. This occurs over time if the oxygen concentration slowly decreases. However, if the person drops into a nitrogen-rich environment with low to no oxygen, the effects will be immediate.

Silo asphyxia can also occur due to nitrogen production by the plant material from a recently filled silo. The nitrogen gas is heavier than air and will settle into the base just above the plant material and form a brown haze. The plant material can also form a carbon dioxide-rich environment after a recently filled silo [2]. Workers in these environments should be wary of entering the silo and at a minimum wear a safety harness with a second safety rope attached, as well as have two people outside the silo to extricate the worker if necessary.

Grain bins filled with grain are also hazardous without safety equipment because the dust can disorient the farmer/worker. The grain can collapse and form an unstable crater, creating a situation of mechanical asphyxia [3]. The grain dust is extremely flammable and can ignite and cause explosions.

Freezers and refrigerators have the same properties of being a closed environment where the exchange of oxygen may be impaired due to the environmental concentration. Typically, this occurs to children who may climb into discarded appliances as a hiding place only to lose consciousness and later be found dead. Occasionally, freezers or sealing boxes may be used to confine a prisoner by an abductor. Storage of these appliances or discards are placed facing a wall so the door is unable to be opened.

Caves can have pockets of lethal gases or even low oxygen saturation and also cause death. Other mechanisms are cave-ins where small rooms are created, which can lead to eventual hypoxic environments. This is why in mining accidents there is an urgency to obtain a shaft to trapped miners to pipe in fresh air and replenish the environment.

PHOTOGRAPHIC DOCUMENTATION

In many asphyxia deaths, there is a potential risk to investigative and rescue personnel. It is imperative that the environment be rendered safe prior to entry. Hazmat may be in attendance and can monitor these situations and verify the status of the scene. The history of what transpired prior to the victim collapsing is important to document, as well as any findings monitored by hazmat. Photographs of the position of the decedent and receipts for purchase of gas-forming materials are relevant to determine an intentional event versus an accidental one. Noting the color of livor at the scene is also important. Photographs of the labels of the chemicals used will aid the determination of the identification of the produced or ingested substance. It is a good practice for the investigator to obtain any type of detergent information that the hazmat team may have used on the decedent to wash away any contamination. This is helpful to the pathologist, as he or she needs to also let the toxicology lab know what was used in the event that there is cross-contamination of tissues and/or blood.

SUICIDE VERSUS ACCIDENT

In some cases it can be difficult to determine the manner of death, especially in carbon monoxide deaths. For instance, was the charcoal grill in the room to produce heat on a cold night, resulting in an accidental death, or was it an intentional act to produce the gas? Scene findings are the key to making these distinctions.

The presence or absence of the ligature and the pattern of its furrow on the neck also give an indication of the course of events. If the ligature is absent, it could have been removed by rescue personnel or the family. If the pattern is suggestive of a horizontal pattern, it is more consistent with it being absent due to it being a homicide and removed by the perpetrator.

REFERENCES

[1] Hazards of Nitrogen Asphyxiation Safety Bulletin. U.S. Chemical Safety and Hazard Investigation Board; 2003. Retrieved from http://www.csb.gov/assets/1/19/SB-Nitrogen-6-11-031.pdf. [August 2013].

[2] Upright Silo Safety. University of Maine Cooperative Extension Publication. Bulletin #2305; 2002. Retrieved from http://umaine.edu/publications/2305e/. [August 2013].

[3] Safety and Health Topics: Grain Handling. Occupational Safety and Health Administration, US Dept of Labor. Retrieved from https://www.osha.gov/SLTC/grainhandling/. [August 2013].

[4] Hydrogen Sulfide Suicide Trend-First Responder Safety Update; 2010. Central Florida Intelligence Exchange, Bulletin No. 10-09-31. Retrieved from http://www.hazmatfc.com/incidentReports/statsTrends/Documents/Hydrogen%20Sulfide%20Suicide%20Incidents.pdf. [August 2013].

CHAPTER 13
Special Circumstances

297

Learning Objectives

- Compare and contrast at least three ways that embalming and cremation alter the body for further investigation.
- A detective from the local agency calls and says a family has accused a caretaker of poisoning their loved one with rat poison containing arsenic. He has investigated and feels there may be some validity to the accusation. The body has been embalmed and buried at the local cemetery. He is asking what the chance of recovery of information might be, as well as what the procedure might be for an autopsy. Outline five items to discuss with the pathologist to return the phone call with further information.

Key Terms
Cremation
Embalming
Exhumation
Conflict of interest
Lethal injection

Chapter Summary

In this chapter various investigation situations are discussed, as well as possible solutions for difficult removals. Also discussed are postmortem disposition issues and scene investigation for in-custody deaths. The various modalities of organ and tissue donation are presented that will provide insight for how it will affect the death investigation in determining the cause and manner of death.

INTRODUCTION

This chapter will discuss multiple unusual, but not necessarily uncommon, death situations an investigator may encounter. The study of these situations prior to actually encountering them or similar situations will give a springboard to troubleshoot for solutions for a body removal or investigation technique. The knowledge will also help the investigator to answer general questions by law enforcement or family members.

CREMATED REMAINS

The **cremation** process involves burning a body at greater than 1,400–1,800°F over a period of two to three hours to reduce the body to ash [1]. At that point, even

FIGURE 13.1
(A) A typical plastic container cremated remains may be stored in. (B) Usually it is lined by a plastic bag to contain the ashes. Identifying tags may be present within the ash remains. It is helpful to X-ray the box prior to opening it to determine if the box contains human identifying materials.

large bones will be brittle and broken but have intact small pieces. Crematoriums generally pass the residual bones through a grinder to also reduce them to fine ash. These cremated remains are then packaged in an urn picked by the next of kin or packaged in a plastic bag inside a square plastic box (usually about 12 × 10 × 5 in.), as shown in Figure 13.1. Inside each box is usually a metal identification tag and the outside usually contains identifying marks. These cremated remains can be stored by the next of kin, buried (with a permit), or scattered (may require a permit). Cremated remains can be shipped, but requirements by the shipping company and local laws may vary and should be verified by each locality. Airlines also ship cremated remains but preauthorization may be required, as well as copies of the death certificate, cremation permit, and any other forms required by Homeland Security or Customs if international [2]. It is best to check with all agencies before assuming remains can be transported and received.

Occasionally these remains are found in a residence, on church steps, or abandoned in other public places. They then fall upon the medical examiner to give final disposition. The issues revolving around this is to confirm whether the remains are human, the identity of the remains, and if there is next of kin who would claim the remains. To make these determinations, it requires the aid of an anthropologist to review the remains to answer at least the first three questions. Many times X-rays may assist with the identification of human artifacts like metal clothing clips or snaps, surgical clips, or hopefully the identification band inside the urn. DNA is destroyed and not able to be retrieved from remains heated to this temperature.

Most house fires approach 750–1,100°F and are not able to reduce adult human remains to the level of incineration seen in a crematorium retort. If an accelerant is used and the fire is stoked over a period of time, a greater percentage of the body can be reduced to ash. The torso is the greatest mass, therefore, even if it is greatly charred on the outside, the majority of the organs and even body fluids may be able to be collected. Infants contain a smaller mass and have little bone and may result in complete incineration at this temperature.

The investigative aspects of these cases will take some true detective work to track down where the deceased originated from and finding next of kin. County tax records may give a clue for a owner who may know information about renters if the remains are found within a building. Discarded remains in public places are very difficult to identify. Remains without identifiers are similar due to lack of clues and very little scientific data to work with.

Disposition of the remains may require assistance from the local county social services agency, which may take control of the disposition for county burial or to assist a family that has no means to make final arrangements. Each state or county has an indigent burial program to assist families with limited means. Public fiduciary or lawyers may close estates where there is no next of kin or appointment of an executor. Power of attorney appointments end at the time of death.

It is important that all county burials falling under the coroner/medical examiner office follow a protocol with a proper chain of custody to the cemetery/funeral home. In addition, the remains should be tagged with identifying wristbands and documentation provided in the investigator's report of the burial plot number. If the policy for disposition of indigents is cremation, it is important that identification measures be undertaken prior to the cremation to ensure the identity of the person, as all information will be gone after.

Cremation authorizations require a permit issued by the local health department, a signed valid death certificate, and, in many states, permission of the coroner or medical examiner that the cause of death is not a reportable case to their office. The latter is hopefully a safeguard to prevent reportable deaths from unnatural causes or homicides to go unreported and investigated.

BURIED BODIES

Clandestine graves are usually associated with a criminal nature as an attempt to dispose of remains in a way they will not be discovered for a period of time, if ever. These cases usually have a great amount of press appeal, especially if they are thought to be associated with a serial killer or have been buried in a noteworthy fashion within a wall, backyard, or basement. John Wayne Gacy was a serial killer of the 1970s in Chicago. He was a contractor and would lure young men to his residence with a promise of work, kill them by strangling them. and then bury them in his crawlspace. Twenty-nine bodies were recovered and a severe stench emanated from the basement. The bodies were in various states of decay and were covered with lime.

Buried bodies decompose much slower than those exposed to air or water, due to lack of exposure to carnivores and insects (Figure 13.2). The rate is further slowed

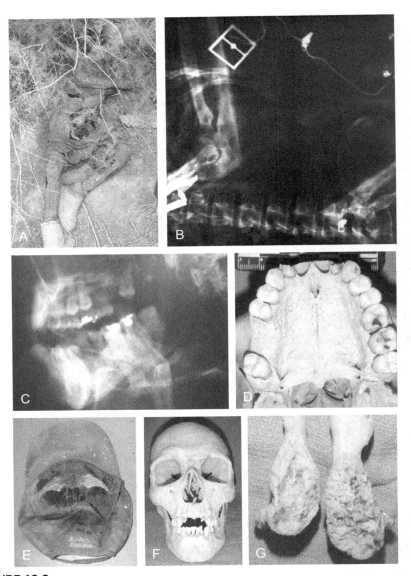

FIGURE 13.2
(A) A partially skeletonized decedent found in a remote area. (B) After removal to the office screening X-rays of the remains inside the body bag with the clothing intact are helpful to screen for projectiles, knives, or sharp objects. (C) The X-rays may also reveal the presence of dental restorations, which are confirmed upon examination of the maxilla (D). (E) Photography of all property including brands and labels is helpful and important to reference in the file for follow-up phone calls, screening the missing person data-bases, and in case the clothing gets separated from the skeletal remains or is lost over time. Anthropology consultation will assist with sex, race, approximate age, and stature using the skull (F), femur, and grooves on the symphysis pubis (G).

if the body is wrapped in protective plastic or a tarp. Sometimes the perpetrator will utilize lime or other materials that decelerate the decomposition rate [3]. It also depends on how deeply the body is buried, as a very shallow grave may not deter carnivores to a great extent. Indications of a grave site include disturbed plant flora, either dead, newly growing, or in some fashion not matching surrounding plants. The area is usually depressed inward and concave due to the body decomposing and shrinking over time, collapsing the overlying dirt.

Recovery of buried remains can be assisted by a local anthropologist or even archaeologist. If none is available, there may be a member of law enforcement or a fellow death investigator with a particular interest or experience with the recovery of buried remains. Initial recovery can begin with shovels, but as materials become evident, smaller trowels and brushes may be needed. It is best to begin at the periphery of the sunken area and work across the surface with gentle shovel digging. It is helpful to have various-size screens to pan the removed dirt looking for expended cartridges, bullets, teeth, or personal effects. If the remains are relatively fresh or largely intact but decomposed, the recovery is much easier than skeletal remains. In either case the dirt under the body can yield useful clues and should be screened as well, looking for any objects. If the decedent was shot while in the grave or on the ground, the expended bullets may have exited into the ground under the body and can still be recovered.

Case Study

Skeletal remains were discovered by construction crews digging a pathway for a new water canal in a rural county. The remains were extricated from their grave by a local archaeologist and sent to the forensic pathologist for examination. X-rays showed no large bullet fragments within the residual skeletal, but small fragments of lead were seen adherent to the internal skull. Gross examination showed an entrance gunshot wound at the back of the left side of the head with internal beveling. An exit wound was noted on the right temporal scalp, which was the portion lying downward in the grave. When the pathologist inquired where the underlying dirt was from that area, he was told the local archaeologist had recovered it for teaching as it showed a perfect outline of the head within the dirt. When it was returned and the dirt X-rayed, a large bullet was visualized and recovered. It was sent to the crime laboratory for comparison to the ballistics database (Integrated Ballistics Database, or IBIS).

FBI and ATF units are working with gun manufacturers to develop a database of each new manufactured gun and record its serial number with the individual rifling of the lands and grooves as gun fingerprints. This would allow the gun to be traced throughout its lifetime, including who it was sold to and what crimes might be related to one another. The FBI and crime laboratories compile the ballistic characteristics of expended bullets/casings/cartridges into a database and can link them to other crimes committed using the same weapon. This has been made possible because of the increased ability of computers to utilize and compare digital images and scan through thousands of images quickly to make comparisons. The only missing link is to use this information and tie it to a particular weapon rather than just a class of guns. Evidence is typically categorized by similarities within a group called class characteristics (e.g., 9-mm handgun) based on the gun's weight and measurements. Individual markings on the bullet or jacket created by the lands and grooves create individual characteristics that can link a particular bullet to a particular gun. The future database would utilize these individual characteristics to improve crime solving.

EMBALMED BODIES

Embalming is the process of replacing body fluids with formalin as a means of preservation. The embalming fluid is a mixture of 18–35% formalin with multiple coloring agents and glutaraldehyde, which is then mixed with water in a small pump apparatus and injected into the arterial system. Different coloring agents are used depending on the desired end result color of the skin. The blood is drained from the body as the formalin mixture is pumped into the arterial system under pressure. The base of the neck is the site of the usual arterial puncture, which is later sutured and glued closed to prevent leakage. Other areas where incisions can be made to improve preservation are the groins or armpits, especially if there is extensive trauma and poor perfusion. The trunk is the next area embalmed by inserting a large suction trocar needle into the organs and removing any feces, fluids, and food in the stomach. The formalin preserves the body's cells by changing the chemical structure of the cellular proteins, which decreases the ability of bacteria to utilize them and in turn slows decomposition.

Bodies being shipped may require higher formalin concentrations and special permits. International shipping usually requires authorization by a physician that the body contains no known infectious disease. Bodies can be shipped to a medical examiner/coroner without embalming or authorization but are usually placed into sealed metal shipping containers similar to caskets but more durable. These containers prevent leakage of biohazardous body fluids or exposure to pathogens as long as the container is intact, however, they are heavy and bulky, and it is difficult to remove a body because of the deep sides.

FROZEN BODIES

Frozen bodies are difficult to maneuver and transport because their position is not malleable. If possible, the goal is to get the body inside a body bag and transport it to the office where it can be slowly thawed for evaluation. If the body will not fit inside a body bag due to its position, it may be necessary to wrap the body in a plastic shroud or tarp for transport. Usually these bodies require an autopsy and retrieval of toxicology, and until the surface and organs are thawed, this is not possible. The length of time to thaw will depend on the body size and the amount of clothing. It may be possible to cut away any thick layers of clothing if the cause is not suspicious. This will greatly shorten the necessary time interval. Use of small portable heaters blowing across the surface and letting the decedent remain at room temperature overnight (an entire weekend is too long, however) will also shorten the defrosting time. If it is the weekend, the body should be placed into the cooler and can be monitored for thawing during a weekday while personnel are present to observe its progress. If prompt identification is imperative, handheld hair dryers can be used to loosen the upper extremities at the shoulders and elbow to retrieve the necessary prints. A fully frozen body can take up to two to three days to defrost. The skin will assume a yellow parchment decomposition pattern as it thaws and dries.

DISMEMBERED REMAINS

Bodies are dismembered usually to dispose of them more easily, to hide their identification, to slow down the investigation, and occasionally to send a message by delivery of a body part. A body can be found in any degree of dismemberment from a single extremity like a finger, head, or torso, to a nearly complete body with only a single item missing. The greater the dismemberment, the greater the challenge to discover a cause of death, the identity of the decedent, and to find a perpetrator. The location the body part is found will result in a huge grid search of the surrounding area to determine if further body parts can be located.

The environment surrounding the body part site needs to be photographed as it is found and after the body part is removed. This will document the amount of blood loss at the site and help determine if it is the location the dismemberment occurred. Special attention should be paid to shoe and vehicle tracks leading to and from the scene. Any surrounding clothing or personal effects that might be related should be examined for identification clues and collected. If the body part is in a plastic or paper bag/box, it should be carefully handled to retain the surface for possible fingerprinting. Trace evidence on the found body part may be the key in linking an eventual suspect with the decedent and include items such as carpet fibers, saw marks, and hairs. Small body parts should be placed in brown paper bags then inside a body bag for transit. They should be handled as little as possible. Larger body parts can be transported as usual.

Recovered torsos and heads should be X-rayed according to the usual trauma panel for suspicious deaths. Recovery of bullets or identification of orthopedic hardware can be the key to the investigation moving forward. Body amputation sites of the dismemberment require close-up detailed photography to demonstrate any tool marks or skin injuries to aid in the identification of the instrument used (Figure 13.3). After photography, the dismemberment site needs to be excised and preserved by freezing rather than formalin fixation. Databases exist for comparison of these tool markings on bone to potential class characteristics of particular instruments if not individual characteristics to compare to a recovered saw or tool. Obviously the morgue saw will create similar saw marks on the excised margins, so to prevent confusion, they should be marked with an "X" across the excision margin. Dr. Symes at the University of Tennessee has done extensive research on this topic and standardized much of the terminology used to describe these types of cut marks [6].

ENTOMBED REMAINS

Disinterment is removal of bodies from the grave where they have been buried for a length of time. This process can also be referred to as **exhumation**. The removal requires authorization from the family or a court order from a judge plus a permit from the health department in the jurisdiction where the body

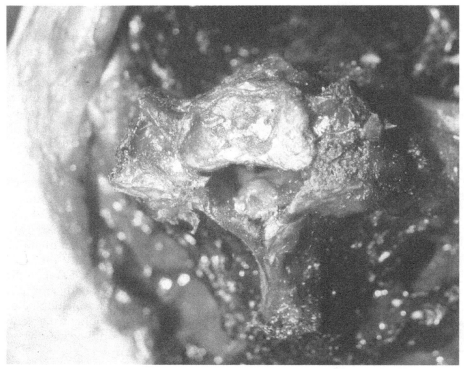

FIGURE 13.3
Tool markings that are present on a dismemberment site on a vertebral body. It is important that they be photographed and preserved for possible comparison to a recovered instrument.

is buried. Bodies are disinterred for a number of reasons, including wanting to bury the person in another location or the burial of a second person in the same burial plot, which is allowed in some locations with the stipulation that the one closest to the surface meet all the burial depth requirements. Cremated remains may also be buried in the same burial plot.

Court-ordered exhumations are done if there is a question of the identity of the person in the plot or for further criminal investigation. If the family is not willing to sign for the exhumation, the judge will want to hear a compelling argument as to the purpose of the investigation and what scientific findings will be sought during the examination. Following the authorization, a disinterment permit will be issued by the health department to the cemetery.

Cemeteries keep detailed records of burial plots with each one denoted by a number on an emblem embedded at one end of the plot. Their assistance will be needed to locate the proper plot prior to beginning any digging. The cemetery map and records need to be reviewed by the person in charge of the exhumation to ensure the proper location and chain of custody to the morgue.

Disinterment requires the use of backhoes to open the grave and remove the first few feet of soil. This is followed by hand shoveling to unearth the casket and expose the perimeter for lifting.

Some caskets are buried with a surrounding plastic liner or concrete vault. This preserves the exterior of the casket and prevents cave-ins over time, and makes it easier to unearth a casket. Depending on the water table of the cemetery, some caskets can be under water for periods of time and lose structural integrity, exposing the remains.

Depending on the purpose of the exhumation, the casket and contents may be removed to the coroner/medical examiner office for examination, or in the case of a reburial, transported to its new location. If the casket is no longer usable, a new one will be needed for the remains to be reburied. The condition of the remains will depend on the soil at the burial site, the type of casket and the presence of a liner or vault, the quality of the embalming, the condition of the body at the time of embalming, and the period of time that has elapsed.

To open the lid of a casket, a casket key is needed and can be borrowed from a funeral home. This key is like a small crank that fits into a small opening at the head end of the casket. A body that has been enclosed in an intact casket for an extended period (five to seven years or longer) in good soil conditions and embalming is strikingly recognizable and intact upon the initial opening of the lid. The body may be covered by areas of mold and have a yellow waxy appearance. The inside of the coffin actually forms a micro-environment, keeping the organisms in balance due to the low oxygen level, lack of sunlight, and relatively uniform environmental temperature. However, upon opening the lid, decomposition will occur rapidly with the skin becoming flaccid and green-black discoloration beginning. It is important to collect evidence and photographs quickly after opening the lid. Internal organs will show the usual embalming trocar artifacts and shrinkage. Calcified areas will retain their architecture better longer than soft tissues like the spleen or gastrointestinal tract.

FAMILIES REPORTING POISONING OR MURDER

It is not uncommon for a family member to call the coroner/medical examiner office and an investigator be faced with him or her accusing another family member of having poisoned or murdered the decedent and the case had gone unreported. The decedent may already have been examined (hopefully autopsied with toxicology) or never even been seen by the office. The motive is purported to be for monetary or emotional gain. This is a difficult position because the body may be buried at the time of the report. If the body is not buried or embalmed, the response is much easier and it can be brought to the office for examination and toxicology. If it was examined already, it is best to immediately call the funeral home and put a hold on embalming, burial, or cremation until the death investigator can speak with the attending pathologist. Most state death investigation laws give the investigator the power to take control of the remains as a suspicious death even under family protest. It may be the person in control of making the arrangements who the other family member is accusing. This can become a very sensitive issue and needs to be handled carefully. The family member calling should be directed to the proper law enforcement to voice his or her concerns. Law enforcement will then call the office to verify information and usually will speak with family members. Depending on the information obtained, the investigator may examine the scene for a potential poisoning. It is best to make sure a pill count and identification is done on all medications submitted with the decedent.

The investigation that is associated with the case will help direct what type of poison was used. Some poisons are not easily detected on routine toxicology screens and need to be targeted for diagnosis. It is best to obtain hair samples and fingernail clippings since long-term poisoning, such as arsenic, can be deposited and identified in these samples. Full toxicology is recommended in an effort to answer the questions of the investigation.

Other times families will note elder abuse or lack of care of the decedent as causing the death, sometimes with underlying monetary gain. This is a very difficult determination in the elderly. Many times they have severe underlying cardiac or respiratory disease, general debilitation, or diabetes mellitus, which makes them prone to lying in bed. It can be very difficult in a home-care situation to prevent bedsores (decubitus ulcers) that in some cases can become massive. In these cases where there are medical community or family concerns, the best course of action is to bring the case to the office for review by the pathologist and include photographs with scales of any ulcers, and a general evaluation of the body for cleanliness, height, weight, etc. In cases where the death investigator goes to a scene and there is a concern of negligent care, it is important to note the condition of the sleeping environment, food conditions, and to confiscate all the decedent's medications.

ORGAN AND TISSUE DONATION

Cases falling under the jurisdiction of the coroner/medical examiner are many times young individuals with few underlying diseases, making their organs desirable for transplantation into other individuals. Older decedents may also qualify for donation depending on their health and cause of death. Each state will have outlined the procedure for approaching the family for this donation [5]. Throughout the United States there are nonprofit companies representing eye donation, organ donation, and tissue donation, all separate companies, and each reviewing a case for potential donation. Organ donation requires that the person is still alive and usually is on a ventilator at the time of brain death. Brain death is determined by a standard protocol of two separate evaluations of the decedent by neurologists demonstrating with a physical exam that there is only brainstem function but a lack of awareness and upper cortical function. A negative drug screen for narcotics and a flat EEG (brainwave scan) is needed to declare brain death. The center for cardiac and respiratory function only requires brainstem function but not higher cortical function where consciousness and awareness of surroundings is present.

After someone is declared brain dead, the family may be approached for their desire to contribute the organs to someone else on the list awaiting a transplant. In some states, the medical examiner/coroner is to be contacted prior to the family to review the case and evaluate the needs of the pathologist as to which organs will be needed to certify the cause of death. The pathologist may place certain restrictions as to which organs may be harvested. Most times toxicology samples need to be requested and acquired prior to the donation. Laboratory specimens for blood and urine are usually held on all patients five to seven days after admission (depending on each hospital's policy) and should be requested as well. In some states this request will require a subpoena from the office to the hospital to acquire them. Admission specimens are valuable because they reflect the toxicology status prior to any blood transfusions or dilution by intravenous fluids. These specimens may also be desired by the donation team because they also reflect the best specimens to test for possible infectious diseases that might be transmitted to the potential recipient. The transplant list is searched for a suitable match based on the blood and HLA (histocompatibility) testing of the decedent and the recipient. If the coroner/medical examiner and family have said yes, the donation may proceed with the organs being removed. The request for organs can include heart, lungs, liver, kidneys, pancreas, and small bowel.

Eye donation follows the same procedure of permission. The request is for the cornea portion of the eye but the extraction needs to be performed during the first 24 hours after death because the cells in the eye are very sensitive to drying and deterioration. During this donation, the entire eye may be removed, or at a minimum the cornea portion of it. The vitreous that is normally present will not be present after the donation unless the donor team obtains it during the harvesting procedure. The vitreous will need to be transmitted from them to the medical examiner/coroner office via a chain of custody. If the coroner/medical examiner obtains the vitreous prior to the harvest, it wrinkles the cornea and renders it unsuitable for transplantation.

Tissue donation is also done following the same permission procedure and performed on decedents within the first 24–48 hours after death. Usual requests are for tendons, arteries, veins, bone, or heart valves. This can also take the form of a request for research and other tissues, including internal organs or extremities and head and neck tissue. Harvesting these tissues destroys the ability of the pathologist to retrieve toxicology specimens, so blood and urine need to be obtained from the femoral vessels and transferred under chain of custody to the office. In cases of requests for heart valves, the pathologist will need to have past cardiac history and the scene investigation findings to assess whether the heart is needed intact for evaluation. He or she may deny donation if the valves are needed for the determination of a cause of death. Requests for valves are approved more stringently on a case-by-case basis. Removal of the heart valves also removes the proximal coronary arteries at the takeoff from the aorta where significant atherosclerosis and variants can occur that may cause death. The residual donated tissue is generally evaluated by a cardiac pathologist provided by the donation company. They will generate a report from the cardiac pathologist that can be supplied to the medical examiner/coroner office. However, the evaluation will not include this vital area since that removal is performed by a technician prior to the cardiac pathologist seeing it. This area can be the key to the cause of death. To wait and hope for a positive toxicology as a cause of death may result in the real cause of death being overlooked. There are many potential causes of death in a case but only *one* real cause of death, and it is the job of the forensic pathologist to render an opinion to the best of his or her ability about the cause. This conflict between donation and retention of organs can lead to strife between the organ procurement agency and the coroner/medical examiner office.

SPECIAL REMOVALS

Some bodies are either very messy or difficult to remove from the position of death. Decomposed bodies have smelly fluids in skin blebs and surrounding them, and maggots and insects may be present. These cases need some care to get the body into a body bag without splashing fluids on clothes. It is helpful to cover the body with a sheet and tie it in place if possible. Position the stretcher with a body bag over the top, grab the body by an arm, and slide it into the bag. If it is necessary to get the outside of the bag dirty by placing it on the floor or ground, it will be necessary to have a second bag nearby to place the decedent in. The body bags are not impermeable and can leak through a cloth zippered area, and lightweight bags tear very easily. The insects also seem to be ingenious in their escaping bags, even in refrigeration. Double bagging may be necessary even inside heavy-duty bags.

Distant removals over rough ground can be done with heavy-duty body bags that have sown-in handles. Depending on the weight, two to four people may be necessary, one on each corner, to remove it to a stretcher that can then be placed inside the removal vehicle. These same bags are useful if there are fragments of glass or metals that may penetrate the usual bag, such as in motor vehicle and airplane accidents.

Decedents positioned in a car are similar to those sitting in a chair. If it is a bloody situation, a sheet, towel, or whatever is available over the front of the decedent will protect everyone as the person is moved. The stretcher can be placed adjacent to the vehicle with the body bag over the top, an arm grasped, and twist the body as if the person was getting out of the vehicle with the legs toward the bottom end of the bag. The body can then be maneuvered onto the stretcher without having to lift it.

Decedents totally or partially in bed are relatively easy as they can be slid directly onto the stretcher that has the bag over the top.

Babies and children dead at a scene or hospital room can be an emotional situation as the parents are nearby. It is important to be as respectful of their feelings as possible and also be cognizant that hospital staff is also very sensitive to this situation. If at all possible, ask the family to step outside while placing the child in a body bag, and wrap a sheet over the top of the body bag. The child can then be lifted onto the usual stretcher and covered, or small infants can be placed into a small basket. When placed into the removal vehicle, the child's body can be transferred onto a stretcher. It is important to have support from law enforcement during the removal phase because families can be very emotional and a scenario may develop that can become threatening. Again, situational awareness is very important at all scenes, but especially with children involved.

Hangings can be challenging because they have all or at least a portion of their weight on the noose. It will take more than one person for the removal and usually, but no more than three. One person will need to use the bolt cutters or knife to cut the noose and the one or two other people to support the decedent under the arms. The decedent's own body weight can be used to ease him or her into an adjacent body bag. It is best to cut the noose in the mid-region, and if duct tape is nearby or in the investigator bag, to encircle the proposed cut site first then cut in the middle of the tape to prevent fraying of the ends (see Chapter 12). A similar approach can be used at the point where it is attached to the suspension point (beam, tree limb, closet rod) and cut again at the circled tape. The entire noose needs to be submitted with the body for the pathologist to review. In cases where the decedent is decomposed, it can be useful to take a body bag and put the decedent's feet in it, have someone else hold the body bag, and have someone zip the bag up all the way until the head is covered inside the bag. Cut the noose and slip it inside the bag. This keeps the mess to a minimum.

Bodies in lakes, rivers, or canals are water soaked and placing a bag in the water does not work. If this is common in your jurisdiction, special mesh tarps can be used to float the decedent on top of the water and lift the body out into a bag. Because huge amounts of water are in and on the body, the bag will become water logged, therefore either two bags are necessary or a heavy-duty one. It is also advisable to take clear photos of the face and any identifying tattoos. These bodies will rapidly decompose once out of the water, with the body not being able to be viewed or the tattoos obscured and unavailable for identification. The hands should be evaluated for possible prints at the same time because they will slough and the surface becomes like gloves of skin. If possible, prior to removing the body from the water, photograph the decedent in the water. The photographs do not have to be taken underwater.

PRISONERS AND EXECUTIONS

Removals from a jail, penitentiary, or even at a law enforcement arrest scene present some unique hurdles. Entrance into a jail or penitentiary requires photo identification, usually a driver's license and an office identification. If the investigator's office is one that allows carrying firearms or knives on the job, those will need to be checked at the admission window. It is important to take stock of all pens, pencils, and other objects an investigator has on his or her person and ensure they are taken back out so they are not made into shivs by other prisoners. The jail or prison personnel will have cleared an entry and exit point from the site of admission to the body and back and will escort the investigator through the building to the site. The other prisoners have usually been placed in lockdown to prevent any issues. It is important for the investigator to show up in full uniform and not casual clothes.

If the death occurs at a law enforcement arrest scene, the situation can be quite volatile and it is important to be cognizant of surrounding bystanders. Tensions may be running high among law enforcement and the community, so it is important to be organized, systematic, and gather the needed data for removing the body as soon as possible. Many times after the body is gone from sight, tensions will start to abate. There may be multiple agencies attending the scene as well as multiple high-ranking officials, depending on the situation. Most agencies have a protocol for in-custody deaths that calls for an outside law enforcement agency to investigate to prevent a question of **conflict of interest**. The coroner/medical examiner office may also have a policy that a forensic pathologist responds to these scenes with the death investigator. It is important for the death investigator as an additional representative from an outside agency to be diligent about photographing the scene, the decedent, any restraints used, and aspects of the scene related to how the person was initially found. If he or she was found hanging in a cell, the noose needs to be photographed and the point of suspension. If the decedent became unresponsive in the back of a patrol car, his or her position in the car needs to be known and appropriate measurements taken, especially if it was the floorboard area. Any emesis, pills, or clothing needs to be photographed, and necessary items collected. Special attention for photographs of the head, neck, and upper extremities are in order. If restraints are still in place at the time of the investigator's arrival, they need to be left in place and the decedent transported as-is to the office. If the death occurred in an interview or restraint room, then overall photographs of the entire scene from multiple vantage points need to be taken, as well as the usual medium and close-up views.

If an officer was involved during an altercation during the arrest, he or she may not be willing to discuss it with the investigator and request a lawyer or union representative be present during any statements. The outside agency will be able to assist the death investigator with obtaining the information needed to relay to the pathologist for evaluation. Most times the outside agency also attends the autopsy to confer with the pathologist. The case is worked like a homicide with full-body X-rays, dirty and clean photographs, evidence collection, and a full autopsy with toxicology.

In executions, the decedent will usually be in the execution chamber. Sometimes the prison has placed the person into a body bag and has cleared the chamber.

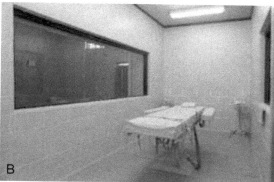

FIGURE 13.4
(A) The gas chamber used by the state of Arizona. (B) The gurney used for lethal injections [4].

In those cases, it is important to do site photography of the body to document any injuries or absence of them. In other cases, the decedent may still be strapped to the execution table with IVs attached. Photographs are obtained, followed by closing all the intravenous bag valves and placing them into the bag with the decedent, including empty bags. Most executions are now done by **lethal injection** but in the past, the gas chamber with hydrogen cyanide gas was another method used (Figure 13.4a). Because the gas is toxic and deposits are formed on the skin surface, the body was hosed down prior to removal in two body bags to prevent diffusion of the gas into the cooler or removal vehicle. Other states used to perform death by firing squad, hanging, or electrical chair, but these have been deemed cruel and heinous punishment and no longer used.

Lethal injection is accomplished by intravenously injecting a barbiturate to induce sleep followed by a neuromuscular blocking agent, such as succinylcholine or pancuronium, which causes paralysis of skeletal and smooth muscles including the diaphragm (Figure 13.4b). This is followed by potassium chloride to cease heart function. The person is then monitored for death and pronounced by medical personnel at the scene. The execution is usually witnessed by invited members such as law enforcement, lawyers, and family members.

DEATH IN THE LINE OF DUTY

A topic that many of us dread are those of personnel dying in the line of duty, including law enforcement officers, firemen, and military personnel. These can be someone known to personnel within the office. Many times they are in uniform, which can make it even more difficult. All clothing and items on the body at the time of death need to remain on the decedent as any other case. Guns may be removed or any other hazards such as shock grenades. If bullets have penetrated gun magazines, they also need to be removed. Bullet-proof vests and clothing need to remain on the body or brought to the autopsy for examination.

These deaths are usually accompanied by an escort of officers. Most times it is after the autopsy and at the time of release and will include a color guard and full police escort to the funeral home. Sometimes, especially in deaths of police officers, they will wish to maintain a guard status by the decedent. This may require the chief coroner or medical examiner to authorize outside personnel to remain in the building after hours. Sometimes a compromise can be reached by the guard outside the door and draping of the body bag with a flag. These bodies should be placed into heavy-duty bags and sealed to prevent any type of alteration while awaiting autopsy. The forensic pathologist on call should be contacted to see if he or she would like to go to the investigation scene or hospital to lend support from the department.

These cases can be very difficult technically and emotionally. Typically, a detective and the agency's photographer not well known to the decedent will attend the autopsy and that fact verified before attendance. The issue of conflict of interest should be addressed early, and if there are any doubts, the investigator's supervisor and/or forensic pathologist needs to be consulted. Many times multiple officers and the officer's upper management may want to participate in the investigation. This can get political, yet privacy of the decedent and the ability to focus on the job needs to be a high priority. Too many people attending an autopsy can be very distracting to the pathologist. It may be necessary to arrange extra personnel to meet with the pathologist in a conference room area after the completion of the autopsy to review findings. Press calls may inundate the investigator and his or her supervisor may be able to assist with a press statement. It is easiest to direct press personnel to the law enforcement public information officer for any information. This prevents "leaking" sensitive information unknowingly about the investigation. Typically law enforcement, chaplains, or military superiors will make or greatly assist with notification in these cases. It is a good idea to keep a new packaged flags within the office for this purpose.

DEATH OF OFFICE PERSONNEL OR FAMILY MEMBERS

This also can be a very difficult scene investigation and follow-through within the office. It usually requires involvement of the investigator's supervisor and/or the chief coroner/medical examiner. To avoid issues of cover-ups and conflict of interest, the body may need to be transported to another office. If the decedent is known to morgue personnel, the body may not be able to be housed within the office and will require early intervention to make these decisions. This will largely depend on the scenario and course of events that transpired leading to the death. Homicide, suicide, accidental, or even natural deaths can be suspicious just because of the knowledge of the personnel involved in the death investigation. If the investigation is managed by the office, the file will need to have restricted access to protect privacy. Any family-related personnel should be given time off until the body is released to a funeral home. Full toxicology should be retained and sent to the laboratory, as well as photographs of any injuries. If the decision is made to manage the case within the office, morgue personnel will need to be on a volunteer basis depending on the identity of the decedent and his or her relationship to the office.

DISASTER SITUATIONS

Each jurisdiction has its own capabilities to deal with a certain number of casualties in a short period of time. The number of casualties can vary and will depend on the maximum occupancy of the morgue cooler and personnel who are available. When that is exceeded, it can be a disaster regardless of size. If the cooler can only handle 2 bodies and a bus accident kills 10, the situation suddenly becomes an immediate issue and will require acquisition of resources. Large offices can deal with these fluctuations and a disaster for them may be a single incident greater than 50 decedents.

The role of the investigator is to have knowledge of the office capabilities and, when exceeded, to contact a supervisor for assistance with coordination of further resources. Sometimes local funeral homes' refrigerators can be utilized or, in larger numbers of deaths, refrigerated semi-trucks can be acquired. Federal resources are also available through the Federal Emergency Management Agency (FEMA), National Transportation Safety Board (NTSB), or even military bases with their Grave's Registration Service. State coroner or adjacent medical examiner systems will also lend assistance and have contingency plans that can be initiated.

Knowledge about what is available is usually within each jurisdiction's procedure manual or through participation in mock drills. It is important to get feedback about the drills so faulty areas can be addressed within a department. The types of disasters that need preparation vary widely from aircraft or train accidents to weapons of mass disaster, including bombs and chemical or biological agents. The investigator may be the first called and enter the area to assess the issue. It is important in these deaths to remember the principles of protection of oneself and responding personnel to prevent further injury by exposure to continued hazards.

Key issues for evaluating decedents in these situations are identification, connecting dismembered remains and their personal effects for eventual return to the family, establishing a cause of death, and aiding investigation techniques to determine the cause of the incident. This may require marking the scene into grids with extensive documentation. This will take a large amount of time, so perimeter safeguards will be necessary to prevent intrusion by press or inquisitive onlookers. Families worried about their next of kin may inundate the phone capabilities of the office. Volunteers may be needed to record contact information and phone numbers. Resources such as body bags, gloves, and biohazard bags may be depleted, so contingency plans will be needed to enlist supplies. Entire courses on mass disaster management are available and further training may be necessary for the investigator to be best prepared.

REFERENCES

[1] Cremation FAQ. National Funeral Directors Association; 2013. Retrieved from http://nfda.org/planning-a-funeral/cremation/160.html#hot. [August 2013].

[2] Transport of Cremated Remains. Cremation Association of North America; 2012. Retrieved from http://www.cremationassociation.org/?page=Transport. [August 2013].

[3] Schotsman EM, et al. Effects of Hydraged Lime and Quicklime on the Decay of Buried Human Remains Using Pig Cadavers as Human Body Analogues. Forensic Sci Int 2012;217(1-3):50–9. doi:10.1016/j.forsciint.2011.09.025. Epub 2011 Oct 24. Retrieved from http://www.ncbi.nlm.nih.gov/pubmed/22030481. [August 2013].

[4] Arizona Death Penalty History. Arizona Department of Corrections; 2013. Retrieved from http://www.azcorrections.gov/adc/history/History_DeathPenalty.aspx. [August 2013].

[5] State Organ Donation Legislation. US Dept of Health & Human Services; 2011. Retrieved from http://www.organdonor.gov/legislation_micro/. [August 2013].

[6] Symes S, et al. Knife and Saw Toolmark Analysis In Bone: A Manual Designed for the Examination of Criminal Mutilation and Dismemberment. Symes-National Institute of Justice Grant #2005-IJ-CX-K016/ National Forensic Academy/Forensic Science Foundation; 2010. Retrieved from http://www.crime-scene-investigator.net/KnifeAndSawToolmarkAnalysisInBone.pdf. [August 2013].

Appendix

CHAIN OF CUSTODY

Decedent's Name: ______________________________

Coroner Case Number: ______________

Date of Death: ______________

Receipt of the following items is acknowledged (list each item):

1. ______________________________
2. ______________________________
3. ______________________________
4. ______________________________
5. ______________________________
6. ______________________________
7. ______________________________
8. ______________________________
9. ______________________________
10. ______________________________

Signature of person/agency receiving: ______________________

Print Name: ______________________________

Signature of person releasing: ______________________

Print Name: ______________________________

Date and time of exchange: ______________________

Date and time returned: ______________________

Reason: (optional) ______________________

FIGURE A.1
Two examples of chain of custody intake forms or worksheets.

CHAIN OF CUSTODY

DATE _____   ML # _____

NAME _____   AGENCY/# _____

_____   _____
_____   _____
_____   _____
_____   _____
_____   _____
_____   _____

FROM   TO

_____ _____ TIME _____ DATE _____
_____ _____ TIME _____ DATE _____
_____ _____ TIME _____ DATE _____

FIGURE A.1, cont'd

		CASE #	
		DATE / TIME	
		Death Investigator:	

DECEASED NAME	LAST	FIRST	MI	SEX	

DEC. ADDRESS	

CITY/ST		ZIP		PHONE	

AGE	DOB	RACE	HGT	WGT	HR	EYES

DRIVERS LIC.#	STATE	SSN#	MARITAL STATUS	VET.

OTHER ID	AKA

SCARS MARKS TATOOS	

IDENTIFIED BY	RELATIONSHIP

DECEASED DENTIST	ADDRESS	PHONE #

DATE OF DEATH	TIME OF DEATH	DEATH PRONOUNCED BY

PLACE OF DEATH	ADMISSION DATE/TIME

DEC. FOUND BY	DATE/TIME

INCIDENT LOCATION	DATE/TIME

AMBULANCE RESPONSE ☐ YES ☐ NO	COMPANY	PHONE

NEXT OF KIN	DOB	RELATIONSHIP

ADDRESS	CITY	STATE	ZIP	PHONE #

NOTIFIED: DATE/TIME	NOTIFIED BY

NEXT OF KIN	DOB	RELATIONSHIP

ADDRESS	CITY	STATE	ZIP	PHONE #

NOTIFIED: DATE/TIME	NOTIFIED BY

INVESTIGATING AGENCY	AGENCY CASE NUMBER

INVESTIGATING OFFICERS	PHONE #

MVA-POSITION ON VEHICLE	RESTRAINT

AIR BAG DEPLOYED	M/C. BICYCLE HELMET

CHILD RESTRAINT	EJECTED

DECEASED TRANSPORTED TO: ☐ OFFICE	☐ MORTUARY	HOLD ☐ YES ☐ NO

MORTUARY	CITY	PHONE

AUTHORIZED BY	RELATIONSHIP

PERSONAL PROPERTY TAKEN	LOCATION

SEAL #	SEALED BY	AGENCY

VEH. LIC. # & STATE	AGENCY STORED VEH.

PRIMARY CARE PHYSICIAN	CONTACT #

PMHx:	

MEDS:	

AUTOPSY	X-RAYS	DENTAL	FINGERPRINTS	PHOTO

COUNTY CREMATION	COUNTY BURIAL	PA REFERRAL	DATE

FIGURE A.2
Two examples of investigative report forms.

DATE RPTD. _____

RPTD. BY _____

TRANSPORT _____

TIME RPTD. _____/_____

TIME COMPLT. _____/_____

FIELD AGENTS _____/_____

DOCTOR _____

INVESTIGATOR _____

COUNTY _____ PROCEDURE _____ DATE _____ FORENSIC ANTHRO _____ DENTIST _____

CASE NUMBER _____

NAME   FN _____ MI _____ LN _____

ALIAS _____ M   S   W   D   OCC _____

ADDRESS _____ CITY _____ STATE _____ ZIP _____

DOB _____ AGE _____ RACE _____ SEX _____ S.S.N. _____

HT (cm) _____ (inches) _____ WT (kg) _____ (lbs) _____ HC _____ EC _____

NOK   FN _____ LN _____ REL _____ PHONE _____

ADDRESS _____ CITY _____ STATE _____ NOTIFIED   Y   N

ID (MEANS & NAME) _____

LOCATION FOUND _____

REASON ME CASE _____

MED. HX _____

MEDS. _____

AGENCY _____ CASE # _____ OFFICER _____

INJURY LOCATION _____ WORK   Y   N

DATE _____ TIME _____ DRIVER _____ PASSENGER _____ PEDESTRIAN _____

WHERE DID DEATH OCCUR?   HOSP. _____ ER _____ OR _____ INPT _____ AT SCENE _____ UNKNOWN _____

LSA DATE _____ TIME _____ LOC. _____ BY _____

FD. DATE _____ TIME _____ LOC. _____ BY _____

PRN. DATE _____ TIME _____ LOC. _____ BY _____

FUNERAL HOME _____ BY _____ RELATION _____

PHOTOS: OME   ID   Y   N   EXAMINATION   OME   Y   N   AGENCY   Y   N

FINGERPRINTS: _____ PALMS _____ FOOT _____ RADIOGRAPHS _____

_____
_____
_____
_____
_____
_____
_____
_____
_____
_____
_____
_____
_____
_____
_____
_____
_____
_____
_____
_____
_____

RELEASED BY _____ RECEIVED BY _____

FIGURE A.2, cont'd

DATE _____   **MEDICATIONS LOG**   ML# _____

NAME _____

ITEM# _____PRESCRIPTION# _____MEDICATION _____
PHARMACY _____PHONE# _____DOCTOR _____
DATE FILLED _____NUMBER REMAINING _____NUMBER ISSUED _____
COMMENTS/DOSAGE _____
_____

ITEM# _____PRESCRIPTION# _____MEDICATION _____
PHARMACY _____PHONE# _____DOCTOR _____
DATE FILLED _____NUMBER REMAINING _____NUMBER ISSUED _____
COMMENTS/DOSAGE _____
_____

ITEM# _____PRESCRIPTION# _____MEDICATION _____
PHARMACY _____PHONE# _____DOCTOR _____
DATE FILLED _____NUMBER REMAINING _____NUMBER ISSUED _____
COMMENTS/DOSAGE _____
_____

ITEM# _____PRESCRIPTION# _____MEDICATION _____
PHARMACY _____PHONE# _____DOCTOR _____
DATE FILLED _____NUMBER REMAINING _____NUMBER ISSUED _____
COMMENTS/DOSAGE _____
_____

ITEM# _____PRESCRIPTION# _____MEDICATION _____
PHARMACY _____PHONE# _____DOCTOR _____
DATE FILLED _____NUMBER REMAINING _____NUMBER ISSUED _____
COMMENTS/DOSAGE _____
_____

ITEM# _____PRESCRIPTION# _____MEDICATION _____
PHARMACY _____PHONE# _____DOCTOR _____
DATE FILLED _____NUMBER REMAINING _____NUMBER ISSUED _____
COMMENTS/DOSAGE _____
_____

FIGURE A.3
Medications log sheet for documenting decedents medications prior to disposal.

Agency Detective Agency Case Number:		**UNIDENTIFED PERSON WORKSHEET**			Case No. _____

Name			DOB:

Est. Age	Sex		Date of Death	
Yrs.	Male// Female // Unknown			
Location Found			**Date of Examination**	**Time** hours

Clothing

Body Length inches	**Body Weight** pounds

Nourishment Normal // Thin // Obese	**Body Preservation** Good // Decomposed// Skeletal

Body Length inches	**Body Weight** pounds

Hair Color and Length Gray // Brown// Black//Blonde // Red Balding _____ cm.	**Head & Neck** Beard: Brown // Black // Gray Stubble or _____cm
Eyes Blue// Brown // Hazel // Indeterminate	Moustache: Tattoos:

Teeth Natural: Restorations: Yes or No Edentulous	Dentures: Yes or No Full Partial

Trunk—Anterior Tattoos:	**Trunk—Posterior** Tattoos: Scars:

Upper Extremities Tattoos:	**Lower Extremities** Tattoos:

Jewelry	**Toxicology Samples Taken** Vitreous/ Urine / Blood/ Liver / Muscle

MANNER OF DEATH   **CAUSE OF DEATH**

NATURAL ☐

ACCIDENT ☐

SUICIDE ☐

HOMICIDE ☐

UNDET. ☐

PENDING ☐

(a)_____
   DUE TO or as a consequence of:

(b)_____
   DUE TO or as a consequence of:

(c)_____

OTHER SIGNIFICANT CONDITIONS:
_____
_____
_____

NOTES:

Dental	Y	NA	Fingerprints	Y	NA
Anthro	Y	N	Photos	Y	N
X-rays	Y	N	NCIC	Y	N
			NAMUS	Y	N

_____   _____
signature   *date*

Identified by:
   Prints
   Dental
   DNA
ID DATE:
Released:

FIGURE A.4
Unidentified person worksheet.

DATE _____

ML # _____

NAME _____

PERSONAL EFFECTS RECEIPT

CLOTHING

MEN

WOMEN

HAT _____	HAT _____
COAT _____	COAT _____
SHIRT _____	BLOUSE _____
PANTS _____	SKIRT/PANTS _____
SUIT _____	DRESS _____
UNDERSHIRT _____	BRA _____
UNDERSHORTS _____	PANTIES _____
SOCKS _____	STOCKINGS _____
SHOES _____	SHOES _____
BELT _____	BELT _____
OTHER _____	OTHER _____

KEYS _____

☐ WALLET _____   ☐ PURSE/HANDBAG _____   ☐ CHECKBOOK _____

CONTENTS _____

JEWELRY	MONEY	
WATCH _____	BILLS	COINS
RINGS _____	$100 _____	$1.00 _____
	50 _____	.50 _____
	20 _____	.25 _____
	10 _____	.10 _____
EARRINGS _____	5 _____	.05 _____
GLASSES _____	1 _____	.01 _____
NECKLACES _____		TOTAL _____

BRACELETS _____

OTHER _____

OTHER _____

SEALED IN BODY BAG ☐   NO PROPERTY ☐

TRANSPORT _____   VERIFIED _____

DATE _____ TIME _____

RELEASE OF PERSONAL EFFECTS

PROPERTY	RECEIVED BY	RELEASED BY	DATE/TIME
_____	_____	_____	_____
_____	_____	_____	_____
_____	_____	_____	_____

FIGURE A.5

Two examples of (A) personal effects receipt and more generic (B) property receipt.

PROPERTY RECEIPT

Date: _____
Name of Deceased: _____ Case # _____

PROPERTY:	Received	Amount		Total	Received
_____	_____	$ 0.01 x _____	=	0.00	_____
_____	_____	$ 0.05 x _____	=	0.00	_____
_____	_____	$ 0.10 x _____	=	0.00	_____
_____	_____	$ 0.25 x _____	=	0.00	_____
_____	_____	$ 0.50 x _____	=	0.00	_____
_____	_____	$ 1.00 x _____	=	0.00	_____
_____	_____	$ 2.00 x _____	=	0.00	_____
_____	_____	$ 5.00 x _____	=	0.00	_____
_____	_____	$ 10.00 x _____	=	0.00	_____
_____	_____	$ 20.00 x _____	=	0.00	_____
_____	_____	$ 50.00 x _____	=	0.00	_____
_____	_____	$ 100.00 x _____	=	0.00	_____
_____	_____		Total =	0.00	_____
_____	_____				
_____	_____	Checks:		Amount	Received
_____	_____	_____	$_____		_____
_____	_____	_____	$_____		_____
_____	_____	_____	$_____		_____
_____	_____	_____	$_____		_____

_____ _____
Signature, Person releasing property

_____
Signature, Person receiving property

_____
Print Name

_____
Witness

_____
Date / Time   By

_____
Relationship to the decedent (Mortuary, Family, Etc.)

FIGURE A.5, cont'd

Per ARS §36-2293, completion of this form is required for any death investigation of children younger than 12 months of age.

Page 1 of 4 (rev. 3/17/10)

Infant Death Investigation Checklist
Arizona Report Form, Version 1.0

Mail or fax completed forms to:
County Office of the Medical Examiner
(fax numbers at the bottom of this page)
Arizona Department of Health Services
(fax: 602-542-1843)

CHILD

Name: SSN:
Home Address:
Incident Address:
Date of Birth: Date of Death: Estimated Time of Death:

MOTHER OR CAREGIVER #1

Name: Other Names Used: SSN:
Address: DL#:
Date of Birth: Other States Where Resided:
Telephone (include area code):   Smoker? ☐ No ☐ Yes
Evidence/History of Substance Use? ☐ No ☐ Yes ☐ Last 24 Hours ☐ Unknown

FATHER OR CAREGIVER #2

Name: Other Names Used: SSN:
Address: DL#:
Date of Birth: Other States Where Resided:
Telephone (include area code):   Smoker? ☐ No ☐ Yes
Evidence/History of Substance Use? ☐ No ☐ Yes ☐ Last 24 Hours ☐ Unknown

CAREGIVER AT TIME OF DEATH (if other than parent)

Name: Other Names Used: SSN:
Address: DL#:
Date of Birth: Other States Where Resided:
Telephone (include area code):   Smoker? ☐ No ☐ Yes
Evidence/History of Substance Use? ☐ No ☐ Yes ☐ Last 24 Hours ☐ Unknown
Relationship to child: How long cared for child:

CAREGIVER(S) AT TIME OF DEATH INFORMATION

1. Primary Caregiver
   Column 1:
   Secondary Caregiver
   Column 2:

One	Two	
☐	☐	Biological parent
☐	☐	Adoptive parent
☐	☐	Step parent
☐	☐	Foster parent
☐	☐	Mother's partner
☐	☐	Father's partner
☐	☐	Grandparent
☐	☐	Sibling
☐	☐	Other relative
☐	☐	Friend/Neighbor
☐	☐	Unknown
☐	☐	Daycare Provider
		☐ Licensed
		☐ Unlicensed
☐	☐	Other Specify:

2. Caregiver(s) age in years
One Two
___ ___ # years
☐   ☐ Unknown

3. Caregiver(s) Sex:
One Two
☐   ☐ Male
☐   ☐ Female
☐   ☐ Unknown

4. Caregiver(s) employment status:
One Two
☐   ☐ Employed
☐   ☐ Unemployed
☐   ☐ On disability
☐   ☐ Stay-at-home
☐   ☐ Retired
☐   ☐ Unknown

5. Caregiver(s) substance use history
One Two
☐   ☐ No
☐   ☐ Yes
☐   ☐ Unknown
If yes, check all that apply
☐ Alcohol
☐ Cocaine
☐ Marijuana
☐ Methamphetamine
☐ Opiates
☐ Prescriptions
☐ Over the counter
☐ Unknown
☐ Other, Specify:

6. Caregiver(s) have prior child death:
One Two
☐   ☐ No
☐   ☐ Yes
☐   ☐ Unknown
If yes, cause(s)
Check all that apply
☐ Abuse #____
☐ Neglect #____
☐ Accident #____
☐ Suicide #____
☐ SIDS #____
☐ Unknown #____
☐ Other #____

MEDICAL EXAMINERS OFFICE FAX NUMBERS

Apache	(520) 243-8610		Maricopa	(602) 506-1546
Cochise	(520) 452-1011		Mohave	(928) 505-5889
Coconino	(928) 679-8798		Navajo	(520) 243-8610
Gila North/South	(520) 243-8610		Pima	(520) 243-8610
Graham	(520) 243-8610		Pinal	(520) 243-8610
Greenlee	(520) 243-8610		Santa Cruz	(520) 243-8610
La Paz	(520) 243-8610		Yavapai	(928) 771-3504
			Yuma	(928) 336-7319

FIGURE A.6
(A) Infant death investigative form from Arizona.

Per ARS §36-2293, completion of this form is required for any death investigation of children younger than 12 months of age.

Page 2 of 4 (rev. 3/17/10)

Infant Death Investigation Checklist
Arizona Report Form, Version 1.0

Mail or fax completed forms to:
County Office of the Medical Examiner
(fax numbers at the bottom of page 1)
Arizona Department of Health Services
(fax: 602-542-1843)

Incident State: ☐ Arizona ☐ Other, Specify Incident County:	Was 911 or local emergency number called? ☐ N/A ☐ No ☐ Yes ☐ Unknown	CPR performed before EMS arrived? ☐ N/A ☐ No ☐ Yes ☐ Unknown	During resuscitation was child: ☐ Injured ☐ Shaken ☐ Jostled ☐ Other, specify:	EMS responded to scene? ☐ N/A ☐ No ☐ Yes ☐ Unknown	Child's activity at time of incident, check all that apply: ☐ Sleeping ☐ Unknown ☐ Playing ☐ Other ☐ Working Specify: ☐ Eating ☐ In vehicle	Total number of deaths at incident event: Children (Ages 0-18): Adults: ☐ Unknown

What led someone to check on the infant? _____

Who was in the home when the child was found? _____

Describe child's appearance when found:	No	Yes	Unknown	Describe/specify location:	First Assessed by:
Discoloration around face/nose/mouth	☐	☐	☐		☐ EMS
Secretions (foam, froth)	☐	☐	☐		☐ ER
Skin discoloration (livor mortis)	☐	☐	☐		☐ PD
Pressure marks (pale areas, blanching)	☐	☐	☐		
Rash or petechiae (small, red blood spots on skin, membranes, or eyes)	☐	☐	☐		
Marks on body (scratches or bruises)	☐	☐	☐		
Infant moved prior to being found	☐	☐	☐		

Time frame information:
_____ Time Found   _____ Last Seen Alive   _____ Time Police Called   Call Type ☐ 911 ☐ Regular ☐ Other, specify: _____
_____ Last Feeding Time   Person Calling _____

What did the child feel like when found? (check all that apply)
☐ Sweaty   ☐ Warm to touch   ☐ Cool to touch   Surface body temperature:
☐ Limp, flexible ☐ Rigid, stiff   ☐ Unknown   Temperature at hospital:
☐ Other, Specify:

SUFFOCATION/ASPHYXIA

A. Type of Event	B. If suffocation/asphyxia, action causing event:		
☐ Suffocation, go to **B**. ☐ Strangulation, go to **C**. ☐ Choking, go to **D**.	☐ Sleep-related (e.g. bedding, overlay, wedged) ☐ Covered in or fell into object, not sleep related ☐ Plastic bag ☐ Dirt/Sand ☐ Unknown ☐ Other, Specify:	☐ Confined in tight space ☐ Refrigerator/freezer ☐ Toy chest ☐ Automobile ☐ Trunk ☐ Unknown ☐ Other, Specify:	☐ Swaddled in tight blanket, not sleep related ☐ Wedged into tight space, but not sleep related ☐ Asphyxia by gas ☐ Unknown ☐ Other, Specify:

C. If strangulation, object causing event:				D. If choking, object causing choking:	
☐ Clothing	☐ High chair	☐ Electrical cord		☐ Food, Specify:	
☐ Blind cord	☐ Belt	☐ Automobile power window or sunroof		☐ Toy, Specify:	
☐ Car seat	☐ Rope/string	☐ Unknown ☐ Person		☐ Balloon	☐ Unknown
☐ Stroller	☐ Leash	☐ Other, Specify:		☐ Other, Specify:	

OTHER CIRCUMSTANCES OF INCIDENT – ANSWER RELEVANT SECTIONS

DID DEATH OCCUR WHILE CHILD SLEEPING OR IN A SLEEPING ENVIRONMENT?   ☐ No   ☐ Yes

A. INCIDENT sleep place:			If adult bed, What type?		C. Child put to sleep:	D. Child found:
☐ Crib	☐ Playpen	☐ Car seat/Stroller	☐ Twin	☐ King	☐ On back	☐ On back
☐ Bassinette	☐ Couch	☐ Unknown	☐ Full	☐ Unknown	☐ On Stomach	☐ On Stomach
☐ Adult bed	☐ Chair	☐ Other, Specify:	☐ Queen	☐ Other, Specify:	☐ On side	☐ On side
☐ Waterbed	☐ Floor				☐ Unknown	☐ Unknown
					By Whom:	By Whom:

E. Was there a crib, bassinette, or port-a-crib in home for child?	☐ No	☐ Yes	☐ Unknown

F. USUAL sleep place:			If adult bed, what type?		G. USUAL sleep position:	H. Child in new or different environment?
☐ Crib	☐ Playpen	☐ Car seat/Stroller	☐ Twin	☐ King	☐ On back	☐ No
☐ Bassinette	☐ Couch	☐ Unknown	☐ Full	☐ Unknown	☐ On Stomach	☐ Yes
☐ Adult bed	☐ Chair	☐ Other, Specify:	☐ Queen	☐ Other, Specify:	☐ On side	☐ Unknown
☐ Waterbed	☐ Floor				☐ Unknown	

FIGURE A.6, cont'd

Per ARS §36-2293, completion of this form is required for any death investigation of children younger than 12 months of age.

Page 3 of 4 (rev. 3/17/10)

Infant Death Investigation Checklist
Arizona Report Form, Version 1.0

Mail or fax completed forms to:
County Office of the Medical Examiner
(fax numbers at the bottom of page 1)
Arizona Department of Health Services
(fax: 602-542-1843)

CIRCUMSTANCES when child found:

Child's airway was:
- ☐ Unobstructed by person or object
- ☐ Fully obstructed by person or object
- ☐ Partially obstructed by person or object
- ☐ Unknown

Child's position most relevant to death:
- ☐ On top of
- ☐ Under
- ☐ Between
- ☐ Wedged into
- ☐ Pressed into
- ☐ Fell or rolled onto
- ☐ Tangled in
- ☐ Unknown
- ☐ Other, Specify:

With what objects or persons? Check all that apply:
- ☐ Adult
- ☐ Child(ren)
- ☐ Animal(s)
- ☐ Blanket
- ☐ Pillow
- ☐ Comforter
- ☐ Mattress
- ☐ Bumper pads
- ☐ Waterbed mattress
- ☐ Air mattress
- ☐ Pillow-top mattress
- ☐ Crib rail
- ☐ Couch
- ☐ Car seat/stroller
- ☐ Stuffed toy
- ☐ Chair, Type:
- ☐ Clothing
- ☐ Cord
- ☐ Plastic bag
- ☐ Wall
- ☐ Unknown
- ☐ Other, Specify:

Child sleeping on same surface with person(s) or animal(s)? Check all that apply:
- ☐ With adults: Number: ___
- ☐ With other child(ren): Number: ___
- ☐ With animal(s): Number: ___
- ☐ Unknown ☐ Number Unknown

Adult obese: ☐ No ☐ Yes ☐ Unknown Alcohol/Drugs? ☐ No ☐ Yes
Child(ren)'s ages:
Type(s) of animals:

What food/liquids was the child fed in the last 24 hours?	No	Yes	Unknown	Quantity (Specify type & brand, if applicable)
Breast milk (one/both sides, length of time)	☐	☐	☐	
Formula (brand, water source – ex. Similac, tap water)	☐	☐	☐	ounces
Was the formula mixed according to directions?	☐	☐	☐	ounces
Cow's milk	☐	☐	☐	
Water (brand, bottled, tap, well)	☐	☐	☐	ounces
Other liquids (juices, teas)	☐	☐	☐	ounces
Solids, specify:	☐	☐	☐	ounces
Other, specify:	☐	☐	☐	ounces

Was a new food introduced in the 24 hours prior the child's death?
☐ No ☐ Yes ☐ Unknown If yes, describe:

Was the child last placed to sleep with a bottle?
☐ No ☐ Yes ☐ Unknown How was formula prepared:

Was the bottle propped on object while feeding?
☐ No ☐ Yes ☐ Unknown If yes, what object used?

What was the quantity of liquid (in ounces) in the bottle?

Did the death occur during: ☐ Breastfeeding ☐ Bottle feeding ☐ Eating solid foods ☐ Not during feeding

RECENT MEDICAL HISTORY

Source of medical information:
☐ Mother/primary care giver ☐ Family ☐ Doctor ☐ Medical records ☐ Other healthcare provider ☐ Other, Specify:

In the 72 hours prior to death, did the child have: (check all that apply)

	No	Yes	Unknown		No	Yes	Unknown
Fever	☐	☐	☐	Diarrhea	☐	☐	☐
Excessive sweating	☐	☐	☐	Difficulty breathing	☐	☐	☐
Weakness or sleeping more than usual	☐	☐	☐	Cough/wheezing	☐	☐	☐
Fussiness or excessive crying	☐	☐	☐	Apnea (stopping breathing)	☐	☐	☐
Decrease in appetite	☐	☐	☐	Cyanosis (turned blue/gray)	☐	☐	☐
Vomiting	☐	☐	☐	Seizures or convulsions	☐	☐	☐
Choking	☐	☐	☐	Other, Specify:			

In the 72 hours prior to death, was the child injured or did child have any other condition(s) not mentioned?
☐ No ☐ Yes If yes, describe:

In the 72 hours prior to the death, did the child receive any vaccinations, medications, or exposure to any chemicals?
(Please include any home remedies, herbal medications, prescription medicines or over-the-counter medications including "cough, cold medicine")
☐ No ☐ Yes If yes, describe/list:

Any recent visit to a medical provider?
☐ No ☐ Yes If yes, When? Doctor/Facility: Why?

FIGURE A.6, cont'd

Per ARS §36-2293, completion of this form is required for any death investigation of children younger than 12 months of age

Page 4 of 4 (rev. 3/17/10)

Mail or fax completed forms to:
County Office of the Medical Examiner
(fax numbers at the bottom of page 1)
Arizona Department of Health Services
(fax: 602-542-1843)

Infant Death Investigation Checklist
Arizona Report Form, Version 1.0

HEALTH INFORMATION

Child's Primary Care Physician: Phone: ( )   Last Visit: When?   Why:

Allergies: Birth defects:

Medications:

Has the child been immunized? ☐ No ☐ Yes ☐ Unknown   Date of last immunization:

Immunizations current? ☐ No ☐ Yes ☐ Unknown   If immunized within the last 30 days, specify type:

Does the child use any home monitors? ☐ No   ☐ Yes   Type/Brand:

   If Yes, was child on home monitor at time of death? ☐ No ☐ Yes

Anyone else in household or other contacts (e.g. daycare) recently ill? ☐ No   ☐ Yes

Family history of genetic/inheritable disease(s)? ☐ No ☐ Yes, Specify:

BIRTH INFORMATION

Birth place (home, hospital name and location):

Birth complications? ☐ No ☐ Yes   If yes, specify:

Gestational Age	Birth Weight:	Multiple Birth?	# of prenatal visits	Month of first prenatal visit
☐ Unknown	☐ Unknown	☐ No	☐ Unknown	Specify 1-9: ____
____ weeks	____ grams	☐ Yes, #____	# ____	☐ Unknown
	____ pounds/ounces			☐ None

During pregnancy, did mother (check all that apply):

☐ Smoke tobacco   ☐ Experience intimate partner violence   ☐ Heavy alcohol use   ☐ Misuse OTC or prescription drugs

☐ Use illicit drugs   ☐ Child born drug exposed   ☐ Child born with fetal alcohol effects or syndrome

☐ During pregnancy, did mother have medical complications/infections? (check all that apply)   Specify type, if known

       Type   **Type**

☐ Lung Disease ____   ☐ Preterm Labor ____

☐ Heart Disease ____   ☐ Premature Rupture Membrane ____

☐ Blood Disorder ____   ☐ Vaginal Bleeding ____

   ☐ Infectious Disease ____   ☐ Diabetes Mellitus ____

   ☐ Familial Genetic Disorder ____   ☐ Other

Were there access or compliance issues related to prenatal care?

☐ No   ☐ Lack of money for care   ☐ Religious objections to care

☐ Yes   ☐ Limited or no health insurance coverage   ☐ Cultural differences

If yes, check all that apply: ☐ Lack of transportation   ☐ Unwilling to obtain care

☐ Unknown   ☐ Lack of child care   ☐ Did not know care needed

     ☐ No phone   ☐ Other, specify:

SCENE DOCUMENTATION

Photos of Death Scene Taken? ☐ No ☐ Yes

Property Seized? ☐ No ☐ Yes   What Agency Seized Property?

Formula? ☐ No ☐ Yes | Bottles/Contents? ☐ No ☐ Yes | Bedding? ☐ No ☐ Yes | Crib? ☐ No ☐ Yes

Other, Specify:

Was there an open CPS case with child at time of death?   ☐ No ☐ Yes ☐ Unk

Was the child ever placed outside of the home prior to death?   ☐ No ☐ Yes Date of Placement:

Were any siblings placed outside of the home prior to this child's death? ☐ No ☐ Yes Date of Placement:

PERSON COMPLETING FORM

Name (please print or type):

Agency:

Telephone: ( )   Fax: ( )   Date:

Signature: Date Signed:

ADDITIONAL COMMENTS: (Include information about additional caregivers/supervisors or circumstances. Attach additional pages as necessary)

FIGURE A.6, cont'd

U.S. DEPARTMENT OF HEALTH AND HUMAN SERVICES
Centers for Disease Control and Prevention
Division of Reproductive Health
Maternal and Infant Health Branch
Atlanta, Georgia 30333

Sudden Unexplained Infant Death Investigation
SUIDI
Reporting Form

INVESTIGATION DATA

Infant's Last Name [ ] Infant's First Name [ ] Middle Name [ ] Case Number [ ]

Sex: [ ] Date of Birth: [ ] Age: [ ] SS#: [ ]

Race: [ ] White [ ] Black/African Am. [ ] Asian/Pacific Isl. [ ] Am. Indian/Alaskan Native [ ] Hispanic/Latino [ ] Other

Infant's Primary Residence:

Address: [ ] City: [ ] County: [ ] State: [ ] Zip: [ ]

Incident Address: [ ] City: [ ] County: [ ] State: [ ] Zip: [ ]

Contact Information for Witness:

Relationship to deceased: [ ] Birth Mother [ ] Birth Father [ ] Grandmother [ ] Grandfather

[ ] Adoptive or Foster Parent [ ] Physician [ ] Health Records [ ] Other Describe: [ ]

Last: [ ] First: [ ] M.: [ ] SS#: [ ]

Address: [ ] City: [ ] State: [ ] Zip: [ ]

Work Address: [ ] City: [ ] State: [ ] Zip: [ ]

Home Phone: [ ] Work Phone: [ ] Date of Birth: [ ]

WITNESS INTERVIEW

1 Are you the usual caregiver?
[ ] No [ ] Yes

2 Tell me what happened:
[ ]

3 Did you notice anything unusual or different about the infant in the last 24 hrs?
[ ] No [ ] Yes Specify: [ ]

4 Did the infant experience any falls or injury within the last 72 hrs?
[ ] No [ ] Yes Specify: [ ]

5 When was the infant LAST PLACED?
Date: [ ] Military Time: [:] Location (room): [ ]

6 When was the infant LAST KNOWN ALIVE(LKA)?
Date: [ ] Military Time: [:] Location (room): [ ]

7 When was the infant FOUND?
Date: [ ] Military Time: [:] Location (room): [ ]

8 Explain how you knew the infant was still alive.
[ ]

9 Where was the infant - (P)laced, (L)ast known alive, (F)ound (write P, L, or F in front of appropriate response)?

[ ] Bassinet	[ ] Bedside co-sleeper	[ ] Car seat	[ ] Chair
[ ] Cradle	[ ] Crib	[ ] Floor	[ ] In a person's arms
[ ] Mattress/box spring	[ ] Mattress on floor	[ ] Playpen	[ ] Portable crib
[ ] Sofa/couch	[ ] Stroller/carriage	[ ] Swing	[ ] Waterbed
[ ] Other - describe:			

FIGURE A.6
(B) Sudden Unexplained Infant Death Investigation form

WITNESS INTERVIEW (cont.)

10 **In what position was the infant LAST PLACED?** ☐ Sitting ☐ On back ☐ On side ☐ On stomach ☐ Unknown
Was this the infant's usual position? ☐ Yes ☐ No What was the usual position? _____

11 **In what position was the infant LKA?** ☐ Sitting ☐ On back ☐ On side ☐ On stomach ☐ Unknown
Was this the infant's usual position? ☐ Yes ☐ No What was the usual position? _____

12 **In what position was the infant FOUND?** ☐ Sitting ☐ On back ☐ On side ☐ On stomach ☐ Unknown
Was this the infant's usual position? ☐ Yes ☐ No What was the usual position? _____

13 **Face position when LAST PLACED?** ☐ Face down on surface ☐ Face up ☐ Face right ☐ Face left

14 **Neck position when LAST PLACED?** ☐ Hyperextended (head back) ☐ Flexed (chin to chest) ☐ Neutral ☐ Turned

15 **Face position when LKA?** ☐ Face down on surface ☐ Face up ☐ Face right ☐ Face left

16 **Neck position when LKA?** ☐ Hyperextended (head back) ☐ Flexed (chin to chest) ☐ Neutral ☐ Turned

17 **Face position when FOUND?** ☐ Face down on surface ☐ Face up ☐ Face right ☐ Face left

18 **Neck position when FOUND?** ☐ Hyperextended (head back) ☐ Flexed (chin to chest) ☐ Neutral ☐ Turned

19 **What was the infant wearing?** *(ex. t-shirt, disposable diaper)* _____

20 **Was the infant tightly wrapped or swaddled?** ☐ No ☐ Yes - describe: _____

21 Please indicate the types and numbers of layers of bedding both over and under infant (not including wrapping blanket):

Bedding UNDER Infant	None	Number	Bedding OVER Infant	None	Number
Receiving blankets			Receiving blankets		
Infant/child blankets			Infant/child blankets		
Infant/child comforters (thick)			Infant/child comforters (thick)		
Adult comforters/duvets			Adult comforters/duvets		
Adult blankets			Adult blankets		
Sheets			Sheets		
Sheepskin			Pillows		
Pillows			Other, specify:		
Rubber or plastic sheet					
Other, specify:					

22 **Which of the following devices were operating in the infant's room?**
☐ None ☐ Apnea monitor ☐ Humidifier ☐ Vaporizer ☐ Air purifier ☐ Other - _____

23 **In was the temperature in the infant's room?** ☐ Hot ☐ Cold ☐ Normal ☐ Other - _____

24 **Which of the following items were near the infant's face, nose, or mouth?**
☐ Bumper pads ☐ Infant pillows ☐ Positional supports ☐ Stuffed animals ☐ Toys ☐ Other - _____

25 **Which of the following items were within the infant's reach?**
☐ Blankets ☐ Toys ☐ Pillows ☐ Pacifier ☐ Nothing ☐ Other - _____

26 **Was anyone sleeping with the infant?** ☐ No ☐ Yes

Name of individual sleeping with infant	Age	Height	Weight	Location in relation to infant	Imparement (intoxication, tired)

27 **Was there evidence of wedging?** ☐ No ☐ Yes - Describe: _____

28 **When the infant was found, was s/he:** ☐ Breathing ☐ Not Breathing
If not breathing, did you witness the infant stop breathing? ☐ No ☐ Yes

FIGURE A.6, cont'd

WITNESS INTERVIEW (cont.)

29 What had led you to check on the infant?

30 Describe the infant's appearance when found.

Appearance	Unknown	No	Yes	Describe and specify location
a) Discoloration around face/nose/mouth				
b) Secretions (foam, froth)				
c) Skin discoloration (livor mortis)				
d) Pressure marks (pale areas, blanching)				
e) Rash or petechiae (small, red blood spots on skin, membranes, or eyes)				
f) Marks on body (scratches or bruises)				
g) Other				

31 What did the infant feel like when found? *(Check all that apply.)*

☐ Sweaty ☐ Warm to touch ☐ Cool to touch ☐ Limp, flexible ☐ Rigid, stif ☐ Unknown

☐ Other - specify:

32 Did anyone else other than EMS try to resuscitate the infant? ☐ No ☐ Yes

Who? Date: Military time:

33 Please describe what was done as part of resuscitation:

34 Has the parent/caregiver ever had a child die suddenly and unexpectedly? ☐ No ☐ Yes

Explain:

INFANT MEDICAL HISTORY

1 Source of medical information: ☐ Doctor ☐ Other healthcare provider ☐ Medical record ☐ Family

☐ Mother/primary caregiver ☐ Other:

2 In the 72 hours prior to death, did the infant have:

Condition	Unknown	No	Yes	Condition	Unknown	No	Yes
a) Fever				k) Apnea (stopped breathing)			
h) Diarrhea				e) Decrease in appetite			
b) Excessive sweating				l) Cyanosis (turned blue/gray)			
i) Stool changes				f) Vomiting			
c) Lethargy or sleeping more than usual				m) Seizures or convulsions			
j) Difficulty breathing				g) Choking			
d) Fussiness or excessive crying				n) Other, specify:			

3 In the 72 hours prior to death, was the infant injured or did s/he have any other condition(s) not mentioned?

☐ No ☐ Yes - describe:

4 In the 72 hours prior to the infants death, was the infant given any vaccinations or medications? ☐ No ☐ Yes
(Please include any home remedies, herbal medications, prescription medicines, over-the-counter medications.)

Name of vaccination or medication	Dose last given	Date given Month	Day	Year	Approx. time (Military Time)	comments:
1.						
2.						
3.						
4.						

FIGURE A.6, cont'd

INFANT MEDICAL HISTORY (cont.)

5 At any time in the infant's life, did s/he have a history of?

Medical history	Unknown	No	Yes	Describe
a) Allergies *(food, medication, or other)*				
b) Abnormal growth or weight gain/loss				
c) Apnea *(stopped breathing)*				
d) Cyanosis *(turned blue/gray)*				
e) Seizures or convulsions				
f) Cardiac *(heart)* abnormalities				

6 Did the infant have any birth defects(s)? ☐ No ☐ Yes

Describe:

7 Describe the two most recent times that the infant was seen by a physician or health care provider:
(Include emergency department visits, clinic visits, hospital admissions, observational stays, and telephone calls)

	First most recent visit	Second most recent visit
a) Date		
b) Reason for visit		
c) Action taken		
d) Physician's name		
e) Hospital/clinic		
f) Address		
g) City		
h) State, ZIP		
i) Phone number		

8 Birth hospital name: _____ Discharge date: _____

Street address: _____

City: _____ State: ___ Zip: ___

9 What was the infant's length at birth? ___ inches or ___ centimeters

10 What was the infant's weight at birth? ___ pounds ___ ounces or ___ grams

11 Compared to the delivery date, was the infant born on time, early, or late?
☐ On time ☐ Early - how many weeks? ___ ☐ Late - how many weeks? ___

12 Was the infant a singleton, twin, triplet, or higher gestation?
☐ Singleton ☐ Twin ☐ Triplet ☐ Quadrupelet or higher gestation

13 Were there any complications during delivery or at birth? *(emergency c-section, child needed oxygen)* ☐ Yes ☐ No

Describe:

14 Are there any alerts to the pathologist? *(previous infant deaths in family, newborn screen results)* ☐ Yes ☐ No

Specify:

Page 4

FIGURE A.6, cont'd

INFANT DIETARY HISTORY

1 On what day and at what approximate time was the infant last fed?

Date: [_____] Military Time: [____:____]

2 What is the name of the person who last fed the infant? [_____]

3 What is his/her relationship to the infant? [_____]

4 What foods and liquids was the infant fed in the <u>last 24 hours</u> (include last fed)?

Food	Unknown	No	Yes	Quantity (ounces)	Specify: (type and brand)
a) Breast milk (one/both sides, length of time)					
b) Formula (brand, water source - ex. Similac, tap water)					
c) Cow's milk					
d) Water (brand, bottled, tap, well)					
e) Other liquids (teas, juices)					
f) Solids					
g) Other					

5 Was a new food introduced in the 24 hours prior to his/her death? [ ] No [ ] Yes
If yes, describe *(ex. content, amount, change in formula, introduction of solids)*

[_____]

6 Was the infant last placed to sleep with a bottle? [ ] Yes [ ] No - if no, skip to question **9** below

7 Was the bottle propped? (i.e., object used to hold bottle while infant feeds) [ ] No [ ] Yes

If yes, what object was used to prop the bottle? [_____]

8 What was the quantity of liquid (in ounces) in the bottle? [_____]

9 Did the death occur during? [ ] Breast-feeding [ ] Bottle-feeding [ ] Eating solid foods [ ] Not during feeding

10 Are there any factors, circumstances, or environmental concerns that may have impacted the infant that have not yet been identified? *(ex. exposed to cigarette smoke or fumes at someone else's home, infant unusually heavy, placed with positional supports or wedges)*

[ ] No [ ] Yes

If yes, - describe: [_____]

PREGNANCY HISTORY

1 Information about the infant's birth mother:

First name: [_____] Last name: [_____]

Middle name: [_____] Maiden name: [_____]

Birth date: [_____] SS#: [_____]

Street address: [_____] City: [_____] State: [____] Zip: [____]

How long has the birth mother been at this address? Years: [____] Months: [____]

Previous Address: [_____]

2 At how many weeks or months did the birth mother begin prenatal care? [ ] No parental care [ ] Unknown

Weeks: [_____] Months: [_____]

3 Where did the birth mother receive prenatal care? *(Please specify physician or other health care provider name and address.)*

Physician/provider: [_____] Hospital/clinic: [_____] Phone: [_____]

Street address: [_____] City: [_____] State: [____] Zip: [____]

FIGURE A.6, cont'd

PREGNANCY HISTORY (cont.)

4 At how many weeks or months did the birth mother begin prenatal care? ☐ No ☐ Yes
(ex. high blood pressure, bleeding, gestational diabetes)
Specify: _____

5 Was the birth mother injured during her pregnancy with the infant? *(ex. auto accident, falls)* ☐ No ☐ Yes
Specify: _____

6 During her pregnancy, did she use any of the following?

	Unknown	No	Yes	Daily		Unknown	No	Yes	Daily
a) Over the counter medications					d) Cigarettes				
b) Prescription medications					e) Alcohol				
c) Herbal remedies					f) Other				

7 Currently, does any caregiver use any of the following?

	Unknown	No	Yes	Daily		Unknown	No	Yes	Daily
a) Over the counter medications					d) Cigarettes				
b) Prescription medications					e) Alcohol				
c) Herbal remedies					f) Other				

INCIDENT SCENE INVESTIGATION

1 Where did the incident or death occur? _____

2 Was this the primary residence? ☐ No ☐ Yes

3 Is the site of the incident or death scene a daycare or other childcare setting? ☐ Yes ☐ No - If no, skip to question **8**

4 How many children (under age 18) were under the care of the provider at the time of the incident or death? _____

5 How many adults (age 18 and over) were supervising the child(ren)? _____

6 What is the license number and licensing agency for the daycare?
License number: _____ Agency: _____

7 How long has the daycare been open for business? _____

8 How many people live at the site of the incident or death scene?
Number of adults (18 years or older): _____ Number of children (under 18 years old): _____

9 Which of the following heating or cooling sources were being used? *(Check all that apply)*

☐ Central air	☐ Gas furnace or boiler	☐ Wood burning fireplace	☐ Open window(s)
☐ A/C window unit	☐ Electric furnace or boiler	☐ Coal burning furnace	☐ Wood burning stove
☐ Ceiling fan	☐ Electric space heater	☐ Kerosene space heater	☐ Floor/table fan
☐ Electric baseboard heat	☐ Electric (radiant) ceiling heat	☐ Window fan	☐ Unknown

☐ Other - specify: _____

10 Indicate the temperature of the room where the infant was found unresponsive:
☐ Thermostat setting ☐ Thermostat reading ☐ Actual room temp. ☐ Outside temp.

11 What was the source of drinking water at the site of the incident or death scene? *(Check all that apply.)*
☐ Public/municipal water ☐ Bottled water ☐ Well ☐ Unknown ☐ Other - Specify: _____

12 The site of the incident or death scene has: *(check all that apply)*

☐ Insects	☐ Mold growth	☐ Smoky smell *(like cigarettes)*
☐ Pets	☐ Dampness	☐ Presence of alcohol containers
☐ Peeling paint	☐ Visible standing water	☐ Presence of drug paraphenalia
☐ Rodents or vermin	☐ Odors or fumes - Describe:	

☐ Other - specify: _____

13 Describe the general appearance of incident scene: *(ex. cleanliness, hazards, overcrowding, etc.)*
Specify: _____

FIGURE A.6, cont'd

INVESTIGATION SUMMARY

1 Are there any factors, circumstances, or environmental concerns about the incident scene investigation that may have impacted the infant that have not yet been identified?

2 Arrival times

Military time

Law enforcement at scene: [:]

DSI at scene: [:]

Infant at hospital: [:]

Investigator's Notes

1 Indicate the task(s) performed

- [ ] Additional scene(s)? (forms attached)
- [ ] Materials collected/evidence logged
- [ ] Notify next of kin or verify notification
- [ ] Doll reenactment/scene re-creation
- [ ] Referral for counseling
- [ ] 911 tape
- [ ] Photos or video taken and noted
- [ ] EMS run sheet/report

2 If more than one person was interviewed, does the information differ? [ ] No [ ] Yes

If yes, detail any differences, inconsistencies of relevant information: *(ex. placed on sofa, last known alive on chair.)*

INVESTIGATION DIAGRAMS

1 Scene Diagram:

2 Body Diagram:

Page 7

FIGURE A.6, cont'd

SUMMARY FOR PATHOLOGIST

Case Information

1 Investigator information Name: [   ] Agency: [   ] Phone: [   ]

	Date	Military time
Investigated:	[ ]	:
Pronounced dead:	[ ]	:

2 Infant's information: Last: [   ] First: [   ] M: [   ] Case #: [   ]

Sex: [ ] Male [ ] Female Date of Birth: [   ] Age: [   ]

Race: [ ] White [ ] Black/African Am. [ ] Asian/Pacific Islander

[ ] Am. Indian/Alaskan Native [ ] Hispanic/Latino [ ] Other: [   ]

1 Indicate whether preliminary investigation suggests any of the following:

Sleeping Environment

Yes	No	
		Asphyxia *(ex. overlying, wedging, choking, nose/mouth obstruction, re-breathing, neck compression, immersion in water)*
		Sharing of sleep surface with adults, children, or pets
		Change in sleep condition *(ex. unaccustomed stomach sleep position, location, or sleep surface)*
		Hyperthermia/Hypothermia *(ex. excessive wrapping, blankets, clothing, or hot or cold environments)*
		Environmental hazards *(ex. carbon monoxide, noxious gases, chemicals, drugs, devices)*
		Unsafe sleep condition *(ex. couch/sofa, waterbed, stuffed toys, pillows, soft bedding)*

Infant History

Yes	No	
		Diet *(e.g., solids introduced, etc.)*
		Recent hospitalization
		Previous medical diagnosis
		History of acute life-threatening events *(ex. apnea, seizures, difficulty breathing)*
		History of medical care without diagnosis
		Recent fall or other injury
		History of religious, cultural, or ethnic remedies
		Cause of death due to natural causes other than SIDS *(ex. birth defects, complications of preterm birth)*

Family Info

Yes	No	
		Prior sibling deaths
		Previous encounters with police or social service agencies
		Request for tissue or organ donation
		Objection to autopsy

Exam

Yes	No	
		Pre-terminal resuscitative treatment
		Death due to trauma (injury), poisoning, or intoxication

Investigator Insight

Yes	No	
		Suspicious circumstances
		Other alerts for pathologist's attention

Any "Yes" answers above should be explained in detail (description of circumstances):

[   ]

Pathologist

2 Pathologist information Name: [   ]

Agency: [   ] Phone: [   ] Fax: [   ]

FIGURE A.6, cont'd

EXTERNAL EXAMINATION WORKSHEET

Case No. _____

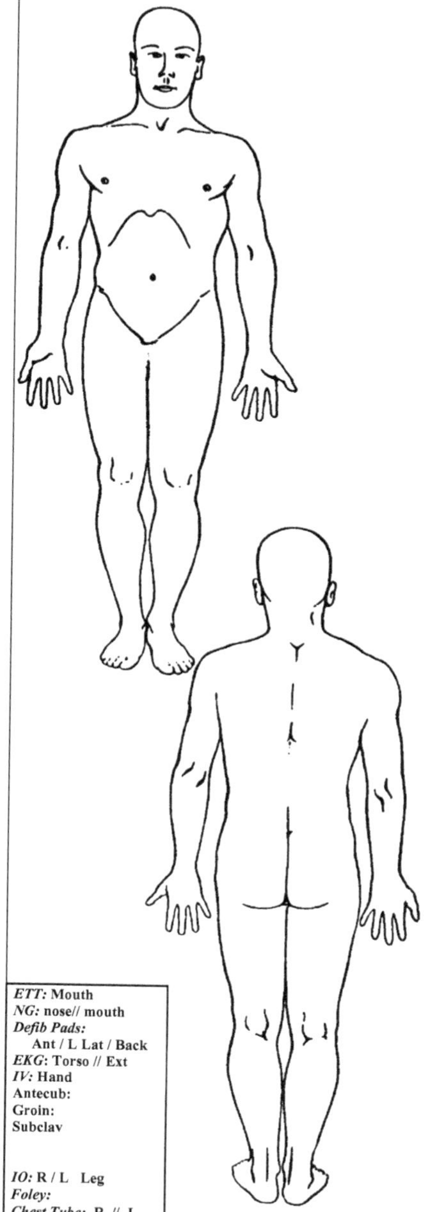

Name	

Age	Sex	Date of Death	
Years	Male// Female		@ hours
Place of Examination	Date of Examination		Time hours

Clothing
Indoor // Outdoor // Pajamas // Underwear// Diaper/// None

Body Length ___ inches | **Body Weight** ___ pounds

Nourishment Normal // Thin // Obese | **Body Preservation** Good // Decomposed// Early Decomposition

Postmortem Lividity Posterior, Anterior Fixed, Blanchable Inferior Warm, Cold | **Postmortem Rigidity** Full: Upper/Lower Ext. & Jaw Easily Broken Absent

Hair Color and Length Gray // Brown// Black//Blonde Balding ___ cm. | **Head** Trauma: Brd brn/blk/gr: stubble/ ___cm// Mstach

Eyes Blue// Brown // Hazel /// ___ cm. ++ // -- petechiae //hemorrhages | **Ears/Nose/Mouth** Trauma:

Teeth Natural: Good // Poor // Moderate Edentulous // + or -- Dentures | **Neck** Trauma:

Trunk—Anterior No trauma // see diagram Tattoos: | **Trunk—Posterior** No trauma // see diagram Tattoos: Scars: See dictation

Upper Extremities No trauma // see diagram Tattoos: | **Lower Extremities** No trauma // see diagram// Tattoos: ___ Edema

Genitalia Normal Male // Normal Female | **Toxicology Samples Taken** Vitreous/ Urine / Blood: Fem or Subclav

MANNER OF DEATH | **CAUSE OF DEATH**

NATURAL ☐   (a)_____ DUE TO or as a consequence of
ACCIDENT ☐   (b)_____ DUE TO or as a consequence of
SUICIDE ☐   (c)_____
HOMICIDE ☐   OTHER SIGNIFICANT CONDITIONS:
UNDET. ☐
PENDING ☐

NOTES:
Place of Death: Scene /// Residence //// Hospital _____
PMHx: HTN //// COPD /// DM /// MI //// CABG //// CA _____
MVA: driver // occupant// pedestrian
GSW: head // chest// abdomen
Xrays:
Cavity Blood: Chest Abdomen

_____ signature   _____ date

ETT: Mouth
NG: nose// mouth
Defib Pads: Ant / L Lat / Back
EKG: Torso // Ext
IV: Hand Antecub: Groin: Subclav
IO: R / L Leg
Foley:
Chest Tube: R // L

FIGURE A.7
External examination worksheet.

Case #		HEIGHT
Decedent:		WEIGHT

ORGAN (weight gms)		Comments
HEART:	RV LV IVS LAD RCA LC	TCV PV MV AV GREAT VESSELS:
LUNGS: Right Left		Pleural Cavities: Right Left
NECK ORGANS:		
THYMUS:		
SPLEEN: Lymph Nodes:		
LIVER: Gall Bladder		
ADRENALS:		
PANCREAS:		
KIDNEYS: Right Left		
PELVIC ORGANS: Uterus F O	Urine: (Color / Vol)	
GI TRACT: Abd. Cav.	Appendix (Y/N) Gastric Contents:	Abdominal Fat

MUSCULOSKELETAL:	Rib Fx: L ant.
	        L lat.
	        L post.
		R ant.
		R lat.
		R post.

BRAIN:		
TOX: Vit Blood: fem sub Urine Liver	Other:	FOC CC AC CR CH WEIGHT IN GRAMS

FIGURE A.8
Worksheet for recording data at the time of the autopsy.

STAB WOUNDS

	# 1	# 2	# 3	# 4	# 5	# 6	# 7	# 8	# 9	# 0
BODY SITE										
DISTANCE WOUND										
Top of Head [H] Right Foot [RF] Left Foot [LF]										
Right Midline [RML]										
Left Midline [LML]										
SIZE OF WOUND										
LENGTH										
WIDTH										
MARGINS										
Square (SQ)										
Acute (A)										
DEPTH OF WOUND										
DIRECTION										
F ->B ↑↓ L ->R B->F R ->L										
ORGANS & FRACTURES										

FIGURE A.9
Notation of stab wounds worksheet.

GUNSHOT WOUNDS

	#	#	#	#	#	#	#	#	#	#
BODY SITE										
Entrance vs. Exit										
Connections										
DISTANCE WOUND										
Top of Head [H] Right Foot [RF] Left Foot [LF]										
Right Midline [RML]										
Left Midline [LML]										
SIZE OF WOUND										
Length x width										
MARGINS										
Marginal Abrasion										
Soot										
Stippling										
Projectiles										
DIRECTION										
F ->B ↑↓ L ->R B->F R ->L										
ORGANS & FRACTURES										

FIGURE A.10
Notation of gunshot wounds worksheet.

Infant Measurements:

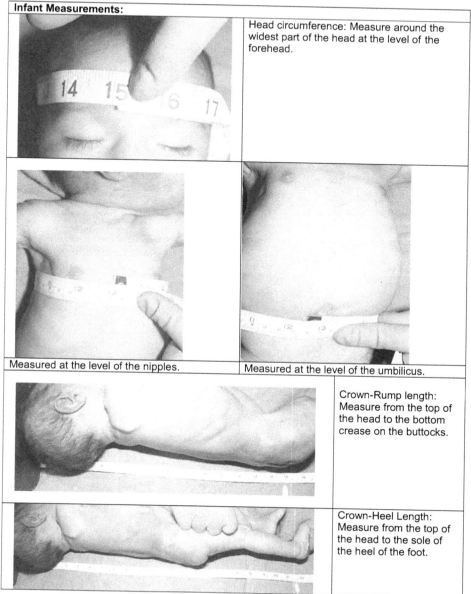

| | Head circumference: Measure around the widest part of the head at the level of the forehead. |

| Measured at the level of the nipples. | Measured at the level of the umbilicus. |

| | Crown-Rump length: Measure from the top of the head to the bottom crease on the buttocks. |

| | Crown-Heel Length: Measure from the top of the head to the sole of the heel of the foot. |

FIGURE A.11
How to obtain various measurements an infant.

Pictoral Overview of an Autopsy

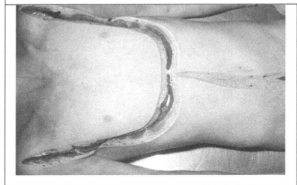

Opening of the body with a Y shaped incision. The upper chest flap is reflected upward to the neck then eventually to the base of the chin to examine the torso and neck organs.

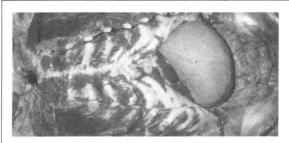

Removal of the chest plate to gain entry into the chest cavity

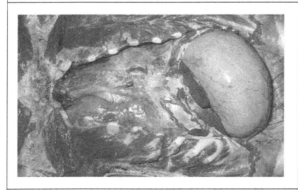

The open chest and abdomen.

FIGURE A.12
Overview of an autopsy.

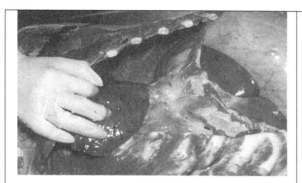

Evaluation of the chest cavity for accumulations of fluid which will need to be measured for quantity.

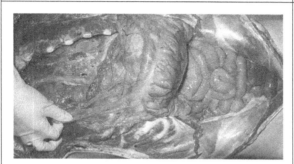

Evaluation of the abdominal cavity for accumulations of fluid. They will need to be measured for quantity.

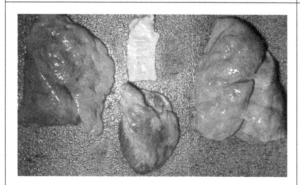

The organs are removed separately, weighed and dissected. Here are the right and left lungs and heart with thoracic aorta.

FIGURE A.12, cont'd

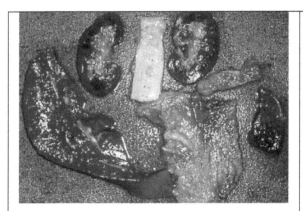

The abdominal organs have been removed and individually dissected looking for pathological processes to contribute to death.

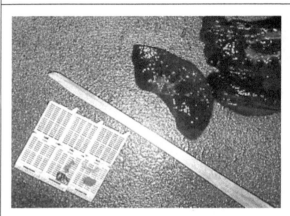

Biopsies of the organs are placed in the plastic cases for submission to histology in a jar of formalin.

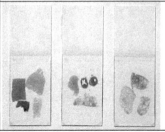

Histology places the plastic cassettes through a series of chemical processes to dehydrate and preserve the specimens. They are then cut into very thin slices and placed onto glass slides, stained and dried. They are then ready for microscopic review by the pathologist.

FIGURE A.12, cont'd

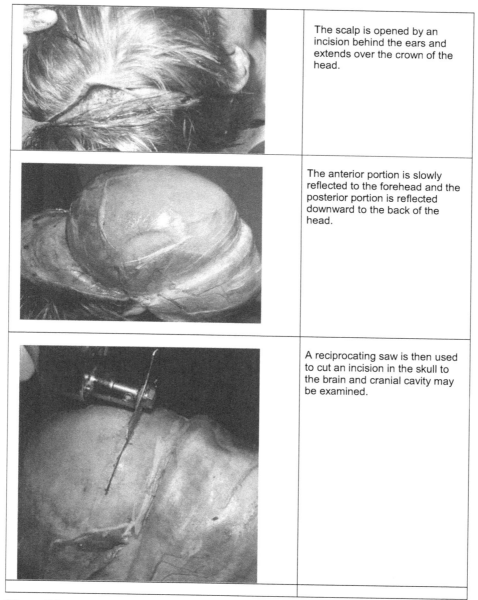

	The scalp is opened by an incision behind the ears and extends over the crown of the head.
	The anterior portion is slowly reflected to the forehead and the posterior portion is reflected downward to the back of the head.
	A reciprocating saw is then used to cut an incision in the skull to the brain and cranial cavity may be examined.

FIGURE A.12, cont'd

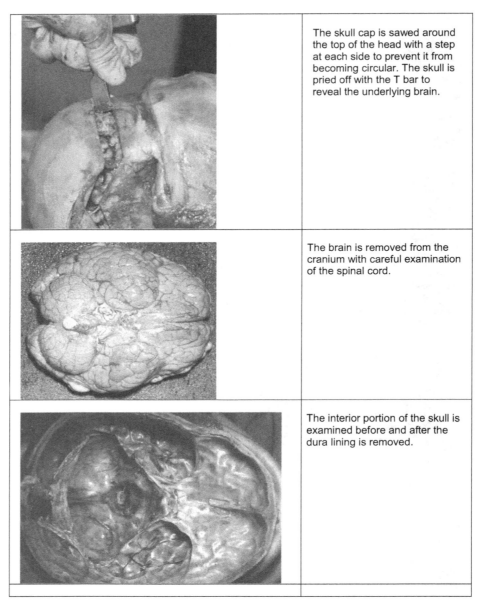

	The skull cap is sawed around the top of the head with a step at each side to prevent it from becoming circular. The skull is pried off with the T bar to reveal the underlying brain.
	The brain is removed from the cranium with careful examination of the spinal cord.
	The interior portion of the skull is examined before and after the dura lining is removed.

FIGURE A.12, cont'd

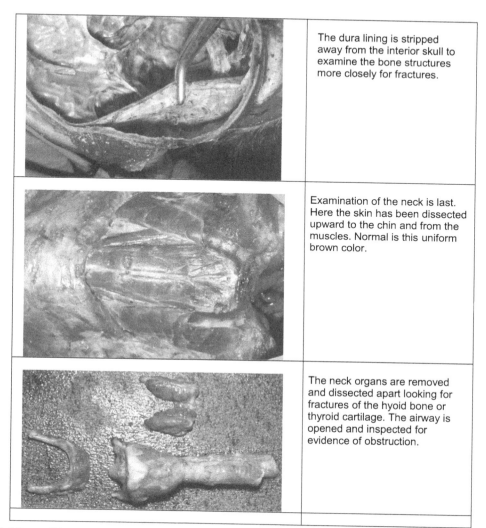

The dura lining is stripped away from the interior skull to examine the bone structures more closely for fractures.

Examination of the neck is last. Here the skin has been dissected upward to the chin and from the muscles. Normal is this uniform brown color.

The neck organs are removed and dissected apart looking for fractures of the hyoid bone or thyroid cartilage. The airway is opened and inspected for evidence of obstruction.

FIGURE A.12, cont'd

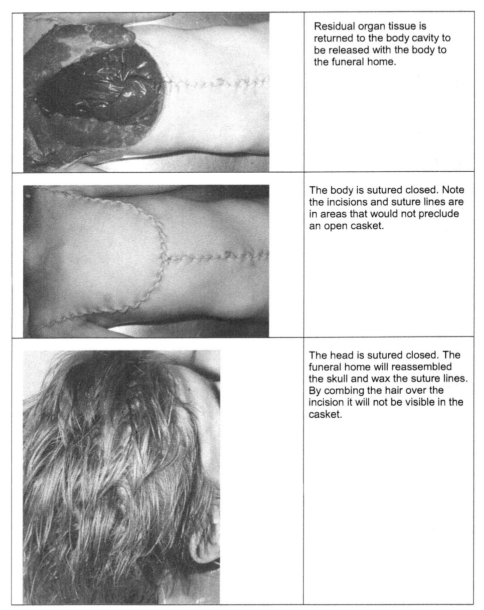

	Residual organ tissue is returned to the body cavity to be released with the body to the funeral home.
	The body is sutured closed. Note the incisions and suture lines are in areas that would not preclude an open casket.
	The head is sutured closed. The funeral home will reassembled the skull and wax the suture lines. By combing the hair over the incision it will not be visible in the casket.

FIGURE A.12, cont'd

Removal of the eyes :

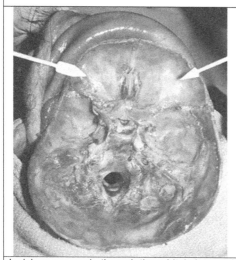 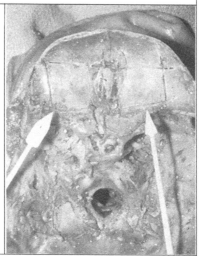

Incisions are made through the orbital plates using the oscillating saw. The plates are removed to loosen the soft tissue around each of the globes, being careful to not incise the eyelids. The eyelids can then be dissected away from the area surrounding the anterior globe. The small muscles on either side of the globe will need to be snipped away to release the globe from the orbital canal.

FIGURE A.13
Overview of removal of certain body parts.

Removal of the internal ear canals:

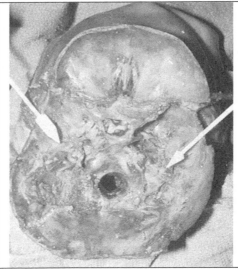 

Wedges of bone at 45 degree angles are incised into the basilar skull over the internal ear canal. The fragments will require decalcification prior to review in microscopic sections.

FIGURE A.13, cont'd

Removal of the spinal cord:

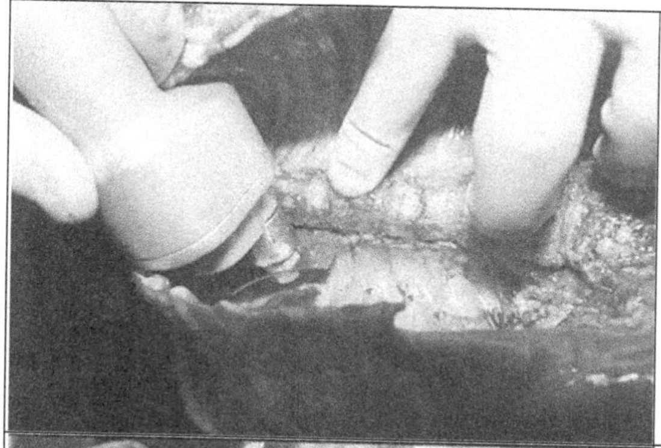

The anterior portion of the vertebral canal must be removed to reveal the underlying spinal cord. A 45 to 60 degree angle incision is made along the edge of the spine.

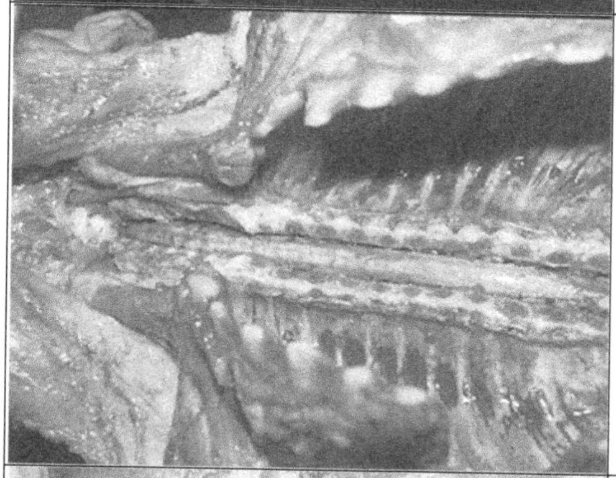

The wedge of bone is lifted off revealing the dura and cord.

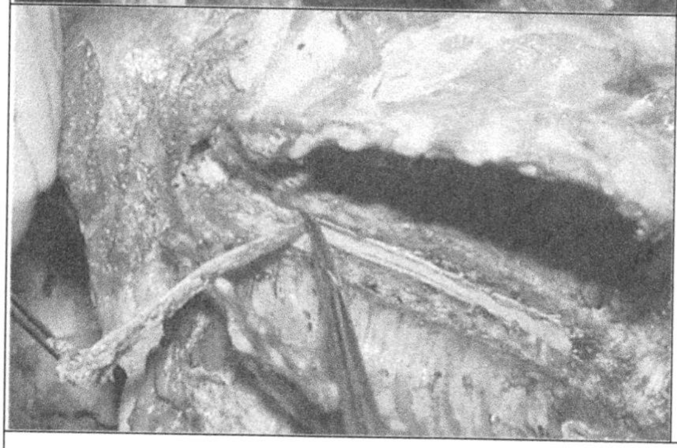

The dura is opened and the cord is able to be removed by snipping the small nerves along the margins.

FIGURE A.13, cont'd

Cerebrospinal Fluid Tap

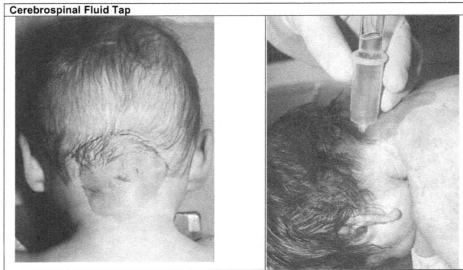

The skin is cleansed with bactericidal soap then a syringe is inserted at the base of the skull into the brain. Clear fluid should be obtained with gentle suciton on the syringe.

FIGURE A.13, cont'd

REHYDRATING MUMMIFIED HANDS FOR FINGERPRINT IDENTIFICATION

(Used with permission Pima County Forensic Science Center, Tucson, AZ)

A. 3% Sodium Hydroxide (NaOH) Solution preparation:

This solution creates HEAT. To prevent spillage, add the sodium hydroxide SLOWLY to the water.

- 60 grams of NaOH (usually in pellet form)
- 2 liters of water (tap water or saline)
- Slowly dissolve the NaOH pellets by adding them into a gallon size container
- Let the solution cool overnight, uncovered. Ready to use the following AM.

Makes 2 liters of the 3% NaOH solution which is enough for a single application.

B. Soaking procedure:

- Disarticulate the hands at the wrist.
- Soak the hands in the 2 liters of 3% NaOH solution. Best if place the pads downward in the container as the hands will float.
- Monitor the hands for suppleness and pliability for next 24-48 hrs. Check frequently after the first 24 hrs to prevent over processing.
- While checking, rinse the hands of debris from the pads and resoak if unable to open from clenched position.
- At the point of suppleness of the pads as well as the hand, remove hands from solution and wrap in a towel and let dry for 24-48 hours.
- After the hands are no longer slick and are pliable they are ready to be printed.
- For best results, use black fingerprint ink applied sparingly to a finger-print slab. Apply the ink to the finger pads using the slab or roller. Print the fingers onto a card. This process may need to be repeated at various intervals to obtain the best prints, allowing the hands to remain wrapped in the towel between attempts.

PROCEDURE FOR OBTAINING PRINTS ON WASHERWOMAN HANDS

1. The day before the autopsy, take a small tub and rest each hand on one so they are located out of the water in the bag.
2. Wrap the hands in a thick towel. It is important to keep the hands from resting in the body bag as it will keep the hands wet.
3. The next morning, massage Goop (usually found at car part stores) into the fingers of the decedent.
4. Use a clean towel to wipe off the Goop. The process of rubbing on the Goop and taking it off may need to be done a couple of times.
5. Using an ink roller, roll a thin layer of ink on the fingertips and print as usual.

ON BEING A WITNESS

1. Make definite arrangements with the attorney who is asking you to testify as to the time and place for the meeting, and whether it is a court or a defense interview. Subpoenas for deposition will state the time and place. Even though you have a subpoena for court, call the attorney prior to going to court to verify the time and place. Wait outside the courtroom until you are called.

2. Become familiar with courtroom proceedings prior to appearing as a witness. Listen and observe some trials either in person or on TV.

3. The witness will be sworn in by the court personnel; the judge will direct you to the correct person. He or she will verify your name and title and you will be sworn in. State "I do" clearly and confidently so the jury can hear.

4. You should wear neat, conservative clothing. Plain, dark colors or small prints are best. For women, a nice dress, suit, or jacket with skirt or pants, minimal makeup, and a small purse. For men, a suit jacket with trousers and a dress shirt with a tie. Your shoes should be neat. Your first impression with the jury is important. You are on a job interview with 12 prospective bosses. Remember you aren't there to impress them with style, you are there to be believable.

5. Try to relax on the witness stand. There is water there for your use if you need it.

6. A witness' testimony is for the benefit of the jury and the court rather than the spectators, attorneys, or judge. Face the jury when testifying. You can face the attorney when he or she is questioning you, and when you reply, shift your attention and body to answer to the jury.

7. Give information to the jury in an air of assurance but do not be arrogant.

8. If you need to refresh your memory, you may bring notes and/or reports to court and utilize them. If you need a moment to locate the passage, state that you need a moment to refer to your notes to answer the question.

9. Be prepared. Review the report and record prior to going to court. Recall what your statements were during pretrial interviews and make notes of them during or after to refer to prior to going to trial. Review your resume so that you can recite your credentials concisely. Always take a copy of a current resume to trial and to a pretrial interview or deposition.

10. A witness should always be courteous and not argumentative. It is the attorney's job to see if he or she can get you riled. Don't let it happen.

11. A witness should always be attentive and interested in what is being said in the courtroom. Do not appear bored or that the questions are tedious. Many times questions are asked and re-asked. Be prepared to state that you have answered the question previously. The court may make you give the answer again; remember what you say and repeat the same words exactly.

12. You are there to give the jury the facts so they can make a decision. Put yourself in a layman's shoes who may have no medical or police knowledge. Help the jury understand the facts without talking down to them. Try to remain neutral in your comments so you are not prejudiced for the defense or prosecution. You aren't there to judge the accused, only to give facts and to represent the decedent or victim.

13. Keep your voice clear. Refrain from using phrases or abbreviations that a juror might not know or understand, and if you must use them, give a very concise explanation of the term in your response.

14. Be direct in your answers. Don't beat around the bush entirely, but give yourself some room if the going gets tough. Don't paint yourself into a corner. Beware of words like "always" or "never." Try to stay away from quantifying with percentages and use general phrases like "more often than not," etc. Attorneys also will take your answer and repeat it back to you changing the wording slightly. Beware!! Repeat it so you can stand behind the statement and in the terms you testified to.

Glossary

abrasion A scrape on the skin causing a loss of the superficial layers of the skin.

adipocere Decomposition of the body in cold, wet environments.

Alphonse Bertillon French law enforcement officer from the late 19th century who performed research in anthropometry.

alveolus Primary unit for gas exchange in the lungs.

aneurysm Bulging of the arterial wall due to weakness of the muscular component.

anoxia A total lack of oxygen in the body.

asphyxia Process causing lack of oxygen to the brain and resulting in unconsciousness and death.

atrophy Loss of muscle or flesh gradually due to lack of use.

avulsion Subtype of laceration in which the tear has created a flap of skin that is able to be lifted from the underlying muscle or bone.

babygram X-ray showing fractures or developmental abnormality of an infant's skeletal system.

bite-mark ruler Standard scale used in forensic photo documentation, helping to prevent misinterpretation of measurements and characteristics.

bullet Small (usually round or elongated) piece of metal used as a projectile in a firearm.

caliber The diameter measurement inside the gun barrel between two lands (usually measured in millimeters).

capital punishment Legal sentencing of a person to death as the result of a crime.

carbon monoxide Tasteless, odorless, colorless gas that is poisonous to humans.

cardiac valve Valve located in the heart located between the chambers and outflow tracts to control the flow of blood.

car pillars Posts supporting the roof of a car.

casing The spent portion of a cartridge that remains inside the cylinder of the gun or is discarded after firing and is usually made of brass or steel.

cause of death Medical description or diagnosis determining why someone is dead, expressed in medical terminology.

Center for Disease Control U.S. federal agency the goal of which is to maintain public health and prevent and control disease.

chain of custody A form listing any seized evidence and listing in a sequential fashion those who have handled or processed it to insure the integrity from the site of origin to its final storage and/or results in report format.

co-sleeping Infants sleeping close to, or in the same bed as, adults or other children.

compression asphyxia Inhibition of the movement of the diaphragm by compression of the chest or abdomen, resulting in lack of gas exchange.

CODIS Combined DNA Index System; an FBI database that stores DNA profiles from multiple sources, including results from crimes scenes and from offenders convicted of violent crimes.

components of air The chemical makeup of air, including nitrogen, oxygen, water vapor, argon, and carbon dioxide.

conflict of interest Situation occurring when the private interests and official responsibilities of a person may clash.

contusion A bruise created by a force being applied to the skin causing the rupture of small blood vessels and bleeding into the tissue under the skin surface.

coroner Elected officials with the legal ability to certify the cause and manner of death on the death certificate.

cremation Burning of a body at greater than 1,400–1,800 °F over a period of two to three hours to reduce the body to ash.

cyanide Colorless toxin that is lethal in high concentrations.

cyanotic Commonly referred to as "blue baby," in which the circulations of oxygenated and deoxygenated blood are mixed.

cylinder Rotating part of a revolver that contains multiple chambers for cartridges to align with the barrel for firing.

defense wounds Stab wounds or incisions that are inflicted by another person on the victim and are characterized by being located on the arms or legs.

dicing wounds Small, superficial cuts on the skin, often caused by shards of glass.

distal Region of the body away from the midline. An example is the hand is distal to the elbow.

edentulous Without teeth.

embalming The process of replacing the body fluids with formalin as a means of preservation.

embolus Detached blood clot transported through circulation.

epi Prefix indicating "outer."

exhumation Removal of a body from the grave where it has been buried for a length of time.

exsanguination Blood loss.

femoral blood Blood found in the femoral vein, which moves blood from the legs to the heart.

fetus An unborn being in the later stages of development.

forensic pathologist Board-certified examiner who performs autopsies as part of the medical examiner or coroner office.

fracture Breaking of a bone due to blunt force.

gauge The inner diameter of a shotgun barrel, expressed as the number of lead balls that will fit in the barrel and make a pound.

gunshot residue Burnt and unburnt particles left behind from the firing of a gun.

hemoglobin Part of the blood containing iron and carrying oxygen through the body.

hemosiderin/hematoidin Colored intracellular pigment caused by the breakdown of hemoglobin from red cells seen on microscopic examination.

hesitation wound Superficial wounds that look like curved abrasions, often surrounding self-inflicted wounds and thought to be tests of a weapon.

hospital pathologist Physician specialized in anatomic pathology working in a hospital who can perform basic autopsies (often deaths that are more likely to be disease related rather than trauma).

hyper Prefix indicating "over."

hypo Prefix indicating "below."

hypoxia A decreased level of oxygen in the body.

IAFIS Integrated Automated Fingerprint Identification System; FBI-sponsored fingerprint identification system that contains fingerprints obtained directly by the FBI and those submitted by various law enforcement agencies.

incision Cut of the skin caused by force applied to the skin by a sharp object. Generally, and that is longer than it is deep (often referred to as slashing injury or as a surgical incision).

infant Very young child.

instar Enlarging cycle of maggots (occurs three times in the life cycle of a blow fly).

jaundice Yellow discoloration of the skin or whites of the eyes.

kinetic energy The energy possessed by an object in motion.

laceration Tear of the skin as a result of a force being applied that exceeds the skin's elastic ability to stretch.

lethal injection Intravenous injection of a barbiturate that induces sleep followed by a neuromuscular-blocking agent such as succinylcholine or pancuronium that causes paralysis of skeletal and smooth muscles including the diaphragm. Potassium chloride is also injected.

live birth Defined as an infant who takes a breath or has a heartbeat upon being born.

livor The postmortem settling of blood

Locard's exchange principle Principle developed by Edmond Locard stating that two items coming into contact with each other will exchange material between them.

macerated Reddening, loss of skin, and feature distortion of a fetus due to retention in the uterus.

magazine Supply chamber of a gun that holds bullets.

manner of death Identification of the way a person died, using one of the following classifications: natural, accident, suicide, homicide, or undetermined.

meconium Thick, dark, tarry stool that a child expels in the early days of life.

medical examiner Forensic pathologist with education as a medical doctor, completion of four years of anatomic pathology, and at least one to two years of subspecialty training in forensic medicine who performs autopsies and has jurisdiction.

mitochondria Small cellular organelles containing DNA.

Model Postmortem Examinations Act The 1954 law outlining the recommended state-mandated reporting of cases to a central investigative agency for adoption of individual state laws.

mummification Decomposition of the body in hot, arid environments in which the body is partially protected from the sun and the air blowing across the body dries it out.

myocardium Muscle layer of the heart.

N-95 mask Mask designed with a very close facial fit used to help control the spread of germs.

next of kin Person or persons who are most closely related to the deceased.

NAMUS National Missing and Unidentified Persons System; National Institute of Justice database that may be viewed by the public as they search for their missing relative.

NCIC National Crime Information Center; FBI database that includes many subfiles including types of crimes for development of statistics regarding various violent crimes and where they are committed, as well as a missing persons database and an unidentified persons database. Available only to law enforcement.

neonate Newborn child.

notification Process of informing next of kin of a death. This is best if done in person, but others should be made aware that the notification is occurring, or a law enforcement officer should also be in attendance.

nucleus Membrane-enclosed organelle performing the information and administrative function of a cell.

pathologic fracture Fracture caused by minimal force applied to weakened bones by osteoporosis or tumor. The amount of force applied would not usually fracture healthy bones.

PCR Polymerase chain reaction, which makes copies of isolated DNA.

peer review Evaluation of content or services by other experts in the field.

positional asphyxia The impairment of oxygen exchange caused by the position of the body.

postmortem After death.

PPE Personal protective equipment; gear worn or used during autopsy to decrease the potential health hazards to those in the room and prevent transmission of biohazards outside the room to clean areas of the office.

premortem Before death.

proximal Located near the center of the body. An example is the elbow is proximal to the hand.

quality assurance Program to monitor the accuracy of and satisfaction with work done by medical examiner/coroner offices. May involve graded case studies or lab samples, peer reviews, and public surveys.

rigor The postmortem muscle stiffening in the body.

Rokitansky technique Style of autopsy developed by Dr. Karl Rokitansky that utilizes a block approach and allows organs to be evaluated in relationship to their interconnections, such as vasculature or ducts.

saponification A soap formation on the body occurring during decomposition in some environments and is due to a chemical change to the composition of body fat.

skeletal survey Scanning the body of a child for acute and healing injuries using a series of X-rays.

stab wound A sharp-force injury that is deeper than it is long.

sub Prefix indicating "lower" or below.

subclavian blood Blood found in the subclavian vessels, is located under the clavicles and represents blood to and from the arms.

therapeutic misadventure Possible additional category of manner of death, meaning and is used when a death is related to a medical intervention.

thrombus Blood clot that forms at the site where it obstructs the vascular lumen.

trace evidence Minute fragments of debris, fibers, hair, vegetation, paint chips, etc. that adhere to the body.

undermining Circumstance in which a segment of skin is lifted from the underlying skeletal structure, forming a pocket.

Virchow technique Style of autopsy developed by Dr. Rudolf Virchow that utilizes an organ-by-organ approach, relying on the natural retraction of the body itself.

vitreous Thick, transparent substance that fills most of the eye and is useful for toxicology, electrolyte and glucose evaluation by the laboratory.

wadding Material used to keep gas behind the projectile of a gun the gunpowder separate from the pellets in a shotgun shell.

Index

Note: Page numbers followed by *f* indicate figures, *t* indicate tables and *b* indicate boxes

CPSIA information can be obtained
at www.ICGtesting.com
Printed in the USA
LVHW021502181219
640939LV00008B/259/P